TO BOULEZ AND BEYOND

Music in Europe Since The Rite of Spring

JOAN PEYSER

Foreword by Charles Wuorinen

BILLBOARD BOOKS
An imprint of Watson-Guptill Publications
New York

Senior Acquisitions Editor: Bob Nirkind
Project Editor: Sarah Fass
Production Manager: Hector Campbell
Cover and book design: Derek Bacchus

First published in 1999 by Billboard Books,
An imprint of Watson-Guptill Publications,
A division of BPI Communications, Inc.
1515 Broadway, New York, NY 10036

Library of Congress Cataloging-in-Publication Data
Peyser, Joan.
         To Boulez and beyond : music in Europe since The rite of spring /
Joan Peyser ; foreword by Charles Wuorinen
              p. cm.
      Includes index.
      ISBN 0-8230-7875-2
            1. Music—Europe—20th century—History and criticism.   2. Boulez, Pierre, 1925- .
      3. Schoenberg, Arnold, 1874-1951—Criticism and interpretation.   4. Stravinsky, Igor,
      1882-1971—Criticism and interpretation.   5. Varèse, Edgard, 1883-1965—Criticism and
      interpretation.   I. Title.
      ML240.5.P49   1999
      780'.9'04—dc21   99-38536
                                                                                                                    CIP

Manufactured in the United States of America

First printing, 1999

1 2 3 4 5 6 7 8 9 / 07 06 05 04 03 02 01 00 99

This book was adapted from *The New Music: The Sense Behind the Sound* (Delacorte Press,
1971) and *Boulez: Composer, Conductor, Enigma* (Schirmer Books, 1976).

To

——— JACQUES

——— BARZUN

CONTENTS

ACKNOWLEDGMENTS   vi

FOREWORD   xiii

INTRODUCTION   xvi

CHAPTERS 1-44   1

PHOTO GALLERY 1900–1950   130

PHOTO GALLERY 1950–1999   264

AFTERWORD   363

INDEX   370

ACKNOWLEDGMENTS

This book originated as two other books I wrote decades ago. The first, *The New Music: the Sense Behind the Sound,* describes the lives and works of Arnold Schoenberg, Igor Stravinsky and Edgard Varèse. Delacorte published it in 1971. In the present volume, the essence of that material appears in chapters 1 through 17. Schirmer Books/Macmillan published the other, *Boulez: Composer, Conductor, Enigma,* in 1976, about eighteen months before Pierre Boulez completed his tenure as Music Director of The New York Philharmonic Orchestra. Occasionally some overlapping occurs. I have edited and transformed these books and added chapter 44, which tells about the last twenty-two years of Boulez's life. I have also added an Afterword in which I briefly describe some first-rate Americans involved in the progressive movement whom I do not include in the body of this mostly European story. Finally, I report here how some younger, very gifted composers, have been nourished by the chromaticism of modern jazz.

In the spring of 1969, during my first interview with Boulez for the Arts & Leisure section of the Sunday *New York Times,* the composer-conductor said, "I have no confidence in those who think they know their goals. You discover your goal as you come upon it. It's out there in front of you; you discover it each day."

Today I understand what he meant more than I did when he made the statement. For it was not until recently I knew my goal was to write compelling histories of the music of my time. Surely I had no sense of this as a goal when, as a child, I was immersed in the music of Bach, Beethoven, Schubert, and Brahms. From the age of five, I practiced the piano every day under the supervision of my mother, a good amateur musician, who helped me prepare for my weekly lessons. Just before I turned thirteen, I played in a recital in New York's Town Hall and just after, I entered the High School of Music and Art, where I chose viola as my second instrument and played in the school orchestras.

Between my twelfth and fifteenth birthdays, four people close to me died: my piano teacher, my two viola teachers, and my mother, whose illness lasted only six weeks. Virtually everyone who taught me music died.

Excising music from my life, I stopped all lessons and left Music and Art. My first two years at Smith College were as devoid of music as my last two years in a private high school. But then, at the start of my junior year, I married, transferred to Barnard College, and reentered my old world. The new route was an academic one. I majored in music, taking courses in harmony, theory, counterpoint, and history.

I went to graduate school at Columbia University, committing myself to musicology under Paul Henry Lang, a distinguished scholar born in Hungary, educated at the Sorbonne, and instrumental in bringing this European discipline to the United States. Lang presided over the International Musicological Society, was then the editor of *The Musical Quarterly,* and was the author of a monumental book, *Music in Western Civilization.* Both in his book and in seminar, Lang shifted the emphasis away from the traditional approach—examining the details within a score—and towards a view of music in the context of cultural history.

I enthusiastically embraced that approach, but I wanted to do something more. I wanted to consider the individual composer's life. Did Mozart compose differently in 1780 than he did in 1770 because of sociological or aesthetic developments? Or did something happen in his own life? Or both?

What happens matters. I knew this only too well from my own experience, and although I never spoke about that to Lang, I continued to press for a more psychological way of approaching history. All of this took place in the 1950s, more than twenty-five years before the burgeoning of the full disclosure biography that swept American publishing in the 1980s and 1990s.

Lang did not subscribe to my idea. So although I submitted pieces on music to small magazines—all of which were published—I had not then made any use at all of what I thought necessary to a full understanding of how a work of art was made. Lang's influence was too strong to permit me to do that.

Several years after I left Columbia, I received a commission to write an article on American music at mid-century. At the time Marc Blitzstein, an American composer, had just been killed in a fight in a bar on Martinique. I knew Blitzstein. We had worked together in an American opera program at the New York City Opera and we were neighbors on lower Fifth Avenue. I wanted to write something to help keep his name alive and decided to base my essay on him.

Here was an opportunity to articulate connections between life and work, to deal with external and internal conflicts, to try to understand why this immensely talented and attractive artist, sponsored by the Ford Foundation to compose an opera for the Metropolitan Opera, left a partially completed score in the trunk of a car he stored in Westchester County rather than do what he told everyone he would do: complete it during his stay on Martinique. In telling his story, I would also be able to reveal the effect on him of the then current relationship between Europe and the United States, between capitalism and communism, between his years of study with Schoenberg and his subsequent commitment to socialist realism, between 12-tone music and tonality.

Exploring Blitzstein's life could also have provided me with the opportunity to deal with the relationship between sexuality and creativity. But in the mid-1960s I did not have the courage to do that.

Published in *The Columbia University Forum,* the essay launched my career. It received the first ASCAP/Deems Taylor Award for excellence in writing on music, brought forth a commission from Delacorte, the hardcover division of Dell Publishing Co., for a work on twentieth-century music, and prompted Seymour Peck, then the editor of the Arts & Leisure section of the *Times,* to ask me to write regularly. I organized the book for Delacorte the same way I had organized the American music essay—through significant composers.

I chose Schoenberg, Stravinsky and Varèse, from the Austro-German, Franco-Russian, French and Greenwich Village domains—and revealed how each of them evolved and affected the others' major moves.

The reader may well wonder why, with a childhood immersed in and limited to old music, music composed no later than Debussy, Satie, and early Stravinsky, I came to concentrate on the new. To understand this requires an acceptance of a mysterious passage from self to symbol. It requires an intuitive sense of why, having experienced what I did in my early teens, I came to equate old (classical) music with death and new (Schoenberg and his followers) with vigor and life.

This is at least part of that story: In the fall of 1998, Merkin Hall, one block north of Lincoln Center, hosted a weekend to commemorate the 124th anniversary of Schoenberg's birth. Some members of the composer's family were there, as was virtually every Schoenberg specialist. Performances and panel discussions excelled. At one point Milton Babbitt, father of Schoenberg-derived serialism in the United States, interrupted himself to ask: "Is Pat Carpenter here? Pat probably knows Schoenberg better than anyone in the house tonight."

Pat Carpenter had been my closest friend when we were graduate students in the 1950s. We remained close long after that. At the start of the friendship, she moved into an apartment just below mine in a small Greenwich Village house. The conversation was continuous and nourishing. Pat had been a music major at UCLA where she studied formally with Schoenberg from 1942 to 1945. Then she worked with him privately and in small groups until 1949. Pat gave one of the first performances of Schoenberg's Piano Concerto Opus 42 while she was still living on the West Coast. Then she studied at Columbia, went on to teach at Barnard, became chairman of the music department there and director of the graduate theory program at Columbia.

Schoenberg had instilled in Pat the same adoration he had in Webern, Berg and others, and she conveyed that awe to me. But that alone would not have propelled me to make the leap to Schoenberg and those who followed in his path. That leap required hearing extraordinary performances, and these were provided, after 1962, by Charles Wuorinen's Group for Contemporary Music, held at Columbia's McMillin Theater. My attachment was reinforced by my growing connection to Babbitt, who headed the Columbia-Princeton Electronic Music Center. I often visited the center and wrote about it for the *Times*.

The section of my book on Schoenberg is indebted to those I credit in the text, as well as to the writings of H. H. Stuckenschmidt. But again my debt to Pat knows no bounds. As I had come to grasp the reasons for her reverence for Schoenberg, she had come to understand the nature of the material I needed to write a full life. To that end she introduced me to Alessandra Comini, on the faculty of the department of fine art, who had slides of portraits of Schoenberg, his wife Mathilde, and their children. They had been painted by Richard Gerstl, an expressionist painter nine years younger than Schoenberg who had lived with the family for an extended period of time. The nature of these paintings, as well as that of a frontal nude self-portrait, led me to believe that something grotesque had happened within the small group. Gerstl burned most of his work, but those that remained were represented by Otto Kallir, owner of the St. Etienne Gallery in New York. Kallir told me the details of the horrific events that occurred in the first decade of this century, events that had never then appeared in print. They had, however, been referred to obliquely by Theodor Adorno, the German philosopher and sociologist, who wrote of "a crisis in personal life whose sorrow, hardly ever mastered, brought Schoenberg's work its full creative weight." The harrowing situation erupted when Schoenberg was at work on his String Quartet No. 2. It was then that he took the decisive step and moved over the border from a clear-cut sense of key in the first three movements to a last keyless movement.

The material on Stravinsky draws on the biography by Eric Walter White, and the section on Varèse builds on one by Fernand Ouellette. But again, the most striking information comes not from any secondary source but from Louise Varèse, the composer's widow. She invariably answered my questions and offered new information to help me understand the sudden changes in Varèse's productivity.

The process of writing about Boulez up to 1976 differed greatly from any other part of this book, as well as from any book I have written. Here there were virtually no secondary sources. Sometimes I described events that took place more than twenty years earlier, such as Boulez getting a job to conduct incidental music for Jean-Louis Barrault and setting up the Domaine Musical with the help of Suzanne Tezenas. Sometimes I wrote about even more recent events than those, the ones connected to his conducting career in the United States. Unless there is a specific attribution in the text, all the quotes that appear in chapters 17 through 43 come from people's conversations with me. I thank all who spoke to me but cite only a few here: Boulez's sister Jeanne Chevalier, his teachers from his Catholic seminary, Jean-Louis Barrault, Suzanne Tezenas, Olivier Messiaen, René Leibowitz, Luciano Berio, Henri Pousseur, John Cage, David Tudor, and all the composers who interacted with him during the early heady days. I also owe a debt to the organizers of the music festivals at Darmstadt and Donaueschingen who gave me more than printed programs; they provided a behind-the-scenes account of the issues and rivalries being fought out there. As for Boulez's career as a major conductor, I am grateful to Sir William Glock of the BBC Symphony, Lawrence Morton of the Monday Evening Concerts in Los Angeles, and Carlos Moseley of The New York Philharmonic for giving me the attention and information they did.

Here is how *Boulez* evolved: As soon as *The New Music* appeared, I sent a copy to Boulez whom I knew from my *New York Times* interview. I suggested he read the book and then decide if he would agree to my writing my next book about him. Boulez replied in a handwritten letter that I should accompany Louise Varèse to Cleveland and attend his all-Varèse concert there. Then, he wrote, he and I would sit down and set the guidelines for my new project. The day after the concert he and I met at Severance Hall. Boulez agreed to open doors for interviews as well as to rehearsals and programming sessions. At that time I did not plan a biography. I wanted to produce a reportage of his experience in New York, where the box office determines the course of events more than anything he had experienced in the past. He agreed he would not ask to see my book before publication. "Of course not," he said, "It is your own work."

At the start Boulez annihilated the guidelines. He locked me out of orchestra rehearsals and the programming sessions with the Philharmonic management. When I told him I had better drop the book he asked me not to, and invited me to less problematic, more toothless events. Later, when I said that these alone could not provide what I needed for the book I had planned to write and was considering a biography instead, Boulez agreed, and arranged for me to stay with his sister for a few days at her house in St. Michel de l'Observatoire, where he was planning to build his own.

At the end Boulez also annihilated the guidelines. Through devious channels, he managed to get hold of the unedited manuscript of the first draft I had submitted to the publisher. In a letter to me, Boulez exploded with great rage, rage you will find him exhibiting time and again throughout the course of this description of his life. He responds this way to any negative criticism, no matter how many positive qualities are recognized by the same author. I felt disappointed at his reaction, of course, but thank him sincerely for the contribution of his time.

Because I have never studied writing in a formal way, I acknowledge my debt to Stanley H. Brown over and above anyone else for teaching me how to avoid the pitfalls of much academic writing and simply and directly say what I mean. Brown, a writer, editor and my friend for thirty-seven years, has served, during that time, as my personal editor, deleting whatever stands in the way of making the narrative driving and clear. Paul Wittke has also played a large role. Senior editor at G. Schirmer for decades, he generously helped me between 1977 and 1984 when I was the editor of *The Musical Quarterly*. Wittke remains a good friend and made significant suggestions as to the shaping and editing of *To Boulez and Beyond*.

Richard Huett and Ken Stuart, then editors at Delacorte and Schirmer Books, oversaw the birth and growth of the biographies that appeared in the 1970s; their work deserves recognition now. Tod Machover, the American composer who heads MIT's Media Laboratory, was once director of musical research at Ircam; he reviewed chapter 44, the one covering Boulez after 1976, filling in whatever gaps in information he found.

William Krasilovsky, an attorney specializing in music, is the author of *This Business of Music*, about to be released in its eighth edition by Billboard Books. Krasilovsky served as a conduit between Billboard Books and me, then negotiated contracts for expanded editions of five of my books. No author can be more indebted to an agent than I am to him for putting these works back in print and for having brought me to the attention of Robert Nirkind, senior editor, whose exceptional staff includes Sarah Fass, Lee Wiggins, and Derek Bacchus.

As with every book of mine that has appeared during the last nine years, I thank Frank Driggs, the noted archivist and man at the center of my life. His work on the photo sections here immeasurably enhances the story of how serious music moved through the twentieth century.

JOAN PEYSER
FEBRUARY 15, 1999

FOREWORD

oan Peyser has long maintained that the debt the world of present-day music owes to Arnold Schoenberg is incalculable. Throughout her writing life, she has been unique among her colleagues (writing in large-distribution publications) in concentrating her attention on living composers—and this gives her special authority in tracing so much of our music back to the irascible Austrian. I should add that while those who know the world of twentieth-century music have no doubt about the crucial importance of Schoenberg's contribution, the larger "music-loving" public has (especially in recent years) been consistently misled by journalists about his music. They have been told repeatedly that his work was a "mistake," that their own conservative tastes embody truths about the eternal nature of music, and that Schoenberg the composer, thinker, and moral force in music is disappearing. With her unique combination of journalistic skill and musical sophistication, Joan Peyser has managed to stand against this knownothingism in exactly the same forum in which it has been promulgated. We are all in her debt.

I am in complete agreement with her position. In what I say below, I summarize not only a few of my own thoughts on Schoenberg, but also reflect the contents of many conversations Mrs. Peyser and I have had over the past thirty years.

Forever is a long time, but almost fifty years after his death, Arnold Schoenberg remains a vivid presence, a composer whose work seems destined to endure "forever"—as long as mankind values art. His music continues to challenge and stimulate, and even the controversy that surrounded him in his life continues, although now joined only by the lower sort of music critic, the kind who thinks that immediate public response determines the value of a work of art. No musician has escaped his influence. direct or indirect; and no serious composer today could make a sound without Schoenberg—even those who would fly from the judgment his beautiful music and his moral presence impose on their own efforts. From the most knowing to the least aware, all musicians have been deeply affected by his life, work and ideals. Schoenberg remains; those who cannot understand him come and go.

Schoenberg's music, which asks so much from the listener and then rewards him so richly, is something of a stranger in the present-day musical polity; and his profound seriousness about composition, about music and musical thought, invoke standards that seem almost beyond the reach of many today, standards against which the tawdriness of our present artistic life and the revolting cultural populism of our present time, measure themselves to their shame. The polity of today has no room in its vision for any art that is not instantly accessible to the ignorant and the indifferent. Indeed, to read much present-day music criticism is to get the impression that the only authentic response to music can be given by those who know nothing about it and don't care. Knowledge and experience are to be feared, skill and professional achievement despised.

Art and entertainment are nowadays hopelessly confounded, and the notion of art as elevated, idealistic, transcendent, is almost completely foreign to us. True, many continue in a higher vision of music; but they have no place today in the public manifestations of the art.

Seriousness about art was axiomatic for Schoenberg, and whatever illusions he may have had about his own eventual "popularity," nothing could shake his fundamental purposes; nor would he be able to understand (as indeed many of us still cannot) the arts-administrator-ridden music world of today, in which musical concerns always give way to marketing and hype. He would find incomprehensible the attitudes of so many young composers, who will adjust their art in any way that secures them performances and notoriety. He would not have kind words for their mixture of sentimental politics and petty ambition. He would find ludicrous the assertion that worth or merit in a work of art is determined by majority vote. And he would be disgusted by a generation of pandering "scholars" who paint a pseudo-intellectual varnish over the vulgarities of contemporary popular music—especially those who say there is no difference in value between the great works of past and present and the latest market-researched media-promoted pop-music manifestation. And I wish he were alive to denounce the perverse and evil notion, now bruited in our leading newspapers, that "quality" in art has no meaning, and is just another notion intended as a strategy for some people to "dominate" others. No, Schoenberg wouldn't fit in at all. The politicization of everything and the valuing of nothing are not conditions he would tolerate.

When one thinks of Schoenberg's contribution to compositional method, it is hard to avoid a comparison with Einstein. The same mighty expansion of materials, methods and horizons that changed the whole world in Einstein's case, changed the littler world of music in Schoenberg's. And the world of enormously expanded pitch-relations opened up by Schoenberg's work, the creation of a musical universe larger than what we had before—that larger new world still including the old one—is very like the embedding of Newtonian physics within the new relativistic Einsteinian universe as a special case, good enough for getting around the galaxy, but on the largest scale, not really true.

And finally, one might paraphrase Alexander Pope's remarks about Newton, with the appropriate substitutions:

> *Music and Music's law lay hid in night;*
> *God said, "Let Schoenberg be," and all was light.*

CHARLES WUORINEN

INTRODUCTION

In a foreword to *The Music of My Time,* a collection of my articles published in 1995, Milton Babbitt of Princeton wrote that he first met me when I was "a graduate student in music history at Columbia." At Princeton the field I pursued is called music history; at Columbia it is musicology. I did not ask Babbitt to correct the error because I prefer to be considered a music historian rather than anything with "ology" attached; that suffix implies all manner and mixes of recently developed disciplines.

To say this is merely to emphasize that what I am writing here is history, and since history recounts the doings of men, it follows that this history is based on my biographies of those who led the way.

Like the law, history is created by the gathering of evidence from as many witnesses as possible. Because its purpose is to tell what's worth remembering, one of the historian's chief tasks is to decide what to leave out. Macaulay said of his own *History of England* that arrangement is everything; it alone makes the welter intelligible and retainable. I note this to anticipate those critics who will complain about the huge spectrum of composers—some of whom wrote beautiful music—who are omitted here. They may begin with Philip Glass, the minimalist composer who is also a practicing Buddhist. Glass's work is specifically incidental to what is happening on the stage and generally incidental to an Eastern philosophy that, to my mind, separates him from the main fare of Western music. The other end of the spectrum might include Thomas Adès, the 27-year-old British composer whose chamber opera, *Powder Her Face,* catapulted him into international renown in 1998. What one hears in this skillfully made, ambitious score is an amalgam of material derived from a plethora of twentieth-century composers going back to Janácek and Berg. It is hard for me to believe that a potpourri of styles of dead composers will wipe out the power of Schoenberg's idea and serve as a model for the music to come.

The reader may well ask why, if Boulez's language is ultimately derived from Schoenberg, the subtitle of this book bypasses the great Viennese in favor of Stravinsky.

During his early period, when Schoenberg composed The Five Orchestral Pieces Opus 16, Anton Webern, his pupil, wrote that these expressive works contained "the experience of Schoenberg's emotional life." Yet when Peters, Schoenberg's publisher, asked the composer on the eve of publication in 1912 to assign them titles, he offered deliberately meaningless ones such as "Chord Colors" and "The Obligato." In his diary Schoenberg wrote that he chose those titles to hide what the music was really about. "For the wonderful thing about music is that one can say everything in it, so that he who knows understands everything; and yet one hasn't given away one's own secrets, the things one doesn't say even to oneself."

Stravinsky took music to the next crucial step, a step that set the tone for what was to come. With him, music did not hide emotions; there were no emotions contained within it to hide. In his *Autobiography,* written in 1934, the composer wrote: "I consider that music is, by its very nature, powerless to express anything at all, whether a feeling, an attitude of mind, a psychological mood, a phenomenon of nature etc. . . . If, as is nearly always the case, music appears to express something, this is only an illusion and not a reality." Stravinsky could have stated this belief twenty years earlier, soon after Schoenberg's Five Orchestral Pieces, when he dazzled the world with *The Rite of Spring.* No repressed thoughts or feelings here; only the most original combination of rhythms ever heard orchestrated under his stunning control.

To Boulez and Beyond: Music in Europe Since The Rite of Spring tells the story of how Schoenberg's secreting of his own powerful passions, corseting them through his carefully constructed method, led Stravinsky and a long line of composers to where we are today: anticipating an art that has more in common with the medieval period than with anything we have known since the beginning of the Renaissance. All indications suggest it will be music of low intensity, not individual but communal, characterized by an anonymity that Boulez says he covets today.

As if to give my prediction some weight, *New York* magazine, in its February 15, 1999, issue, quotes sources at the Juilliard School that the number of Americans who "consider themselves composers of classical music . . . [ranges] between an astonishing 20,000 and 40,000." Who are they? And if we found all of them, would any one possess the genius of a Mozart, a Brahms or, yes, a Schoenberg?

CHAPTER 1

It was inevitable that tonality would outlive its role as the foundation on which serious music was based. But it was an accident that at the very time this happened—during the first decades of the twentieth century—a man emerged who not only had an insight into the aesthetic requirements of the time, but also the unshakable faith that he was put on earth to proclaim these requirements to the world. Arnold Schoenberg was convinced of his destiny as lawgiver: "I am the slave of an internal power stronger than my education; it compels me to obey a conception which, inborn, has greater power over me than any elemental artistic formation."

Schoenberg regarded himself as the figure whose duty it was to reestablish the formerly undisputed hegemony of Austro-German music. Born in Vienna, a direct descendant of Wagner and Brahms, Schoenberg viewed this goal in mystical terms. But his sense of destiny: "I have a mission . . . I have a task . . . I am but the loudspeaker of an idea. . . ." is not to be interpreted merely as a symptom of megalomaniacal thinking; it should be considered in the context of the milieu in which he grew up.

Friedrich Nietzsche had repudiated nineteenth-century ideology and demanded the reorganization of human society under the guidance of exceptional leaders. Richard Wagner answered the call. Arrogant beyond measure, Wagner became the German superhero, the embodiment of the Dionysian ideal for which Nietzsche yearned. Schoenberg, by the age of twenty-five, had heard each of Wagner's operas between twenty and thirty times, and had inherited Wagner's tyrannical mien.

1

Yet Schoenberg was also a confirmed Brahmsian. This appears to be a paradox, for the conflict between Wagner and Brahms revolved around such crucial artistic principles that any conciliation seemed, in Schoenberg's youth, to be impossible. Brahms was considered a conservative; Wagner a revolutionary. Brahms chose the classic molds of the sonata, string quartet and symphony, rather than the popular "moments musicales" and symphonic tone poems of other contemporaries. Wagner experimented with a musical idiom that moved away from diatonicism and toward an all-embracing chromaticism totally threatening to the tonal system. Brahms did not generally use notes to create sensuous effects.

The balance of power was divided. On the one hand the critic Eduard Hanslick defended the classicist; on the other hand a host of imposing figures rallied for the musical revolution. Richard Strauss, ten years older than Schoenberg, started as a strict Brahmsian and became a confirmed Wagnerian, and Anton Bruckner consistently praised the new in music. Hugo Wolf, song composer and music critic of the fashionable journal the Viennese *Salonblatt,* expressed disdain for Brahms's conservatism: "The leaders of the revolutionary movement in music after Beethoven (in which Schumann indeed expected a Messiah and thought he had found one in Brahms) have passed our symphonist by without leaving a trace on him. Brahms writes symphonies regardless of what has happened in the meantime."

Yet Schoenberg clearly perceived a common factor in the work of both classicist and rebel; each exhibited a linear, horizontal orientation in his compositional procedures which was, in a most conscious sense, derived from the late works of Beethoven. It is this polyphonic emphasis— the musical realization of a germinal motive—that Schoenberg inherited, via Brahms and Wagner, from the late Beethoven. In an analysis of Beethoven's String Quartet in F Major, Opus 135, Schoenberg articulated his debt to Beethoven.

He used the work to illustrate his belief that its composition was not motivated by divisions into architectonic tonal areas, but that it was derived from the first three notes of the first theme of the first movement. In another essay, "Brahms, the Progressive," Schoenberg cited a number of examples in which Brahms subjected a single germinal motive to the technique of perpetual variation and gave examples to illustrate what he considered to be Brahms's sense of "unitary perception." He points out that the primary melodic idea in Brahms's First Symphony is not restricted to the usual single movement but binds all four.

It is less easy at first to see Wagner's debt to Beethoven than to see

Brahms's, for Wagner was devoted to opera while Beethoven, like Brahms, shunned the genre. (Beethoven wrote one; Brahms none.) But on closer inspection the affinity between Beethoven and Wagner becomes clear. Despite the fact that Wagner wrote for the theater, his focus was centered on what was played by the orchestra—not what was sung on the stage. The popularity of the orchestral version of the "Love-Death" duet from *Tristan und Isolde*—to cite one example—attests to the importance of the purely musical in Wagner's work. His musical fabric is a complex one, held together by leitmotifs which not only identify particular characters and situations in the drama but unify the purely musical texture the way the thematic material unifies a symphony or chamber work. Wagner recognized the essentially abstract nature of his music. He claimed that he was not continuing the tradition of Gluck, Mozart or Carl Maria von Weber. Instead, his music-dramas stemmed directly from Beethoven's Ninth Symphony. In fact, Wagner considered Beethoven his immediate precursor; he viewed Beethoven's inclusion of voices in the last movement of this symphony as the first step in the revival of the Greek ideal, the inclusive work embracing the compass of all the arts, Wagner's Romantic creation, the *Gesamtkunstwerk*.

Thus the musical idea, an intellectual concept that had its genesis in Beethoven's art, developed through both Brahms and Wagner. Because of the importance accorded "theme" in Brahms's instrumental works and the leit-motif in Wagner's sensuous music-dramas, and despite the different styles of the two Romantic men (Wagner snidely referred to Brahms as the "chaste Johannes"), Schoenberg drew lavishly from both and repudiated everything outside of Austro-German composition. One of his earliest pupils has reported that the composer once said to him: "Either what we do is music or what the French do is music. But both cannot be music." And when Schoenberg wrote to Josef Stransky, conductor of the New York Philharmonic, suggesting he perform works by his two most gifted pupils, Schoenberg asked: "Would you not like to look at scores of works by Dr. Anton von Webern and Alban Berg, two real musicians—not Bolshevik illiterates, but men with a musically educated ear!"

The attitude that excluded France and Russia from the center of Schoenberg's musical orbit was founded not only on traditional German prejudice, but on what were for him the most valid artistic principles: "Today the majority strive for 'style, technique and sound,' meaning thereby something purely external and striking in character, for the sake of which all old culture displayed in presenting a thought is neglected." Casting aside with contempt the Stravinsky-inspired music that received so much attention during the 1920s, '30s, and '40s, Schoenberg, in both his writing and teaching, continued to stress the old German masters. Throughout his life he never thought of himself as a radical, but as a traditionalist in the classic sense. In 1937 he wrote to Nicolas Slonimsky: "I personally hate to be called a revolutionist, which I am not."

"The Method of Composing with Twelve Tones Related Only to Each Other," which Schoenberg formulated when he was fifty years old, dramatically altered the course of composition in the twentieth century. Schoenberg never "taught" the technique, which he regarded as a private affair. But Anton Webern, his pupil, described both its genesis and its nature with clarity in lectures he gave in Vienna during the early 1930s:

> Just as the church modes disappeared and made way for major and minor, so these two have disappeared and made way for a single series, the chromatic scale. Relation to a keynote, tonality, has been lost. . . . Schoenberg expressed this in an analogy: double gender has given rise to higher race. . . .
>
> Now I'm asked: "How do I arrive at this row?" Not arbitrarily, but according to certain secret laws. (A tie of this kind is very strict, so that one must consider very carefully and seriously, just as one enters into marriage, the choice is hard!) How does it come about . . . speaking from my own experience, I've mostly come to it in association with what in productive people we call "inspiration."
>
> What we establish is the law. Earlier, when one wrote in C Major, one also felt "tied" to it; otherwise the result was a mess. One was obliged to return to the tonic, one was tied to the nature of this scale. Now we base our invention on a scale that has not seven notes but twelve, and moreover in a particular order. That's "composition with twelve notes related only to each other."
>
> . . . The basic shape, the course of the twelve notes, can give rise to variants—we also use the twelve notes back to front—that's cancrizans—and then inverted—as if we were looking in a mirror—and also the cancrizans of the inversion. That makes four forms. But then what can one do with these? We can base them on every degree of the scale. Twelve times four makes forty-eight forms. Enough to choose from! Until now we've found these forty-eight forms

sufficient, these forty-eight forms that are the same thing throughout. Just as earlier composition was in C Major, we write in these forty-eight forms.

As applied in the 1950s and early 1960s, the 12-tone technique was a numerical, proportional one, with no extra-musical elements. Yet Schoenberg was a Romantic composer who wrote such grand and lavish pieces as the *Gurrelieder* and *Pelleas und Melisande* at the beginning of his career and the expressive String Trio, Opus 45, at the end. Schoenberg was aware of his public image as abstract philosopher but he was unconcerned: "A problematic relationship between the science of mathematics as expressed by Einstein and the science of music as developed by myself has been suggested. There may be a relationship between the two fields of endeavor but I have no idea what it is. . . ."

Several of Schoenberg's original group became disenchanted in the 1920s after Schoenberg proclaimed the 12-tone technique. Alfredo Casella accused the Viennese master of confining music in a narrow prison, and the Marxist Hanns Eisler, shifting to the principle of socialist realism, commented that his teacher had gone to the trouble of bringing about a revolution in order to be a reactionary. But Schoenberg did not develop dodecaphony to be perverse; the technique was indissoluble from what he considered to be the well-expressed idea: "Music essentially consists of ideas. Beethoven called himself a 'brain proprietor.' It is no use to rail at new music because it contains too many ideas. Music without ideas is unthinkable."

In the following conversation with the music critic José Rodriguez, Schoenberg elucidated his point:

SCHOENBERG: We all have technical difficulties which
arise not from the inability to handle the material, but from some
inherent quality in the idea. And it is this first idea, the
first thought, that must dictate the structure and texture of
the work.
RODRIGUEZ: In the beginning was the Word. . . .
SCHOENBERG: What else? What else can I do but express the
original Word, which to me is a human thought, a human idea or
a human aspiration?

Thus it can be seen that Schoenberg's theme was a musical translation of an idea which, in its origin, was the Word of God. Schoenberg was a profoundly religious man and his most ambitious works were religious subjects. *Moses und Aron,* on which he worked throughout his life, ends: "But even in the wasteland you shall be victorious and achieve the goal: unity with God."

Although in conversation and in his letters, Schoenberg frequently indicated a sense of despair at being chosen God's emissary on earth, he never questioned the fact that he was. He often repeated a story from his days in the army during World War I: a colonel asked him whether he was really *the* Arnold Schoenberg, and he replied: "Somebody had to be. Nobody wanted to. So in the end I agreed to take on the job." At other times he was far more mystical about his mission: "I was content when I wrote in the period of the Chamber Symphony. But I hardly had written so when I began to compose in a new style without knowing it. In the time of the Chamber Symphony I understood better what I had written and had more personal pleasure with that than with the music that followed. Then to compose was a great pleasure. In a later time it was a duty against myself. It was not a question of pleasure. . . ."

But Schoenberg's sense of mission was not only a burden; it brought moments of supreme inspiration. "I am," he wrote in an essay, "Heart and Brain," "the creature of inspiration. I compose and paint instinctively. When I am not in the mood I cannot even write a good harmony example for my pupils. There are times when I write with the greatest fluency and ease. My third quartet was composed in six weeks. They say I am a mathematician. Mathematics goes more slowly."

The actual speed with which he composed confirms his claims; except when a psychological block interrupted the course of a work, which generally occurred while he was at work on a religious text—only *Die Jakobsleiter, Moses und Aron,* and *Modern Psalms* were not completed—Schoenberg claimed that he would spend one week writing a sonata movement, ten days on a short opera, and between one and three hours on a song. His students have said that his teaching was also affected by these periods of inspiration. One reports that several lessons could be prosaic. "Then, suddenly, Schoenberg would get up, pace back and forth with his hands clasped tightly behind his back, and with eyes that were frightening in the force they had, begin to explain something in a very special way. It was intuition that made the whole thing tick."

Schoenberg held his mystical convictions in concrete terms. An American interviewer asked him, toward the end of his life, whether he thought he would have become as good a painter as he was a composer. Schoenberg answered yes—because he could paint a perfect circle without the aid of a compass. He was, in fact, a most precise painter and executed a portrait of Mahler which Mahler's widow claimed surpassed any photograph in realistic detail. He also painted a self-portrait from the back, with the aid of a mirror, which friends report portrays his bald spot and crooked stance with deadly accuracy.

The literal characteristics that played a role in his painting were in evidence in his approach to composition. Whether composing in a chromatically embellished tonal framework, or in a thoroughly atonal one, specific programs determined many of the works he wrote before 1912. Not only were *Gurrelieder* and *Pelleas und Melisande* program works; *Verklärte Nacht, Das Buch der hängenden Gärten, Erwartung, Die glückliche Hand,* and *Pierrot Lunaire* were also organized around nonmusical material. Even at the end of his life this penchant for literalism returned: Thomas Mann has written that Schoenberg told him that the seemingly abstract Trio, Opus 45, depicted a recent illness and included musical references to a male nurse and hypodermic needle.

Schoenberg's emphasis on form rather than literal content after 1912—when he began to evolve the 12-tone technique—concealed his own experience and emotion; thus the method should be considered in the context of Schoenberg's tendency to withdraw: "There are some things I have not finished," he wrote on his fiftieth birthday in *Die Musikblätter des Anbruch.* "Thus, I have published less than I have written and written less than I have thought."

His revolutionary method of composing music may be interpreted, as Hans Keller has suggested, as a method to hide rather than to communicate the deepest emotional responses of its creator. That this was his objective is borne out in an essay published in the collection *Style and Idea*; in it Schoenberg refers to music as a "language in which a musician unconsciously gives himself away." The composer predicts that "one day the children's children of our psychologists will have deciphered the language of music. Woe, then, to the incautious who thought his innermost secrets carefully hidden and who must now allow tactless men to besmirch his most personal possessions with their own impurities. Woe, then, to Beethoven, Brahms, Schumann—when they fall into such hands—these men who used their human right of free speech in order to conceal their true thoughts. Is the right to keep silent not worthy of protection?"

The 12-tone technique put an end to a several-hundred-year period in which music was devoted to a dramatic-expressive ideal. The technique, as extended by Schoenberg's musical descendants of the 1950s and 1960s, developed into an abstract language devoid of extra-musical implications. Music was not alone, among the arts, in developing along a more abstract path. It was a logical counterpart of that movement in the development of art in which its function, as Arnold Hauser has stated, "of being true to life and faithful to nature has been questioned for the first time since the Middle Ages."

Although some of the developments of dodecaphony provide a kind of music appropriate for a scientific, technologic age, the roots of that system lay in one man's way of viewing the world and his compelling manner of systematizing that view. The method which solidified Schoenberg's position in the history of music can best be understood—in terms of the personal dynamics that motivated it—by investigating the life that Schoenberg began to give to letters and numbers about 1912, just before he set about creating his new system.

Before 1912, Schoenberg's ritualistic behavior was not apparent. The names of his first two children, Gertrude and George, appear to have been chosen on an arbitrary basis. Several decades later, after Schoenberg married a second time, he chose Ronald as the name of his first son by this marriage and Roland as the name of the second, both anagrams of his first name. Upon discovering adverse numerological implications in the name Roland, he changed the child's name to Lawrence Adam, which contains all the letters of Arnold except the o.

In symbolism, numbers are not merely expressions of quantities, but idea forces, each with a particular character of its own. The actual digits are only the outer garments. The most generally accepted symbolic meaning of the number 13, one which figured prominently in Schoenberg's life, is that of death. And to the composer, 13 did represent the height of malevolent magic. Born on September 13, he considered this to be an evil portent and was so convinced of the inherent destructive power of the number that he claimed if he interrupted a composition and left it for a week or two, he invariably found that he stopped on a measure that was a multiple of 13. This prompted him to number his measures, later in life, as 12, 12A and 14. "It is not superstition," he often said, "it is belief."

The belief was of such an overpowering nature that the composer feared he would die during a year that was a multiple of 13. He so dreaded his sixty-fifth birthday that a friend asked composer and astrologer Dane Rudhyar to prepare Schoenberg's horoscope. Rudhyar did this and told Schoenberg that although the year was dangerous, it was not necessarily fatal. Schoenberg survived it. But in 1951, on his seventy-sixth birthday, the Viennese musician and astrologer Oscar Adler wrote Schoenberg a note warning him that the year was a critical one: 7 plus 6 equals 13. This stunned and depressed the composer, for up to that point he had only been wary of multiples of 13 and never considered adding the digits of his age. He became obsessed with this idea and many friends report that he frequently said: "If I can only pull through this year I shall be safe."

On Friday, July 13, of his seventy-sixth year, Arnold Schoenberg stayed in bed—sick, anxious and depressed. Shortly before midnight his wife leaned over and whispered, "You see, the day is almost over. All that worry was for nothing."

He looked at her and died.

Placing a musical note held as much magical significance to Schoenberg as placing a letter or number. He admitted that shortly after he evolved the 12-tone technique, he wanted to destroy the Chamber Symphony because he could see no relationship between the two themes. But then he made a happy discovery. He saw that the fourth, twelfth, thirteenth, fourteenth, and eighteenth notes of the first theme, when altered in rhythm and inverted, gave him his second theme. As far-fetched as this relationship may appear to an outsider, it caused Schoenberg's agony about the piece to abate.

Schoenberg identified his ways with God's, and was as impatient with critics who questioned him as he was with anyone questioning God's ways. "Everything which we do not understand we take for error," he wrote. "Everything which makes us uncomfortable we take for a mistake of its creator. And we do not stop to think that since we do not understand the meaning, silence, respectful silence, would be the only fitting response. And admiration—boundless admiration."

Viewing Schoenberg's mystical beliefs in light of the fact that he was not attached to a single religion throughout his life (Schoenberg converted from Judaism to Lutheranism and back to Judaism, and the children from his second marriage were educated in Jesuit schools), one is struck with his obsessional behavior, a carefully ordered system that influenced his every thought and action. Drawn to a belief in this kind of magic Schoenberg attempted to control his powerful inner drives as well as what happened during the course of his life and possibly even the moment of his death.

How meaningful it must have been to this man that the number of semi-tones into which the scale is divided is 12—that celestial number preceding 13! And how fortuitous for the history of music that this compelling, self-pronounced emissary of God arrived at the appropriate moment and ordered into being what composer Ernst Krenek has described as "the only method by which the idiom of atonality could be brought clearly and unmistakably under control."

"We shall not have our hero in a housecoat."

Thus Felix Greissle, Schoenberg's son-in-law, articulated why members of Schoenberg's family and close circle of friends had maintained Schoenberg's obsession with secrecy beyond the grave.

Although little personal biographical information is available, it is known that Samuel Schoenberg, the composer's father, came from Pressburg, a stronghold of Jewish orthodoxy in Hungary. A nephew, Hans Nachod, has described him as a "genius, a dreamer, a thinker, a sort of anarchistic idealist." Schoenberg's mother, Pauline Nachod, came from Prague, where her family had been cantors for several hundred years. Arnold's parents arrived in Vienna shortly after the enactment of the 1867 Constitution which removed the legal inequities against the Jews.

But anti-Semitism continued unabated. Sigmund Freud was denied the post of associate professor at the University of Vienna although he had been teaching for seventeen years without a formal appointment. The world of music was also closed to Jews: Mahler had to renounce Judaism and be baptized to be eligible for the director's post of the Vienna Court Opera, a powerful organization administered by the Court Chamberlain.

Vienna, birthplace of Haydn, Mozart, Beethoven and Schubert, became the center of the musical life of Europe after the Napoleonic wars. Aristocratic families gave concerts in their palaces, patrician families held recitals in their homes, concert halls opened, and the Viennese press began to exert considerable influence on musical events, with the music critic achieving an unprecedented position in the life of the art.

Arnold Schoenberg, oldest son of Samuel (then a shopkeeper in Vienna), has been described by his cousin Nachod as wild, energetic, witty and brash. At eight he began to study the violin and a little later learned the cello. Young Schoenberg taught himself to compose duets, trios and quartets so he would have chamber music to play with his friends.

When Arnold was sixteen, his father died poor. The boy left school at the end of the year in order to help support his mother. He took a job which a friend, David Joseph Bach, has described as that of an "underpaid clerk in a tenth-rate bank." Bach reported that one day Schoenberg entered the name of Beethoven in the principal ledger instead of the name of his client and announced to his friends: "I am so happy to have lost my job. The firm is insolvent anyhow and no one will ever drag me into another office."

Thus, at twenty-one, Schoenberg committed himself to a life of music and its consequences, including little prospect of making a living. He couldn't play any one instrument well, although he made an effort to play them all. He took a job conducting a chorus of metal workers in Stockerau, a community just outside Vienna, but had trouble playing the piano. Nevertheless, he got them to sing Brahms.

Schoenberg joined an orchestral society, the Polyhymnia, where he met Alexander von Zemlinsky, conductor and well-known avant-garde musician. Zemlinsky persuaded him to study music seriously and became his one and only teacher, instructing him in counterpoint for several months. Zemlinsky told friends and colleagues that Schoenberg learned everything quickly and with little apparent effort.

In 1895 and 1896, when Schoenberg was conducting the workers in the suburbs, he became involved in progressive music circles in the city. In the Cafés Landtmann and Griensteidl, where he and his contemporaries gathered, conversation focused on *Tristan und Isolde*, the Wagnerian music-drama that had used an advanced harmonic language steeped in sensuous chromaticism. During these years the programs of the Vienna Philharmonic included Bruckner's symphonies, Richard Strauss's tone poems and Max Reger's orchestral works, all richly chromatic and polyphonic in the Austro-German tradition.

In 1897, while on a summer holiday with Zemlinsky, Schoenberg produced the piano score for Zemlinsky's opera, *Sarema*, and composed a string quartet in the familiar vocabulary of the time. It was well received at its first performance in Vienna. That year Brahms died, and Schoenberg began to move in a new path. He composed his first mature works, a group of lieder. He gave them the opus numbers 1, 2 and 3. At about that time he left Judaism to become a Lutheran.

The Opus 1, 2 and 3 Lieder, performed at a recital with Zemlinsky at the piano, got a hostile reception. The clean and contrapuntal texture of the songs heightened the intensity of the dissonances. These dissonances were not qualitatively different from Wagner's, but they were more obvious, because they were not obscured by lush orchestrations. Secondly, the melody startled; notes were used to create intervals that were not only difficult to sing but often very unfamiliar to the ear. Thirdly, the rhythmic treatment was new; notes no longer depended upon the bar line. These harmonic, melodic and rhythmic devices, which were to become hallmarks of Schoenberg's later style, shocked the Viennese audience. Schoenberg's own response proved characteristic. He proudly proclaimed to his pupil René Leibowitz—reportedly with a smile—that "ever since this performance the riots have never stopped."

Verklärte Nacht, Schoenberg's first major large-scale work, composed in 1899, fulfilled the composer's desire for recognition only after an initial hostile response. He introduced the American recording of the work in 1950 with the following notes:

> At the end of the nineteenth century, the foremost representatives of the Zeitgeist in poetry were Detlov von Liliencron, Hugo von Hofmannsthal, and Richard Dehmel. But in music, after Brahms' death, many young composers followed the model of Richard Strauss by composing program music. This explains the origin of *Verklärte Nacht*; it is program music, illustrating and expressing the poem of Richard Dehmel.
>
> My composition was, perhaps, somewhat different from other illustrative compositions firstly, by not being for orchestra but for chamber group, and secondly, because it does not illustrate any action or drama but was restricted to portray nature and express human feelings. It seemed that, due to this attitude, my composition has gained qualities which can also satisfy if one does not know what it illustrates or, in other words, it offers the possibility to be appreciated as "pure music." Thus it can make you forget the poem which many a person today might call rather repulsive.

Schoenberg ends his notes with the following admonition: "It shall not be forgotten that this work, at its first performance in Vienna, was hissed and caused riots and fist fights. But very soon it was successful."

Verklärte Nacht, Opus 4, is a sextet for strings, written during a three-week holiday spent with Zemlinsky during the summer of 1899. The poem, taken from Richard Dehmel's novel *Zwei Menschen*, tells the story of a man's forgiveness of the sin committed by the woman he loves and of how, by this forgiveness, the world appears transfigured. The work is a literal one, despite Schoenberg's claims to the contrary. There are five sections: the first, third and fifth portray the couple wandering in the moonlight; the second contains a confession by the woman, the fourth the lover's response. The dialogue between the man and the woman is expressed by cello and violin.

The difference between *Verklärte Nacht*'s delicate chamber structure and Wagner's gigantic stage apparatus should not obscure the fact that the musical language of Schoenberg's early work is similar to that of Wagner. One harmonic innovation in *Verklärte Nacht* is an inversion of a ninth chord in which the ninth is in the bass position. A concert society refused permission to perform the piece on the basis of the inclusion of this "forbidden" chord. Later Schoenberg facetiously explained: "It is self-evident; there is no such thing as an inversion of a ninth chord; therefore there is no such thing as a performance of it; for one cannot perform something that does not exist. So I had to wait for several years."

The year after completing *Verklärte Nacht,* Schoenberg began to work on his monumental *Gurrelieder*. He completed it in the spring of 1901 but took another decade to finish the orchestration. The reason for the delay lay in the nature of the score. Responding, most likely, to the influence of Mahler's overwhelmingly large symphonies, Schoenberg called for a huge complement of performers: an orchestra of 140 players, five vocal soloists, one speaker, three male choirs and one mixed choir. He even specified "heavy iron chains," imitating Mahler's use of cowbells in his Sixth Symphony. Schoenberg ordered specially made score paper—with 48 staves.

In 1901, Schoenberg married Zemlinsky's sister, Mathilde. In order to make a living he left Vienna and moved to Berlin, where he had been offered a job scoring and conducting light music in an artistic cabaret. The position was probably not as offensive to him as many scholars assume it to have been. In his youth Schoenberg admired Franz Lehar and Leo Fall and later he frequently expressed admiration for Gilbert and Sullivan. Nevertheless, the orchestration of some 6,000 pages of operetta interfered considerably with his serious work.

Schoenberg took *Gurrelieder* with him when he went to Berlin. The exuberant, emotional Romantic work, a cantata set to a text by Danish poet Jens Peter Jacobsen, tells a typical story: King Waldemar of Denmark, passionately in love with Tove, is forced, for political reasons, to marry Helvig. Wild with jealousy, Queen Helvig causes Tove's death. The program note continues: "The grief of Waldemar was terrible to witness. He uttered many fearful blasphemies, which provoked Divine punishment and Waldemar was condemned to death to hunt nightly from dusk to dawn, galloping with his henchmen in a wild chase across the skies." But love proved to be stronger than death and Waldemar was reunited with his beloved Tove.

Gurrelieder is a three-part work. The first section contains an Orchestral Prelude, the statements of the lovers' passion and Tove's death. The second portrays Waldemar's curse and the third the tale of the nightly hunt. Although *Gurrelieder* is divided into these sections in its most apparent form, it is, as the contemporary theorist George Perle has pointed out, "entirely novel in form, a cycle of songs that are individually self-contained numbers in the tradition of the German lied but collectively a single large-scale work based on the Wagnerian technique of the leitmotif." Even in this very early work, Schoenberg focuses on what becomes the *idée fixe* of his life in music: the perpetual variation of a melodic idea. Waldemar's opening theme is related to material originally heard in the Orchestral Prelude, and Tove's theme, heard when she first expresses her love, becomes the major motive of the work, appearing in countless manifestations as leading melodic idea and subsidiary material as well.

Shortly after he arrived in Berlin, Schoenberg met Richard Strauss and showed him the first two sections of this formidable work. On the basis of what he saw, Strauss recommended Schoenberg to the Sterne Conservatory as a teacher and to the Liszt Foundation for a scholarship. Schoenberg was grateful for the position and the grant, for the cabaret had closed and his wife was pregnant. Their first child, Gertrude, was born in 1902.

At the same time that Schoenberg began teaching at Sterne, he began to work on a project suggested to him by Strauss, the setting of Maurice Maeterlinck's *Pelléas et Mélisande*. Debussy's opera, based on the same poem, was performed in Paris in 1902, the year that Schoenberg began work on the theme. Years later Schoenberg evaluated the difference between his *Pelleas* and Debussy's: "I had first planned to convert *Pelléas et Mélisande* into an opera, but I gave up this plan, although I did not know that Debussy was working on this opera at the same time. I still regret that I did not carry out my initial intention. It would have differed from Debussy's. I might have missed the wonderful perfume of the poem, but I would have made my characters more singing."

The program approach to music characteristic of *Verklärte Nacht* and *Gurrelieder* is pushed to extremes in *Pelleas*. In the notes he prepared for the American recording, Schoenberg wrote, "I tried to mirror every detail of it . . . the three main characters are presented in the manner of Wagner's leitmotifs." Not only are people represented by musical motives but "Golaud's jealousy" is pictured by one melodic idea and "destiny" by another. The story echoes the romantic legend of the doomed lovers. It centers on a beautiful young woman, lured into marriage with a much older man whom she does not love. Golo, the husband, and Pelleas, the lover, are half brothers. Thus the final catastrophe is inevitable; Melisande must die.

Schoenberg's *Pelleas,* Opus 5, orchestrated for a very large ensemble, is densely polyphonic, with every melodic idea surrounded by numerous other melodies. Despite the fact that this work, like *Verklärte Nacht,* begins and ends in the same key and is, therefore, a "tonal" composition, Schoenberg moves further away from conventional tonality, building chords on fourths, thus replacing the harmonic scheme of superimposed thirds.

In 1946, in a lecture at the University of Chicago, Schoenberg said: "I always attempted to produce something conventional and it always, against my will, became something unusual."

Whether or not the composer consciously tried to be conventional is irrelevant; the fact is that he always did produce something unusual. Even in these early days of his career, when he was still steeped in the Romantic tradition, Schoenberg introduced at least one radical procedure into each of his works. The searching quality and restless energy manifested in *Verklärte Nacht, Gurrelieder,* and *Pelleas* were reflected in his life as well. In July, 1903, Schoenberg left Berlin with his wife and child and returned to Vienna, the city that had been so unfriendly to him.

During their first year there—while living in Zemlinsky's house—Schoenberg met Gustav Mahler. The renowned composer-conductor, having heard his brother-in-law Arnold Rosé conduct a rehearsal of *Verklärte Nacht,* asked Zemlinsky to introduce him to Schoenberg. Dika Newlin, one of Schoenberg's American disciples, writes of a curious relationship that developed, in which Mahler referred to Zemlinsky and Schoenberg by the diminutives "Eisele and Beisele." At first Schoenberg expressed extreme irritation at Mahler's condescending manner but soon he became utterly devoted to him and courted his attention in a most impassioned way. He orchestrated *Gurrelieder* in a characteristically Mahlerian manner, and in 1904, wrote to Mahler:

> Honored Herr Direktor: In order to do any justice to the unheard of impressions which I received from your symphony, I must speak, not as musician to musician, but as man to man. For I have seen your soul naked, stark naked. It lay before me like a wild, mysterious landscape with its frightening crevasses and abysses. . . .

And in the summer of 1906: "Nothing would please me more than your saying we had come closer together."

The evidence is that they had. Rosé's quartet performed Schoenberg's Quartet No. 1 in February 1907, and Alma Mahler described the event:

> The critic yelled "Stop it!" when the audience was registering quiet but unanimous amusement. An unpardonable error! For his shouts were followed by such a whistling and racket as I have never heard before or since. A fellow parked himself in front of the first row and hissed at Schoenberg, who insisted on coming back for innumerable bows, cocking his head—the head of a Jewish Bruckner—this way and that, as though asking pardon and at the same time unobtrusively pleading for consideration. Mahler jumped up, stood beside the man, and said, "I'd just like to get a good look at a fellow who hisses."

Later, after a performance of Schoenberg's Chamber Symphony which was attended by as unruly an audience as the one attending the First Quartet, Mahler stood up ostentatiously in his box and applauded loudly until the last of the hostile demonstrators had left the hall. Despite this enthusiastic behavior toward Schoenberg, Mahler privately admitted to him that he did not understand the Opus 7: "I'm accustomed to reading thirty-voiced scores, but the four voices of your quartet give me at least twice as much trouble."

In 1903 Rosé conducted *Verklärte Nacht* in Vienna for the first time. The audience response was predictably unpleasant. It was after this occasion that a formidable decision was made: for what may have been the first time in history, a group of composers decided to organize a society, the Union of Creative Musicians, to educate listeners and critics. Mahler was the honorary president; among its members were such avant-garde composers as Schoenberg, Zemlinsky and Bruno Walter. Under these auspices Schoenberg conducted the first performance of his *Pelleas und Melisande* and Mahler directed the premier of his own *Kindertotenlieder* and Strauss's *Sinfonia Domestica*. Forty years later Schoenberg described the reaction to *Pelleas*: "The first performance, under my direction, provoked great riots among the audience and even the critics. Reviews were unusually violent and one of the music critics even suggested putting me in an insane asylum and keeping music paper out of my reach."

After his return to Vienna, Schoenberg avoided the program format and began to order his music along classic lines. His String Quartet No. 1, Opus 7, in D Minor, finished in 1905, shows the composer's affinity for Mahler, with sudden shifts of tempo, interrupted tunes and abrupt modulations. But Brahms still affected his work; a four-beat rhythm combined with triplets in the viola and cello is reminiscent of Brahms.

In 1906, the year his second child was born, Schoenberg wrote his Chamber Symphony, Opus 9. In this work for fifteen solo instruments, the composer used the whole-tone scale, almost completely negating the E Major signature. Chords which had formerly been used simply as passing harmonies were now allowed to stand quite alone. Another important aspect of the work lay in the fact that it started the trend toward the chamber form in Germany, six years before Stravinsky began to score for groups of solo instruments. Schoenberg's reaction against the super-orchestra was one of the factors that led the way to the overwhelming concern for instrumental color which has characterized much twentieth-century work.

Also in 1906, Webern, according to his own later testimony, showed Schoenberg a movement of a new work inspired by the Chamber Symphony. (Webern, Alban Berg, Erwin Stein and Heinrich Jalowitz all began to study under Schoenberg in 1904.) Its tones were not related to any particular key. It was, in effect, an "atonal" piece. Schoenberg finally rejected it and Webern wrote his next piece in the key of C Major, but it is probable that his experiment affected Schoenberg's own next work, the String Quartet No. 2, Opus 10, in F-sharp Minor. The first three movements bear the traditional key signatures, but the fourth enters into another domain, which Schoenberg characterized as having been inspired by Mahler's "pantonal" realms of composition.

In his writing Schoenberg demonstrated that pantonality was one of Mahler's particular contributions to composition, by contrasting the classic symphony, which begins and ends in the same key or begins in a minor key and ends in the related major, with Mahler's symphonies. The First begins in D Minor and ends in F Minor; the Fourth begins in G Major and ends in E Major; the Fifth begins in C-sharp Minor and ends in D Major. Thus Schoenberg considered the fourth movement of his quartet to have been derived from Mahler. Schoenberg's attempted break-up of the tonal system in this movement is actually more closely related to Mahler's post-Romantic tonal experiments than to Webern's more radical compositional thinking. The conductor Robert Craft has written, "It is interesting today to listen to parts of Schoenberg's Second Quartet and mark the stray excursions into atonality and the rather sheep-like return to the tonal fold whose border is, of course, as arbitrary as the ear's education."

To specify his gratitude to Mahler, Schoenberg used two of Mahler's most striking devices in the F-sharp Minor Quartet. He introduced a soprano into the third and fourth movements, as Mahler introduced the human voice into his symphonies. And he quoted the folk tune "Ach, du lieber Augustin" in the Scherzo movement as Mahler had quoted another folk tune in his First Symphony. The tune's banal qualities stand out in sharp relief against the context of Schoenberg's otherwise difficult, angular writing.

It should be noted that the Quartet, Opus 10, was the work that followed the Chamber Symphony; Schoenberg himself described the transition: "In the time of the Chamber Symphony I understood better what I had written and had more personal pleasure with that than with the music that followed. Then to compose was a great pleasure. In a later time it was a duty against myself. . . ." The emotion that lay behind this crucial, revolutionary, atonal movement was accurately reflected by the soprano's words. The piece is set to a poem by Stefan George:

> *I feel the air of other spheres . . .*
> *I dissolve into tones, circling, wreathing . . .*
> *yielding involuntarily to the great breathing . . .*
> *The earth shakes, white and soft as foam.*
> *I climb across huge chasms.*
> *I feel as if I were swimming beyond the farthest*
> *cloud in a sea of crystalline brilliance.*
> *I am only a flicker of the sacred fire.*
> *I am only a mumbling of the sacred voice.*

CHAPTER 3

Theodor W. Adorno, the German philosopher, sociologist and composition student of Alban Berg, has written that the Quartet No. 2 was an "echo of a crisis in personal life whose sorrow, hardly ever mastered, brought to Schoenberg's work its full creative weight."

Its genesis took place in 1906, when Zemlinsky introduced Schoenberg to Richard Gerstl, a painter nine years younger than Schoenberg and a man so withdrawn that he did not sign the front of his paintings, nor did he ever exhibit. Alma Mahler has said that although she knew Gerstl well, she never saw any of his work. Gerstl lived with the Schoenberg family during the summers of 1907 and 1908; under his guidance, Schoenberg began to paint.

Gerstl began a love affair with Mathilde Schoenberg and revealed the pain of the ensuing relationship in a number of wild works. Paintings of Arnold, Mathilde, and the couple with their children were followed by a naked self-portrait and finally by a portrayal of his face in a grotesque state of laughter. This was Gerstl's last work, a painting of a deeply disturbed man. In the fall of 1908, Mathilde left her husband to live with her lover.

Several days later, Gerstl gathered his paintings together in a pile on the floor, set his studio on fire, plunged a kitchen knife into his heart, and hanged himself over the burning debris. (Gerstl's family salvaged fifteen paintings and stored them in a cellar in Vienna where they were discovered in 1931.)

Gerstl's tortured relationship with Schoenberg, whom he adored, was similar to Schoenberg's relationship with Mahler and consistent with the cult of suffering implicit in the Romantic agony that had been cultivated by Goethe, Byron, Berlioz, and Wagner's Tristan. Coincident with the Gerstl affair, Mahler left Vienna for New York. It was during this traumatic time that Schoenberg tentatively entered the atonal world with the last movement of his Second Quartet.

Schoenberg's next and crucial work is a cycle of songs set to Stefan George's *Das Buch der hängenden Gärten*. Schoenberg's notes indicate his awareness of the profundity of his own stylistic change:

> In the Georgelieder I have succeeded for the first time in approaching an ideal of expression and form that has hovered about me for some years. Hitherto I had not sufficient strength and sureness to realize the ideal. Now, however, I have definitely started on a new journey, I may confess to have broken off the bonds of a bygone aesthetic; and, if I am striving towards a goal that seems to me to be certain, nevertheless, I always feel the opposition I shall have to overcome.

It is in the thirteenth song of the cycle, "Du lehnest wider eine Silberweide," that there is no key signature at all; it is the first literally "atonal" piece. As the number 13 marked the birth and death of Schoenberg, it also marked the birth of atonality and the death of the tonal scheme. In all the other songs of the cycle, the principle of tonality is simply suspended. Composed in 1908, immediately after Gerstl's death, it is Schoenberg's most extended work for voice and piano. (Milton Babbitt, according it a position with the song cycles of Beethoven, Schubert and Schumann, points out that it combines the human voice—the most restrictive instrument in register—with the piano—the most restrictive instrument in timbre—and marvels at the diversity which the composer was, nevertheless, able to achieve.)

Schoenberg disclaimed responsibility for the term "atonal," noting that it was as absurd to call music atonal as to call painting aspectral. He preferred the term "atonical," implying an absence of a tonic center, or "pantonal," referring to a merging of all the keys.

Thus music entered a state of crisis in 1908. The breakdown of the tonal system confirmed the annihilation of law and order in the Austro-German musical world. The absence of all formal restrictions in the non-harmonically conceived works that followed permitted a great discharge of emotional tension. An era of highly expressionistic music began that paralleled the art of Kokoschka and Kandinsky.

The Gerstl affair not only precipitated Schoenberg's move into the atonal world; according to a member of the Schoenberg family, it also generated his involvement in painting, and he entered the field as a full professional. Between 1908 and 1910 Schoenberg produced about sixty paintings and drawings. In a letter to his publisher, Emil Hertzka, in which he sought Hertzka's aid in obtaining commissions for portraits, he displayed the same arrogant, defensive attitude that characterized his dealings in the world of music:

> It is much more interesting to have one's portrait done or to own a painting by a musician of my reputation than to be painted by some mere practitioner of painting whose name will be forgotten in twenty years whereas even now my name belongs to the history of music. For a life-size portrait I want from two to six sittings and from two hundred to four hundred kronen. That is really very cheap considering that in twenty years people will pay ten times as much for these paintings. I am quite sure you realize this, and I hope you won't make any feeble jokes about a matter as serious as this, but will treat it as seriously as it deserves.

Art was a serious business for Schoenberg. His interest in painting led him to Wassily Kandinsky, the Russian abstract expressionist who was living in Munich, and Schoenberg became a member of the Blaue Reiter group. His paintings were exhibited in 1910 at the bookstore and art gallery of Hugo Heller. Kandinsky commented on his work:

> Schoenberg's pictures fall into two categories: on the one hand the portraits and landscapes painted directly from nature; on the other hand, heads imagined intuitively, which he calls "visions." The former Schoenberg designates as finger exercises, which he feels he needs, but which he does not particularly value, and which he does not like to exhibit. The others he paints (just as rarely as the first sort) to express emotions that find no musical form. These two categories are extremely different. Internally they stem from one and the same soul, caused to vibrate in one case by external nature and in the other by nature within. . . .

Schoenberg and Kandinsky followed remarkably similar paths in their moves away from representation to abstraction and from the single focuses of perspective and tonality in painting and music to the subsequent afocal attributes of both. Both artists had received the initial impulses in these directions as early as the last years of the nineteenth century, and neither one achieved the full realization of his purpose until many years later.

_As Kandinsky formulated the principles of an abstract style for the first time in 1910 in his treatise *On the Spiritual in Art,* so Schoenberg first set down the theory of the emancipation of the dissonance in his *Theory of Harmony (Harmonielehre)* published in 1911. In this work Schoenberg analyzes what he refers to as the "function of tonality": "Tonality does not serve; on the contrary it demands to be served. . . . It has always been the referring of all results to a center, to an emanating point of tonality, which rendered important service to the composer in matters of form. All the tonal successions, chords, and chord successions in a piece achieve a unified meaning through their definite relation to a tonal center and also through their mutual ties. . . . That is the unifying function of tonality. . . ."

Schoenberg asks whether one could "write a piece which does not use the advantages offered by tonality and yet unifies all other elements so that their succession and relation are logically comprehensible." He answers yes, if the composer substitutes melodic motive for tonal structure: "It could be easily shown that a work might have tonal unity, but nevertheless still be confused in content, incoherent, superficial, external, yes, even without sense. . . . I am rather inclined to believe that one may sooner sacrifice logic and unity in the harmony than in the thematic substance, in the motives, in the thought-content."

In this treatise Schoenberg defined "consonance" as the clearer and simpler relation with the ground note, and "dissonance" as the more remote and complicated, holding a quantitative rather than a qualitative distinction between the two. Removing the qualitative distinction between consonance and dissonance eliminates the concept of the one being beautiful and the other ugly. The physical basis that Schoenberg thus provided for atonal composition resulted in the "emancipation of the dissonance," a process that was taking place in the most advanced composition in France (Debussy) and Russia (Scriabine) but without the accompanying verbal justification. The freeing of notes from obligations that derive from the seven-note scale implies that the historic process of tonality had finally come to an end. Schoenberg's important 500-page treatise was dedicated to Mahler, who died at the age of fifty just before the book was completed:

> This book is dedicated to the memory of Gustav Mahler. It was hoped that the dedication might give him some small joy while he still lived. It was intended, thereby, to do honor to his immortal compositions and to show that his work, at which cultivated musicians in their superiority shrugged their

shoulders and which they even passed by with contempt, was revered by one who, perhaps, to some extent understood it.

During his last illness, Mahler asked his wife to take care of Schoenberg after his death. She carried out his wish, setting up a fund for him.

Between 1908 and 1912, Schoenberg produced at least three of the great pieces from which, as Stravinsky has claimed, subsequent generations of composers have taken their bearings. Although Richard Strauss was, at the time, the most important Establishment figure, Schoenberg was the central creative musician around whom all advanced musical activity in Germany took place. With *Der Rosenkavalier*, which Strauss composed in 1911, the latter repudiated the advances he had made in *Salome* (1905) and the wildly dissonant *Elektra* (1909). At the same time, Schoenberg continued to move ahead, increasing the harmonic complexities as he decreased his instrumental forces.

The striking reduction in size from his earlier, grandiose program works to the atonal, short, nonprogram pieces indicates the power that tonality—however much extended—had been able to provide in Schoenberg's Romantic works. Once having abandoned the tonal frame- work, the composer relied on the musical motive alone as the source of unity for his composition. This is clearly in evidence in the first of these works, the Piano Pieces, Opus 11, and, most particularly, in the second of these pieces. Here an initial idea, a swift upbeat followed by a melodic tritone, is introduced in the first four measures and sustains the rest of the short com- position. The "theme" is Schoenberg's *Grundgestalt*, the creative idea which undergoes perpetual variation but never repetition. It was in the Preface to Opus 11 that Schoenberg wrote that he was following "an inner compulsion that is stronger than my education, stronger than my artistic training." The move into the atonal world had extramusical implications for him.

Schoenberg then moved away from the piano, the instrument on which he first applied his most radical ideas, and composed an "atonal" work for orchestra, the Five Orchestral Pieces, Opus 16, the only purely orchestral work of this period.* That each of these pieces bears a poetic title should not, however, misdirect the listener. In an entry in his diary just before the publication of the work in 1912, Schoenberg wrote:

---

* *In a program note to Opus 16, Webern wrote that these pieces contained the "experience of Schoenberg's emotional life."*

Letter from Peters, making an appointment with me for Wednesday in Berlin, in order to get to know me personally. Wants titles for the orchestral pieces—for publisher's reasons. Maybe I'll give in, for I've found that titles are at least possible. On the whole, unsympathetic to the idea. For the wonderful thing about music is that one can say everything in it, so that he who knows understands everything; and yet one hasn't given away one's secrets—the things one doesn't even admit to oneself. But titles give you away! Besides—whatever was to be said has been said, by the music. Why, then, words as well? If words were necessary they would be there in the first place. But art says more than words. Now, the titles which I may provide give nothing away, because some of them are very obscure and others highly technical. To wit:

I.	Premonitions	*(everybody has those)*
II.	The Past	*(everybody has that, too)*
III.	Chord-Colors	*(technical)*
IV.	Peripetia	*(general enough, I think)*
V.	The obbligato	*(perhaps better the "fully developed" or the "endless recitative)*

However, there should be a note that these titles were added for the technical reasons of publication and not to give a poetic content.

The Five Pieces for Orchestra, together with the Three Piano Pieces, represent a clean break with the past. In each of the orchestral pieces an original cell gives rise to the whole. In one, Schoenberg's *Grundgestalt* is only a five-part chord; he achieves variety through a constantly shifting instrumentation. Schoenberg wrote of the importance of tone color in his *Treatise on Harmony*, predicting its growth as a structural element in composition: "I cannot unreservedly agree with the distinction between color and pitch. I find that a note is perceived by its color, one of whose dimensions is pitch. Color, then, is the great realm, pitch one of its provinces. . . . If the ear could discriminate between differences of color, it might be feasible to invent melodies that are built of colors *(klangfarbenmelodien)*. But who dares to develop such theories?"

Not grounded in tonality, the Opus 16 pieces were not encased in the formal framework that serves to articulate tonal areas. These instrumental pieces are revolutionary in their free formal structure as well as in the soloistic treatment of instruments within the orchestral fabric. They were not performed until 1912, and then not in Germany but in London under the direction of Sir Henry Wood. The work received bad press in London. *The Times* described it as "incomprehensible as a Tibetan poem," and Berlin musicologist Hugo Leichentritt wrote: "How poor our descendants will be if they take this joyless, careworn Schoenberg as the sensibility of our age."

Both sets of abstract, atonal works, the Opus 11 and Opus 16, contained only very short pieces. Schoenberg found, at the beginning of 1910, that the perpetual variation of a melodic motive could not alone sustain more extended works. The composer later described the predicament which he faced and how he came to depend on extramusical sources to provide the unity which he sought: "Formerly the harmony had served not only as a source of beauty, but, more important, as a means of distinguishing the features of the form. . . . Hence it seemed at first impossible to compose pieces of complicated organization or of great length. A little later I discovered how to construct larger forms by following a text or a poem."

The first of the large, atonal works was *Erwartung,* a monodrama set to a text by Marie Pappenheim, the wife of a Viennese psychiatrist. (This was the golden age of psychoanalysis in Vienna.) The piece, written in the strikingly short span of seventeen days, describes a hysterical woman's terrified thoughts. The angular melodies and profusion of dissonances mirror the anxiety, depression, love and hate which she experiences as she searches for her lover on a dark and moonlit night. In *Erwartung* Schoenberg uses ten- and eleven-note chords which destroy any trace of traditional consonance. No musical idea is ever repeated in exactly the same way; the text is what holds the work together.

Schoenberg composed his next piece, *Die glückliche Hand,* in the same atonal idiom as *Erwartung,* only this time he wrote the libretto as well, a strongly autobiographical one. The Man is obviously Schoenberg who, at the beginning, lies prone on the stage with the monster of dissatisfaction gnawing at his back. A Greek chorus upbraids him for desiring worldly things—recognition and acclaim—when he knows that fulfillment can only come to him through spiritual and intellectual paths.

The women of the chorus begin the work, intoning:

> *Be still, won't you, You know how it always is, and yet*
> *you remain blind.*
> *So many times already! And once again?*
> *Once again the same ending.*
> *Once again trusting in the same dream.*

Once again you fix your longing on the unattainable.
Once again you give yourself up to the sirens of your
thoughts, thoughts that are unworldly but thirst for
worldly fulfillment.
You poor fool—worldly fulfillment!
You, who have the divine in you, and covet the worldly!

The humiliation which Schoenberg, who had "the divine in him," must perpetually suffer is the theme of this curious musico-dramatic work. Schoenberg's involvement in the visual arts profoundly affected his realization of *Die glückliche Hand*, for he specified the lighting effects in the score. Color, both instrumental and spectral, was of primary importance during these expressionistic, productive years.

Around 1910 Schoenberg's career began to improve. The Union of Art and Culture in Vienna produced part of *Gurrelieder* with piano accompaniment, and Oscar Fried, champion of new music, conducted *Pelleas und Melisande* in Berlin. In 1910 Schoenberg began making carbon copies of his letters, obviously intending them for posterity.

In 1911, Schoenberg received the news of Mahler's death. He expressed his reaction verbally in an essay in the journal *Der Merker* and musically in the Six Little Piano Pieces, Opus 19. The most notable characteristic of these pieces is their brevity and musical concentration: the longest is eighteen measures and the shortest only nine. In the last piece Schoenberg records his impressions at Mahler's funeral by setting an angular five-note melody against a series of bell-like chords built on fourths.

During the summer of 1911, Schoenberg and his family moved back to Berlin. His situation in Vienna had not improved; he had only a few pupils and no chance for a steady position. The fact that he was "permitted," but not engaged, to teach at the Academy was particularly humiliating to him. Financial prospects in Berlin were not much better. He had only two pupils waiting for him there, but the progressive atmosphere in general and Fried's performance in particular, motivated him into making the change.

Shortly after his arrival in Berlin, his two pupils—Eduard Steuermann and Edward Clarke—arranged for him to give a series of public lectures. When his Five Orchestral Pieces was published in an inexpensive edition, the scores sold well, indicating that the lectures were exerting a profound effect. Schoenberg's first Berlin composition, the lied "Herzgewächse," Opus 20, was a setting of the Maeterlinck poem for the unusual combination of soprano, celeste, harmonium, and harp, with the voice covering an enormous range. The work provides a beautiful connecting link between the Piano Pieces, Opus 11—about which he wrote that he was following an "inner compulsion" and which heralded his atonal period—and *Pierrot Lunaire*, which culminated this most productive era in Schoenberg's life.

In March, 1912, Schoenberg started *Pierrot Lunaire*. Like the Man in *Die glückliche Hand*, Pierrot, with his tormented soul, clearly reflects Schoenberg's picture of himself. The composer chose to set a cycle of poems by Albert Giraud which had been published in 1884. Of the fifty poems in the cycle, he chose twenty-one, but that number corresponds to the opus number of the work and is a reversal of the digits of the year of its appearance. Schoenberg grouped these pieces into three parts of seven poems each, and to ensure that no one should miss the number mysticism which had begun to affect his life seriously, he entitled the piece "Dreimal sieben Gedichte aus Albert Girauds Pierrot Lunaire."

Schoenberg's Pierrot is a far cry from the clown of the commedia dell'arte. This Pierrot presents many apparently psychotic features whose significance was being brought to light by psychoanalytic psychology. Stravinsky, whose *Petrushka,* composed the previous year, featured an altogether simpler kind of clown, heard a rehearsal of *Pierrot Lunaire*. Although he reported different reactions to this hearing at various times, he consistently praised the instrumentation. Written for piano, flute, piccolo, clarinet, double bass clarinet, violin, viola, and cello, the work also celebrates *Sprechstimme*, a technique Schoenberg introduced into the chorus of *Die glückliche Hand*.

Reciting a text to instrumental accompaniment was not new. The spoken word, given a relatively free range within a certain allocation of bars, had been used during the eighteenth and nineteenth centuries. But in *Pierrot Lunaire,* Schoenberg ensures that the recitation will take place in strict time by using traditional notation. He places crosses on note heads to indicate the particular line of speech melody. This speaking voice is not only notated rhythmically, but with sharps, flats and returns to naturals. Schoenberg directed: "The sung note keeps to the level of the note without changing; the spoken note gives it, yet immediately leaves it to fall or rise."

In its musical form, *Pierrot Lunaire* represents a shift from Schoenberg's recent expressive compositions to a new emphasis on form. Piece No. 1 is based on an ostinato, while some others are strictly canonic. Schoenberg displays a virtuoso handling of polyphonic procedures; in the piece "Moonspot," when Pierrot looks around and discovers a white spot on his back, his action is accompanied by the piano playing a three-part fugue, the clarinet and piccolo forming canons in diminution with the first two voices of the fugue, and a third canon, independent of the others, handled by the violin and cello. Halfway through the piece, the clarinet and piccolo, proceeding at twice the speed of the canonic partners, run out of notes and begin running backwards, an auditory parallel for Pierrot frantically trying to rub the moonspot off his back.

Each of the stanzas contains thirteen lines; the seventh and last lines repeat the first and the eighth repeats the second. Both in the text and the music, strictness of form is combined with freedom of content. The musical content is tonally free, although, as is apparent in the use of canons and fugues, the forms in which the content is contained are frequently very strict.

Thus in 1912 Schoenberg had complete tonal freedom and used it in *Pierrot Lunaire*. At the same time he knew he had not found a purely musical way to sustain works with large dimensions. It was perhaps in the context of this stylistic crisis that Schoenberg chose the following verse as the last in the cycle, and underscored the attraction of "days of yore" with the use of parallel thirds and a recurring E Major triad, nostalgic reminiscences of an earlier, more comfortable musical time.

> *O fragrance old from days of yore,*
> *Once more you intoxicate my senses.*
> *A prankish troop of rogueries*
> *Is swirling through the air.*
>
> *A cheerful longing makes me hope*
> *For joys which I have long despised;*
> *O fragrance old from days of yore*
> *Once more you intoxicate me.*
>
> *I have abandoned all my gloom*
> *And from my window framed in sunlight*
> *I freely gaze on the dear world*
> *And dream beyond in boundless transport—*
> *O fragrance old from days of yore.*

After *Pierrot Lunaire*, Schoenberg's compositional pace slowed down dramatically. In the decade that followed he completed only one work, the Orchestral Songs, Opus 22, of 1914 and early 1915. As World War I began, his position and that of Austria and Germany were threatened by the spectacular artistic production of the French. Marcel Proust finished his monumental novel *À la recherche du temps perdu*, Debussy composed the great and revolutionary ballet *Jeux*, and in Paris, the Ballet Russe presented Stravinsky's colossal *Le Sacre du Printemps*.

"Vorgefühl" (Premonition), one of the Opus 22 songs with a text by Rainer Maria Rilke, expresses anxiety:

> *I feel the winds that come, and must endure them.*
> *While things on earth must rest in utter stillness.*
> *The doors close softly, in the room is silence;*
> *The windows yet unmoved, the dust is heavy.*
> *But I live the storm—I am stirred like the sea—*
> *I stretch forth my arms—am thrown back on myself—*
> *I cast myself forth—and remain all alone*
> *In the greatest of storms.*

CHAPTER 4

uring the next decade, Schoenberg evolved the 12-tone technique. He began working out the method in an oratorio, *Die Jakobsleiter,* which he never completed. The project originated in 1912, when poet Richard Dehmel wrote Schoenberg a letter: "Last night I heard *Verklärte Nacht* and I should feel it a sin of omission if I did not send you a word of thanks for your wonderful sextet." Schoenberg replied to Dehmel, thanking him and requesting him to serve as librettist once again, this time for an oratorio which he described the following way:

> Modern man, having passed through materialism, social-ism, and anarchy, and despite having been an atheist, still having in him some residue of ancient faith (in the form of superstition) wrestles with God (see also Strindberg's *Jacob Wrestling*) and finally succeeds in finding God and becoming religious, learning to pray! It is not through any action, any blows of fate, least of all through any love of woman, that this change of heart is to come about.

Dehmel would not agree to the project, so Schoenberg wrote the libretto himself. Like the Man in *Die glückliche Hand,* and the tortured clown in *Pierrot Lunaire,* Gabriel, the protagonist in *Die Jakobsleiter,* is identifiable as the martyred composer, the sole human being called upon to proclaim the new to the world, the ultimate musical lawgiver of our time.

Die Jakobsleiter, which Schoenberg worked on intermittently during the second decade of the twentieth century (he was in and out of the Austrian army twice), is, as Bertold Viertel has written, an allegory of his mission as an artist. The work opens with a group of dissatisfied people wandering about in considerable confusion. They are tired but strive on, not knowing where the journey leads. Gabriel is among them, giving help and advice, judging and leading them.

Although Schoenberg structured the work as an oratorio, the language is far from traditional and indicates the curious pathological nature of his relationship with God and man: "Union with Him awakes magnetically the currents of the mind by induction," is interwoven with "My Word I leave here; make what you can of it. My form I take with me. In any case it must remain beyond you until it reappears in your midst with new words—the old ones over again—to be newly misunderstood."

Between 1915 and 1923, Schoenberg did not publish a single composition. He appears to have been exclusively concerned with the development of the dodecaphonic principle which he desperately hoped would reestablish Germany as the undisputed center of the musical world and himself as its sole redeemer.

The first measures of *Die Jakobsleiter,* written in 1917, reveal the nature of the 12-tone technique. Karl Rankl, Schoenberg's student during that year, has pointed out that the first half of the 12-note scale is played by cellos, which repeat the same six notes six times in succession. The other six are built up vertically, from the second bar onward, and are handled by brass and woodwinds. "These bars clearly show," Rankl writes, "the exposition of a 12-tone scale divided into two halves." Schoenberg, in what appears to be a strikingly ingenious double entendre, described the nature of the technique in the opening words of the oratorio:

> *Whether right or left,*
> *Forwards or backwards,*
> *Uphill or downhill,*
> *We have to go on without asking*
> *What lies beyond or ahead.*
> *It will remain hidden from you.*
> *You should, you must forget it*
> *To fulfill your task.*

Egon Wellesz, another early Schoenberg pupil, tells an interesting story about the development of the 12-tone technique in an August, 1961 issue of *The Listener*:

> It was in 1915 that a private in the Austrian army was sent to me because the military psychiatrists found that he was so neurotic and talked about music in such a peculiar

way that they did not know what to do with him and wanted my advice. The man was Josef Hauer. Hauer had developed in his compositions the idea of 12-note rows which, according to his theory, had the same function as the nomoi, the type-melodies in Greek music. Though Hauer expressed his views in a very amateurish way, I found his ideas very interesting and his attitude toward music reminded me of Erik Satie. I think that my favorable report helped to get Hauer released from his work in an army office. Reti, of whose judgment Schoenberg thought highly, told him about Hauer's theories and compositions, and Schoenberg began to develop these ideas which led him to introduce the system of composition with twelve tones.

There can be no doubt that Hauer was the first to construct rows of twelve notes—rather haphazardly—and to choose which one of them suited him best for a composition.

Hauer, in fact, did not choose a single row for a musical work, nor did he work with the "row" as we know it. Unlike Schoenberg, who insisted that one row provide all the material and thus ensure a sense of unitary perception, Hauer allowed that any number of 12-tone melodies could be combined within a single movement.

In 1920, Hauer published an essay, "On the Nature of Music," in which he argued that the notion of equal temperament, the division of the scale into twelve equal parts, which had developed during the nineteenth century (as opposed to the division of the scale into unequal intervals, which pulled all the notes to a single tonic) necessitated a new compositional system. In describing what he had in mind, Hauer used the word "atonal" for what we generally designate as 12-tone: "In atonal music . . . which stems from "totalities," intervals alone are relevant. Music expression is no longer achieved through the use of major and minor keys and of specific instruments with a single timbre: it is founded on the totality of intervals and timbre, and this is best and most clearly realized by using one single, tempered instrument. . . . The "law" or "*nomos*" is that all twelve notes of the temperament are to be repeated over and over again."

The question of priority—of who conceived the 12-tone idea first—is not the crucial one. What is interesting is Schoenberg's desire to be first in announcing the technique in light of the fact that he postponed publishing any 12-tone work until 1923, years after he began using the method. A letter

Schoenberg wrote to Hauer in December, 1923, gives such a full picture of the uses to which Schoenberg put his theory that it is quoted in full:

Dear Herr Hauer:
Your letter gave me very, very great pleasure. And I can give you proof of this. The fact is that about 1 1/2 or 2 years ago I saw from one of your publications that you were trying to do something similar to me, in a similar way. After coming to terms with the painful feeling that someone else, by also being engaged in something I had been thinking about for pretty well fifteen years, was jeopardizing my reputation for originality, which might cause me to renounce putting my ideas into practice if I did not want to pass for a plagiarist—a painful feeling, you will admit—after having come to terms with this feeling and having come to see wherein we differ from each other and that I was in a position to prove the independence of my ideas, I resolved to make the following suggestion to you:

"Let us write a book together, a book in which one chapter will be written by one of us, the next by the other and so on. In it let us state our ideas, exactly defining the distinctive elements, by means of objective but courteous argument trying to collaborate a little bit in spite of these differences: because of what there is in common a basis can surely be found on which we can get along smoothly and with each other."

And I meant to say also: "Let us show that music, if nothing else, would not have advanced if it had not been for the Austrians, and that we know what the next step must be."

Then, however, I had qualms (there are always mischief-makers and gossips) lest I would be exposing myself to a refusal, and so the letter was never written. Perhaps now, your suggestion of a school is even better. Above all, because in that way an exchange of ideas would come about spontaneously, more frequently, and without the agitatory contributions of a public maliciously looking on and provoking one to stubbornness. But the idea of the book, for the purpose of establishing the present point of view, should not be completely rejected either.

We are perhaps both in search of the same thing and have probably found related things. My point of departure was the attempt to replace the no longer applicable principle of tonality by a new principle relevant to the changed conditions, that is, in theory. I am definitely concerned with no other theories but the methods of "twelve-note composition" as—after many errors and deviations—I now (and I hope definitively) call it. I believe— for the first time again in fifteen years—that I have found a key. Probably the book to be entitled *The Theory of Musical Unity* originally planned about ten years ago, often sketched out and just as often scrapped, time and again newly delimited and then enlarged, will in the end have just the modest title: *Composition with Twelve Notes*. This is as far as I have got in the last approx- imately two years, and frankly, I have so far—for the first time— found no mistake and the system keeps on growing of its own accord, without my doing anything about it. This I consider a good sign. In this way I find myself positively enabled to com- pose as freely and fantastically as one otherwise does only in one's youth, and am nevertheless subject to a precisely definable aesthetic discipline. It is now more precise than it has ever been. For I can provide rules for almost everything. Admittedly, I have not yet taught this method, because I must still test it in some more compositions and expand it in some directions. But in the introductory course for my pupils I have been using a great deal of it for some years in order to define forms and formal elements and in particular to explain musical technique.

Please do believe that my wish to reach an understanding with you springs above all from the urge to recognize achieve- ment. This is something I have proved often enough; among other cases, also where you were concerned (I mention this in order to show you that the two occasions when you tried to find an approach to me were, after all, not wasted), in my *Theory of Harmony* I argue (on page 488 of the new edition) against the term "atonality" and then continue with an appreciation of you personally: you will realize that I did this for no one's sake but my own, out of the need to be fair: and this makes the value of my praise objectively even greater! My friends will be able to confirm, too, that although I have put my head down and charged like a bull at what I am opposed to in your ideas, in conversation I have acknowledged your achievements at least as much as I have done in my book.

It is a pleasure to give you proof of all this, for your amicable advance is of a kind that should remove all misunderstanding and all grudges; and so I shall gladly contribute a share as large as yours. I should be very pleased if we could now soon also have a further discussion about further details. It is in particular the project of the school that I have a good deal to say about, having long been turning over the idea of starting a school for the development of style. Perhaps you will yourself name some afternoon next week when you would care to visit me (excepting Tuesday and Friday). Although I may be in Vienna next week, I do not know whether I shall have the time then.

I am looking forward very much to the further development of our understanding and remain, with kindest regards, yours sincerely,

ARNOLD SCHOENBERG

N.B. This letter was not dictated, but written by me personally on the typewriter, thus respecting your wish that for the present I should not mention our discussions to any third person.

Neither the book nor the school materialized.

Schoenberg and Hauer were not the only two musicians independently to formulate the 12-tone technique; Webern later claimed that he was composing 12-tone music as early as 1911 but was not then conscious of the underlying law. What made dodecaphony such an extraordinary innovation in the history of music in Western civilization was that the man who first did become conscious of the law and its importance in a generative sense, had a special arrogance of manner stemming from a mystical conviction that he had been chosen by God to proclaim it to the world. Until Mahler's death, Schoenberg played the role of the follower, an idolator of the great Viennese musician. But after Mahler's death Schoenberg stepped into a new role, the adored leader, the subject of idolatry on the part of a group of utterly devoted disciples.

As he proceeded to develop his system during these years, he institutionalized his leadership by establishing—directly after the Armistice—the Society for Private Musical Performances in Vienna. Webern and Berg were both members and Berg has described the aims of the society: "The Society was founded in November, 1918, for the purpose of enabling Arnold Schoenberg to carry out his plan and give artists and music lovers a real and exact knowledge of modern music."

At these meetings, experienced musicians played exceptionally well-rehearsed works by a diversity of composers including Berg, Debussy, Webern, Zemlinsky, Stravinsky, Scriabin, Strauss, Max Reger, Hans Pfitzner, Josef Hauer and Schoenberg. Those entering the group were aware of its stringent regulations: "Upon joining this Society, members must fill in and mail the appended form, declaring knowledge and willingness to abide by the statutes. February 16, 1919, Arnold Schoenberg." The statutes cited that "a completely free hand in the direction of the Society, and all decisions of the General Assembly including elections, changes in statutes, dissolution of the Society, require for their validity the consent of the President."

Schoenberg's growing megalomania and paranoid manner of thinking manifest themselves not only in the authoritarian nature of the society but in the suspicious nature of the regulations. The most striking one is that each member had to come to each performance armed not only with an identification card but with an accompanying photograph as well, so that no hostile outsider could slip into the hall unnoticed.

In a collection of articles published by Schirmer in 1937, César Searchinger described Schoenberg's personality during these years in which he was completing the formulation of the 12-tone technique:

> My first experience with Schoenberg was in Amsterdam at the Mahler Festival of 1921. Here, surrounded by his disciples Schoenberg went around, revered as a musical prophet. . . .
>
> A few months later I saw Schoenberg again in Vienna, ruling with the iron hand of the musical pedant, the concerts of the Society for Private Musical Performances, insisting on innumerable rehearsals and the strictest precision and perfection in the delivery of the works of his contemporaries of all nationalities—an artistic tyranny such as I have never witnessed before or since.

The society dissolved in 1922, primarily because of the devastating devaluation of Austrian currency. The short-lived history of this minuscule dictatorship has never been revealed.

Schoenberg's tyrannical manner during these critical years just before the release of his 12-tone technique is understandable in the light of his sense of possession and mystical convictions concerning the system. Then how curious it is that although he began to formulate the technique during the writing of the libretto to *Die Jakobsleiter* in 1915, and developed it further in various sketches and movements composed after that, he kept all of this music under wraps until 1923, when the firm of Wilhelm Hansen in Copenhagen published the Five Piano Pieces, Opus 23. One would expect that his desire to preempt Hauer, whose article on 12-tone composition appeared in 1920, and anyone else working in a similar vein would have motivated him into releasing his first 12-tone piece almost as soon as it was written.

Yet, clearly, this was not the case.

A study by Jan Maegaard published in 1962 in the *Dansk Aarbog for Musikforskning* reveals all of the dates of composition of the various movements included in Schoenberg's first three 12-tone works: Five Piano Pieces, Opus 23; Serenade, Opus 24; and Suite for Piano, Opus 25. Schoenberg's care to date his finished drafts, his hesitancy to throw anything away and the fact that his handwriting changed recognizably all helped Maegaard identify the manuscripts.

From this study one learns these facts: Schoenberg completed the first and third of the Five Piano Pieces in July 1920, but did not publish them until 1923. He finished the last piece of Opus 24 in April 1923, but did not publish the work until 1924. And he completed the last movements of the Opus 25, the Trio and Gigue, on March 3 and March 2, 1923, but the Suite was not published until 1925.

In a letter to Nicolas Slonimsky, Schoenberg described his early attempts to formulate the 12-tone technique:

> As an example of such attempts (i.e., to base the structure consciously on a unifying idea) I may mention the Piano Pieces, Opus 23. Here I arrived at a technique which I called for myself "composition with tones," a vague term, but it meant something to me. . . .
>
> The fourth movement, "Sonett," (i.e., of the Serenade, Opus 24) is a real composition with twelve tones. The technique is here relatively primitive, because it is one of the first works written strictly in harmony with this method, though it was not the very first. There were some movements of the Suite for Piano which I composed in the fall of 1921.

Schoenberg informs Slonimsky that he had actually composed various kinds of 12-tone works between 1914 and 1923. One of them, he wrote, was an uncompleted symphony which included a Scherzo written in late 1914 or early 1915 that was built on a 12-note theme; but he adds that other themes were used in the work. "My conscious aim," he claimed, "was always to build up my musical structures from one unifying idea which was the source of all the other ideas and also governed the accompaniment and chords or the 'harmonies.' I made many attempts to achieve this. But few of them were completed or published."

Why were they not completed or published? In 1909, Schoenberg had concluded his first agreement with Universal Edition, the publishing house which handled the most important composers in Vienna. Yet, as late as 1921, no work of Schoenberg's written after 1915 appeared in their catalogues. Schoenberg's biographer, H. H. Stuckenschmidt, said of these curious circumstances: "Even the pupils and friends of Schoenberg's closest circle did not know how to explain this fact. Some of them had been allowed a glimpse of *Die Jakobsleiter*—the work of the war years 1915–1917. After that Schoenberg's inspiration seemed to have dried up."

It was during the summer of 1922, almost five years after he had begun the score for *Die Jakobsleiter,* that Schoenberg confided to his close friend Josef Ruter: "I have discovered something that will guarantee the supremacy of German music for the next hundred years." In relating this incident, Stuckenschmidt goes on: "There followed an indication of the 'method of composing with twelve notes.' At the time he had written a number of works in which the method had been consciously used. Schoenberg had not made any of them public: he hesitated for years before he spoke of a discovery and before showing its results, which he knew would take the technique of composition along quite new lines."

The composer's obsession with numbers, so evident by now, seems to have caused the delay: he waited until 1923 to publish his Opus 23, 1924 to publish his Opus 24, and 1925 to publish his Opus 25, magically ensuring the success of the 12-tone technique by having the opus numbers of the first three works composed in that system coincide with their years of publication.

In October, 1923, Mathilde Zemlinsky Schoenberg, who had betrayed Schoenberg with Gerstl sixteen years earlier, died alone in a hospital. Schoenberg refused to go to her. In August, 1924, the composer married Gertrude Kolisch. She was the sister of the violinist Rudolf Kolisch, who proved to be as much a friend and promoter of his brother-in-law's music as Alexander Zemlinsky had been.

The unity provided by the recently evolved 12-tone technique made it possible for Schoenberg to return to the use of larger forms without the aid of a text and thus permitted him to work with classic structures. The Piano Suite, Opus 25, an eighteenth-century suite with a Prelude, Gavotte, Musette,

Intermezzo, Minuet and Gigue, is unified by a single row that provides construction material for the whole work. The Woodwind Quintet, Opus 26, closely approaches the sonata with its Allegro, Scherzo, Adagio and Rondo. Jan Maegaard considers this as the first thoroughly pervasive application of dodecaphony: "Here Schoenberg reached the goal for which he strives, since his music had been doomed to aphoristic shortness by the expressionistic style—viz. a method of composing large forms without sacrificing either atonality or the possibility of considerable tightness of expression."

At fifty, Schoenberg had found the solution he had sought. Certain basic tenets prevail:

1. Each row represents an ordered arrangement of all twelve notes of the chromatic scale.
2. The row may be presented in any or all of four ways: original, inverted, backwards or backwards and inverted.
3. The row may be stated in any of these ways on any degree of the chromatic scale.

Schoenberg's fiftieth year, surely a notable occasion for a ritualistic man, marked a number of significant achievements. The composer had crystallized his compositional technique, published his first pieces written in this method, and married a young woman. To celebrate his birthday, friends and disciples published a celebratory volume, *The Special Schoenberg Birthday Book*, in which adulatory articles appeared by Webern, Berg, Alfredo Casella and G. F. Malipiero. Universal Edition opened an Arnold Schoenberg Library of Modern Music available to students free of charge. And only a short time elapsed between the publication of a work of his and its first public performance. Unlike the Five Orchestral Pieces, which had to wait three years for its first performance, the Woodwind Quintet, Opus 26, a lengthy and complex work, was conducted by Webern soon after its completion. Schoenberg's fame was spreading beyond Austro-German borders for the first time. In Rome, the Saint Cecilia Academy conferred an honorary membership upon him.

Meanwhile, in Paris, Igor Stravinsky startled the public with his Octet, and in 1925, he toured the United States, both as composer and pianist.

The revelation of the 12-tone technique had not secured for Schoenberg unequivocal control.

CHAPTER 5

The progressive conductor Hermann Scherchen and composer Paul Hindemith organized a major festival in Frankfurt-am-Main to honor Schoenberg's fiftieth birthday. After receiving notice of these plans, Schoenberg wrote Scherchen expressing his gratitude, admittedly a curious kind of gratitude:

> Now let me thank you again most warmly and ask you to tell Hindemith too that I am extremely pleased with him. By doing this he is making a splendid sign of a proper attitude towards his elders, a sign such as can be made only by a man with a genuine and justifiable sense of his own worth; only by one who has no need to fear for his own fame when another is being honored and who recognizes that precisely such an honor does honor also to him if he associates himself with it. I once said: "Only he can bestow honor who himself has a sense of honor and deserves honor. Such a man knows what is due to him and therefore what is due to his peers."

The festival and various published accolades succeeded in mellowing the fifty-year-old Schoenberg. He himself noticed the change. In the Introduction to *The Special Schoenberg Birthday Book*, he wrote: "I cannot hate any more the way I used to; and worse yet, I can sometimes understand things without holding them in contempt."

In June 1930, a Berlin newspaper wrote to Schoenberg asking him to comment on the "musical life and the shift of the center of gravity from Vienna to Berlin."

Schoenberg replied:

> Even before the war people in Vienna were rightly and wrongly proud and ashamed of being less active than Berlin.

Even at the time Berlin showed a lively and intense interest in recognizing and explaining the symptoms of a work of art, something that was missing in Vienna, thanks to centuries of experience in composing.

Even in those days whatever was new was derided after several performances in Berlin, whereas in Vienna it needed only one performance. In extreme cases—in both places—no performance at all.

Even in those days, in both cities, the public had discovered that there is always plenty of time to honor a great man after he is dead. Presumably it had been recognized even in those days that it can be done more effectively and decoratively, and, what is more to the point, more lucratively.

The Society for Private Performances in Vienna had three hundred members, two hundred of them good ones. But they could not keep it afloat.

1/10,000 of 2 millions is 200.

1/10,000 of 4 millions is 400.

Perhaps four hundred can keep an artistically pure enterprise going?

I am looking for a center of gravity and find them all too light.

What didn't get shiftily shifted in the inflation! Perhaps, behind my back, some lighter centers of gravity as well.

Berlin in the 1920s became the center of progressive activity in all of the arts. It not only supported the Berlin Philharmonic, under the direction of Wilhelm Furtwängler; it also housed two of the foremost opera houses in Europe, the International Society for Contemporary Music, and the Novembergruppe, the intellectual organization that enthusiastically supported new music. In 1920 Scherchen founded the periodical *Melos*, which spearheaded the cause of contemporary music, and in 1925 the Prussian State Academy of the Arts appointed Schoenberg a director of the master class in composition, a position left vacant by the death of Ferruccio Busoni, whose revolutionary views on the aesthetics of music had made Berlin progressive two decades before.

Schoenberg accepted the appointment with delight. In a letter to the Prussian Minister for Science, Art and Education, he expressed his gratitude for the "great honor and distinction accorded me by this appointment to such an eminent position."

When Schoenberg arrived in Berlin in 1925, he was accompanied by several pupils and his long-time friend and colleague, Josef Rufer, who was to handle the more rudimentary teaching of harmony, counterpoint and form in order to provide Schoenberg with the free time he needed to compose. At this point in his career, Schoenberg could make stringent demands; in this case they included six months free each year so that he might spend the winters in the South. Schoenberg suffered severely from asthma.

During 1925, Erich Kleiber, in Berlin, conducted the world premiere of Alban Berg's *Wozzeck,* the most spectacular product to come from the Schoenberg school. The work received tremendous attention and Schoenberg was suddenly in great demand as a teacher. During the next few years he had among his pupils Winfried Zillig, Roberto Gerhard, Walter Goehr, Walter Gronostay, Peter Schacht, Adolphe Weiss, Joseph Zmigrod, Norbert von Hannenheim, Charilaos Perpessa, Erich Schmid, Niko Skalkottas, Rudolph Goehr, Fred Walter, Henry Cowell and Marc Blitzstein.

But just as his prestige grew and his work was performed more, a totally opposed movement, commonly labeled "neoclassicism," was developing in other parts of Europe. Igor Stravinsky defined neoclassicism at precisely the time Schoenberg crystallized dodecaphony: the need for formal principles was felt at the same time by the many other figures in the musical world, despite their divergent backgrounds and different personalities.

Neoclassicism relied on key centers. In contrast to dodecaphony, which plunged into the future, neoclassicism drew from the past through its retention of some aspects of the old tonal system. Schoenberg expressed his disdain for this kind of composition in his *Satires* for Mixed Chorus, Opus 28, spelling out his aesthetic position in a Prologue in the unlikely event that any listener would miss the point of the music. The *Satires,* scored for viola, cello, piano, mixed chorus, and tenor and bass solos, is a 12-tone work in which diatonic and dodecaphonic writing exist side by side. In the first two bars, the viola plays a seven-note scale while the cello plays the missing five notes—also diatonic—but seemingly in a different "key." At the same time the piano plays the twelve notes against the strings in an entirely different grouping. Schoenberg ends his fugue with a C after introducing all other eleven notes of the chromatic scale. Thus he mimics the neoclassic composer who, in Schoenberg's view, ends absurdly with a classic tonic chord after endless meaningless cacophonous music.

Perhaps in an effort to underscore the fact that he knew, only too well, where the true values of classicism lay, Schoenberg continued to compose a number of works which adhered quite closely to the classic forms, while using the 12-tone technique. The Suite, Opus 29, for E-flat Clarinet, B-flat Clarinet, Bass Clarinet, String Trio and Piano contains four movements: Overture, Tanzschritte, Langsam and Gigue. The first chord consists of the first six notes of the row while the piano figure that follows supplies the last six notes. Thus Schoenberg was able to superimpose his new discipline over broad, flowing, eighteenth-century forms. In doing this he confirmed his basic musical tenet: the presence of form in music does not depend on tonality.

Schoenberg's String Quartet No. 3, Opus 30, continues the practice of his Opus 29 Suite, rejecting the free forms of his atonal days and embracing the stricter, eighteenth-century structures. This work, composed at the request of the American patron Elizabeth Sprague Coolidge, was performed by the Kolisch Quartet in 1927. In it Schoenberg introduced a freer treatment of the row: five notes (not twelve)—G E D-sharp A C—form an ostinato which continues for twelve measures.

Schoenberg had never denied the possibility of introducing such liberties into his method of composition. In the mid-1920s he told Roberto Gerhard: "The reason why we must not use any of the traditional chords without the greatest precaution, why, in fact, I think we had better do without them altogether, is not difficult to discover. Our new musical language is in its early stage of development; promiscuity with elements of the older system could, at this stage, only obstruct and delay its natural growth. But when it consolidates itself the time will come, no doubt, for the reintegration of many elements of the older system which, for the present, we must firmly discard."

During 1927 and 1928 Schoenberg worked on his first 12-tone piece for orchestra, the densely polyphonic orchestral Variations, Opus 31. It contains an Introduction, a thematic statement and nine Variations, as well as an important Coda. The work explores all the possibilities inherent in the variation technique within a dodecaphonic framework. Furtwängler and the Berlin Philharmonic first played it in December, 1928.

In this first work for orchestra in fifteen years, Schoenberg used the motif B A C H as his musical theme; Bach did the same in his *Art of the Fugue*. (In German musical nomenclature, B-flat is represented by H.) The composer's great respect for Bach, who he once said could be described as the first 12-tone composer, is reflected again in the work that followed, an instrumental transcription of Bach's E-flat Major Organ Prelude and Fugue.

During the 1920s, some of Schoenberg's disciples defected. Alfredo Casella abandoned him, accusing Schoenberg of being mad. Hindemith started on a more accessible path and Hanns Eisler left the fold to embrace socialist realism. In 1930 César Searchinger wrote: "The phrase 'professor of modernity' has probably been coined for him. Not radicalism but academicism is the charge leveled at Schoenberg by his colleagues today."

Schoenberg did not tolerate criticism. Eisler indicated his disenchantment with Schoenberg to Zemlinsky during a talk on a train. Zemlinsky reported the conversation to Schoenberg, who wrote Eisler two enraged letters during March, 1926, in which he made the following remarks:

> . . .Then this is the way it is: you hold opinions deviating from me, wherefore I shall presumably reject them out of hand, and on the basis of these opinions, as on the basis of everyone's right to freedom of speech, you spoke about them freely to Zemlinsky. . . . Views diverging from my own are something that I should never resent, as little as I resent anyone having any other disability! One short leg, a clumsy hand, etc. I could only be sorry for such a person, but I couldn't be angry with him. . . . I described your proceedings as treason. But now I consider it was not me you betrayed, it was yourself you betrayed in a "chat on the train"; in such chat, in fact, you were not capable of not betraying your opinion of me, you actually had to blazon it abroad.

The increasing opposition to Schoenberg's new formal principle affected the course of his own work. Only a short time after the radical and complex orchestral Variations, he wrote a comic opera, *Von Heute auf Morgen*. Under the pseudonym Max Blonda, his wife created the libretto about the domestic entanglements of a bourgeois German couple. Such a dramatic departure can be understood in the light of the musical life of the time. American jazz had arrived in Europe and was captivating art composers. In Paris Stravinsky and Milhaud incorporated it into their work and in Germany the enthusiasm of Kurt Weill was shared by other serious composers like Ernst Krenek and Hindemith. Schoenberg wrote *Von Heute auf Morgen*—the orchestra includes a saxophone—the year after Brecht and Weill wrote their *Three Penny Opera*. Krenek had just succeeded with *Jonny Spielt Auf* and Hindemith had written a light opera, *Neues vom Tage*.

Schoenberg's effort in this genre may justly be interpreted as his initial attempt to come to terms with a new aesthetic. But he failed completely. Although the plot was simple, the music was full of contrapuntal invention. Built on a 12-note row, canonic forms flowed; *Von Heute auf Morgen* was hardly light opera.

And in 1931, in response to a commission from a Magdeburg publishing house (Richard Strauss and others were similarly commissioned), Schoenberg made another effort to reach a large public through a 12-tone but programmatic approach. His *Accompaniment to a Film Scene,* Opus 34, depicts three different episodes: Imminent Danger, Fear and Catastrophe. (It accompanied no actual film.)

In an effort to work out a solution to his problems, Schoenberg went to work, once again, at the piano, where he handled his initial forays into both atonality (Piano Pieces, Opus 11) and dodecaphony (Piano Pieces, Opus 23). In his Opus 33 Piano Pieces, certain principles of combination govern the way in which the row is handled. One finds sections organized around different permutations of the row in much the same manner that sections in eighteenth- and nineteenth-century composition were organized around different tonal areas. George Perle writes that in these pieces the "composer has created a music in which the structure of the 12-tone set has the same total relevance as the diatonic scale and triadic harmonies have in the major-minor system. All the 12-tone works that Schoenberg wrote after his arrival in the United States are based on these principles."

In 1930 Schoenberg composed Six Pieces for Male Chorus, written for unaccompanied male voices. The last of the group, "Verbündenheit," seems to veer even more strongly toward the past. It includes conventional triads and even ends on a D Minor chord, although the chord is admittedly in an inverted position. The words reflect the composer's state of mind:

> *Everything comes once, but what does it matter?*
> *One has luck, another has delusions.*
> *Is everything hopeless?*
> *Does it matter that one found luck and I found nothing?*

Such a specific question must surely have been motivated by Stravinsky's rise in prestige and his own decline.

With national socialism on the rise, and the retrograde aesthetic of mass taste on the march, Schoenberg pleaded for recognition as a truly German artist who was determined to keep Germany the center of the musical world. In a document published in February 1931, in the journal *National Music,* Schoenberg stated his curiously poignant case:

> It is strange that nobody has yet observed that my music, grown on German ground and untouched by foreign influences as it is, constitutes an art which has sprung

entirely from the traditions of German music, and which effectively opposes the striving for hegemony on the part of the Romance and Slav schools.

The general failure to perceive this is due not so much to the difficulty of my scores as to the indolence and arrogance of the observers. For the facts are self-evident.

But let me, for once, recount them myself:

My masters were in the first place Bach and Mozart, in the second Beethoven, Brahms, and Wagner.

Schoenberg then methodically listed each of the musical techniques he had learned from each of these eminent German musicians. He concluded:

I have learned much from Schubert, too, and from Mahler, Strauss and Reger . . . . I am convinced that the time will come when people will realize how intimately my discoveries are related with the best that was handed down to us. I claim the distinction of having written truly new music which, based on tradition, as it is, is destined to become tradition.

But the Prussian Ministry of Culture did not respond to his plea. In May 1933, Schoenberg was dismissed from his post at the Prussian State Academy of the Arts. With his wife and year-old daughter, he left Berlin and traveled first to France. There, in a Paris synagogue, he converted back to the religion of his birth.

This formality was not the first manifestation of Schoenberg's recommitment to Judaism; this had occurred as early as 1923, in an angry exchange with Kandinsky, who sought Schoenberg's entrance into the Bauhaus at Weimar. Schoenberg had heard the unlikely fact that some of its members were anti-Semitic and expressed his rage at those intellectuals who exempted him from the onus of being a Jew.

I have learned at last the lesson that has been forced upon me this year and I shall never forget it. It is that I am not a German, not a European, indeed, perhaps, scarcely a human being (at least, the Europeans prefer the worst of their race to me), but I am a Jew. I am content that it should be so! Today I no longer wish to be an exception. . . .

When I walk along the street and each person looks at

me to see whether I'm a Christian or a Jew, I can't very well tell each of them that I'm the one that Kandinsky and some others make an exception of . . . and you join in that sort of thing and "reject me as a Jew"? Did I ever offer myself to you? Do you think someone like myself lets himself be rejected?

Schoenberg was rejected all his life. But he had supreme faith in his mission and his faith sustained him in the most difficult times. A few years before leaving Germany, Schoenberg began *Moses und Aron*, the work that occupied his attention for the rest of his life. In it he expresses his lifelong commitment: "My love is for the idea. I live just for it."

The words are sung by Moses, the biblical lawmaker and leader of his people who enforced upon them a discipline which they bitterly resented. Schoenberg identified with Moses. It was not far-fetched for him to do so; there was much of Moses in Schoenberg's own nature.

CHAPTER 6

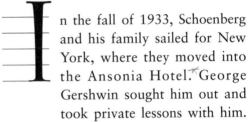

In the fall of 1933, Schoenberg and his family sailed for New York, where they moved into the Ansonia Hotel. George Gershwin sought him out and took private lessons with him. Schoenberg had accepted a position in a little known conservatory that had recently opened in Boston's Back Bay, the Malkin Conservatory of Music. Although the Malkin brothers had the foresight and courage to hire Schoenberg from abroad, they lacked the necessary funds to make his stay comfortable. They could not even afford a small orchestra. Then, too, Schoenberg found the climate disagreeable and the weekly trip between Boston and New York, where he also held classes, arduous. During his first winter in the United States, Schoenberg became ill and was forced to postpone conducting a performance of his *Pelleas* until the spring. The Juilliard School of Music finally offered him a teaching position, but he decided to leave the Northeast and settle in California.

Before moving West, the Schoenbergs spent the summer in Chautauqua, a resort that offers its guests lectures, recitals, music courses and orchestral concerts. There he met Martin Bernstein, music professor at New York University, who told him of the problems he had in finding good contemporary scores for his student orchestra. Bernstein mentioned that the orchestra had played works by Bloch, Porter, Ravel and Hindemith, and was continually in search of new material.

Before leaving Chautauqua, Schoenberg assured Bernstein that he would write a piece for the NYU group. Once in California, he wrote to Bernstein, saying that the work was not as easy as he had hoped it would be, but was very good nevertheless. The composer added that he would not send it to the publisher "on speculation"; he was, he proclaimed, "no amateur." Bernstein replied that the honorarium, during these Depression days, could only be the $50 which had been collected from the students themselves. Gertrude Schoenberg finally ended the affair with a note to Bernstein informing him that her husband had given the work to the Juilliard School and that Schirmer would publish it.

But the Juilliard School orchestra never performed the Suite in G Major. Otto Klemperer conducted the Los Angeles Philharmonic in one of the work's few performances during the spring of 1934. Schoenberg's piece of the newly fashionable *Gebrauchsmusik* turned out not to be *Gebrauchsmusik* (simple to perform "music for use") at all; in his negotiations the composer had defeated his own purpose. Because of its obvious tonal organization—it was Schoenberg's first piece with a key signature since 1907—and because it was also his first work written in the United States, it was widely interpreted (possibly correctly) as Schoenberg's attempt to join the "neotonal" movement that pervaded the country at that time.

Oscar Levant's view of Schoenberg's life in Hollywood is one of the rare glimpses we have of the man from someone outside his intimate circle of close friends and relatives:

> There is rarely a period in Hollywood when all the orchestrators and most of the movie composers are not studying with one or another of the prominent musicians who have come there to live. At one time the vogue was for Schoenberg, who came with a great reputation, of course, as a teacher. However, most of the boys wanted to take a six weeks' course and learn a handful of Schoenberg's tricks. They were sorely disappointed when they discovered that it was his intention to give them instruction in counterpoint, harmony, and chorale, which meant that they would have to expend considerable effort themselves in doing assigned work. . . .
>
> When Schoenberg arrived in California it was the desire of his friends to see him employed in the movies and well paid for it. He was invited to an important premiere following which the producer intercepted him and asked what he thought of the score. Schoenberg replied that he hadn't noticed it, thus bearing out the average producer's theory of what constitutes a good score only in reverse. . . .

Schoenberg severed relations with the film community altogether when, at his wife's suggestion, he asked $50,000 and "not a note changed" in return for composing a score for a film. The price was so outrageous that, according to his own estimate of the incident, it saved him from "a destructive course of action."

Schoenberg complained during his California years that the United States had not proven the haven he expected. In 1936 the composer wrote to Hermann Scherchen: "Artistically I am more dissatisfied than ever, and, as for what I am doing here, well, I have been teaching at one University [USC] and next year shall be teaching at the other of the two universities here [UCLA]. But unfortunately the material I get has had such an inadequate grounding that my work is as much a waste of time as if Einstein were having to teach mathematics at a secondary school."

Like other European composers, Schoenberg was confronted with the problem of writing music that satisfied his own criteria in a predominantly alien world. In the United States, Russia and other parts of Europe, retrogressive artistic movements took hold. In the United States the musical results were clear-cut: composers wrote simple, accessible and folklike works. Radio and movies contributed to the implementation of these ideas and the WPA commissioned such works. In 1937 the American composer Roger Sessions attributed the success of these reactionary artistic pressures to the "reaction of a public which, for the first time in musical history, had found itself completely out of touch with modern music itself." Sessions added that musicians desired a new and closer relationship with audiences.

Different composers, of course, responded differently. Some went along with the movement, inhibiting their advanced ideas. Some stopped composing altogether or, like Varèse, threw their scores into the wastebasket as they continued to produce them. Others, for example the Schoenberg-trained Blitzstein, motivated by a combination of social guilt and what he felt to be a genuine need for social change, went all the way and wrote completely tonal, tuneful music. Neoclassicism, with its enormous tonal umbrella, provided the "ism" into which all of this music could be drawn. In the late 1930s Schoenberg responded to the neotonal pressure; the Suite in G Major anticipated several impassioned program works which he composed in an idiom of extended tonality.

But immediately after the Suite in G Major, composed in 1934, he returned to the 12-tone technique. Schoenberg's Violin Concerto, Opus 36, was published in 1936 and dedicated to Webern. It was the most significant work of Schoenberg's first years in the United States. A 12-tone composition in three classic movements, it was practically unplayable. Even Schoenberg conceded that it needed a sixth finger. Louis Krasner, playing with the Philadelphia Orchestra under the direction of Leopold Stokowski, gave the work its first performance in 1941. The performance was not broadcast and Schoenberg did not hear his piece until shortly before his death when he heard a tape of a performance by the Cologne Radio Orchestra. Friends say he wept as he listened. Schoenberg said it was his favorite work.

The String Quartet No. 4, Opus 37, was completed before the 1936 Opus 36 Violin Concerto, again suggesting that Schoenberg manipulated events in order to give crucial works opus numbers corresponding to the years in which they were published. The Opus 37 String Quartet is a masterful 12-tone work written in the traditional four movements.

Kol Nidre, based on the ancient melody sung at the beginning of the Jewish Day of Atonement, is written in G Minor and ends in G Major. Schoenberg's next piece, Variations on a Recitative for Organ, is not a 12-tone work either; there are notes in the harmony that create a distinctly tonal effect. Although the *Ode to Napoleon,* which Schoenberg composed immediately after he became a United States citizen, is constructed on a 12-note row, it is handled in such a manner that the listener can hear the tonalities of E-flat Minor, G Minor and B Minor. The poem by Byron is a passionate denunciation of dictatorship scored for speaking voice, string quartet and piano. World War II moved even those most dedicated to abstract form to compose music with a programmatic content.

Schoenberg, in his sixties, did more than compose and teach. With Gershwin now in Beverly Hills, he played tennis once a week on the American composer's courts. Schoenberg liked chess and devised a new system requiring a hundred chessmen; and he opened his Brentwood house on Sunday afternoons to play music with his friends and colleagues. Among the musicians gathering there were Edgard Varèse, Henry Cowell, Roger Sessions, Darius Milhaud, David Diamond, René Leibowitz, Fritz Stiedry, Eduard Steuermann, Rosalyn Tureck and Arthur Schnabel. Another friend who visited him was Thomas Mann, as well as his old friend Alma Mahler Werfel. Yet, in the fall of 1937, when invited to Denver to deliver a lecture at a festival in his honor, he chose a characteristic title: "How One Becomes Lonely."

In 1944, when Schoenberg celebrated his seventieth year, former pupil Heinrich Jalowetz and composer Darius Milhaud wrote commemorative essays in *The Musical Quarterly,* musicians Kurt List, Lou Harrison and Ernst Krenek contributed articles in his honor to *Modern Music,* and Roger Sessions paid him a tribute in the journal *Tempo.* Schoenberg's life still left much to be desired. He was forced to retire from UCLA at the age of seventy and therefore had to take on many more private pupils during 1944 and 1945. ASCAP increased his royalties, friends raised funds in order to help out, but it was not until Schoenberg sold several manuscripts to the Library of Congress that he felt he received any financial aid.

In January, 1945, Schoenberg applied to the Guggenheim Foundation for a grant to enable him to give up his pupils and complete *Moses und Aron, Die Jakobsleiter,* and several theoretical works. He specified that his pension from UCLA was $38 a month and that he had a wife and three children, aged thirteen, eight and four, to support. The Guggenheim Foundation rejected his request; of the works mentioned in the application, he finished only the *Structural Functions of Harmony.*

Schoenberg did not turn the other cheek. He was as vocally bitter about his treatment in the United States as he had been about his treatment in Vienna. In a letter to Henry Cowell he wrote:

> It seems as if I have to celebrate a comeback in New York. It is time. It's a comeback because I have never been there, you know. I was so seldom performed in New York that nobody knows whether my music is worth hearing or not.
>
> It is worse here in Los Angeles. Mr. Wallenstein is six years here in Los Angeles and has not yet played one piece of mine.

And, in a letter to Kolisch, Schoenberg sums up his accurate assessment of the U.S. situation:

> They (la Boulanger's pupils, the imitators of Stravinsky, Hindemith and Bartók as well) have taken over American musical life lock, stock and barrel. The only person who can get an appointment in a university department is one who has taken his degree at one of them, and even the pupils are recruited and scholarships awarded to them in order to have the next generation in the bag. The tendency is to suppress European influence and encourage nationalistic methods of composition constructed on the pattern adopted in Russia and such places.

Perhaps because of his disenchantment with this situation, Schoenberg spent a great part of his last years compiling his writings for a book, *Style and Idea,* published in 1950. From time to time he turned to composition. In 1946 he became seriously ill. After he recovered he wrote to his biographer, H. H. Stuckenschmidt: "I have risen from real death and now feel very well." During the five weeks of the summer that followed, Schoenberg wrote the String Trio, Opus 45. It is short, dodecaphonic, in one movement, and uses unusual registers and varying tone colors with harmonics, pizzicati, bowed and struck col legno. Thomas Mann spoke about Schoenberg's own view of the Trio: "One must bear in mind here a meeting with Schoenberg at which he told me of his new, just completed Trio, and of the experiences of life that he secreted in this composition; this work in a certain sense is a repetition of them. He declared that he described his medical treatment including his 'male nurse' and the rest in it."

During 1947 Schoenberg finally received an official accolade, $1,000 from the American Academy of Arts and Letters. Schoenberg wrote a letter of acceptance:

> . . . That you should regard all I have tried to do in the last fifty years as an achievement strikes me as in some respects an overestimate. My own feeling was that I had fallen into an ocean of boiling water; and as I couldn't swim and knew no other way out, I struggled with my arms and legs as best I could. I don't know what saved me, or why I wasn't drowned or boiled alive—perhaps my own merit was that I never gave in. Whether my movements were very economical or completely senseless, whether they helped or hindered my survival, there was no one willing to help me and there were plenty of people who would have gladly seen me go under. I don't think it was envy—what was there to envy?—and I doubt whether it was lack of good will, or worse, positive ill will on their part. Perhaps they just wanted to get rid of the nightmare, the agonizing disharmony, the unintelligible thinking, the systematic lunacy that I represented, and I must admit that those who thought in that way were not bad men—though, of course, I could never understand what I had done to them to make them so malicious, so violent, so aggressive. . . . Please don't call it false modesty if I say that perhaps something was achieved, but that it is not I who deserves the credit. The credit must go to my opponents. It was they who really helped me.

The letter, in which Schoenberg diagnoses his own "systematic lunacy," reveals that his suspicious nature was still very much part of his personality. It has been publicly claimed that Schoenberg and Freud never met. This is incorrect. An interview was arranged by a member of the Schoenberg family during the 1920s. After it was over—the meeting was characterized as friendly, polite, respectful, cool, focusing on art and music—

Schoenberg turned to his relative and said: "Freud is certainly an interesting man but what has that got to do with me?"

In 1947, Schoenberg composed the dramatic cantata, *A Survivor from Warsaw*. Scored for speaker, male chorus and orchestra, the work deals with the heroic episode of the Polish Jews during the last days of the Warsaw ghetto. Hebrew songs are heard against the cacophonous sounds of the murderers. Schoenberg's use of different languages—the narrator's English and German juxtaposed with the chorus intoning the Hebrew chant—contributed a terrifying naturalism. A Survivor from Warsaw, first performed at the University of Mexico in 1948, made a thunderous impact on the audience. It was dramatic, expressive, rhetorical music, not far removed from the Romantic tradition into which the composer had been born.

During the last months of his life he worked on both text and music to a religious work *Modern Psalms*, scored for speaker, chorus and orchestra. The work is addressed to God, the "unimaginable (Unvorstellbaren) of whom I cannot and must not make an Image." The text includes a discussion of prayer, a request to God to punish all offenders, a description of the Chosen People, an essay in praise of superstition, a treatment of the miracle as a calculated chess maneuver on the part of God, and several statements concerning racial identity.

Modern Psalms reveals Schoenberg's thoughts at the end of his life. The setting remains unfinished in precisely the same textual context as that point at which Schoenberg stopped composing *Moses und Aron*. The words "And nevertheless, I pray," are set, but the rest of the sentence, "because I do not want to lose the rapturous feeling of oneness, of unity with you," remains unset. *Die Jakobsleiter, Moses und Aron*, and the *Modern Psalms* are the only major works that Schoenberg began and did not complete.

The clearest expression of the composer's inner life is in the libretto for *Moses und Aron*. Moses (Schoenberg) sees and understands everything but he cannot convey his vision. (Moses had a speech impediment in the Bible.) Aron, glib, articulate, able to sway the people, claims that the tablets containing the Ten Commandments are images, "just part of the whole idea." "Then," said Moses, "I shall smash to pieces both these tablets and I shall also ask Him to withdraw the task given to me." At the end of the second act (Schoenberg never wrote the third), Moses falls to the ground in total despair. It is not that he doubts the existence of one God; it is that he despairs of ever being able to communicate his vision to the world: "O word, thou word, that I lack."

Moses is a speaking-voice part; Aron is a bel canto tenor. The entire score of *Moses und Aron* realizes the compelling musical idea for which Schoenberg lived: the whole opera is based on a single row. Schoenberg began it in Germany in 1930, when the Prussian government considered his music degenerate. He continued to work on it in the United States during a period in which Americans rejected his music. But Schoenberg's vision persisted; in reply to a South African correspondent he wrote in 1949: "The kind of tonality which is preferred today, which uses all kind of incoherent dissonances and returns without any reason to a major or to a minor triad, and rests then for a time and considers this the tonality of the piece, seems to me to be doomed. I cannot believe that this will last very long. . . . May I add that I believe, when the movement of the reactionaries has died away, that music will return to composing with twelve tones."

His letter was prophetic: The method of composing with twelve tones related only to each other was to be, for many years, the impetus behind the music written by many of the most articulate and powerful composers in Europe and the United States.

CHAPTER 7

The Viennese composer Ernst Krenek once characterized Schoenberg's students as docile men who displayed "sectarian fanaticism and spineless devotion to their master." All the evidence supports his claim. After 1910, when Schoenberg began to make carbon copies of his letters and to demand high fees for his paintings ("even now my name belongs to the history of music"), his personal manner and perfectionistic demands resulted in a paralysis of creativity among many of his pupils.

In 1933, Marc Blitzstein, a former Schoenberg pupil, wrote in the American music journal *Modern Music* of Schoenberg's anticipated arrival in the United States: "A danger for his pupils lies in his insistence on genius, on perfection, in his ruthlessness with the near-perfect; the danger of paralysis and despair. Most of Schoenberg's Berlin and Vienna pupils have given up composing, convinced the master is right, composing is too hard, it is hopeless; one can never reach the goal and so on." Lois Lautner, one of Schoenberg's first American pupils, confirmed Blitzstein's fear. In an article published in the Winter 1967 issue of the *Michigan Quarterly Review* she wrote, "Although Schoenberg offered to teach me free of charge wherever he was, I had decided that I was not creating 'new beauty' for this century or any other. I would teach, after all."

Most of his pupils did exactly the same thing. But two musicians of great stature did emerge—Viennese composers Alban Berg and Anton Webern—whom Schoenberg began to teach in 1904. Berg's music sprang from the world of German Romanticism; but his ties to the tonal world, like Schoenberg's, were never severed completely. Webern, on the other hand, looked directly into the future. In a strikingly passionate article published in 1952, Pierre Boulez, a prime mover of the "new music," expressed his disdain for Schoenberg and reverence for Webern:

. . . We can see why Schoenberg's 12-tone music was bound to come to a dead end. In the first place he explored the new technique in only one direction. Rhythm was neglected, and even such questions as intensity, dynamics etc. considered in a structural sense. Perhaps it would be better to dissociate Schoenberg's work altogether from the phenomenon of the tone row. The two have been confused with obvious pleasure—sometimes with unconcealed dishonesty—and a certain Webern has only been too easily forgotten.

Perhaps we might convince ourselves that the tone row is a historical necessity. Perhaps, like Webern, we might succeed in writing works whose form arises inevitably from the given material. Perhaps we could enlarge the field of 12-tone compositions to include other intervals than the semi-tone: micro-intervals, irregular intervals, complex sounds. Perhaps the principle of the tone row could be applied to the five elements of sound: pitch, duration, tone production, intensity and timbre. Let us, then, without any wish to provoke indignation, but also without shame or hypocrisy, or any melancholy sense of frustration, admit the fact that SCHOENBERG IS DEAD.

Stravinsky supported Boulez's judgment. In 1955, commemorating the tenth anniversary of Webern's death in the avant-garde German journal, *Die Reihe*, Stravinsky wrote:

The 15 of September 1945, the day of Anton Webern's death, should be a day of mourning for any receptive musician.

We must hail not only this great composer but also a real hero. Doomed to a total failure in a deaf world of ignorance and indifference he inexorably kept on cutting out his diamonds, his dazzling diamonds, the mines of which he had such a perfect knowledge.

As late as 1961, Stravinsky still had only praise for Webern: "He is the discoverer of a new musical distance between the musical object and ourselves, and therefore of a new measure of musical time."

Anton Webern was born in Vienna in 1883, the year that Wagner died and nine years after Schoenberg was born. Early in his career he discarded tonality, which Wagner had extended to its ultimate limits.

Webern's father was a mining engineer and administrator in the Austrian Imperial regime. By the time Anton was eighteen, he had studied piano, cello and music theory, and was composing constantly. His early songs, written before he met Schoenberg, indicate that even at that time he never chose easy solutions to compositional problems: not one of them, written between 1899 and 1904, is constructed in the traditional a b a pattern.

Webern was thoroughly educated in music history, one of the first composers to pursue such studies. In 1902 he began to study musicology at the University of Vienna under the scholar Guido Adler. He completed his dissertation in 1906; it treated Heinrich Isaac's *Choralis Constantinus,* a monumental work written at the beginning of the sixteenth century. Isaac's use of a Gregorian chant as a *cantus firmus* for these fifty-eight pieces bears some similarity to the perpetual variation of a single idea that characterizes 12-tone music.

As soon as Webern began to study with Schoenberg in 1904, the results showed in his work. One of his earliest pieces, *Im Sommerwind,* reveals a careful study of *Pelleas und Melisande*; both works introduce melodic ideas that are later combined, four and five at a time. His String Quartet, written in 1905, shows a similar debt to *Verklärte Nacht*; both are built on the principle of perpetual variation and are based on traditional tonal harmonies. A major theme in the Webern quartet is, in fact, derived from a subsidiary motive in the Schoenberg work.

The significant interplay between teacher and student is revealed in a lecture Webern delivered in the early 1930s, in which he described the effect that Schoenberg's Chamber Symphony had on him:

> In 1906 Schoenberg came back from a stay in the country, bringing the Chamber Symphony. It made a colossal impression. I'd been his pupil for three years and immediately felt "You must write something like that, too." Under the influence of the work I wrote a sonata movement the very next day. In that movement I reached the farthest limits of tonality.
>
> At that time Schoenberg was enormously productive. Every time we pupils came to see him something else was there. It was frightfully difficult for him as a teacher; the purely theoretical side had given out. By pure intuition, amid

frightful struggles, his uncanny feeling for form told him what was wrong.

Both of us sensed that in this sonata movement I'd broken through to a material for which the situation was not yet ripe. I finished the movement—it was still related to a key—but in a very remarkable way. Then I was supposed to write a variation movement, but I thought of a variation that wasn't really in a key at all. Schoenberg called on Zemlinsky for help, and he dealt with the matter negatively.

Now you have an idea of how we wrestled with all of this. It was unendurable. Indeed, I did go on to write a quartet in C Major—but only in passing. The key, the chosen key note, is invisible—so to speak—"suspended tonality."

It was thus shortly after Webern's "keyless" movement that Schoenberg wrote his own keyless movement in the Second Quartet, and soon after that that he composed his first "atonal" works, the Piano Pieces, Opus 11, and the Georgelieder, Opus 15. In these works the harmony is free from all tonal ties and the melody contains notes "foreign" to the harmony. In numbers 2 and 5 of the Georgelieder, Schoenberg does not return to the tonic. In his lectures Webern explains why: "Everyone feels the end anyway."

The work that appears to have had an even more crucial effect on Webern than the Chamber Symphony is Schoenberg's Five Pieces for Orchestra. The composition had sprung from a discussion with Mahler in which Schoenberg held that it was possible to create an actual melody by sounding a single tone on different instruments. This was his initial application of the idea that "a note is perceived by its color, one of whose dimensions is pitch. Color, then, is the great realm, pitch one of its provinces. . . ."

The effects of economy and concentration of the orchestral pieces reached their zenith in Schoenberg's Three Pieces for Orchestra, written in 1910 and only discovered after his death, as well as in the Opus 19 Piano Pieces, written in 1911 after the trauma of Mahler's death. But these compositions represent the end of the road for Schoenberg. Robert Craft has written: "After his Opus 19 Pieces, Schoenberg was to return to the rhetoric and time-scale of Brahms, whereas Webern inhabited ever after a completely new time-world begotten only with the materials of 12-tone composition. However close Webern was to Schoenberg, their paths had already diverged."

The story that Webern tells of his particular path during a lecture on

February 12, 1932, is a fascinating one:

> About 1911 I wrote the Bagatelles for String Quartet Opus 9, all very short pieces, lasting a couple of minutes—perhaps the shortest music so far. Here I had the feeling "When all twelve notes have gone by, the piece is over." Much later I discovered that all this was part of the necessary development. In my sketchbook I wrote out the chromatic scale and crossed off the individual notes. Why? Because I had convinced myself, "This note has already been there." It sounds grotesque, incomprehensible and it was incredibly difficult. The inner ear decided quite rightly that the man who wrote out the chromatic scale and crossed off individual notes was no fool. Josef Matthias Hauer, too, went through and discovered all this his own way. In short, a rule of law emerged; until all twelve notes have occurred, none of them may occur again The most important thing is that each "run" of twelve notes marked a division within the piece, idea or theme.
>
> My Goethe song, "Gleich und Gleich" (Four Songs, Opus 12, No. 4, composed in 1917), begins as follows: G-sharp A D-sharp G, then a chord E C B-flat D, then F-sharp B F C-sharp. That makes twelve notes: none is repeated. At that time we were not conscious of the law, but had been sensing it for a long time. One day Schoenberg intuitively discovered the law that underlies twelve-tone composition. An inevitable development of the law was that one gave the succession of twelve notes a particular order. . . .
>
> Today we've arrived at the end of the path, i.e. at the goal; the twelve notes have come to power and the practical need for this law is completely clear to us today. We can look back at its development and see no gaps.

Schoenberg's response to the Six Bagatelles is contained in a curious mystical preface, published in June 1924:

> Though the brevity of these pieces is a persuasive advocate for them, on the other hand that very brevity itself requires an advocate.
>
> Consider what moderation is required to express oneself

so briefly. You can stretch every glance out into a poem, every sigh into a novel. But to express a novel in a single gesture, a joy in a breath—such concentration can only be present in proportion to the absence of self-pity.

These pieces will only be understood by those who share the faith that music can see things which can only be expressed in music. These pieces can face criticism as little as this—or any—belief. If faith can move mountains, disbelief can deny their existence. And faith is impotent against such impotence.

Does the musician know how to play these pieces, does the listener know how to receive them? Can faithful musicians and listeners fail to surrender themselves to one another?

But what shall we do with the heathens? Fire and sword can keep them down; only believers need to be restrained.

May this silence sound for them.

Schoenberg's pupil Erwin Stein made the following comment about Webern: "Ecstasy was his natural state of mind. His compositions should be understood as mystical visions." Not only did Schoenberg and Webern share a mystical view of the world; they also had in common the instinct to adore. As Schoenberg adored Mahler, so Webern adored Schoenberg. Hans Moldenhauer, director of the Webern Society, writes that Webern had an "almost fanatical regard" for Schoenberg, and a letter that Berg wrote to Webern in 1910 testifies to the love both pupils felt for their imposing master:

> How despondent you must be again, far away from all those divine experiences, having to forego the walks with Schoenberg and miss the meaning, the gestures, the cadence of his talk. Twice a week I wait for him at the Karlplatz, before teaching begins at the Conservatory, and for the 15 to 30 minute walk, the hubbub of the city is drowned by the "roar" of his words. But to tell you all this is only to increase your sense of deprivation. . . .

Webern's adoration brought with it an identification in the most personal psychological terms. His statement, "With me things never turn out as I wish, but only as ordained for me—as I must," is strongly reminiscent of Schoenberg's frequently expressed claim that he had been driven into a painful path on "orders from the Supreme Commander."

If Webern's music had simply realized Schoenberg's principles, his path would have been an easier one, the challenge nullified, the identification with the ever-rejected Schoenberg destroyed. But instead of following in Schoenberg's footsteps, Webern chose a new, highly individual path and forged altogether new routes for the evolution of music in this century.

Webern's works were unprecedentedly short and incredibly quiet. Boulez has written that Webern's unique rhythmic innovation is "this conception whereby sound and silence are linked in a precise organization directed toward the exhaustive exploitation of our powers of hearing. The tension of sound is enriched to the extent of a genuine respiration, comparable only with Mallarmé's contribution to poetry."

Webern filled the few measures of his pieces with the uncomfortable intervals of the major seventh and minor ninth and placed enormous expressive value on each sonority. Each tone was assigned its special function in the overall scheme; no note was ever wasted. The instruments, used at the extremes of their registers, play only one note at a time, with the dynamics and tempi frequently changing from note to note. Webern, the composer of the *ppp* sixteenth note, often used crescendo and diminuendo on one tone. The instructions that accompanied the score were usually "Like a whisper" or "Dying away." Webern created a distilled and lonely lyricism that was not understood for years, awaiting a postwar generation of musicians.

His Symphony, Opus 21, written after Schoenberg had published a number of 12-tone works, was more tightly constructed than anything composed by Schoenberg himself. Scored for clarinet, bass clarinet, two horns, two harps, violins, violas and cellos, the work lasts only ten minutes. Webern describes the second movement:

> The row is F A-flat G F-sharp B-flat A; E-flat E C C-sharp D B. It's peculiar in that the second half is the cancrizans of the first. This is a particular intimate unity. So here there are only twenty-four forms, since there are a corresponding number of identical pairs. In the accompaniment to the theme, the cancrizans appears at the beginning. The first variation of the melody is a transposition of the row starting on C. The accompaniment is a double canon. Greater unity is impossible. . . . In the fourth variation there are constant mirrorings. This variation is itself the midpoint of the whole movement after which everything goes backwards. So the entire movement is itself a double canon by retrograde motion.

It was later, however, in his Opus 27 Piano Variations, that other composers assert Webern extended the same tightly knit organization he had given to pitch, to other attributes of the musical tone. The work has been analyzed by musicians and theorists who claim to have discovered in it precedents for the serial organization of duration, density and register as well. Although Webern never said that he was extending the serial organization of pitch to other structural elements of the musical tone, he might have been doing so unconsciously, in much the same manner as he intuitively wrote his first 12-tone work.

Boulez has claimed that Webern was not tied to the row as "theme." Webern, himself, acknowledged that:

> I can work without thematicism, that is to say, much more freely, because of the unity that's now been achieved in another way: the row ensures unity.
>
> Adherence is strict, often burdensome, but it's *salvation!* We couldn't do a thing about the dissolution of tonality, and we didn't create the new law by ourselves—it forced itself overwhelmingly on us. This compulsion, adherence, is so powerful that one has to consider very carefully before finally committing oneself to it for a prolonged period, almost as if taking the decision to marry; a difficult moment. Trust your inspiration! There's no alternative!

In 1930 Webern was appointed reader and "specialist adviser" to the Austrian radio on all questions to do with new music. In April 1931, he was honored by the first concert devoted to his own compositions, performed by Kolisch, Steuermann and others. In May 1932, he received Vienna's Music Prize. Even after Hitler came to power, he continued to teach. Schoenberg never forgave him his sympathy with the Nazis, and after Webern's death, refused to help the family on moral grounds.

Webern's death has been recorded by Moldenhauer; the scholar spent years tracking down the story: increased bombings of Vienna had forced the composer to move to Mittersill, a small town eighty miles southwest of Salzburg where his daughter and her family lived. One evening, shortly after the end of the war, Webern stepped outside the house to smoke a cigar after dinner. American soldiers, approaching to intercept Webern's son-in-law in a black market transaction, unaccountably killed Webern by mistake.

Webern remained tied to Schoenberg throughout his life. The ambivalence Schoenberg felt for Mahler, Webern felt for Schoenberg. The younger man tried repeatedly to break away and on one occasion a quarrel lasted for three years. Such a relationship is infinitely complex; one cannot adore without deeply resenting the beloved who holds one so captive. Still, in 1944, the year before his untimely death, Webern wrote to a friend asking about plans to commemorate Schoenberg's birthday: "How will you celebrate September 13th? Pass on my deepest remembrances, which possess me night and day, my unspeakable longing! But also my unwearying hopes for a happy future."

CHAPTER 8

People always expect the wrong thing of me. They think they have pinned me down and then all of a sudden—au revoir!

IGOR STRAVINSKY
Modern Music, 1946

In *Moses und Aron* Schoenberg pits two brothers against one another. Moses, who understands the God of the Jews, cannot communicate his vision. Aron, who is seductive and manipulative, distorts that vision and gives the people what they want: the idol of the Golden Calf, a vulgar realization of the invisible deity that possesses enormous mass appeal.

There may be something of Igor Stravinsky in this Aron, for Stravinsky, like Aron, is as uncommitted a theoretician as he is a great musician.

Stravinsky's attitude toward Schoenberg's commitment to the "idea" is revealed in a conversation between Mallarmé and Degas related in Stravinsky's autobiography, which he wrote when he was fifty-two years old "Degas, who, as is well known, liked to dabble in poetry, one day said to Mallarmé: "I cannot manage the end of my sonnet and it is not that I am wanting in ideas." Mallarmé, softly, "It is not with ideas that one makes sonnets but with words." So it is with Beethoven. It is in the quality of his musical material and not in the nature of his ideas that his true greatness lies. It is time that this was recognized, and Beethoven was rescued from the unjustifiable monopoly of the "intellectuals" and left to those who seek in music for nothing but music."

These two giants of twentieth-century music were locked in a power struggle that began before the onset of World War I and lasted until Schoenberg's death. Schoenberg saw the once securely entrenched hegemony of the Austro-Germans threatened by *Le Sacre du Printemps*. He was correct in his assessment of Stravinsky's threat, although few shared his perception of the event. Boris de Schlœtzer, an eminent Stravinsky authority, has written that the real significance of the *Sacre,* not generally grasped at the time, lay in the reaction the work created against chromaticism and atonality.

Between 1940 and 1951 Schoenberg and Stravinsky lived only ten miles apart in Los Angeles. It is no accident that they met only once—at the funeral of a mutual friend. Each avoided the other conscientiously and visitors to one never mentioned having paid a visit to the other. They were not only recipients of altogether different national characteristics and artistic gifts; they also were strikingly different men.

In contrast to the extraordinary secrecy that always surrounded Schoenberg and the paucity of material about him, Stravinsky is accessible in the extreme. Essays in journals and books about him have proliferated throughout the century.

Whereas Schoenberg's relatively few words represent his deepest convictions about the most serious matters, Stravinsky's many verbal expressions reflect a restless, changeable, volatile figure who accepts the fluctuating nature of his personality apparently without difficulty. In the foreword to his autobiography he acknowledged his infidelities: "As I call my recollections to mind, I shall necessarily be obliged to speak of my opinions, my tastes, my preferences, and my abhorrences. I am but too well aware of how much these feelings vary in the course of time. This is why I shall take great care not to confuse my present reactions with those experienced at other stages of my life."

At sixty-two, in the American journal *Modern Music,* the composer wrote: "I do not have any ultimate viewpoint of composition and when I write my next symphony it will be an expression of my will at that moment. And what that will is going to be I do not know. I wish people would let me have the privilege of being a little bit unconscious. It is so nice, sometimes, to go blind, just with the *feeling* for the right thing."

Later, in *The Observer* (London) on the occasion of his eightieth birthday: "My agenbite of inwit is that I do not know, am not aware, while composing, of any question of value. I love with my whole being whatever I am now composing, and with each new work I always feel that I have just found the way, just begun to compose. I love all my children, of course, and like any father I favor the backwards and imperfectly formed ones. But I am excited only by the newest—Don Juanism—and the youngest—nymphetism."

Unlike the conflicted, visionary Schoenberg, Stravinsky always responded with instinct, deftness and musicianship to the musical matter at hand. When the Russian ballet master Serge Diaghilev asked him to assemble a number of eighteenth-century pieces, he complied and wrote *Pulcinella.* When his friend and colleague, Ernest Ansermet, returned from the United States with some jazz material, Stravinsky responded with *Ragtime.* When, in the 1930s, Stravinsky made his first contact with a commercial recording company, he produced the Serenade in A, in which the length of each movement corresponded to one side of a 78-r.p.m. disc. And when Ringling Brothers commissioned him to write a polka for a group of elephants wearing tutus in the circus, he did just that. Finally, in 1952, when his devoted amanuensis, Robert Craft, introduced him to large doses of Anton Webern, he repudiated his hostile attitude to "the three Viennese" (Schoenberg, Webern and Berg) and embraced the serial procedure.

Stravinsky's essentially receptive nature has been commented upon by Craft, who lived as a member of the Stravinsky family for much of the period that followed their meeting in 1948: "The initial agony [of composition] could be softened by imposition from without. Stravinsky seemed to seek imposition." This was true not only of his musical composition but of his prose writing as well. The composer readily acknowledges that his autobiography and the *Poetics of Music* were written in collaboration with others, and, after 1957, he allowed Craft to speak for him.

None of the stylistic changes that Stravinsky made during his long and productive life affected the nature of his working habits. Unlike Schoenberg, he finished just about everything he began. And unlike Schoenberg, he suffered no long periods when he couldn't create music. Writing of the sketchbooks, Craft said, "Most sketch entries are dated, and it is possible to determine in them exactly what was composed on what date. The dates show that Stravinsky has been able all his life to produce about the same amount of music each day."

Stravinsky was as rooted in Russia as Schoenberg was rooted in Vienna and Berlin. Although he left St. Petersburg in 1914 and, as he declared in 1966, "fled every reminder of my past until a decade ago," he obviously maintained very deep ties to his native land.

He never repudiated his Russian forefathers. According to Eric Walter White's biography, Stravinsky's first teacher, Rimsky-Korsakov, "became a sort of father-figure in Stravinsky's life following the death of his own father in 1902." Stravinsky's affection for Rimsky is supported by Erik Satie, who wrote in 1923: "Stravinsky remembers Rimsky very kindly and always speaks of him with great affection and filial gratitude."

Stravinsky's feeling for Rimsky was only exceeded by his admiration for Tchaikovsky, who was as revered in Russia as Wagner was in Germany. In 1921, Stravinsky praised Tchaikovsky's *Sleeping Beauty*: "It is a great satisfaction to me as a musician to see produced a work of so direct a character at a time when so many people, who are neither simple, nor naive, nor spontaneous, seek in their art simplicity, 'poverty,' and spontaneity. Tchaikovsky in his very nature possessed these three gifts to the fullest extent. That is why he never feared to let himself go, whereas the prudes, whether raffiné or academic, were shocked by the frank speech, free from artifice, of his music."

That praise, expressed in a letter written just after Stravinsky completed his "neoclassic" Octet, quickly became notorious. People had assumed that the composer would be against everything emotional and subjective, everything Tchaikovsky stood for. But Stravinsky's respect for the older composer remained intact. He dedicated his comic opera, *Mavra*, to the three Russian artists he most admired—Pushkin, Glinka and Tchaikovsky—and dedicated *Le Baiser de la Fée* to Tchaikovsky, many of whose melodies he quoted in the piece.

In the 1936 *Autobiography*, Stravinsky wrote of his first and only contact with Tchaikovsky, which occurred at a gala performance of Glinka's *Russlan and Ludmilla* at the Imperial Opera in St. Petersburg in 1893:

> Besides the excitement I felt at hearing this music that I already loved to distraction, it was my good fortune to catch a glimpse in the foyer of Peter Tchaikovsky, the idol of the Russian public, whom I had never seen before and was never to see again. He had just conducted the first audition of his new symphony, the Pathetic, in St. Petersburg. A fortnight later my mother took me to a concert where the same symphony was played in memory of the composer, who had been suddenly carried off by cholera. Deeply though I was impressed by the unexpected death of the great musician, I was far from realizing at the moment that this glimpse of the living Tchaikovsky—fleeting though it was—would become one of my most treasured memories.

In 1962 Stravinsky returned to Russia for a brief visit. In *Newsweek* he was quoted as saying: "My wish to go there is due primarily to the evidence I have received of a genuine desire or need for me by the younger generation of Russian composers. No artist's name has been more abused in the Soviet Union than mine, but one cannot achieve the future we must achieve with the Russians by nursing a grudge." Vera Stravinsky implied that her husband masked considerable feeling under these cool words. She said that he hesitated before accepting the Russian invitation because he was worried that "he would become too emotional" when he returned to his country. In a speech delivered before the Soviet Ministry of Culture on

October 1 of that year, Stravinsky declared himself to be more a Russian than a Frenchman or American:

> "The smell of Russian earth is different; and such things are impossible to forget. . . . A man has one birthplace, one fatherland, one country—he can have only one country—and the place of his birth is the most important factor in his life. I regret that circumstances separated me from my fatherland, that I did not bring my works to birth there, and, above all, that I was not there to help the new Soviet Union create its new music. But I did not leave Russia by my own will, even though I admit I disliked much in my Russia and in Russia generally. But the right to criticize Russia is mine, because Russia is mine and I love it. I do not give any foreigner that right."

That evening Craft entered the following note in his diary: "I am certain that to be recognized and acclaimed as a Russian in Russia, and to be performed there, has meant more to him than anything else in the years I have known him."

The Russia into which Stravinsky was born, because of its relative geographic isolation, fathered a rich and varied folk idiom, a wealth of liturgical song, but virtually no art music. Before the middle of the nineteenth century, such music was a foreign commodity, imported from other countries for the pleasure of the upper classes.

Modish, Western European art and thought first began to intrude upon Russian life only at the end of the seventeenth century. When Catherine II became Empress in 1762, she brought with her a snobbish but infectious love for French culture, which persisted in Russia well into Stravinsky's own lifetime.

By the nineteenth century nationalistic concerns began to displace the international musical idiom of the century before; people wanted to hear their own sounds in artistic settings. Smetana appeared in Bohemia, Grieg and Sinding in Scandinavia, and Mikhail Ivanovich Glinka incorporated Russian folk tunes into the classical and early grand opera forms he had learned while he was living in Paris, Berlin and Italy. His first work, *A Life for the Tsar,* the first significant musical work written by a Russian composer, was created less than sixty years before Stravinsky's birth.

Soon after the appearance of *A Life for the Tsar,* it became apparent that two philosophies of music were emerging which reflected the age-old division of Russian thought on everything ranging from art to politics. One group was committed to a Pan-Slavic orientation that precluded Western influences; the other was in favor of assimilating the wealth of the West. Supporting the former premise, a group known as "The Nationalist Five" rose to prominence: Alexander Borodin, Modest Moussorgsky, César Cui, Nikolai Rimsky-Korsakov, and Mili Balakirev. Moussorgsky was the most original musician in the group. Responding to the inspired nationalism of the 1860s, he sought to make art the servant of the people: "To seek assiduously the most delicate and subtle features of human nature—of the human crowd—to follow them into unknown regions, to make them our own: this seems to me the true vocation of the artist . . . to feed upon humanity as a healthy diet which has been neglected—there lies the whole problem of art."

Throughout his life, Moussorgsky refused to submit to the discipline of a European musical education, which the Westernized Russian composers actively sought. This second group of musicians was headed by Anton Rubinstein and Peter Ilich Tchaikovsky. Tchaikovsky was the foremost Russian composer of the nineteenth century to receive worldwide acclaim; the manner in which he incorporated Russian sentiment and Russian folk melodies into European musical forms carried his art across national boundaries.

Even Rimsky-Korsakov, Stravinsky's teacher and a leading figure in the Nationalist Five, was not immune to the pull from abroad, and in 1864, he wrote the very first Russian "symphony." In Rimsky's case, the form provided a shell into which he inserted a literal or sequential repetition of folk melodies. He never developed his material in the generic "symphonic" sense.

The Russian Revolution, in 1917, deprived Stravinsky of his property, and he no longer received an income from his estate. It was at this time that the composer built on his sympathy with French culture and crystallized a pro-Western identification. In the *Autobiography* he argues for the Western approach and writes of his admiration for Pushkin, who was in that same tradition:

> . . . By his nature, his mentality, and his ideology, Pushkin was the most perfect representative of that wonderful line which began with Peter the Great and which, by a fortunate alloy, has united the most characteristically Russian elements with the spiritual riches of the West.
>
> Diaghilev unquestionably belongs to this line, and all his activities have only confirmed the authenticity of that origin.

As for myself, I have always been aware that I had in me the germs of the same mentality only needing development and I subsequently cultivated them.

Thus the basic ingredients of Schoenberg's and Stravinsky's musical diet were as strikingly different as German and Russian food. The most apparent difference lies in the fact that, during his student years, Stravinsky was completely under Rimsky-Korsakov's control, and Rimsky was oblivious to the Germanic idea that underlay Schoenberg's creative life: the perpetual variation of a single melodic idea.

But the more profound difference may well be this: Schoenberg was born at the end of a long and distinguished Austro-German musical tradition, which gave birth to an enormous literature for symphony, chamber and solo instruments. When Schoenberg reached his artistic maturity, tonality, the language on which this tradition was based, appeared finally to be exhausted. Schoenberg thus attempted to forge ahead and create a new musical language which would respectably uphold a very lengthy tradition.

Stravinsky, on the other hand, was born in Russia during a period when Tchaikovsky and Rimsky-Korsakov both borrowed melodies from popular sources and musical forms from Western Europe. It is no wonder, then, that throughout the course of his life, Stravinsky adopted exactly what he chose to and imbued the adopted form with his own dazzling, individual sound.

CHAPTER 9

My real answer to your questions about my childhood is that it was a period of waiting for the moment when I could send everyone and everything connected with it to hell.

IGOR STRAVINSKY
Memories and Commentaries,
1960

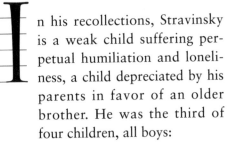 n his recollections, Stravinsky is a weak child suffering perpetual humiliation and loneliness, a child depreciated by his parents in favor of an older brother. He was the third of four children, all boys:

I was baptized by a prelate of the Russian Orthodox Church in Oranienbaum (a suburb of St. Petersburg) a few hours after my birth, which occurred at noon (June 17, 1882). My parents summoned a [priest] to say prayers for me, to sprinkle my head with anointed waters, and to draw a cross on my forehead in anointing oil. . . . According to custom in the Russian Church, frail babies were sometimes baptized summarily in this fashion. (The fact of my frailty, thus established at my first hour, was insisted upon throughout my youth, until it became a way of thinking about myself; and even now, as a healthy octogenarian leading an active and strenuous life, I sometimes remind myself that, in fact, I am much too frail and had better stop.)

Stravinsky describes his father, Feodor Ignatievich, as nervous and irritable and his mother, Anna Kholodovsky, as cold and unloving. His assessment of his mother gains support from this incident: In 1938, when Anna Stravinsky was about to attend her first performance of her son's *Le Sacre du Printemps* on the occasion of its twenty-fifth anniversary, she told a friend that she did not expect to enjoy it, because it was not her "kind of music." The composer George Antheil, a friend of Stravinsky, reports that

Stravinsky's mother frequently chided her son about his lack of appreciation of the advanced, chromatic Scriabin, saying that he was obviously not capable of "recognizing his betters."

Despite this, Stravinsky enjoyed some advantages in being a child of this cultivated, musical couple. On both sides the families had been landed gentry or artists, and Stravinsky's father possessed a library of between 7,000 and 8,000 books, including many first editions. Feodor was a famous bass singer at the Imperial Opera House in St. Petersburg, where the Stravinsky family lived. Tchaikovsky gave him an inscribed photograph and wrote a letter to a friend in which he lavishly praised Feodor's talent. Indeed, Feodor Stravinsky was so admired by Tchaikovsky that he served as a pallbearer at his funeral.

Igor grew up in large, comfortable, glamorous surroundings. Tchaikovsky's photograph stood on a table in his father's studio, Rimsky-Korsakov visited from time to time, and the child was allowed the run of his father's library. But Stravinsky also recalls the sounds of his city. And it is sound, not idea, that is at the core of his creative life:

> The first such sounds that record themselves on my awareness were those of the drushkis on cobblestones or blackwood parquetry pavements. Only a few of those horse-carriages had rubber tires, and those were doubly expensive; the whole city crackled with the iron hoops of the others. The loudest diurnal noises of the city were cannonades of bells from the Nikolsky Cathedral . . . but I recall with more nostalgia the sound of an accordion in a suburban street on a lonely Sunday afternoon, or the trilling of wires of the balalaika orchestra in a restaurant café.

Stravinsky writes that he first became conscious of himself as a musician when he was two years old: "My nurse brought me home from the village where we had been perambulating one afternoon, and my parents, who were then trying to coax me to talk asked me what I had seen there. I said I had seen the peasants and heard them sing, and I sang what they had sung. Everyone was astonished and impressed at this recital, and I heard my father remark that I had a wonderful ear."

His musical gifts were supplemented by a continuous exposure to serious music. In his infancy and early childhood, Stravinsky heard his father, whose study was near the nursery, rehearse roles from the Russian repertory—Glinka, Rimsky-Korsakov, Tchaikovsky, Dargomizhsky, Borodin and Moussorgsky—as well as from the standard Italian works. At seven, Igor made his first trip to the Maryinsky Theater, across the street from his apartment, to attend a performance of Tchaikovsky's *Sleeping Beauty*; he cites that occasion as the one at which he developed a lifelong attachment to both ballet and Tchaikovsky. A year or so later his mother took him to *A Life for the Tsar,* an opera he was already able to play on the piano: "It was then that I heard an orchestra for the first time. And what an orchestra—Glinka's! The impression was indelible, but it must not be supposed that this was due solely to the fact that it was the first orchestra I ever heard. To this day [1936] not only Glinka's music in itself, but his orchestration as well, remains a perfect monument of musical art. . . ."

At nine, Igor began to study piano with a pupil of Rubinstein's, who refused him permission to improvise. Although he was unhappy at this, he learned to play the piano well enough to cope with the standard European literature: Mendelssohn's Piano Concerto, and works by Mozart, Haydn, Beethoven, Schumann and Schubert. In his early teens, an uncle, an avid music lover and Russian liberal, took Igor under his wing and introduced him to the works of the Russian Five. It was through this uncle and his circle of friends that the young musician's horizons widened; the lines of communication were open between Russian nationalism and German academicism:

> Was it Glazounov, adopted son of the Five, with his heavy German academic symphonies, or the lyrical symphonies of Tchaikovsky, or the epic symphonies of Borodin, or the symphonic poems of Rimsky-Korsakov, that imbued this group with its taste for symphonism? Who can say? But however that may be, all these ardently devoted themselves to that type of music. It was thanks to this environment that I got to know the great German composers.

He also learned about German music through his private lessons with Vassily Kalafaty, who worked with him on counterpoint, invention, fugue and the harmonization of chorale melodies. Stravinsky reports that Kalafaty was very suspicious of any "new" chords but adds that he is grateful to him for teaching him to appeal to his ear as the first and last test.

The most crucial foreign influence on Stravinsky was French. At fifteen, he met Ivan Pokrovsky, then twenty-three: "I was still in the Gymnasium when we met and he was already being graduated from the university. My life at home was unbearable (even more unbearable than usual, that is) and Pokrovsky appeared to me as a kind of shining Baudelaire versus the *esprit Belge* of my family."

Pokrovsky introduced Stravinsky to Charles Gounod, Georges Bizet and Emmanuel Chabrier and, through playing four-handed arrangements at the piano, to Offenbach's *Tales of Hoffmann* and Delibes's *Lakmé* and *Coppélia*. It was at this time that Stravinsky recognized his attraction to French music: "I found in [it] a different type of musical writing, different harmonic methods, a different melodic conception, a freer and fresher feeling for form. This gave rise to doubts, as yet barely perceptible, with respect to what had up till then seemed unassailable dogma. That is why I am eternally grateful to Pokrovsky; for from my discussions with him dates my gradual emancipation from the influences that, all unknown to myself, the academicism of the time was exercising over me."

Thus, in his late teens, Stravinsky was an able pianist, an educated musician, and a connoisseur of musical style. But he had not yet begun to compose.

When he was twenty, during a vacation with his family at Heidelberg, Stravinsky met Rimsky-Korsakov and showed him a few pieces he had written. He was enrolled in law school at the time; his parents never took seriously his interest in music:

> During this visit I showed Rimsky my compositions, short piano pieces, "andantes," "melodies," and so forth. I was ashamed of myself for wasting his time but I was also extremely eager to become his pupil. He looked at these tender efforts of mine with great patience, and then said that if I would continue my work with Kalafaty I might also come to him two times a week for lessons. I was overjoyed, so much so, in fact, that not only did I apply myself to Kalafaty's exercises, but I also filled several note books with them by the end of the summer.

Shortly after this meeting, Stravinsky's father, who had been suffering from cancer for over a year, died. Rimsky-Korsakov stepped quickly into the parental role and proved to be no more loving and encouraging than Feodor had been. Stravinsky never criticized this attitude, attributing it to some hidden effort to spur him on to do better things. He writes that Rimsky was always very careful not to encourage him with the loose use of the word "talent." But Rimsky went even further than avoiding complimentary words; he made public unfavorable opinions of his student's work. In 1907 one

Russian critic wrote: "In the opinion of Rimsky-Korsakov, the talent of Igor Stravinsky has not yet taken clear shape. Rimsky thinks that the fourth part of his symphony imitates Glazounov too much and Rimsky himself."

It is not surprising that the Stravinsky of that time sounded a little like Rimsky. Just consider Rimsky's method of teaching Stravinsky:

> Rimsky adopted the plan of teaching form and orchestration side by side, because in his view the more highly developed musical forms found their fullest expression in the complexity of the orchestra. . . . My work with Rimsky-Korsakov consisted of his giving me pieces of classical music to orchestrate. I remember that they were chiefly parts of Beethoven sonatas, and of Schubert's quartets and marches. . . . A year and a half later I began the composition of a symphony. As soon as I finished one part of a movement I used to show it to him, so that my whole work, including the instrumentation, was under his control.

Thus Stravinsky's early work shows a classical, international orientation with touches of Rimsky in the instrumentation. He composed his first Piano Sonata, not given an opus number, in the traditional four movements. His first published work, Symphony in E-flat, opens with a theme borrowed from Richard Strauss and a polyphonic texture reminiscent of Wagner's. In *Faun and Shepherdess*, Opus 2, written during 1906–7, Stravinsky set verses of Pushkin for mezzo-soprano and orchestra in a French, impressionistic way; Debussy and Ravel had obviously affected him.

In 1905, when he was twenty-three and had just finished his studies at law school, he married his first cousin, Catherine Nossenko, who was one year older than he. He describes their relationship as being "like sister and brother." In the fall of 1908, Stravinsky visited Rimsky-Korsakov to tell him he was working on a new piece to celebrate the approaching marriage of Rimsky's daughter. He took the work with him on a vacation with his wife and finished it within six weeks, but between the time Stravinsky sent off the score and it arrived in St. Petersburg, Rimsky-Korsakov died.

Almost immediately, Stravinsky abandoned the German and French influences and assumed a most pronounced Rimsky-like sound. His teacher had, on occasion, complained of plagiaristic tendencies on Stravinsky's part. And even after he died, Rimsky's family persisted in this complaint. Their attitude was succinctly expressed by Mme Rimsky-Korsakov. On seeing Stravinsky in tears at her husband's funeral, she made a remark which

Stravinsky later characterized as the cruelest ever made to him: "Why so unhappy? We still have Glazounov."

But Stravinsky's next aesthetic mentor was not to be Glazounov. The winter that followed Rimsky's death, *Fireworks* was performed on the same program with another Stravinsky dazzler, *Scherzo Fantastique.* Serge Diaghilev was in the audience. *Fireworks* impressed the ballet master of the newly formed Russian Ballet. He asked Stravinsky to arrange two piano pieces by Chopin for his ballet, *Les Sylphides,* for the Paris Opera during the spring of 1909. The ballet was to open with the Chopin/Stravinsky Nocturne in A-flat and close with the Valse Brillante in E-flat.

At the time Stravinsky was also working on *The Nightingale,* an opera he had started while still with Rimsky. With the help of his friend Stepan Mitusov, he had written a libretto based on a Hans Christian Andersen story about a sick Chinese Emperor who could be cured only by the song of the nightingale. The first act was completed in 1909. But because of Diaghilev's other commissions, Stravinsky could not finish the work until 1914.

Stravinsky abandoned the development of a motive, in the traditional symphonic sense, in *The Nightingale.* The fishermen repeat their air frequently from the beginning with no change. The nightingale's motive doesn't change either. And the Three Chinese Marches are really one march and two echoes rather than three distinct musical pieces. This nondevelopmental aspect of his work persisted throughout the composer's life. Béla Bartók described the basis of Stravinsky's style: "He seldom uses melodies of a closed form consisting of three or four lines but short motives of two or three bars and repeats them *à la ostinato.* These short, recurring, primitive motives are very characteristic of Russian music of a very certain category." And, referring to Stravinsky's *Perséphone,* composed in 1934, Bartók pointed out that a five-bar phrase is repeated four times. "We perceive that the repetitions are only incidents in a continuous line, which because it is not directed to any climax and is devoid of all harmonic tension, seems endless. Such melodies, undramatic in structure, are rare in other composers." Repeating melodic fragments in this way, avoiding the development of a single idea, Stravinsky, quite naturally, separated himself from Schoenberg as early as 1909, before each of the men recognized and coped with the threat of the other.

After *Les Sylphides,* Diaghilev commissioned Stravinsky to write a full-length ballet, *The Firebird.* Diaghilev originally wanted Liadov, then a more famous composer, to do it, but he was afraid that Liadov would not deliver it on time. Stravinsky was frightened by the nature of the commission—it was his first with a deadline—but he could not resist the glamour:

"It was highly flattering to be chosen from among the musicians of my generation, and to be allowed to collaborate in so important an enterprise side by side with personages who were generally recognized as masters in their own spheres."

Following the practice of Rimsky-Korsakov, Stravinsky took his literary theme from an old Russian legend. He wrote the music in the form of a *ballet d'action,* in which the music followed the stage action bar by bar. Stravinsky's arrival in Paris to participate in rehearsals put him in daily contact with the exciting world of French impressionistic music. Although he had been attracted to French culture while still in St. Petersburg, his taste was heightened by close association with Debussy, Ravel, Satie and Florent Schmitt. At close to fifty, Debussy epitomized French culture and specifically the French challenge to Wagner. Stravinsky has touched on his relationship with Debussy in *Expositions and Developments,* written with Craft in 1960:

> I was called to the stage to bow at the conclusion [of *Firebird*] and was recalled several times. I was still on stage when the final curtain had come down, and I saw coming toward me Diaghilev and a dark man with a double forehead whom he introduced as Claude Debussy. The great composer spoke kindly about the music, ending his words with an invitation to dine with him. Some time later, when we were sitting together in a box during a performance of *Pelléas,* I asked him what he had really thought about *Firebird.* He said, "Que voulez-vous, il fallait bien commencer par quelque chose." Honest, but not extremely flattering. Yet shortly after the *Firebird* premiere, he gave me his well-known photo (in profile) with a dedication: "à Igor en toute sympathie artistique." I was not so honest about the work we were then hearing. I thought *Pelléas* a great bore as a whole, and in spite of many wonderful pages.

Despite the carping words on both sides, Stravinsky adopted French Impressionism, absorbing it into his own personal style. Virgil Thomson has written that by the time he was thirty, Stravinsky had "so firmly proved himself a master of French Impressionism that he scared the daylights out of Claude Debussy."

Although Stravinsky's additive, nondevelopmental form is related to Debussy's, there are striking differences in style between the works of the two composers. Stravinsky discussed these differences in an interview published in 1968: "Debussy referred to me as a 'primitive' and 'instinctual,' rather than a 'schooled' composer. And he was right. Like Ramanujan, who did his mathematics without any formal mathematical education, I have had to depend on natural insight and instinct for all the learning I would have acquired if I had taken a Ph.D. in composition. . . ."

Thus, at the start of his career, without a set of intellectual premises, Stravinsky created an altogether new kind of continuity in music. Despite manifold changes throughout his career, he never abandoned this mosaic structure that came so unselfconsciously to him.

Although Debussy composed *Pelléas* in 1902 and his works were performed throughout Europe during the first decade of the twentieth century, the French composer failed to dispel the Wagnerian mystique. In a lecture at Harvard in 1939, Stravinsky described the situation that prevailed at that time:

> Even the admirable music of *Pelléas et Mélisande*, so fresh in its modesty, was unable to get us out into the open, in spite of so many characteristics with which it shook off the tyranny of the Wagnerian system. . . . I am not without motive in provoking a quarrel with the notorious *Synthesis of the Arts* [Wagner's *Gesamtkunstwerk*]. I do not merely condemn it for its lack of tradition, its nouveau riche smugness. What makes its case much worse is the fact that the application of its theories has inflicted a terrible blow on music itself. . . . We can speak of these things all the more freely in view of the fact that the halcyon days of Wagnerism are past, and that the distance which separates us from them permits us to set matters straight.

The halcyon days of Wagnerism were past because, between 1910 and 1914, Stravinsky succeeded in shifting the focus of the musical world away from the German Romantic agony to Paris and the Diaghilev Ballet.

ike Stravinsky, Diaghilev studied music while enrolled in law school and then drifted into journalism. He founded a journal, *Mir Isskustva*, that was against academicism and for the avant-garde: Moussorgsky, Rimsky-Korsakov, Prokofiev, Stravinsky, as well as contemporary French composers and painters. Diaghilev went to Paris in 1908 and organized a series of concerts of Russian music including a performance of *Boris Godunov* with Chaliapin playing Boris. The following year, he formed the Ballet Russe. Diaghilev's impeccable taste and formidable powers of organization produced a new kind of ballet that made dance, music, theater and scenic design equally crucial to the overall production.

The Ballet Russe never performed in Russia, but it did play most of the great cities of the West: Madrid, London, Rome, Berlin, Monte Carlo, Buenos Aires, New York, Philadelphia and Paris. Its dancers and choreographers included Pavlova, Karsavina, Lopokouva, Balanchine, Fokine, Massine, Bohm, Lifar, Nijinsky and Nijinska. Its scenic designers were Picasso, Braque, Utrillo, di Chirico, Juan Gris, Rouault, and the Russians (Bakst, Benois, Larionov, Goncharova, among others). Its composers also were the major talents working outside the German domain, and included Debussy, Ravel, Satie, Poulenc, Milhaud, de Falla, Rieti, Schmitt, Prokofiev and Stravinsky. Stravinsky wrote more music for the company than any other composer, including his three major ballets—*Firebird, Petrushka,* and *The Rite of Spring.*

During the winter of 1909–10, before he even received the contract, Stravinsky began *Firebird.* As soon as he finished, he left St. Petersburg for Paris to attend the rehearsals with Fokine, scenarist and choreographer for *Firebird.* Alexander Benois has described his impressions of the composer: "In those days he was a very willing and charming 'pupil.' He thirsted for enlightenment and longed to widen his knowledge. . . . But what was most valuable in him was the absence of the slightest dogmatism."

Based on a Russian legend in which a good fairy comes into conflict with an ogre, *Firebird* became an immediate success. Parisians loved its driving motor rhythms, so different from Debussy, as well as its lush Rimsky-like orchestration. The composer later said the orchestra was "wastefully large," with its triangulo, tamburo, campanelli, tamtam, piatti, xylophone, celesta, piano, three harps, sixteen first violins, sixteen second violins, fourteen violas, eight cellos, eight double basses, three trumpets, two tenor tubas and two bass tubas. Stravinsky dedicated the work to Andrey Rimsky-Korsakov, son of his late teacher, as though to compensate the family for what he had borrowed from the father. Eric Walter White notes that Stravinsky here adopts a technique Rimsky had used in his last work, *Le Coq d'Or,* of associating human elements with diatonic themes and magical elements with chromatic material.

The Ballet Russe performed *Firebird* for the first time on June 25, 1910, at the Paris Opera House, with Karsavina in the leading role. (Pavlova refused to dance it, criticizing the music as complicated and meaningless.) The audience applauded loudly, Debussy came backstage to compliment the composer, and the publishing house of Jorgenson hastily printed the score. Unlike Schoenberg, Stravinsky did not have to wait long for worldwide acclaim.

"One day when I was finishing the last pages of *Firebird* in St. Petersburg," Stravinsky writes,

> I had a fleeting vision which came to me as a complete surprise, my mind at the time being full of other things. I saw in imagination a solemn pagan rite: sage elders, seated in a circle, watched a young girl dance herself to death. They were sacrificing her to propitiate the God of Spring. Such was the theme of *The Rite of Spring.* . . .
>
> "Before tackling [it] . . . I wanted to refresh myself by composing an orchestral piece in which the piano would play the most important part—a sort of *Konzertstück.* In composing the music I had in mind the distinct picture of a puppet, suddenly endowed with life, exasperating the patience of the orchestra with diabolical cascades of arpeggios. The orchestra, in turn, retaliates with menacing trumpet blasts. The outcome is a terrific noise which reaches its climax and ends in the sorrowful and querulous collapse of the poor puppet.

Surprised that Stravinsky had not proceeded with the *Sacre du Printemps,* Diaghilev was nevertheless delighted with the imagery for

Petrushka and decided to make a ballet of it. He chose Benois to work with Stravinsky on the scenario and Fokine to choreograph the piece. *Petrushka* is organized according to classical symphonic structure. It is in four movements: Allegro, Andante, Scherzo and Trio, and Rondo.

Stravinsky worked on the score in Switzerland, the Riviera, St. Petersburg and Rome. Diaghilev presented it in Paris a year after the *Firebird,* with Nijinsky and Karsavina dancing and Pierre Monteux conducting. The composer scored it for a *Firebird*-like orchestra but this time he created a special effect, that of a mechanistic, soulless world. Bubbling flutes set the first scene. Dolls and barrel organs on stage are accompanied by angular melodies and short, repetitive rhythms. Piano passages for Petrushka's movements suggest watches and other ticking things. The story of love, murder and resurrection could not fail in Paris. One critic wrote that it treated human material as "inextricable and precise as a dream," and in Rome the futurist poet Marinetti carried a banner: "Down with Wagner, Long Live Stravinsky!"

Petrushka's major musical innovation lay in the bitonal effect which represented the mechanical and human elements of Petrushka's personality. Stravinsky knew exactly what he was doing:

> I had conceived of the music in two keys in the second tableau as Petrushka's insult to the public, and I wanted the dialogue for trumpets in two keys at the end to show that his ghost is still insulting the public. I was, and am, more proud of these last pages than of anything else in the score.
>
> Diaghilev wished to have me change the last four pizzicato chords in favor of a "tonal ending," as he so quaintly put it, though, two months later, when *Petrushka* was one of the Ballet's greatest successes, he denied he had ever been guilty of his original criticism.

Bitonality was new to the audience, and the rhythmic innovations surpassed those in *Firebird*. But the melodies in *Petrushka* were familiar. The score quotes heavily from folk tunes (at least they sound like folk tunes), from barrel organ pieces and from lilting waltzes. White specifies their origins: the first hurdy-gurdy tune is from a Russian chanson; the second from the French pop song, "Elle avait un jambe en bois"; the first theme of the waltz in Scene Three from Joseph Lanner's *Tanze,* Opus 165; and the waltz's second theme from Lanner's Opus 200. Stravinsky obviously had nothing against borrowing. He has always acknowledged that his theatrical ideas, like the one behind *The Rite of Spring* or the one that prompted *Histoire du Soldat*, appeared to him through dreams or in visions but that his melodic material was derived from folk songs or the music of other composers.

Petrushka was Stravinsky's first score to be published by Russischer Musik Verlag, the publishing house that had been established by Serge and Natalie Koussevitzky.

Stravinsky has written that the "primus inter pares" of the musical world between 1906 and 1912 was Arnold Schoenberg. But by 1914 it was Stravinsky whom Sir Osbert Sitwell matter-of-factly identified as "the master of the epoch." Thus, between 1912 and 1914, the center of the new musical universe had apparently shifted from Schoenberg to Stravinsky. *The Rite of Spring* made the difference.

All that began with *Firebird* and developed in *Petrushka* culminated in *The Rite of Spring*. Its spontaneity, bitonality, and unconventional rhythms established the work as one of the artistic landmarks of its time.

The *Rite* is divided into two major sections: "The Adoration of the Earth" and "The Sacrifice." Stravinsky scored it for his largest orchestra, particularly heavy on percussion instruments. The composer collaborated in the scenario with Nicolas Roerich, the painter and archeologist. In a letter to Diaghilev, Roerich wrote:

> In the ballet of the *Rite of Spring* as conceived by myself and Stravinsky, my object is to present a number of scenes of earthly joy and celestial triumph as understood by the Slavs. . . . My intention is that the first set should transport us to the foot of a sacred hill, in a lush plain, where Slavonic tribes are gathered together to celebrate the spring rites. In this scene there is an old witch who predicts the future, a marriage by capture, round dances. Then comes the solemn moment. The wise elder is brought from the village to imprint his sacred kiss on the new-flowering earth. During this rite the crowd is seized with a mystic terror. . . . After this uprush of terrestrial joy, the second scene sets a celestial mystery before us. Young virgins dance in circles on the sacred hill and enchanted rocks; then they choose the victim they intend to honor. In a moment she will dance her last dance before the ancients clad in bearskins to show that the bear was man's ancestor. Then the greybeards dedicate the victim to the God Yarilo.

Many critics attribute the scenario to Stravinsky's love for the Russian spring, for the composer once said to Craft that spring, in Russia, "seemed to begin in an hour and was like the whole earth cracking." But there is another dimension to *The Rite of Spring*; it picks up where *Petrushka* left off in treating the dehumanization of man. The music suggests physical action rather than a reflective spirit. Rhythms of an intensity never heard before in Western music attempt to convey the instinctual forces forging ahead unimpeded by man's intellect and reason. The rhythm is everywhere revolutionary: when the victim dances herself to death at the close of the work, she does so in bars originally marked 3/16, 5/16, 3/16, 4/16, 5/16, 3/16, 4/16. (The score has subsequently been revised for easier readings.)

In retrospect, the most striking aspect of *The Rite of Spring* was Stravinsky's adherence to a diatonic idiom at a time when the Schoenberg school was thoroughly atonal. Stravinsky's score, generated by rhythm, uses a harmonic bass; the final cadence of the sacred dance moves from dominant to tonic, the essence of classic tonality.

The Ballet Russe first performed *The Rite of Spring* at the Théâtre des Champs Élysées on May 29, 1913. But Stravinsky said that Nijinsky choreographed it inappropriately. It is difficult to determine whether the choreography—Nijinsky's first attempt—or the music caused the commotion that night. The following account of the disturbance is taken from Stravinsky's *Expositions and Developments*:

> Mild protests against the music could be heard from the very beginning of the performance. Then, when the curtain opened on the group of knock-kneed and long-braided Lolitas jumping up and down (Danse des Adolescents), the storm broke . . . I heard Florent Schmitt shout "Taisez-vous garces du seizième"; the "garces" of the sixteenth arrondissement were, of course, the most elegant ladies in Paris. The uproar continued, however, and a few minutes later I left the hall in a rage; I was sitting on the right near the orchestra and I remember slamming the door. I have never again been that angry. The music was so familiar to me; I loved it, and I could not understand why people who had not yet heard it wanted to protest in advance. I arrived in a fury backstage, where I saw Diaghilev flicking the house lights in a last effort to quiet the hall. For the rest of the performance I stood in the wings behind Nijinsky holding the tails of his *frac*,

while he stood on a chair shouting numbers to the dancers, like a coxswain.

The review in *Le Figaro* was as negative as the response of the audience:

> Bluffing the idle rich of Paris through appeals to their snobbery is a delightfully simple matter. Take the best society possible, composed of rich, simple-minded, idle people. . . . By pamphlets, newspaper articles, lectures, personal visits and all other appeals to their snobbery, persuade them that hitherto they have seen only vulgar spectacles, and are at last to know what is art and beauty. Impress them with cannibalistic formulae. They have not the slightest notion of music, literature, painting and dancing; still, they have heretofore seen under these names only a rude imitation of the real thing. Finally assure them that they are to see real dancing and hear real music. It will then be necessary to double the prices of the theater, so great will be the rush of shallow worshippers at this false shrine.

But Stravinsky's score was vindicated within a year. The discordant complexity of the harmonic texture set against the simplest themes, the artful, sophisticated instrumentation used to create the most primitive effects, the profoundly original rhythm and meter were revealed clearly at the Casino de Paris in April 1914, when Pierre Monteux conducted *Le Sacre* again in a concert version. Without the distraction of sets and dancing, *The Rite of Spring* scored a tremendous success. Stravinsky wrote:

> At the end of the Danse Sacrale the entire audience jumped to its feet and cheered. I came on stage and hugged Monteux, who was a river of perspiration; it was the saltiest hug of my life. A crowd swept backstage. I was hoisted to anonymous shoulders and carried into the street and up to the Place de la Trinité. A policeman pushed his way to my side in an effort to protect me, and it was this guardian of the law Diaghilev later fixed upon in his accounts of the story: "Our little Igor now requires police escorts out of his concerts, like a prize fighter."

During the 1912–13 season, Stravinsky went to Berlin for a performance of *Firebird* and *Petrushka* which the Kaiser and Kaiserin were scheduled to attend. It was during this visit that he met Schoenberg for the first time and heard his *Pierrot Lunaire*. Stravinsky recalls in his *Dialogues*: "I was aware that this was the most prescient confrontation of my life." He met that confrontation with *The Rite of Spring*; with the triumph of this work, music with a tonal center prevailed over music that was without one. Schoenberg felt the effect immediately; after Monteux's celebrated performance he set Rainer Maria Rilke's "Vorgefühl": "I cast myself forth and remain all alone—in the greatest of storms."

In a lecture delivered at Harvard in 1939, Stravinsky acknowledged the promotional aspect of his role: "Whatever field of endeavor has fallen upon our lot, if it is true we are intellectuals, we are called upon not to cogitate but to perform."

CHAPTER 11

After the 1917 Russian Revolution, Stravinsky dissociated himself from his country and committed his art to the traditions of Western Europe. Stravinsky then led the development of the neoclassical movement. Schoenberg crystallized dodecaphony and Stravinsky neoclassicism at precisely the same time. The difference between them was the fundamental one of direction: Schoenberg plunged into the future, declaring the twelve tones to be equal, while Stravinsky drew from the past, reexploring tonality as a viable language. Both composers aspired to a common end: order in place of anarchy and cliché. And both explored their paths by dramatically reduced means. Before Stravinsky finished *The Rite of Spring,* he composed the Three Japanese Lyrics for Soprano and Piano.

In his *Autobiography,* Stravinsky writes that "the Three Japanese Lyrics were very close to my heart. . . . The graphic solution of problems of perspective and space shown by their art incited me to find something analogous in music." The brevity of these pieces—the longest poem is only forty syllables with each getting only one quarter note—is reminiscent of the Schoenberg and Webern pieces of the time. And in the Japanese Lyrics, Stravinsky clearly moves toward atonality. The first is tonally ambiguous although it is written with a key signature while the other two have no key signatures at all. It may well have been these pieces, as well as the similarly treated *Le Roi des Étoiles,* that prompted Debussy to comment: "One wonders into whose arms the music of our time is going to fall. The young Russian school holds out its arms; but in my view they've become as little Russian as possible. Stravinsky himself leans dangerously in the direction of Schoenberg." But Stravinsky did not proceed in that direction at this time.

Just before the war, Stravinsky returned to Russia in search of folk sources for a grand *divertissement.* In Kiev he located the Kireievsky and Afanasiev collections of folk poetry and brought them with him to

Switzerland. The poetry served as a source for his wedding cantata, *Les Noces,* and for *Pribaoutki, Les Berceuses du Chat,* and *Renard,* all composed during the following few years. Stravinsky attributes his reassertion of his Russianness, after his involvement with French Impressionism, to political events: "My profound emotion on reading the news of war, which aroused patriotic feelings and a sense of sadness at being so distant from my own country, found some alleviation in the delight in which I steeped myself in Russian folk poems."

The Stravinsky family, now including two sons and two daughters, moved into a house in Clarens, Switzerland. There the composer began to work on *Les Noces.* The theme is similar to that of *The Rite of Spring*: both works focus on public ritual and away from matters of heart and mind. *Les Noces* celebrates a peasant wedding, but only in the most abstract, ritualized terms. Stravinsky never identifies any single voice with a particular character on stage; singers and chorus continually change roles. The listener grasps bits of ritual and clichés, but nothing that would individualize the characters in the ceremony. The involvement he had with *Petrushka* is missing in this piece composed a few years later.

In *Les Noces,* Stravinsky captures the spirit of the Russian folk song with one pervasive motif: a minor third and a whole tone within the interval of a fourth. Four three-note figures form the skeleton of almost all the themes in *Les Noces,* a compositional principle similar to that which Schoenberg was working on at the same time.

Stravinsky's avoidance of human material continues in *Renard,* a ballet about a cock, cat, fox and goat, and *Les Berceuses du Chat,* which treats of sparrows, geese, swans and more cats. Stravinsky's ultimate removal from things human is epitomized in his interest, in 1917, in the player piano. He wrote a Study for Pianola and followed that with many pianola transcriptions of his works. In an interview in the *New York Herald Tribune* in 1925, Stravinsky expressed his unbound admiration: "There is a new polyphonic truth in the player piano. There are new possibilities. It is something more. It is not the same thing as the piano. The player piano resembles the piano but it also resembles an orchestra. . . . The soul of it is the soul of an automobile. Besides the piano, it is practical. It has a future, yes. It has its utility. Men will write for it. But it will create matter for itself."

Although the themes of his post-1914 work continue to be similar to *The Rite of Spring,* the music takes a very different turn. It is elegant, subtle and contrapuntal, and no longer depends on a stage. His rhythms grow increasingly intricate. In place of a large orchestra he chooses tones that are stark and lean.

This economy was partly due to artistic considerations—where could he go after *The Rite of Spring*? But it was also caused by financial conditions: Stravinsky wanted his music performed. (Even the Ballet Russe had serious financial problems during World War I.) The composer began to score his pieces for unusual combinations of instruments and to use these instruments in novel ways. For *Les Noces* he chose four pianos and percussion and for *Les Berceuses du Chat* a contralto and clarinets. In *Renard* he treated the voice in an unconventional buffo manner, and *Histoire du Soldat* called for violin, double bass, clarinet, trombone, bassoon and a single percussionist playing two side drums, a bass drum, cymbals, tambourine, and triangle.

Perhaps stimulated by the successful concert performance of the *Rite*, and certainly stimulated by lack of money, Stravinsky immersed himself in the folk material he brought out of Russia. Writing about the appeal of the poetry, he voiced the belief that music had no expressive powers, a concept that shocked the musical world:

"What fascinated me in this verse," he wrote in the *Autobiography*,

> was not so much the stories, which were often crude, or the pictures and metaphors, always so deliciously unexpected, as the sequence of words and syllables, and the cadence they create, which produces an effect on one's sensibilities very closely akin to that of music. For I consider that music is, by its very nature, powerless to express anything at all, whether a feeling, an attitude of mind, a psychological mood, a phenomenon of nature etc. . . . . Expression has never been an inherent property of music. This is by no means the purpose of its existence. If, as is nearly always the case, music appears to express something, this is only an illusion and not a reality. It is simply an additional attribute which, by tacit and inveterate agreement, we have lent it, thrust upon it, as a label, a convention—in short, an aspect unconsciously or by force of habit, we have come to confuse with its essential being.

Despite the fact that Stravinsky drew from the tonal past, in articulating this nonexpressive function of music he looked farther into the future than Schoenberg did during his entire life. And Stravinsky was on this path as early as 1914–15. In Three Pieces for String Quartet, he does not call the work a string quartet to emphasize a break with the traditional quartet form.

(Stravinsky is reported to have said that if he had his way, he would cut out the development sections of Mozart's symphonies.) The *Pribaoutki* also avoids development; the Russian title means "Say it quickly," a game in which one person said one word, a second said another and a third still another—all very rapidly. In writing down these verses no attention is paid to the traditional rules of prosody, and Stravinsky plays with the rhythmic variety that results. In the Three Easy Pieces for Piano Duet, written for his two older children to play, a simple, unchanging ostinato in the left hand accompanies extended figurations in the right. These pieces represent the composer's first excursion, since his student days, into a non-Russian, international idiom. Later he identified them as the moment at which "neoclassicism was born."

However artistically productive the time was, Stravinsky had many trying days. Financial problems precipitated a crisis with Diaghilev. The Ballet Russe was signed for an American tour and scheduled to play the Metropolitan Opera House in New York. Stravinsky wanted to conduct his own ballets. Although he insisted that the Met wanted him, the management never sent him a contract. Just before the company's second American tour, which was marked by the same neglect, Stravinsky asked Diaghilev to boycott the engagement but Diaghilev refused. Nijinsky's new wife reports a Stravinsky visit: "He insisted that if Vaslav [Nijinsky] were a real friend he would make it a condition to go to America only if Stravinsky was asked also. I thought this rather stretching the bonds of friendship. Stravinsky talked, raged, cried; he paced up and down the room cursing Diaghilev: "He thinks that he is the Russian Ballet himself. Our success has gone to his head. What would he be without us, without Bakst, Benois, you, myself? Vaslav, I count on you."

Nijinsky sent a wire to New York, asking for Stravinsky to be included in the arrangement, but nothing ever came of it. The Ballet Russe left for New York, with Diaghilev, Nijinsky and Ansermet, but without Stravinsky. Despite his bitterness at this, Stravinsky went to Spain to greet Diaghilev on his return; the composer always swallowed abuse when it was practical to do so—whether it came from his father, his mother, Rimsky, Debussy or Diaghilev. On that score he was far different from Schoenberg.

The 1917 Revolution deprived Stravinsky of his property. In the same year the nurse who tended him and his children died. His favorite brother died in Russia, and Nijinsky retired from dancing because of increasing mental problems. The composer said: "This period, the end of 1917, was one of the hardest I have ever experienced. Overwhelmed by the successive bereavements that I had suffered, I was also now in a position of the utmost pecuniary difficulty. The Communist Revolution, which had just triumphed in Russia, deprived me of the last resources that had still, from time to time, been reaching me from my country and I found myself, so to speak, face to face with nothing, in a foreign land and right in the middle of war."

Stravinsky enlisted the help of the Swiss writer Charles Ferdinand Ramuz, who had translated for him the Russian texts to *Renard, Pribaoutki,* and *Les Berceuses du Chat,* to collaborate in the creation of a miniature mobile theater which would produce works accessible to people in all different countries. Stravinsky found a patron, and Ramuz agreed to write the libretto for *Histoire du Soldat,* a Faustian tale of a soldier who trades his violin for material wealth and is subsequently destroyed for having made the choice.

Just before he started work on the score, inspired by the piano reductions of jazz that Ansermet brought back from the United States, Stravinsky wrote *Ragtime* for cimbalon, nine solo instruments, and percussion in 1918, and *Piano Rag-Music* for Artur Rubinstein in 1919. And *Histoire* exhibits specifically American jazz effects. In this self-consciously non-Russian work, the composer not only makes musical reference to the United States, but quotes South American tangos, Swiss brass bands, Spanish pasadobles, Lutheran chorales and Viennese waltzes.

Although *Histoire* proved to be one of the composer's most popular works, it did not serve its original purpose. Stravinsky attributes its failure to the great influenza pandemic that attacked performers, agents and managers. He was still in financial trouble the following year; this notice appeared in *Musical America*: "Word has just come to this country that Igor Stravinsky, composer of *Petrushka* and *The Nightingale* etc., is in dire need. A cable just received from an American attaché of the embassy reads: 'Cable money to Stravinsky in desperate circumstances—care of American consul in Geneva.'"

But soon his luck improved. Diaghilev, who had delivered Stravinsky from anonymity in 1909 by providing him with a theatrical base, came to the rescue once again. He commissioned him to string together a number of pieces then thought to be by the eighteenth-century Italian composer Giovanni Pergolesi. Diaghilev thus pointed to a rich and varied source of material, distinct from indigenous art, from which Stravinsky was to derive inspiration for the next thirty years.

Stravinsky's neoclassicism, his use of material from the past, was not an original device in music. Roman Vlad, one of Stravinsky's biographers, specifies the *Missae Parodiae*, Bach's transcriptions of Vivaldi and Marcello, Liszt's paraphrases, and the innumerable classic theme and variations as other occasions on which musicians borrowed from the past. And in 1962, Stravinsky mentioned T. S. Eliot in this context in an interview in *The Observer* (London):

> Were Eliot and myself merely trying to refit old ships while "the other side," Webern, Schoenberg, Joyce and Klee sought new forms of travel? I think that distinction, much traded on a generation ago, has disappeared. Our era is a unity of which we are all a part. Of course, we seemed, Eliot and myself, to have made art out of the *disjecta membra*, the quotations of other poets and composers, the references to earlier styles (hints of earlier and other creation), the detritus that betokened a wreck. But we used it and anything that came to hand to rebuild. We did not invent new conveyors, new means of travel. But the true business of the artist is to rebuild old ships. He can say, in his way, only what has been said.

Although Stravinsky did not refer to Picasso in this article, the great Spanish painter also played a major role in the classicism of the 1920s. Picasso said: "The artist is a receptacle for emotions from all over the place, from the sky, from the earth, from a scrap of paper, from a passing shape, from a spider's web. . . . Where things are concerned there are no class distinctions. We must pick out what is good for us where we find it. . . . When I am shown a portfolio of old drawings, for instance, I have no qualms about taking anything I want from them."

Stravinsky first met Picasso in 1917 when the painter came to join the Diaghilev Ballet to design sets for Satie's *Parades*. Cocteau, the librettist, introduced him into the company. It was then that he drew the first of his famous Stravinsky portraits and designed the cover for *Ragtime*.

Diaghilev's idea for *Pulcinella* was a practical one. It grew out of his success with two similar ballet projects, for he had commissioned Respighi to arrange Cimarosa for the *Astuzie Femminili* and Tommasini to arrange Scarlatti for *The Good-Humored Ladies*. The "Pergolesi" manuscripts, which included two three-act operas and twelve trio sonatas, were found in the Naples Conservatory and the British Museum.

In the *Autobiography*, Stravinsky explains what brought him back to Diaghilev:

> The proposal that I should work with Picasso, who was to do the scenery and costumes and whose art was

particularly near and dear to me, recollections of the walks together and the impressions of Naples we had shared, the great pleasure I had experienced from Massine's choreography in *The Good-Humored Ladies*—all this combined to overcome my reluctance. For it was a delicate task to breathe new life into scattered fragments and to create a whole from the isolated pages of a musician for whom I felt a special liking and tenderness.

Not only was the score eighteenth-century; the scenario was eighteenth-century as well. Diaghilev and Massine created it from a Neapolitan manuscript dating from around 1700, which involved impersonations, mistaken identities and other devices common to opera buffa. In *Pulcinella*, several men conspire to kill the protagonist out of jealousy, but he tricks them by having a double stand in for him. At the end Pulcinella miraculously emerges, marries off all the possible couples, and keeps the lovely Pimpinella for himself.

The work consists of eight tableaux. It begins with an Overture for orchestra. The tableaux that follow adhere to the traditional eighteenth-century forms and are marked according to tempo: Allegro, Andantino, Scherzino, etc. Stravinsky retained the original melodies and bass lines and introduced his own tissue between, a tissue basically diatonic. There is virtually no chromatic writing and polytonal passages are equally rare. *Pulcinella*, the first Stravinsky/Diaghilev production since *The Rite of Spring*, breaks with both Romanticism and Impressionism. The public was not to be treated to rich colors and sensuous effects but to the precise lines associated with eighteenth-century music and thought.

The Russian Ballet performed *Pulcinella* at the Paris Opera House in 1920. Stravinsky was delighted by the results: "*Pulcinella* was one of those productions—and they are rare—where everything harmonizes, where all the elements—subject, music, dancing and artistic setting—form a coherent and homogenous whole. . . . As for Picasso, he worked miracles and I find it difficult to decide what was most enchanting—the coloring, the design, or the amazing inventiveness of this remarkable man."

In 1920, when Schoenberg wrote his first 12-tone movement, Stravinsky produced his first "neoclassic" work, a work nourished by the eighteenth century. As with dodecaphony, the neoclassical idea in music was certainly in the air. As early as 1912, Busoni, in Berlin, had composed his *Fantasia Contrapuntistica*, a bold attempt to complete Bach's *Art of the Fugue,* and in 1920 Busoni followed his own lead in a call for a "young classicism." In a letter to music critic Paul Bekker, he demanded that the "results of all earlier experiments should be classified, exploited and mastered, and should be converted into lasting, beautiful forms."

Thus, it was reasonable that Stravinsky, separated both physically and spiritually from Russia and in close contact with artists from Western Europe, should borrow their musical forms and ideas. Ingesting melodies and adapting structures from the past, Stravinsky went on to compose many neoclassic masterpieces.

"Neoclassicism" implies an objective, detached musical style that depends on a diatonic idiom. The movement was anti-Romantic, repudiating the emotional, subjective music of the past, and anti-dodecaphonic as well. Composers who considered themselves part of neoclassicism revived opera buffa, with its set arias, and the oratorio, too, while avoiding grand opera and program music.

As Hauer and Webern anticipated Schoenberg's composition with twelve tones, so Ravel and Satie anticipated neoclassicism. Ravel, with his *Tombeau de Couperin,* used the old dance forms *forlane, rigaudon* and *minuet,* while Satie's *Socrate,* a "drame-symphonie," anticipated Stravinsky's "opera-oratorio," *Oedipus Rex.*

But Hauer, Webern, Ravel and Satie did not establish schools of musical thought. To do that required the unbridled narcissism of Schoenberg or Stravinsky. Stravinsky could not have followed Schoenberg's lead, despite several pieces that indicate he considered that direction, because Schoenberg's personality allowed room only for followers, not colleagues. Determined, therefore, to stake out his own territory, Stravinsky moved from Switzerland to France, where he "felt the pulse of the world beating most strongly."

Soon after his arrival in Paris, he met Vera de Bosset, the actress and wife of Russian painter Serge Sudeikine. Hastily, the composer asked Ramuz to send her chocolates from Switzerland, and he admits in his *Dialogues* that, in 1923, he secretly dedicated his *Octuor* to her.

In his 1918 diary, Nijinsky writes that Stravinsky did not love Catherine as she loved him. Stravinsky's increasing estrangement from his wife, particularly after meeting Mme Sudeikine, may have motivated his new career, that of conductor and pianist. During the 1920s and 1930s, the composer spent at least half of each year on tour spreading neoclassicism throughout Europe and the United States.

His last musical ties to Russia were the folk tunes quoted in the *Symphonies of Wind Instruments,* written in 1920 in memory of Debussy. The following year, Stravinsky proclaimed his identification with the Russian artists of Western European sympathies in a letter published in *The Times* (London). The letter was prompted by Diaghilev's production of *The Sleeping Beauty,* in which Vera Sudeikine appeared in the nondancing role of the Queen. Stravinsky followed his praise of Tchaikovsky with a comic opera, *Mavra,* dedicated to the Westernized Russian artists. In his dedication, Stravinsky described *Mavra* as an attack on Wagnerian music-drama, "which represented no tradition at all and fulfilled no necessity at all from the musical point of view." But forty years later, in *Expositions,* he recalled that the major motivation for the piece came not from his opposition to the *Gesamtkunstwerk,* but from his distaste for the Russian nationalists. Calling *Mavra* a "piece of propaganda," Stravinsky told Craft: "I wanted to show a different Russia to my non-Russian, and especially to my French, colleagues who were, I considered, saturated with the tourist office orientalism of the *maguchia kuchka,* the 'powerful clique,' as Stassov used to call the Five. I was, in fact, protesting against the picturesque in Russian music and against those who failed to see that the picturesque is produced by very small tricks. Tchaikovsky's talent was the largest in Russia, and with the exception of Moussorgsky's the truest."

Mavra, a one-act opera based on Pushkin's *Little House in Kolomna,* contains melodies from both Tchaikovsky and Glinka. The story revolves around a Russian girl who disguises her lover as a maid and brings him into her parents' house. One day, when the parents are out, the young man shaves. Surprised by the reentry of the mother, he quickly flees. *Mavra* is divided into arias, duets and quartets in the traditional Italian style and includes bits of jazz, gypsy music and Italian bel canto.

Mavra was first produced at the Paris Opera House in June 1922, and failed completely. Stravinsky attributed the poor reception to its having been squeezed between *Petrushka* and *The Rite of Spring,* two spectacular romantic ballets. But he writes that he was pleased with it: "For my own part, I was glad to see that I had completely succeeded in realizing my musical ideas, and was, therefore, able to develop them further—this time in the domain of the symphony. I began to compose my *Octuor pour Instruments à Vent.*"

The composer Alfredo Casella has singled out the *Octuor* as the quintessence of neoclassicism. It is indeed cool and intellectual in the extreme, exactly what Stravinsky himself had in mind:

I remember what an effort it cost me to establish an ensemble of eight instruments, for they could not strike the listener's ear with a great display of tone. In order that this music should reach the ear of the public, it was necessary to emphasize the entries of several instruments, to introduce breathing space between phrases (rests), to pay particular attention to the intonation, the instrumental prosody, the accentuation—in short, to establish order and discipline in the purely sonorous scheme to which I always give precedence over elements of an emotional nature.

Such intellectuality was nowhere present in *Petrushka* or *The Rite of Spring*, where the protagonists had danced themselves to death. With *Octuor*, Stravinsky promoted the remote and heady at the expense of the warm and passionate. By 1923 an emphasis on form prevailed: dodecaphony and neoclassicism were both sides of the same anti-expressionist coin.

Although Stravinsky chose an ensemble of flute, clarinet, two bassoons, two trumpets and two trombones for *Octuor*, he writes that he composed the work without any instrumentation in mind. In the *Dialogues* he tells Craft that the instrumentation only came to him later in a dream. Thus the composer had arrived at a point where abstraction engaged him above all else. No longer involved in stage spectacle or body gesture, Stravinsky made music in the purest, most intramusical terms.

In 1923, for the first time, Stravinsky conducted his own work at the Paris Opera House. Press and public attacked the *Octuor*, but Satie, in an issue of *Vanity Fair*, was among those who defended him vigorously:

> I love and admire Stravinsky because I perceive that he is a liberator. More than anyone else, he has freed the musical thought of today which is sadly in need of development.
>
> I am glad to have to recognize this, I, who have suffered so much from the Wagnerian oppression, or rather, from that of the Wagnerians. For, a few years ago, the genius of Wagner was miserably admired by the combined Mediocrity and Ignorance of the crowd. . . .
>
> Wagner's dictatorship was the sole power and odiously dominated the general taste. An era of desolation, during which the classics themselves seemed blasted. . . . Today things have changed: a happy sunlight illumines the recesses of our souls.

That year Diaghilev presented the ballet *Les Noces.* Although Stravinsky had begun this work almost ten years earlier, he finished orchestrating it only several months before the premiere. A grand dinner for Stravinsky held on a barge in the Seine attracted as guests many luminaries of high society and art, including Picasso, Diaghilev, Cocteau and the Princesse de Polignac. With *Les Noces,* Stravinsky could bring the world to its feet; with *Octuor* he received silence or disdain. But the composer did not change his route: a sober intellectualism displaced the Romanticism of an earlier time.

In 1923 Stravinsky became the center of considerable attention. *La Revue Musicale* devoted an entire issue to him, with famous musicians attacking or defending him. And Stravinsky began to justify his old works on the basis of the new ideology. In this journal, Michel Georges Michel quotes the composer as saying that when he wrote *The Rite of Spring,* the musical idea preceded the theatrical vision: "Note well that this idea came from the music, the music did not come from the idea. My work is architectonic, not anecdotal; objective, not descriptive construction."

In 1924, in *The Arts,* Stravinsky again emphasized form: "I turn to form because I do not conceive or feel the true emotive force except under coordinated musical sensation. This sort of music has no other aim than to be sufficient in itself. In general, I consider that music is only able to solve musical problems, and neither the literary nor the picturesque can be in music of real interest. The play of musical elements is the thing."

At this time, Stravinsky began a new career as a pianist. For his first work he composed the Concerto for Piano and Wind Instruments, which uses the piano percussively in a three-part toccata-like theme reminiscent of Scarlatti and Bach. The composer introduced the piece at a Koussevitzky concert in Paris during the spring of 1924 and played it forty times during the next five years.

After the Piano Concerto, Stravinsky wanted another touring piece. He composed a piano sonata, of which he wrote, "I gave it that name without, however, giving it the classical form such as we find it in Clementi, Haydn and Mozart. . . ." Bach, not Mozart, pervades the piece. Stravinsky played the sonata at a 1925 festival in Venice sponsored by the recently formed International Society for Contemporary Music, an outgrowth of Schoenberg's defunct private concerts. Although Schoenberg attended the event, the two musicians did not meet. The Piano Sonata's eighteenth-century contrapuntal style provoked much talk of a "return to Bach."

Schoenberg responded with his *Three Satires,* written during

1925–26. The second, "Vielseitigkeit," is a mirror canon ridiculing Stravinsky:

> *But who's this beating the drum?*
> *It's little Modernsky!*
> *He's had his hair cut in an old fashioned queue,*
> *And it looks quite nice,*
> *Like real false hair—*
> *Like a wig—Just like (at least Little Modernsky thinks so)*
> *Just like Father Bach!*

Stravinsky confided to friends that Schoenberg's attack hurt him deeply, far more than any attack from the press. To the press attacks, Stravinsky responded with a now-famous manifesto, "L'Avertissement," published in the journal *The Dominant*, in which he discussed neoclassicism:

> There is much talk nowadays of a reversion to classicism, and works believed to have been composed under the influence of the so-called classical modes are labeled neoclassic. . . .
>
> It is difficult for me to say whether this classification is correct or not. With works that are worthy of attention, and have been written under the obvious influence of the music of the past, does not the matter consist in a quest that goes deeper than in a mere imitation of the so-called classical idiom? . . .
>
> If those who label as neoclassic the works belonging to the latest tendency in music mean by that label that they detect in them a wholesome return to this formal idea, well and good . . . .

Many American composers embraced the Stravinsky aesthetic. In 1921, Aaron Copland began to study composition at the Fontainebleau in Paris under Nadia Boulanger, a formidable proponent of Stravinsky's ideals. In 1925 Stravinsky toured the United States and appeared in New York, Boston, Chicago, Philadelphia, Cleveland, Detroit and Cincinnati. Within a few years, Leopold Stokowski, under the auspices of the League of Composers, conducted *The Rite of Spring* and *Les Noces*. The Metropolitan Opera produced *Petrushka* and *The Nightingale*. During the tour Stravinsky made contact with a commercial recording company and arranged to write his Serenade in A, the divertimento in which each movement would be the length of one 78-r.p.m. disc.

In 1927, Roger Sessions paid tribute to the now thoroughly Westernized Stravinsky in *Modern Music*:

> Younger men are dreaming of an entirely different kind of music—a music which derives its power from forms beautiful and significant by virtue of inherent musical weight rather than from intensity of utterance; a music whose impersonality and self-sufficiency preclude the exotic; which takes its impulse from the realities of a passionate logic; which, in its authentic freshness of mood, is the reverse of the ironic, and, in its very aloofness from the concrete preoccupations of life, strives rather to contribute form, design, a vision of order and harmony.

Neoclassicism attracted composers in all countries. Hindemith, earlier a follower of Schoenberg, adopted the neotonal, neoclassic idea. Bartók incorporated his Hungarian folk material into a neoclassic frame, and in the United States, Copland was only the most prominent member of the growing anti-dodecaphonic school. Stravinsky went on to create the major, mature pieces of his second period: *Oedipus Rex, Apollon Musagète, Le Baiser de la Fée*, the *Symphony of Psalms* and *Perséphone*, all written between 1927 and 1934. Each was composed for a practical purpose. He wrote *Oedipus* in collaboration with Cocteau to celebrate Diaghilev's twentieth year in the theater. The American patron Elizabeth Sprague Coolidge commissioned *Apollon Musagète*, French impresario Ida Rubinstein *Le Baiser de la Fée* and *Perséphone*, and Koussevitzky, by then conductor of the Boston Symphony Orchestra, the *Symphony of Psalms* in commemoration of the orchestra's fiftieth anniversary. The pieces were all characterized by restraint: stage effects were static and many musical ideas were derivative. A Capriccio for Piano and Orchestra, written during the same period to provide himself with another piece to perform, not only brings to mind the seventeenth-century composer Praetorius, who used the same title, but also Beethoven, Tchaikovsky and Carl Maria von Weber.

Stravinsky sought a static quality in all of these works. In *Oedipus* he uses Latin, a "monumental" language, and a narrator to tell the audience just what is going to happen—in the style of the classical Greek chorus, reducing the stage action to a minimum. His harmony often rests on a single chord for many measures and the rhythmic alterations are not more ambitious than moving from 3/4 to 4/4. In *Apollon Musagète,* the language is predominantly diatonic and the orchestra is limited to strings. For the *Symphony of Psalms,* Stravinsky uses another unusual orchestra, devoid of violins and violas, and adds a chorus to balance it. *Perséphone,* based on Gide's "Hymn to Demeter," imposed an additional limitation: the title role was to be assumed by Mme Rubinstein herself, who could not sing and would not dance. Stravinsky had her speak and mime the role.

Although these works are among the most lyrical and spiritual of Stravinsky's career, the initial response was primarily negative. Diaghilev agreed with the cool audience and branded *Oedipus* as "un cadeau très macabre." The other works did not fare much better. In 1934, when European commissions were about to run dry, Stravinsky issued the following "Manifesto," a defensive Introduction to *Perséphone:*

> This score, as it is written and as it must remain in the musical archives of our time, forms an indissoluble whole with the tendencies repeatedly asserted in my previous works. . . . It is a sequel to *Oedipus Rex,* the *Symphony of Psalms* and to a whole progression of works whose musical autonomy is in no way affected by the absence of a stage spectacle. . . . Nothing of all this originates in a caprice of my own. I am on a perfectly sure road. One does not criticize anybody or anything that is functioning. A nose is not manufactured: a nose just is. Thus too, is my art.

Nevertheless, *Perséphone* received only three performances, plus an official rejection for its composer: the Institut de France appointed Florent Schmitt to the post of director (vacant since the death of Paul Dukas). Stravinsky had made it clear that he wanted the job; he and his wife even became French citizens, a requirement for the position.

In Russia, Stravinsky's reception was even worse than in France. During the 1920s, when the artistic life of the Soviet Union had been bold and experimental, the composer was still held in high regard. The chief music theorist, Boris Asafiev, promoted him with enthusiasm. But the situation changed radically in 1932 when Stalin became increasingly distrustful of foreigners. His xenophobia became paranoia, and the monstrous purges that followed affected art: the Union of Soviet Composers took over Russian music and began its own music journal, *Sovietskaya Muzyka,* the following year. Its premise was socialist realism and its musicologist, Arnold Alshvang, repudiated Asafiev on Stravinsky, calling the expatriate "an important and near comprehensive artistic ideologist of the imperialist bourgeoisie."

Stravinsky was hurt by this and all the other criticism. Samuel Dushkin, a young violinist for whom the composer wrote the Violin Concerto and the *Duo Concertante* during the early 1930s, said, "I sensed very soon something tense and anguished about him, which made one want to comfort and reassure him."

But this aspect of himself Stravinsky rarely showed to the world. His haughty manner continued unabated and was given full expression in the *Perséphone* manifesto. Nevertheless, he seemed to have lost his way; Diaghilev's death, in 1929, may have led to a lessening of his creative energy. The fact that at the end of 1934 Stravinsky could find the time to write his *Autobiography* indicates that neoclassicism had ceased to provide much impetus for him.

Stravinsky often said of himself: "I am a Maker. I am a Doer. I am an inventor of music." But turning to a book of memoirs did not sound as if he meant that anymore.

CHAPTER 13

By the mid-1930s, composers everywhere were under the spell of Stravinsky. After Aaron Copland, other American musicians flocked to Boulanger. During 1935–36, Stravinsky himself taught one class a month at the École Normale, where Boulanger presided over two classes a week. A pupil, Maurice Perrin, recalls that

> under the influence of Nadia Boulanger, nearly all of us admired Stravinsky with an almost religious fervor. . . . What struck us most was his air of intense seriousness. . . . Sometimes he would sit at the piano and try to improve a certain passage. It was at such moments that he would astonish me most. He did not say: do this, use this or that chord; no: he would play a chord, listen to it, change a note, listen again, change another note, go back to the earlier chord, alter a different note etc., all the time listening with the utmost attention. . . . The result of these essays at the piano left us amazed; the fourth or fifth attempt would produce an admirable chord, of such surprising beauty that none of us could have invented it. (Stravinsky used to speak, in such cases, precisely of inventing a chord.)

Walter Piston, Virgil Thomson, and Marc Blitzstein were among the Boulanger pupils. Their accessible, melodic music, unencumbered by harsh dissonance, drowned out dodecaphony in the United States. The Boulanger school had its counterparts in New England: Harold Shapero, Irving Fine, and Arthur Berger taught at Harvard where Leonard Bernstein was a student. At Tanglewood, in Lenox, Massachusetts, Aaron Copland led the "neoclassic" school. Vladimir Ussachevsky has said that a student at the Eastman School of Music in Rochester, New York, could not hear any

Schoenberg, Webern, or Berg during the late 1930s and early 1940s. Stravinsky was delighted with the Americans' attention and, in the *Autobiography*, complimented their taste: "The serious interest of the Americans in music is displayed, among other ways, in the judicious selection of those to whom they apply for instruction. A large number of young people have come to France to complete their musical education—indeed, since the War, this has been almost a tradition . . . ."

In 1935, with a sympathetic public awaiting him, Stravinsky returned to the United States to undertake a second American tour; *Time* magazine covered the story. In 1936, the composer began negotiations with Lincoln Kirstein and Edward Warburg for a ballet, *The Card Party,* for the newly formed American Ballet Company. In 1937, *Jeu de Cartes* was produced at the Metropolitan Opera House with George Balanchine choreographing and Stravinsky conducting. *Jeu de Cartes* was accompanied by *Apollon Musagète* and a newly choreographed production of *Le Baiser de la Fée,* both by Balanchine.

In 1938, millionaire Robert Bliss paid Stravinsky $1,000 to write a concerto, the *Dumbarton Oaks,* to celebrate Bliss's thirtieth wedding anniversary; Bliss followed this with an even more handsome commission, $2,500, to commemorate the fiftieth anniversary of the Chicago Symphony Orchestra, a work to be ready for the 1940–41 season. Stravinsky's last European commission had been in 1933.

In 1939, before he began the Symphony in C, Stravinsky received the Charles Eliot Norton professorship at Harvard, given annually to men who have achieved high international distinction in the arts. Stravinsky, the first musician to be so honored, received $10,000 to deliver six lectures.

The late 1930s, attractive years for the composer in the United States, were especially grim for him in Europe. Not only had commissions stopped flowing, but in 1939 *La Revue Musicale* devoted an issue to him which was harshly critical. And personal tragedy struck in incredible profusion: between November 1938, and June 1939, Stravinsky's mother, wife and daughter died. With few meaningful ties left in Europe, Stravinsky moved to the United States. Vera de Bosset joined him a few months later. They married and settled in Los Angeles, in the heart of the movie community, just a short distance from Arnold Schoenberg.

Stravinsky writes that the Symphony in C reminds him of the unhappiest period of his life. He had been in poor health when he accepted the Bliss commission and did so to pay the medical bills for his wife and daughter, both of whom were in a tuberculosis sanitarium near Paris. The composer, too, became ill. Shortly after *The Card Party's* premiere, doctors discovered a lesion in his left lung and ordered him to join his family in the sanitarium. But he refused and worked on the *Dumbarton Oaks* piece and the Symphony in C. Although Stravinsky borrows nothing specifically from Franz Josef Haydn, the musicologist Edward Cone has demonstrated, in an analysis published in 1963, how the spirit of Haydn pervades the work. Cone points out that the traditional framework is retained, with diatonic melodies, metric regularity, harmonic simplicity and typical patterns. But he adds that Stravinsky injects sudden harmonic shifts, persistent but mild dissonances, and his own distinctive instrumental sound.

American commissions for Stravinsky dried up during World War II, so he turned to the film industry; but all his efforts there failed. A score for a film, *The Moon Is Down,* based on a novel by John Steinbeck, about the Nazi invasion of Norway, was rejected; so he converted it to *Four Norwegian Moods.* Another with a Russian setting became *Scherzo à la Russe.* The score for Orson Welles's *Jane Eyre* ended up as the middle movement of the *Ode,* and the music he wrote for Franz Werfel's *Song of Bernadette* was salvaged as the second movement of his Symphony in Three Movements.

But Stravinsky kept hammering away because he needed money: "I have never regarded poverty as attractive," he writes. "I do not want to be buried in the rain, unattended as Mozart was. . . . The very image of Bartók's poverty-stricken demise, to mention only one of my less fortunate colleagues, was enough to fire my ambition to earn every penny from a society that failed in its duty to Mozart."

Stravinsky arranged the *Firebird* as a love ballad, "Summer Moon," so that it would turn up on jukeboxes and deliver him large royalties. He wrote his polka for the Barnum and Bailey circus and the *Ebony Concerto* for Woody Herman in an effort to tap Tin Pan Alley.

But even Stravinsky became enmeshed in the production of "meaningful" and "relevant" music. The Symphony in Three Movements, which he conducted at Carnegie Hall in 1946, shows the power that socialist realism exerted even on one committed to Western formalism. Stravinsky writes that the first movement was inspired by a documentary film of "scorched earth tactics in China," and the episode for clarinet, piano and strings was conceived "as a series of instrumental conversations to accompany a cinematographic scene showing the Chinese people scratching and digging in their fields." The second movement came from the rejected *Song of Bernadette* score, and the third, the composer continues, was partly a "musical reaction to the newsreels and documentaries that I had seen of goose-stepping soldiers," while the latter part of the movement was associated "with the rise of the Allies after the overturning of the war machine."

In 1945, Stravinsky became an American citizen and signed a contract with the firm of Boosey & Hawkes, who took over all of his works published by Édition Russe de Musique. The composer was bitter about the lack of a U.S./Russia copyright agreement which prevented him from collecting royalties on his earlier popular pieces. To rectify this, he re-orchestrated these frequently played compositions to collect payments on the revised versions. Among them were *Petrushka, Symphonies of Wind Instruments, Apollon Musagète, Pulcinella, Oedipus Rex, Symphony of Psalms, Le Baiser de la Fée, Octuor,* and *The Nightingale*. But the sparer orchestrations of the 1940s did not compete with the lusher treatments of his younger days, and conductors generally preferred to use the original scores. That he devoted his time to re-orchestrating old pieces indicated the artistic bankruptcy that threatened him.

In 1946 Stravinsky received his first European commission since *Perséphone*; Paul Sacher asked for a concerto for orchestra. Stravinsky's letter to Sacher about the Concerto in D reveals his depression at that time: ". . . What can be said other than that the work is composed for a string orchestra (that—one will see immediately), that it is in three movements (that—one will read in your programs in any case), that it is not in the least atonal (but that—don't you think that the public should have the pleasure of discovering this for themselves?)" Thus, in 1946, Stravinsky appeared to be at an aesthetic impasse.

But before he could find a solution to this neoclassic impasse, he wrote a work which represents the culmination of his interest in eighteenth-century music. In 1947, at the Chicago Art Institute, Stravinsky saw Hogarth's prints depicting *The Rake's Progress* and thought he might use them as a series of tableaux for his first opera in English. His neighbor, Aldous Huxley, recommended W. H. Auden as librettist, and Auden asked his friend the poet Chester Kallman to collaborate with him. Boosey and Hawkes agreed to finance the project and Stravinsky began work in 1948. In an interview before the premiere in September, 1951, the librettists said that they considered operatic tradition to have been carried by Verdi, Puccini and others to a point at which it had exhausted itself, so they had retreated to the eighteenth century for inspiration. So did Stravinsky. During the entire period of the composition of the work, he listened repeatedly to Mozart's *Cosi fan Tutte*.

The premiere in Venice was a star-studded event. Mme Stravinsky, in a charmingly malicious tone, reports that Boulanger was there carrying

Stravinsky's valises and the rest of the world seemed to share Boulanger's adoration. But the glitter could not hide the failure that many saw in *The Rake's Progress*. Even Virgil Thomson has described the story as "an incredible melange of Little Red Riding Hood, Dr. Faustus and Oedipus Rex . . . in which the hero murders not his father but the woman in his motherly sweetheart and marries, in the form of a bearded lady, his father's image." Thomson suggests that the score did not compensate for the libretto.

In 1948, still revising old works, Stravinsky met his new Diaghilev, the bright, young conductor Robert Craft, and the composer's life took a turn. As Diaghilev had pointed him to Pergolesi and the eighteenth century, so Craft directed the sixty-six-year-old musician to Schoenberg and his disciples Webern and Berg.

Just after Stravinsky crystallized his plans for *The Rake's Progress,* Craft wrote to him asking for the score for the *Symphonies of Wind Instruments*. Stravinsky replied that he was finishing a new version of the piece and would like to have the pleasure of conducting it himself. Craft, director of a small chamber ensemble, the Chamber Art Society, wrote that he had no money to offer him. But Stravinsky—obviously anxious for some musical action—uncharacteristically answered that he would do it for nothing. They first met in Washington, D.C., where Stravinsky was introduced to Craft by Auden. Craft, according to his own testimony, was overwhelmed:

> On the subject of Stravinsky I lived and breathed a mimiety, as Coleridge would call it, enough to perturb anyone of my acquaintance. I must have been guilty of displaying my admiration to Stravinsky, but I also must have shown genuine knowledge of his music, for he invited me to come to Hollywood to stay in his house, and to accomplish certain tasks for him. I did go there, I became famulus. . . .
>
> When I first moved there Los Angeles was divided, like the rest of the musical world, into twin hegemonies of Stravinsky and Schoenberg. The dividing line was Los Angeles' and the world's doing, of course, not the masters . . . the fact remains that they were kept separate and isolated. Paris and Vienna had crossed the world with them, establishing small and exceedingly provincial Viennas and Parises separated by only ten miles of Hollywood no man's land, but as far apart as ever. Musicians came from all over the world

to visit them, not mentioning to one composer their meetings with the other. . . .

A curious relationship began among Stravinsky, his wife, and Robert Craft, in which identities spilled over onto one another: the writings of all three seem to emerge from the same pen. Friends reported that Craft would anticipate what Stravinsky would say and that Stravinsky would consider an idea to be his when Craft articulated it only moments before. The Craft/Stravinsky conversations, published in the late 1950s and through the 1960s, reveal the extraordinary intimacy of this union. (Stravinsky had used other people as media before: the *Autobiography* and *Poetics of Music* were both written through other men.) Thus Stravinsky made use of a virtuoso in the English language—Robert Craft—to express his thoughts to the American public. But it is wrong to conclude from this fact that the young and erudite Craft played the sole and controlling role in Stravinsky's shift from neoclassicism to serialism.

On Friday, June 13, 1951, shortly before *The Rake's Progress* premiere, an event of enormous consequence occurred: Arnold Schoenberg died.

Schoenberg's death set in motion a chain of events that led Stravinsky to abandon neoclassicism and embrace what he referred to as "seriality," just as almost half a century before, Rimsky-Korsakov's death had led him to abandon a Germanic structure and adopt the style of the Rimsky orchestra. While Schoenberg was still alive, Stravinsky seemed unable to adopt his idea; hubris prevented him from doing so. But once that formidable figure was dead, Stravinsky could readily incorporate and assimilate his technique without the slightest loss of identity. The adoption of the serial idea by the giant of the neoclassic movement has been characterized by Hans Keller as "the most profound surprise in the history of music," and by others as a form of prostitution.

A surprise, perhaps, but not prostitution. Stravinsky never deprecated either Schoenberg or dodecaphony. As early as February 1913, in an interview in London's *Daily Mail,* he attacked Vienna for ignoring Schoenberg, "one of the greatest creative spirits of our era." And, as late as 1939, when neoclassicism was at its peak and dodecaphony anathema everywhere, Stravinsky spoke highly of Schoenberg at Harvard:

> Whatever opinion one may hold about the music of Arnold Schoenberg (to take as an example a composer evolving along lines essentially different from mine, both aesthetically and technically), whose works have frequently

given rise to violent reactions or ironic smiles—it is impossible for a self-respecting mind equipped with genuine musical culture not to feel that the composer of Pierrot Lunaire is fully aware of what he is doing and that he is not trying to deceive anyone. He adopted the musical system that suited his needs and, within this system, he is perfectly consistent with himself, perfectly coherent. One cannot dismiss music that one dislikes by labeling it cacophony.

Stravinsky's motivating artistic credo did not lie in "impressionism," "neoclassicism" or "serialism." "Rape," he claimed, "may be justified by the creation of a child." Thus Stravinsky, a great polyphonist and profoundly original creator of rhythms and new sounds, "raped" Schoenberg and Webern in the early fifties. He even raped their heritage. In a 1966 film produced by Richard Leacock and D.A. Pennebaker, Stravinsky pointed to a photograph of Wagner in his studio and said: "I have Wagner in my head. I have Wagner in my ears. I think very much more of Wagner today than I did twenty years ago."

But Stravinsky's own musical identity has never been in question. His serial works are as Stravinskyan as his impressionist and neoclassic pieces. Jean Cocteau recognized this as early as 1922 when writers and musicians attacked the composer for his conversion from the impressionistic works to the spare, lean, neoclassic sound. In *La Revue Musicale*, Cocteau wrote: "There is no disorder in this Slavic genius. He sounds his organs, takes care of his muscles and never loses his head. He knows that an artist who spends his whole life in the same costume ceases to interest us. Consequently he transforms himself, changes his skin and emerges new in the sun, unrecognizable by those who judge a work from its outside."

Stravinsky did not make those changes overnight. In *Themes and Episodes* he describes what happened:

> I have had to survive two crises as a composer, although as I continue to move from work to work, I was not aware of either of them as such, or indeed, of any momentous change. The first—the loss of Russia and its language of words as well as of music—affected every circumstance of my personal no less than my artistic life, which made recovery more difficult. Only after a decade of samplings, experiments, amalgamations, did I find the path to *Oedipus*

Rex and the *Symphony of Psalms.* Crisis Number Two was brought on by the natural outgrowing of the special incubator in which I wrote *The Rake's Progress* (which is why I did not use Auden's beautiful Delia libretto; I could not continue in the same strain, could not compose a sequel to the *Rake,* as I would have had to do.) The period of adjustment was only half as long as this time, but as I look back on it I am surprised at how long I continued to straddle my "styles." Was it because one has to unlearn as well as to learn, and at seventy the unlearning is more difficult?

Some of Stravinsky's followers felt betrayed by the composer's shift to the serial idea; neoclassicism and dodecaphony had too long been promulgated as polar opposites with each side fighting for the other's annihilation. But many more composers followed Stravinsky's lead.

CHAPTER 14

Polyphony reasserted itself in Stravinsky's music even before he met Robert Craft. Just before *The Rake's Progress*, he composed the contrapuntal ballet *Orpheus* and the weighty, polyphonic *Mass*. But the death of Schoenberg and the goading of Craft precipitated his actual conversion to the serial procedure, which he treated with increasing comprehensiveness from that time on. Stravinsky's appropriation of the musical system that originated with Schoenberg did not, however, imply an appropriation of Schoenberg's expressive, Romantic style. Stravinsky repudiated the rhetoric and gesture of Schoenberg's Violin Concerto, Opus 36. He told Craft: "The pathos is last century's and since pathos is created by language, the language in essence must be last century's too; harmonize the second movement in a purely Brahmsian manner—you have only to move a few notes over a bit—and the theme is happily restored to its true habitat. Schoenberg is the evolutionary center but only up to a period many years before this concerto."

So Stravinsky bypassed Schoenberg in favor of Webern.

Craft attributes what he refers to as Stravinsky's "deep impression" of the serial technique to his hearing Webern's Quartet, Opus 22, several times in January and February, 1952. In April the composer began the Cantata for Soprano, Tenor, Female Chorus and Orchestra, in which he first used the row technique but limited his row to less than twelve notes. In this piece, Stravinsky's self-conscious adoption of the serial technique is not only apparent from the structure of the work but from the highly technical language he uses in the program note: ". . . the piece begins with a one-bar introduction by the flutes and cello, the statement of the canonic subject which is the subject of the whole piece. This subject is repeated by the tenor over a recitative style accompaniment of oboes and cello, in original form, retrograde form (or cancrizans, which means that its notes are heard in reverse order, in this case, in a different rhythm), inverted form and finally, in retrograde inversion. . . ."

But the new technique did not alter the old sound: Stravinsky's interest in sonority continued to compete with his interest in pitch, and the repetition of small phrases, brought about by the use of words with repeated refrains, motivated the repetition of small phrases of music, a feature that Bartók noted in early Stravinsky scores. In *In Memoriam Dylan Thomas*— Stravinsky was planning to write an opera with Thomas when he died— the composer set the line "Rage, rage against the dying of the light" almost identically four different times. In addition to the repeated refrain, a two-bar instrumental phrase occurs seven times: as Introduction, Ritornelli between each verse, and Coda. The nondevelopmental, mosaic-like structure of *The Rite of Spring* and *The Nightingale* persists in Stravinsky's late serial work.

In Memoriam Dylan Thomas, the Septet, and *Three Songs from William Shakespeare*, written just after the Cantata, are all based on a row limited to fewer than twelve notes. But in the *Canticum Sacrum* of 1955, Stravinsky adopted the entire chromatic scale in his first comprehensive 12-tone work.

Based on texts from the Old Testament, the *Canticum Sacrum* was commissioned by and heard at the ISCM Festival in Venice, the same auspices under which Stravinsky introduced his "Bach-like" Sonata in 1925. The first movement of the *Canticum Sacrum* pronounces God's command-ment and the last His fulfillment. The last is treated by cancrizans of the first, making the piece not only cyclical in form but suggestive of a literal reversal of time. Rhythms and pitch flow backward as easily as forward.

In a speech celebrating Stravinsky's eightieth birthday, Milton Babbitt referred to the significance of the *Canticum Sacrum* and Stravinsky's use of the 12-tone row:

> There is little point, in the name of discretion, in attempting to minimize the results of the appearance of an incontrovertibly 12-tone work by Stravinsky. . . . That Igor Stravinsky should now be creating works which were instances of a musical system originally associated with the name of Arnold Schoenberg, appeared to destroy a funda-mental preconception of how the activity of contemporary music has long since been compartmentalized and assigned, and how the issues had been patly and permanently drawn. Composers, presumably, are competitors, and never

colleagues; their primary activity is that of consolidating their holdings while attempting to depreciate the value of the holdings of other composers.

One musicologist maintained that Stravinsky's use of dodecaphony was a way to mourn Schoenberg's death, while another ridiculed the serialists: "There is great swagger about this conversion which the partisans celebrate in the musical equivalent of 'from log cabin to the White House motif.'" But Stravinsky was not deterred; he confirmed his allegiance to 12-tone writing with his next work, *Agon*, written in close collaboration with Balanchine. *Agon* begins diatonically, turns chromatic and 12-tone, and then returns to the original diatonic bars. Stressing his interest in the number 12, Stravinsky arranged twelve movements in four groups of three and prescribed the choreography for twelve dancers. The New York City Ballet presented the piece in 1957; it has remained in the repertory ever since.

Despite the fact that the same popularity does not hold for Stravinsky's unchoreographed serial pieces—they still receive few performances—serialism won the battle in Stravinsky's mind. *Threni: Id Est Lamentationes Jeremiae Prophetae* no longer presents the serial portion framed between diatonic passages as did *Canticum Sacrum* and *Agon*. In *Threni* the whole work is based on a series derived from a single thematic idea.

Stravinsky has identified his next work, *Movements for Piano and Orchestra,* as the "cornerstone" of his late period, as *Oedipus* was the cornerstone of his middle period. With *Movements* he extends the serial principle into the other elements of music: "My polyrhythmic combinations," he told Craft, "are meant to be heard vertically," and he cited as a parallel the second Agnus Dei in Josquin's *Missa l'homme armé*. Babbitt celebrated Stravinsky's *Movements*: "Never before have his linear—and above all—his ensemble rhythms been so intricate. . . . Never before have registral, timbral and, as a result, dynamic elements been so manifestly ordered and organized."

After *Movements*, Stravinsky wrote a few short, concentrated pieces: the *Epitaphium für das Grabmal des Prinzen Max Egon zu Furstenberg*, the patron of the Webern-inspired Donaueschingen Festival, and a Double Canon in memory of Raoul Dufy. Each is serial and lasts only one minute and sixteen seconds. Even the weightier work that followed, *A Sermon, a Narrative and a Prayer,* one of Stravinsky's most lyrical serial works, lasts only sixteen minutes. The piece is divided into two sections, both of which are followed by the same refrain: "And the substance of things hoped for, the evidence of things not seen, is faith. And our Lord is a consuming fire." These short works show his assimilation of Webern's ideas.

In 1961 Stravinsky received a commission from NBC to write a musical play with choreography by Balanchine. He spoke to Craft about writing music for television:

> Visually it offers every advantage over stage opera, but the saving of musical time interests me more than anything visual. This new musical economy was the one specific medium which guided my conception of the *Flood*. Because the suspension of visualizations can be instantaneous, the composer may dispense with the afflatus of overtures, connecting episodes, curtain music. I have used only one or two notes to punctuate each stage in the Creation, for example, and so far, I have not been able to imagine the work on the operatic stage because the speed is so uniquely cinematic.

For *The Flood*, Stravinsky wove a strong tonal feeling into this serial score through the use of certain "harmonic" intervals. He did the same in his next work, Abraham and Isaac, a sacred ballad in Hebrew for the Israel Festival Committee. In his notes he defends these harmonic intervals: "Octaves, fifths and double intervals can be found but they are not in contradiction to the serial basis of composition, being the result of concordances from the several serial forms, or what I call serial verticals."

With *Variations*, written in memory of his friend Aldous Huxley, Stravinsky attacks his unresponsive listener in much the same manner as he did in connection with *Perséphone* ("I am on a perfectly sure road. One does not criticize anything or anybody that is functioning."). In referring to the density of the extraordinarily complex *Variations*, he touches on the question of musical information and reasserts his strong anti-Romantic attitude: "The question of length (duration) is inseparable from that of depth and/or height (content). But whether full, partly full, or empty, the musical statements of the *Variations* are concise, I prefer to think, rather than short. They are, whatever one thinks, a radical contrast to the prolix manner of speech of our concert life: and there lies the difficulty, mine with you no less than yours with me."

During the middle and late 1960s, Stravinsky continued to write in memory of many dead: the *Elegy for JFK,* an *Introitus for T. S. Eliot,* and the

Requiem Canticles for several friends. And for his wife, he composed *The Owl and the Pussycat*. In 1967, he served as the subject of *Bravo Stravinsky,* written by Craft in collaboration with photographer Arnold Newman. Craft asked the composer:

> CRAFT: Having composed with series for so many years now, are you aware of any compulsiveness in certain combinations of numbers?
>
> STRAVINSKY: All composers eventually become obsessed with numbers, I suspect, that rapport expressed between them being so much greater than expressions of rapport in reality. I cannot explain this to non-musicians. . . . It may be that my love of combining twos, threes, fours and sixes is compulsive, and that I am behaving in music like the man who has to lock his door three times or step on all of the cracks of the sidewalk. . . .

Craft's question and Stravinsky's reply bring the reader back to Schoenberg's magical use of numbers and to the impetus behind his treatment of the twelve notes of the chromatic scale.

In interviews published in *The New York Review of Books,* Stravinsky depreciates the new trends in musical composition; referring to the work of Karlheinz Stockhausen, he said he is bored with these "note-clumps and silences." Suggesting that the resources of serial writing have not yet even been tapped, Stravinsky has maintained that "those younger colleagues who already regard 'serial' as an indecent word, in their claim to have gone far beyond, are, I think, greatly in error."

An anti-Stravinsky cynic might ask: If Stravinsky were to outlive Stockhausen, might he not create "note-clumps and silences" just as he appropriated Rimsky's orchestra and Schoenberg's series after their deaths? There is little doubt that he would not. Stravinsky's need to control his material was too great to allow him to embrace the "aleatoric" idea. The importance of chance in music, probably initiated by John Cage and adopted by Stockhausen and many others, culminated in an approach to art in which significance lies only in what the spectator perceives. The only meaning found in the work is that imposed upon it by the outside. But Stravinsky's self-conscious commitment to form was diametrically opposed to such negations of it. Always striving for the ultimate in form, Stravinsky lent added weight to the serial procedure with the choice of many sacred subjects for his serial compositions.

In *The Observer,* on his eightieth birthday, Stravinsky remarked:

> I was born to causality and determinism and I have
> survived to probability theory and chance. I was educated
> by the simple "fact": the trigger one squeezed was what shot
> the gun; and I have had to learn that, in fact, the universe
> of anterior contributing possibilities was responsible.
>
> I do not understand the composer who says we must
> analyze the evolutionary tendency of the musical situation
> and go from there. I have never consciously analyzed any
> musical "situation" and I can "go" only where my musical
> appetites lead me.

CHAPTER 15

While Schoenberg was developing the 12-tone technique and Stravinsky was responding to his musical appetites, Edgard Varèse forged an even more radical path. Through experiments in electronic music, he came to be known as the father of this new technological medium.

Varèse was born in 1883, nine years after Schoenberg, one year after Stravinsky, and the same year as Anton Webern. His revolution was ahead of anything dreamed of by his contemporaries: "Scientists are the poets of today. 'Art' means keeping up with the speed of light." In 1917 the composer described the quest that was to pervade his entire life: "I dream of instruments obedient to my thought and which, with their contribution to a whole new world of unsuspected sounds, will lend themselves to the exigencies of my inner rhythm."

Varèse began his career by questioning the principles that underlay Western music. He did not accept the fact of twelve equal semitones; he regarded it as an arbitrary division of the octave. Nor did he accept the tempered fifth. He repudiated the physical principles on which his music was based, and thus made a clean break with the past. Varèse pointed the way to a pitchless music, with an emphasis on pure sound and rhythm, and thus led the move toward a growing involvement of serious composers in electronic music. It is significant that Varèse, unlike Schoenberg and Stravinsky, did not wait until he was driven from Europe. He came to the United States well before that, arriving in New York in 1915. Varèse considered *Amériques*, which he completed in 1922, his first truly representative work, written when Schoenberg was composing his first dodecaphonic movements and Stravinsky his first neoclassic compositions.

Varèse enjoyed America. "The people here," he said, "have a sense of optimistic realism. In Europe they bellyache." But even the United States, with its preoccupation with technology, did not meet Varèse's standards. He once told an audience of concert goers: "Contrary to the general belief, an artist is never ahead of his time but most people are far behind theirs! Einstein once said, 'Our situation cannot be compared to anything in the past. We must radically change our ways of thinking, our methods of action.' Yet Einstein, who played the violin and had a predilection for Mozart, did not see that the world was standing still, that it was obstinately refusing to change its thinking or actions."

For Varèse that refusal meant that he was unable to produce many of the sounds he imagined. During the greater part of his life this composer was forced to operate within the fixed values of the tempered system and with conventional instruments that dictated the duration, dynamics and timbre of his notes.

Even so, he could still make some remarkable sounds. After World War II, Varèse received his first tape recorder and interpolated taped sounds into his orchestral work *Déserts*. The difficulty for the listener in determining when the orchestra stops and when the electronic interpolations begin testifies to Varèse's skill in producing revolutionary sounds with conventional means.

Today a composer is free to use all aural phenomena as raw material for his creative work. The current interest in pitchless composition can be traced directly to Varèse and his relentless pursuit of his goals.

In his speech at Princeton in 1959, Varèse said that he had often been criticized for disparaging the past and insisted that he had never done so: ". . . that [the past] is where my roots are. No matter how original, how different a composer may seem, he has only grafted a little bit of himself on the old plant. But this he should be allowed to do without being accused of wanting to kill the plant. He only wanted to produce a new flower. . . ."

But in fact Varèse's roots go no farther back than Claude Debussy. An aberrant strain characterizes French music since the beginning of the twentieth century. Committed to both letters and ideas, the French have consistently fought the mainline. Debussy turned away from the Wagnerian music-drama that was sweeping Europe in favor of sounds from outside Western tradition.

On his visit to the Bayreuth Festival in 1888–89, Debussy realized the necessity for a musical language diametrically opposed to the grand pathos and histrionic extroversion of the *Gesamtkunstwerk*. *Pelléas et Mélisande*, completed in 1902, anticipated developments soon to come from Vienna. Debussy used the whole-tone scale and suspended tonality in Western music about five years before Schoenberg's Quartet No. 2. He turned away from the full triad in favor of the fourth and fifth, apparent in the opening measures of *La Cathédrale Engloutie*. This produces an effect similar to the medieval organum of the twelfth- and thirteenth-century musicians Leonin and Perotin. Debussy treated the chord as an independent sonority, as a vertical conglomerate in itself, independent of its harmonic context.

His free treatment of rhythm (no longer did bar lines determine rhythmic units) were matched by innovations in timbre. Such was the nature of the mind of the man whose musical ideas influenced Varèse .

Henri Varèse, Edgard's father, was, like Webern's, an engineer. The two most advanced musical figures of the first half of the century were raised with a respect for mathematics and science.

Varèse has described his father as "a kind of Prussian sergeant, the drill-master type," and his mother as retiring and frightened of her husband. When he was only a few weeks old, his parents sent Edgard to live with an aunt in Villars in Burgundy, where Debussy was also raised. His maternal grandfather, whom the boy loved, ran a bistro in Paris, and Edgard spent much of his time traveling between Burgundy and the capital.

When he was nine years old, Edgard was sent to Turin to live with his parents. Henri Varèse, who had studied at the Polytechnicum in Zurich, wanted Edgard to follow in his path. He was so unnerved at any display of his son's interest in music that he locked the grand piano, covered it with a shroud, and hid the key.

Edgard attended musical events at the Turin conservatory and opera house. He began secretly to visit the director of the conservatory, Giovanni Bolzoni, who gave him harmony and counterpoint lessons. Varèse became a member of the percussion section of the opera house orchestra and conducted a rehearsal when the conductor fell ill.

Edgard's mother died when he was fourteen. Varèse remained with the family for a few years after her death but left when the antagonism between him and his father became unbearable. According to Louise Varèse, the composer's widow, the father bullied Edgard in such a depreciating way that the boy grew up "not liking himself." She quotes him as saying, "I believe I have an allergy to myself." Varèse's only biographer, Fernand Ouellette, writes that the composer's attitude toward his father colored all future professional father-son relationships: "As soon as any man established a relationship with Varèse involving authority over him (Rodin or d'Indy, for example), that relationship was bound to fall apart very quickly. Behind the face of a d'Indy lurked the features of his father, hated since birth. Because of this, it took very little—a simple criticism which Varèse disliked intensely—

to make all his aggressiveness, his willfulness, and his violence burst through to the surface."

Such feelings might well have contributed to the strength of Varèse's rebellion against the music of the status quo.

When he was seventeen, Varèse visited the Paris Exposition, which had so affected Debussy. Two years later he settled in Paris. Although the first performance of *Pelléas et Mélisande* had just created a scandal, there was little other musical excitement for him there. The new composers were undistinguished. The old—d'Indy, Saint-Saens, Lalo, Charpentier, Widor, Dukas and Chausson—were producing nothing that interested him.

Nevertheless, Varèse's exposure to science led him to think about the actual materials of music:

> When I was around 20, I became interested in a book by Wronsky, a disciple of Kant. Wronsky had written his own theories of philosophy, and while reading the book, I was struck by a phrase he coined to describe music. It was this: "the corporealization of the intelligence in sounds." I liked that phrase, and later it set me to wondering what, if anything, existed between sounds; or in other words, was there a sound between the C key and C#, or a difference between C# and D flat?
>
> The question led me to Helmholtz's *Physiology of Sounds*: I then began to think of the opposite of sound, of silence, and of how it can be used. . . . Now, to me, the climax of a crescendo can be a space of absolute silence.

In 1904 Varèse entered the Schola Cantorum, where he studied counterpoint, fugue, medieval and Renaissance music, and composition and conducting with d'Indy. Quickly, he became disenchanted with d'Indy: "The reason I left him was because his idea of teaching was to form disciples. His vanity would not permit the least sign of originality, or even independent thinking, and I did not want to become a little d'Indy. One was enough."

After one year at the Schola Cantorum—which Debussy described as the "citadel of the mandarins who made music into a pedantic science," Varèse changed to the Conservatoire. But the Conservatoire did not represent much of a change; to a man who was to consider music the true "art-science" and refer to himself as an "organizer of sounds," one established school was not very different from another.

Through the recommendations of Massenet and Widor, Varèse received the Premiere Bourse Artistique de la Ville de Paris when he was only twenty-three years old. During that year he married his first wife, Suzanne Bing, and set up housekeeping in an unheated room. Varèse soon became restless and depressed. Louise Varèse, his second wife, reports that whenever this happened, he would move. This time—1907—the young couple left France for Berlin.

In Berlin, Ferruccio Busoni's *Sketch of a New Aesthetic of Music* had just created considerable attention in musical circles. Busoni, who preceded Schoenberg at the Berlin Academy, was not only an extraordinary pianist but also a champion of new music. In this revolutionary tract, Busoni discussed the possibility of new scale formations, microtones (tones smaller than a half step), and new instrumental possibilities. He stated that the progress of music could eventually be impeded by the physical limitations of existing instruments. Busoni applied his ideas by building a "harmonium," an instrument that anticipated electronic instruments no longer tied to the halftone scale. With the whole tone divided in three, the octave C–C would be composed of eighteen third-note steps. Busoni never composed in this system.

Varèse described Busoni's importance to him: "I had read his remarkable little book, *A New Aesthetic of Music* (another milestone in my development), and when I came across his dictum: "Music was born free and to win freedom is its destiny," I was amazed and very much excited to find that there was someone besides myself—and a musician at that—who believed this. It gave me courage to go on with my ideas and my scores."

There were, of course, differences between the two men. Varèse explains: "It was Busoni who coined the expression 'The New Classicism' and classicism new or old was what I was bent on avoiding."

During the years 1907 to 1915, Varèse traveled between Berlin and Paris. In Berlin he was friendly with Busoni, Hugo von Hofsmannsthal, Richard Strauss, and the conductor Karl Muck; in Paris with the author Romain Rolland, as well as Debussy and Ravel. But these impressive contacts produced no practical results.

In 1910, the year his only child was born, Varèse did not have a single pupil. His intensity may have put students off: "I became a sort of diabolical Parsifal on a quest, not for the Holy Grail, but for the bomb that would explode the musical world and allow all sounds to come rushing into it through the resulting breach. . . ."

Varèse's first bomb exploded in December 1910, when Josef Stransky presented Varèse's *Bourgogne* to a conventional concert audience. Although

Schoenberg's *Pelleas* was introduced that same week, *Bourgogne* created the larger scandal. Critics complained of "caterwauling" and "din"; later Varèse repudiated this early work, and destroyed it.

In 1912, in the Choralionsaal in Berlin, Stravinsky and Varèse heard the first performances of the atonal *Pierrot Lunaire*. Varèse was impressed. In 1913 he attended the premiere performance of *The Rite of Spring*, the work that reaffirmed a tonal center and deified its composer the following year.

In 1914, Schoenberg stopped publishing. At the same time, Varèse turned to a conducting career; the milieu did not encourage radical musical ideas. Varèse conducted a successful concert of contemporary music in Prague, but World War I interrupted his career. Inducted into the French army, he was quickly discharged because of a respiratory problem. Louise Varèse said that even in his youth, Varèse suffered from claustrophobia and gasped for breath as he walked down the rue de Rivoli.

The musical traditions of Western Europe may also have been smothering him. In 1915 he left Paris alone—his marriage having broken up two years before—and arrived in the United States. Varèse found a more sympathetic environment in New York City than he had in Paris or Berlin.

CHAPTER 16

Varèse arrived in the United States in 1915 with ninety dollars, thinking he could pick up a conducting career that had been cut off in Prague. He planned to bring new music to America, and because he brought many letters of reference from European musicians, Varèse received the assignment to conduct the Berlioz *Requiem*. At his disposal was the musical army that Berlioz had prescribed. Varèse was much at home with this large-scale work, so dependent upon huge masses of sound.

The performance in April 1917, received rave notices. Paul Rosenfeld, one of the most advanced American music critics, wrote that the conductor possessed the "inspiration of genius." But even this success did not help Varèse's career. Eleven months later, he was out of work.

In 1917 he met Louise Norton; they married and lived in New York. Mrs. Varèse went on to become an outstanding French translator, but he would not use her income for family expenses. Earning a living was a continual struggle.

In April 1919, Varèse became conductor of the New Symphony Orchestra. The idea of performing well-rehearsed contemporary works was the same as that behind Schoenberg's society. But whereas Schoenberg limited attendance to an enlightened few, Varèse tried to reach the largest possible audience. He wanted to spread new music everywhere and to stress American works in an international context. But Varèse's plan did not materialize. The musicians were as unfriendly as the public; they did not want to learn new scores.

During this period Varèse began his most important work: "With *Amériques* I began to write my music and I wish to live or die by my later works." *Amériques* is written in sonata form, but is characterized by a new preoccupation with sound. In the *Christian Science Monitor,* Winthrop Tyron wrote: "Now this work, dispassionately regarded, may be said to mark a date in the history of art. In all reason it may be accounted the first original score for grand orchestra that has been made in America since the twentieth century began. Everything else can be referred to some European model. But here we are completely out of the field of borrowed, derived, imitated thought."

Despite his advanced ideas, Varèse was a romantic man. In the 1950s, Varèse confided that he did not delight in the technology that had materialized. Louise Varèse reports that he was an emotional man and wanted his music to produce an "emotional effect."

With the harpist Carlos Salzedo, the composer started the International Composers Guild. In July 1921, the Guild published a manifesto in which Varèse praised composers and attacked performers: "The composer is the only one of the creators today who is denied direct contact with the public. When his work is done, he is thrust aside and the interpreter enters, not to try to understand the work but impertinently to judge it. . . . Dying is the privilege of the weary. The present day composers refuse to die. . . . It is out of such collective will that the International Composers Guild was born."

The Guild attracted substantial financial and artistic support. Financier Adam Gimbel and painter Joseph Stella served on the administrative board, and Carlos Salzedo, with composers Ruggles and Casella, joined Varèse on the technical board. Mrs. Harry Payne Whitney and a friend, Mrs. Christian Holmes, backed the costly operation.

The ICG held its first concert at the Greenwich Village Theater in February, 1922, before an audience of three hundred people. During the next six years it presented works by Ruggles, Riegger, Stravinsky, Satie, Honegger, Poulenc, Milhaud, Schoenberg, Webern, Berg, Chavez and Revueltas. It also presented the first American performances of Schoenberg's *Pierrot Lunaire,* Stravinsky's *Les Noces,* Webern's *Movements for String Quartet,* and Berg's *Chamber Concerto.* The ICG arrangement gave Varèse what he needed; during these years, he wrote *Offrandes, Hyperprism, Octandre* and *Intégrales,* each of which was introduced at an ICG concert.

Varèse's style did not vary much from work to work. He tackled problems in the late *Déserts* that were similar to those in the early *Amériques.* He thought always in volumes and densities of sound, ignoring conventional harmonies and melodies; and created what has been characterized as "sonorous objects moving in a new sound-space."

Offrandes, performed in April 1922, was divided into two sections, each based on a poem. No longer did melody prevail over duration and timbre. The orchestra's balance of power shifted, with strings subservient to the percussion. In *Offrandes,* Varèse worked with the entire frequency range, from trumpets in high registers to contrabass trombones and tubas in very low ones, with passages that included notes at the extremes of the range held for relatively long periods of time. Varèse looked forward to a time when the composer would no longer be dependent upon the capacity of a human lung. He told the *Christian Science Monitor:* "What we want is an instrument that will give us a continuous sound at any pitch. The composer and electrician will have to labor together to get it. At any rate, we cannot keep working in the old school colors. Speed and synthesis are characteristic of our epoch. We need twentieth-century instruments to realize them in music."

Varèse then wrote *Hyperprism,* in which he rejects all thematicism, and looks directly into the future. The use of the siren gave Varèse the gradation of pitch Busoni had referred to many years before. The *New York Herald Tribune* reported: "After the Varèse number a large part of the audience broke into laughter, which was followed by hisses and catcalls. The supporters of the musicians began to applaud and amid the uproar Salzedo jumped to his feet, and after calling to the audience to be quiet, cried: "This is serious." Apparently for the purpose of restoring order, the musicians played the Varèse number again while half the audience left the building."

Paul Rosenfeld claimed that "Varèse undoubtedly has done as much with the aural sensations of contemporary nature as Picasso with the purely visual ones."

Eugene Goossens conducted *Hyperprism* in London in 1924. He told a reporter from the *Musical Advance:* "Varèse is near the Schoenberg camp but a very great difference exists between the two. They have written of Schoenberg that his music emanates from a sick mind whereas, of Varèse, whatever criticism has been provoked of him, there has been no solicitude as to the state of his health."

Varèse followed *Hyperprism* with *Octandre,* composed at the end of 1923; the work is divided into three general sections, characterized by an unusual use of instruments. An oboe opens the first slow movement, a low piccolo the lively second, and after a slow, subdued passage, a bassoon announces the flamboyant third. Varèse introduces an innovation in the metric markings of the flute part: 1/4 1/2; 3/4 1/2; 4/4 1/2. The extra half represents an added half beat or an eighth note at the end of the measure, but 1/4 and 1/2 is not the same as 3/4. The former is conducted by one long and one short stroke of the baton, while the latter is conducted with three even strokes. Providing his own means to get precisely the results he had in mind was characteristic of Varèse.

The composer's next work, *Intégrales,* written in 1925, contains high-volume screams, short stops, wild crescendi and rapid decrescendi. Varèse's description of what he had in mind was strikingly clairvoyant in terms of the objectives of many of today's composers. *Intégrales,* he said, was conceived for "spatial projections" and was constructed to "employ acoustical means" which did not then exist but which he knew would do so some day.

Stokowski conducted *Intégrales* at Aeolian Hall in March, 1925. Winthrop Tyron, critic of the *Christian Science Monitor,* wrote that it was the "first original score for grand orchestra that had been made in America since the twentieth century began. Here we are completely out of the field of borrowed, derived, or imitated musical thought." But Olin Downes of *The New York Times* and Deems Taylor of the *Herald Tribune* ridiculed Varèse's work. When Stokowski conducted *Amériques* in 1926, Downes wrote that the piece reminded him of "election night, a menagerie or two, and a catastrophe in a boiler factory."

The following winter Varèse completed a gigantic work, *Arcana,* which Stokowski conducted in 1927. On the title page of the score, the composer included a quotation from Paracelsus's *Hermetic Astronomy.* Varèse perhaps identified with the medieval physician, alchemist and mystic.

Arcana was scored for 120 players and even more instruments; Stokowski later admitted that his musicians and the audience detested the piece. By 1927 the handwriting was on the wall: "neoclassicism," taught by Boulanger in Paris, boosted by Stravinsky on his 1925 American tour, and promulgated through the recently formed League of Composers, triumphed over Varèse and his advanced musical colleagues.

By the late 1920s the concept of socialist realism had gained momentum. Art for the social good was not best implemented by experimentation in sound but by "borrowed or derived musical thought." From this time on, neoclassicism grew in the United States, nourished by the League of Composers, which was presided over by Claire Reis. She had been an administrator of the ICG but broke with the parent group in 1923 because she and Varèse did not get along and because she did not agree with his "first performance only" policy. Twenty-five years later, Reis wrote in *The Musical Quarterly*: "The new League preferred to repeat good works rather than to present compositions too immature for public performance."

The ascendancy of neoclassicism can be seen in the fact that the League flourished while the ICG died. Pitts Sanborn, a New York music critic, wrote an article in the League's official journal, *Modern Music,* in which he attacked Varèse as being prepared to "score for a bird-cage, an ash-can, or a renuncible carpet sweeper, provided any of these entities can make a desired contribution to his sonorous whole."

In the fall of 1927, Varèse dissolved the ICG and began to search for another outlet for his music. In a last attempt to provide a "new" music group, he collaborated with Ives, Riegger, Cowell, Salzedo and Nicolas Slonimsky to found the Pan-American Association of Composers. Advocating experimentation, Varèse explained the reason for the group: "The Pan-American was born because I realized that Europe was drifting back to neoclassicism, or rather what is so-called, there really being no such possible thing. You can't make a classic; it has to become one with age. What is called neoclassicism is really academicism. This influence we wish to combat is an evil thing, for it stifles spontaneous expression. . . . It is not that we believe music should be limited to a passport, but rather, that today very little is alive, musically, in Europe. . . ."

A few months later, Varèse left New York for Paris with a $2,000 gift from Stokowski and a small income of his own. He told the newspaper *Le Figaro* of his negotiations with an electric company "to do research into certain instruments which we hope will have a voice more in conformity with our age."

He was referring to machines for synthesizing sounds which he had been talking about with Harvey Fletcher, the acoustical director of the Bell Telephone Laboratories. The project did not materialize, so Varèse formulated his own ideas for a laboratory in Paris. But he failed to attract financial backing.

Varèse's fascination with scientific phenomena appeared not only in his titles, but also in a work for which he never actually wrote the music, *L'Astronome*. Set in an observatory, it had as protagonist an astronomer who raked the sky with his telescope. In the final scene, when the astronomer is thrust into space, factory sirens and airplane propellers were to sound. The music was to be "as strident and unbearable as possible, so as to terrify the audience and render it groggy."

Still limited to conventional instruments, Varèse began *Espace* and *Ionisation*. Scored exclusively for percussion, *Ionisation is* sonority. Varèse uses instruments of definite and indefinite pitch—celesta, piano, and tubular chimes—as well as instruments of pitch. The work is structured according to different qualities of sound: metal, wood, heavy, light. It is Varèse's most familiar work. The title refers to atomic fission; scientists report that a recording of *Ionisation* was frequently played at Oak Ridge while they were at work on the atom bomb.

As the bomb symbolized a revolution in technology, so *Ionisation* symbolized a revolution in music. But the man behind these strikingly new sounds did not exude the one quality—the absolute knowledge that he possessed the only truth—that appears to be essential to gain worldwide renown. Varèse was a personable man who liked to cook, drink wine with friends, and listen to the works of others as well as to his own. Louise said, "He was egocentric but not conceited, not the egoist that Schoenberg was. Varèse had doubts; I wonder whether Schoenberg ever had doubts."

In 1933, during Varèse's last year in Paris, Nicolas Slonimsky conducted *Ionisation* at Carnegie Hall. According to the *Musical Courier,* it "moved even earnest devotees of the musical esoteric to smiles."

When Slonimsky conducted *Arcana* in Berlin in 1932, the audience was outraged. And in Paris the situation was such that Varèse wrote to a friend: "It is disheartening to see the young school here in France becoming zealously academic. It is perhaps normal at a time of world-wide hesitancy to wish to escape into the categorical past, but life with its exigencies goes on and in the end will sweep away all that is static, all that does not move with the rhythm of life."

In the fall of 1933, Varèse and his wife returned to New York. His first large-scale work on his return was *Ecuatorial,* for which the Russian professor of electronics, Leon Theremin, created two instruments. Slonimsky conducted it in April, 1934, and it was very badly received; even his partisans turned against him.

Receiving fewer performances, Varèse turned again to electronics, and applied to the Guggenheim Foundation for help. His request stated the following objectives:

> To pursue work on an instrument for the producing of new sound. To inspect other new inventions in certain laboratories in order to discover if any of them could serve any new sound conceptions. To submit to the technicians of different organizations my ideas in regard to the contribution which music, mine, at least, looks for from science, and to prove to them the necessity of closer collaboration between composer and scientist.

Although Varèse applied several times, the Guggenheim denied his requests. Desperate for a laboratory, Varèse even tried to get into the Hollywood sound studios but could not interest anyone there in his ideas.

The advance in musical thought that had begun in the early years of the century had come to a paralyzing halt.

In 1934, Varèse indulged in some wishful thinking: "I think that Stravinsky is finished and I believe Schoenberg is of much greater importance." But the realities of American political life—the Depression, socialist realism and the WPA—forced American music to become conservative if it was to be accepted and supported. Accessibility was the keynote of the age and radio its primary medium.

Varèse had helped make New York City a mecca of contemporary music during the 1920s, challenging the life of Paris or Berlin. But that activity came to an end in the early 1930s. He frequently repeated the admonition that new instruments were needed "to liberate sound and free the composer from the tempered system." But he appeared to be speaking in a vacuum.

At this time Varèse was profoundly depressed. Continuing to produce scores, he destroyed the pages as he went along. In 1937, in the depths of despair, the composer subjected himself to an unnecessary vasectomy, which, Louise Varèse said, destroyed his sexual potency. This powerful and emotional man, desperately in need of public acclaim, waited for time and technology to catch up with him. It never did during his lifetime. Only after his death did he receive recognition as the initiator of electronic music.

Ferruccio Busoni, whose 1907 Sketch of a New Aesthetic
of Music *helped make Berlin a mecca of progressive
musical thought, attracting Schoenberg and Varèse.*

FRANK DRIGGS COLLECTION

Gustav Mahler, whose emotionally searing music and huge orchestral forces influenced Schoenberg's early work. Mahler publicly defended the younger composer while privately admitting to him that he could not understand his String Quartet No. 1. FRANK DRIGGS COLLECTION

Nikolai Rimsky-Korsakov, Stravinsky's most important teacher. His colorful, nationalistic compositions influenced his pupil's Firebird, Petrushka, *and* The Rite of Spring. FRANK DRIGGS COLLECTION

Arnold Schoenberg, in Mödling, Austria, 1922, with pupils Walter Goehr and Eduard Steuermann. FRANK DRIGGS COLLECTION

Alban Berg, c. 1935.
Berg began to study under
Schoenberg in 1904. His opera,
Wozzeck, *which premiered*
in Berlin in 1925, is generally
considered to be the most
successful creation to emerge
from the Schoenberg school.
FRANK DRIGGS COLLECTION

Along with Berg, Anton Webern was an early pupil of Schoenberg, who became the inspiration for the revolution in music begun by Boulez and his followers just after World War II. FRANK DRIGGS COLLECTION

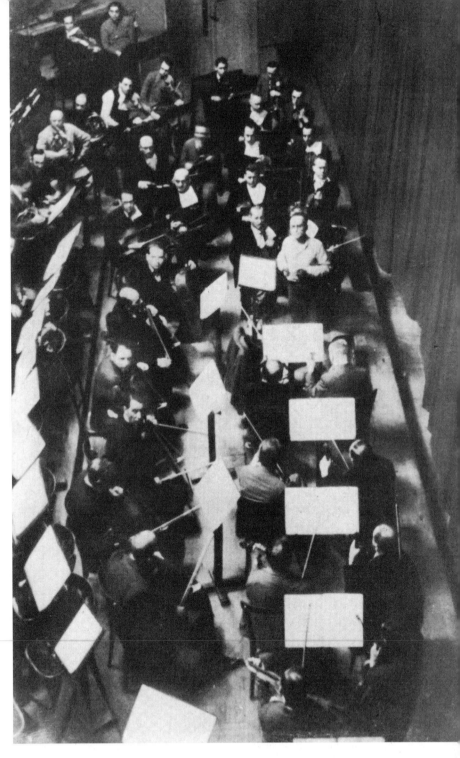

Anton Webern, conducting the Vienna Philharmonic c. 1933. The composer of short, quiet pieces, Webern said the sound of a full orchestra caused him actual physical pain. FRANK DRIGGS COLLECTION

Paris 1913

Igor Stravinsky, 1913, the year of the world premiere of
The Rite of Spring *in Paris, which precipitated a spectacular
scandal. One year later, in the same city, Pierre Monteux
conducted the work in a concert version, vindicating the score
and blaming Nijinsky for clumsy and provocative choreography.*
COURTESY ROBERT CRAFT

In the second decade of the century, Stravinsky responded to American jazz with Ragtime *and* Piano-Rag Music. *Here he is in 1946 with clarinetist and bandleader Woody Herman, whose commission of a Stravinsky work resulted in* The Ebony Concerto. FRANK DRIGGS COLLECTION

Paul Hindemith, c. 1946, with the Berlin Philharmonic. Initially drawn to modernism, Hindemith, by 1927, distanced himself from Schoenberg, becoming an advocate of Gebrauchsmusik, *music designed for day-to-day situations, capable of being played by able amateurs.* FRANK DRIGGS COLLECTION

American composer Henry Cowell, in the 1920s, playing his "tone clusters" on the piano. Bartók asked Cowell for permission to use them. Cowell replied that he had no patent on them. Cage acknowledged Cowell to be a primary influence.

FRANK DRIGGS COLLECTION

Dmitri Shostakovich and Aaron Copland in New York City, 1949, were among
the most important anti-12-tone composers of the pre-World War II period.
In 1957, with his Piano Fantasy, Copland *wrote the first of three 12-tone works.*
Then he stopped composing.   FRANK DRIGGS COLLECTION

*Associated with no school of composition,
Bela Bartók, a giant of the first half of
the 20th century, assimilated his studies
of folk music with his concert work. The
Concerto for Orchestra, composed in
1942 on commission by Serge Koussevitzky
and the Boston Symphony orchestra,
appears to be the most recent creation by
any composer to enter the general repertoire.*

FRANK DRIGGS COLLECTION

Stefan Wolpe's students encompass such diverse musicians as Ralph Shapey, David Tudor, Morton Feldman, Ezra Laderman, and film composer Elmer Bernstein. Wolpe died in 1972. CLEMENS KALISCHER

Edgard Varèse, whose goal was to make us "forget what we know," in a youthful photograph in which he appears to be hypnotizing the public to follow his lead. More than any other single figure, Varèse can be said to have been the pioneer of electronic music. COURTESY CHOU WEN-CHUNG

144

Until Déserts, *in which the tape recorder was used,* Varèse *was limited to primitive materials. Here he is shown in his Greenwich Village house working with unsophisticated means of producing new sounds.* FRANK DRIGGS COLLECTION

CHAPTER 17

On June 1, 1969, the New York Philharmonic announced the appointment of Pierre Boulez as its music director. He was to succeed Leonard Bernstein, the ebullient, gifted musical personality who had begun his career in the 1940s as the protégé of Serge Koussevitzky. For Bernstein, the first American to assume the post, it was very definitely a step up in prestige. For Boulez it was, in some people's view, a step down. As a critic, an organizer of musical thought, Boulez had no equal in the 1950s. And as a member of the postwar avant-garde, he had led the way to a new musical grammar that had been accepted by many of the most talented and aggressive composers in the world.

Boulez built his conducting career in the 1960s when aleatory music threatened the idea in which he believed. Olivier Messiaen, Boulez's teacher at the Paris Conservatoire, suggested what lay behind his virtual shift of profession: "Boulez is a great composer. He is also a very intelligent man. He understands all the changes and they make him suffer. There are people who go unperturbed through change. Like Bach. Like Richard Strauss. But Boulez cannot. He thinks that advancing the language is all. He feels he must be in the advance guard and he doesn't like what is happening there."

The desire to escape from the severe discipline into which Boulez's idea had led moved whole sections of the new music world toward what he viewed as theatrical gimmickry and nihilism. Boulez accepted the Philharmonic post primarily to attack this situation. His purpose was to promote his own cause, to make familiar to large audiences the modern language in which he believed, in which form exercised a centripetal role.

Boulez's commitment allows for no shift in taste. He personifies the control of mind over body, just as Bernstein personified the reverse. Bernstein reportedly lost seven pounds a performance because he perspired so freely. Boulez rarely perspires at all. Bernstein had a family and a highly styled social life. Boulez lives only for his work, and he lives alone. Bernstein said

"I love you" to those he met in corridors. There's no evidence that Boulez has ever said "I love you" in his life.

Thus it is fitting that Boulez—not anyone else—promulgate the most crucial musical idea of the century, one that replaces tonality, the traditional method of composition in Western civilization, with a newly created scheme. New York was the place and the 1970s the time for him to make his point momentously. Because of Boulez's talent, his energy, his position, and his devotion to that language, he was better suited to test it than any other musician in the world.

CHAPTER 18

*I believe a civilization that conserves is
one that will decay because it is afraid of
going forward and attributes more
importance to memory than the future.
The strongest civilizations are those without memory—those capable of complete
forgetfulness. They are strong enough
to destroy because they know they can
replace what is destroyed. Today our
musical civilization is not strong; it shows
clear signs of withering. . . .*

*The more I grow, the more I detach myself
from other composers, not only from the
distant past but also from the recent past
and even from the present. Conducting has
forced me to absorb a great deal of history,
so much so, in fact, that history seems more
than ever to me a great burden. In my
opinion we must get rid of it once and
for all.*

PIERRE BOULEZ
1975

The art of the past haunts both composer and listener. Even Stravinsky, less than ten years after composing as radical a work as *Le Sacre du Printemps*, was drawn back to music of earlier times. In 1920 Stravinsky launched the "neoclassical" movement that dominated music for at least thirty years. Despite his own shift—at sixty-six years old—from neoclassicism to serialism, Stravinsky's bias toward older music remained intact. During the last years of his life he listened to nothing more advanced than Debussy and spent most of his time with recordings of the late Beethoven sonatas and quartets.

Soon after Stravinsky's death, the *Saturday Review* asked Boulez to write a commemorative article. Convention did not prevent Boulez from attacking Stravinsky for quoting old scores, even when done in a spirit of irony. Later, with associates, he embellished his point: "It is not enough to deface the Mona Lisa because that does not kill the Mona Lisa. All the art of the past must be destroyed."

The comment was quoted in the Sunday *New York Times,* and the media questioned Boulez. To *Newsweek* he replied, "I must abandon the past. In the beginning in the womb you are tied to an umbilical cord. You're fed through it. Eventually you cut it. You can still love your mother but you have to feed yourself." To *Time* he revealed his yardstick for art: If a work advances the language, it is good; if it does not, it is bad. "History is much like the guillotine," he said. "If a composer is not moving in the right direction he will be killed, metaphorically speaking. The evolution of music and everything else, for that matter, depends on people who are gifted enough to understand that change is an absolutely irreversible process. You cannot ignore the historical landmarks of music because if you ignore them, then history will ignore you. . . . The dilemma of music is the dilemma of our civilization. We have to fight the past to survive."

Thus Boulez promoted Schoenberg, Webern, and Berg because they crystallized the language that moved music in a new direction. And he celebrated Mahler and Wagner, for they are the ones who led the way. But Brahms and Verdi—and particularly Tchaikovsky—go to the guillotine.

Along with the eminent social theorist Theodor Adorno, whom he knew and admired, Boulez was out to kill the musical past because of aesthetic necessity: tonality was exhausted after a few hundred years and a new musical grammar was needed in its place. But Boulez's impassioned assault on the old was imbued with a fanatical fervor, because it stemmed from a need to destroy his own past.

When Boulez was first acclaimed in France as the greatest musical genius since Debussy, a music critic asked him about his youth. "I shall be the first composer in history," he replied, "not to have a biography." His attitude has never altered. He told *Newsweek*'s Hubert Saal, "I have gigantic powers of forgetfulness. I think everyone's childhood is the same. The important decisions are the ones you make when you are no longer a child." "How did you come to be?" asked Mr. Saal. "By myself," Boulez answered. "Neither heredity nor environment played any role at all. It is just a seed," he went on. "The most important things need no explanation."

Residents of the French town in which he grew up say that his nature is not typically French. "The French are reserved; Boulez is closed." Like his handwriting, which is so small that it can hardly be read without a magnifying glass, everything serves to hide the ferment inside. In discussing a great work of art Boulez said: "If it were necessary for me to find a profound motive for such a work, it would be the search for anonymity.

Perhaps I can explain it best by an old Chinese story: A painter drew a landscape so beautifully that he entered the picture and disappeared. For me that is the definition of a great work—a landscape painted so well that the artist disappears in it."

Boulez was born on March 26, 1925, in an apartment over a pharmacy on Rue Tupinerie, the main street of the Loire town of Montbrison, which had then a population of seven thousand five hundred and a winding stream that cut through its center. His father, Léon, was an engineer and technical director of a steel factory. He was taller than any of his children are and cut an extremely authoritative figure. Léon had received a strict Catholic upbringing and placed great stress on a structured family life as well as on a classical education for his children. Politics was one of the many subjects not considered suitable for discussion at the dinner table. A rigid but preeminently just man, he prevailed at the top of a tight family pyramid.

Boulez's mother, Marcelle, was, according to her children, "half-Catholic and half-nothing." She was, above all, deferential to her husband. Those who know her describe her as "simple, direct, very talkative . . . like a bull who grabs you by the arm as she talks . . . a woman whom you could never believe would have produced such a son as that!"

The Boulez family is invariably branded as bourgeois by Boulez's contemporaries in a country where the aristocracy passionately promotes the avant-garde, and the avant-garde passionately despises the bourgeoisie. This may explain Pierre Boulez's efforts to erase his historical origins from the face of the map, virtually to "kill off" his contemptible bourgeois past. Boulez's most pejorative comments are reserved for those who, in his words, are afflicted with a "shopkeeper's mentality." But that alone does not explain his refusal to touch on his childhood, his hatred of the way he was as a boy. What he seems to want most to erase is evidence of his former devotion to God and any manifestation of docility before authority.

According to family friends, Pierre was not a strong infant. He didn't walk until he was three, and once, when burned in an accident, his mother rushed him to a priest to be blessed. Perhaps because he was the first boy born after her first son died, Marcelle Boulez seems to have thought that, in the second Pierre, she had produced a special person. She treated him accordingly. In the traditional school system, where winning is the sine qua non, the boy flourished. Freud's statement that "a man who has been the indisputable favorite of his mother keeps for life the feeling of a conqueror, the confidence of success that often induces real success," receives confirmation here.

Of four children, three survived. The original Pierre was born and died in 1920. Jeanne was born in 1922, Pierre in 1925, and Roger in 1936. When Pierre was four the family moved from above the pharmacy to a private house, 46 rue Alsace Lorraine, a pink building on a tree-lined street. Boulez recalled it being built. With his hand in his father's, he would stand on the scaffolding of the top floor and look down with wonder through the levels below. The house, covered with ivy, had shutters, French windows, and a small garden. In it the family prospered in every way. Neighbors report envy at their admirable state. The Boulezes were united, economically solvent, and generally in excellent health. In 1931 Léon Boulez made his first trip to the United States and brought back a radio. It was the first time Pierre heard orchestral music. Theirs was the simple, provincial life, Boulez emphasizes, with nothing unique about it.

But there was something special in his early life that he did not reveal to me: his knowledge that a brother had died before he was born. When I told him I had learned of this fact, he made the statement, "I have his name." Then he recalled an incident that occurred when he was five years old and visited the town graveyard for the first time. Although he had known the brother had died in infancy, the child had never been referred to by name. At an age when children first become aware of death, Pierre stood at the head of this tiny grave and read on the headstone, Pierre Boulez. He spoke of the moment almost in a whisper—but then shook his head, vigorously denying he had been affected by it. "I am a Darwinian," Boulez explained. "I believe I survived because I was the stronger. He was the sketch, I the drawing."

At seven Boulez began his studies at the Institut Victor de la Prade, named for a minor Romantic poet. It was a Catholic seminary, but because there was no lycée in Montbrison, it filled the role of the traditional highly competitive secular high school.

Here he received his First Communion. His days were devoted to study and prayer. He said he knew nothing at all about sex until well into his adolescence. "Our lives were surrounded by a sense of sin everywhere."

Each morning at 5:40, when it was still completely dark, Pierre made his way down a winding dirt road, and twenty minutes later arrived at a gray, monastery-like building. There he spent thirteen hours each day. A brilliant student, he remained at the seminary until he was fifteen, when he passed the first part of his baccalaureate. Although he was younger than the minimum age of sixteen, he graduated at the top of his class in physics and chemistry. His desk was unfailingly neat, with nothing but his work exposed at any time. According to his childhood associates, he was authoritarian from the time he could talk. Like his father he would brook no argument.

In most solid European bourgeois families, children were given piano lessons, and the Boulez family was no exception. Pierre's sister Jeanne began to study when she was six and encouraged her younger brother to do the same. Pierre began at the same age and was playing better than his sister within a year. At first he studied with a local teacher, and by nine he was playing difficult Chopin. His musical experience was not limited to the piano. At thirteen he was soprano soloist at the seminary and at fourteen began to make weekly visits to nearby St. Étienne, a much larger town, where he studied with a more sophisticated musician. By then, music was the central fact of his life. Although he excelled in mathematics, he generally hid his grades from his father because he suspected, even then, that he did not want what his father wanted for him—an engineering career. Boulez denies his mathematical gifts today, for his enemies have used his talent in science to attack his "feeling" as a musician.

Boulez disclaims intellectuality. "I am like my peasant grandfather," he said, "my grandfather on my father's side. My sister is the real intellect." Jeanne Chevalier, Boulez's sister, delights in recalling their childhood days. "Pierre was disciplined in a headstrong way, not in a submissive way. He was never bad or at all rebellious. When he was struck, he never struck back. He was the best child I ever knew.

"By the time we were fifteen," Jeanne Chevalier said, "both of us were skeptical about religion. Pierre never liked sports. He didn't like to swim because he hated the spatial limitations of a swimming pool. He showed no important likes or dislikes but he enjoyed vacationing with his family. In those days we toured virtually all of France.

"He had a few comrades at school but friends were not at all important to him. His relations with them were not at all intense. I was the most important person in his life. It was with me that he shared everything—his games, hopes, and deepest dreams. We still travel together—Scotland last year and Mexico this—and we get along very well. He is strong. But I am strong too."

After completing the first part of his baccalaureate, Boulez spent the school year of 1940–41 at the Pensionnat St. Louis at St. Etienne and the next year at the University of Lyon taking courses that would prepare him for an engineering career. Lyon, with a population of one million, was forty-five miles from Montbrison; Pierre would come home every three or four weeks. It was in Lyon that Boulez heard a live orchestra for the first time and attended his first opera, *Boris Godunov*. It was also there that he met a singer, Ninon Vallin, who had performed *Godunov* with Chaliapin. Vallin asked the boy to accompany her in arias from *Aida* and *The Damnation of Faust*. Even then Verdi struck him as "melodramatic"; more recently he dismissed him as "dum de dum, nothing more." Still, impressed with the boy's musicianship, Vallin persuaded his father to allow him to apply to the Lyon Conservatoire. But the Conservatoire rejected Pierre, supporting the father's assessment of his son's musical gifts. Jeanne Boulez confronted the director and pleaded for a reversal but was unsuccessful.

In 1942 Jeanne and Pierre made the first decisions that precipitated a separation, both from each other and from their parents. Jeanne met and decided to marry Jack Chevalier. When Pierre was home for his holiday, his sister interceded with their father in support of a career in music. Pierre wanted an additional year in Lyon, pursuing not engineering but piano, harmony, and counterpoint, with one course in mathematical theory on the side. Vallin recommended a teacher for his musical studies and once again the authoritarian father acquiesced. It was, as Jeanne Chevalier recalled it, "a clear-cut decision against his father." In reconstructing the battle, Boulez spoke with pride of his own and his sister's strength. "Our parents were strong. But finally we were stronger than they."

In the spring of 1940 Germany invaded France, occupying Paris and the north and setting up the Vichy government in the south. Germany took over the south in 1942, when Boulez was in Lyon for his second year. Boulez speaks of the invasion dispassionately, noting simplistically that the French sank their fleet in order not to help the Germans and that, in the spring of 1943, the Germans "decided to have a kind of administration of the south and north." But how is one, on the threshold of manhood and raised in a school system that values the "battle" over everything else, to cope with his country's grotesquely humiliating defeat?

Still, Boulez's subsequent repudiation of France and identification with German culture cannot be attributed to the German victory. Boulez has often said that if you are a sensual person, France may be the country for you, but if you are concerned with more profound matters, France is woefully inadequate. He has been explicit about music in this regard: "From the point of view of form, what influenced me most was German music, in fact what's most German in German music—the continuity, the proliferation of material from a small musical cell. There is also an extraordinary continuity in the rich history of German music, whereas in France there is Rameau, then after a long period Berlioz, then after another long period Debussy."

Boulez saw benefits in the German occupation of Paris. "The

theaters were crowded. People could not leave the cities and all of them jammed into concert halls. I went to a concert given by my own piano teacher and could hardly get into it. The Germans virtually brought high culture to France."

Thus, by the time he was eighteen, Boulez had turned against his father, his country, and everything else that had been held up to him as sacred. Indeed, the young man who had "never struck back" struck back with passion. He repudiated Catholicism, spouting Latin obscenities when he was drunk. He flung epithets at France, attacking people in high places. Although he didn't join the Communist party, he attended its meetings, he has said, as a substitute for church-going. He never studied under any one man for any length of time, "detesting the father-son relationship." And as for the musical language itself, he literally tried to kill off the old works by mocking them through distortions at the piano.

When he first heard 12-tone music in 1945 he found the answer he had been searching for on both aesthetic and psychological grounds. "It was a revelation," he explains. "Here was a music of our time, a language with unlimited possibilities. No other language was possible. It was the most radical revolution since Monteverdi, for all the familiar patterns were now abolished. With it, music moved out of the world of Newton and into the world of Einstein. The tonal idea was based on a universe defined by gravity and attraction. The serial idea is based on a universe that finds itself in perpetual expansion."

Erik Erikson has written that ideas fill the mind and attach themselves to the strongest feelings. "Ideas form systems and systems absorb lives. A believer in a system supports it with all of his instincts. He is no longer alone in his struggle against the world. He has found liberation from uncertainty. . . . With this moral conceit, the idea makes him superior to everyone else."

This is what happened to Boulez, who has devoted his life to forging and implementing an idea. Boulez promulgated this idea as Moses promulgated the idea of one God. And he did it in ways that were familiar to him—rising before dawn and working throughout the day, living the life of the religious celibate, ignoring clothes, entertainment, and food, moving without friends, permitting no dialogue. Boulez said that throughout his life he has refused to define himself through interaction with others. Instead he has defined himself through "personal breaks," breaks that were as filled with rage as the one "against" his father when he was eighteen.

CHAPTER 19

There is little to be learned from professors. Personally, in two years, I learned all I could from teachers. Between the ages of 18 and 21, I discovered the Viennese school, Stravinsky, and Messiaen—that is to say, I discovered a literature I had no idea existed before I was 17. . . . Now, more than twenty-five years later, I find those choices have hardly changed at all. . . .

It was during those same years that I first saw the works of Klee, Kandinsky, and Mondrian. Again, I knew immediately that these figures were the capital ones in the evolution of painting. They are, in my opinion, still the most important of that period.

The same is true of my first encounters with Joyce and Kafka. I believe I was defined by the period immediately preceding me. What these composers, painters, and writers did enabled me to move quickly on, because history had been liquidated by them and one had only to think of oneself.

PIERRE BOULEZ
1975

When Boulez arrived in Paris in 1943, the musical climate was much the same as it had been before the war. Nadia Boulanger, who had taught neoclassicism in the 1920s and '30s and was the pillar of the salon of Marie Blanche de Polignac, continued to teach neoclassicism then. Milhaud, Poulenc, Auric, and Honegger still dominated the musical scene. Henri Sauguet, the only active surviving pupil of Erik Satie, and the most successful composer of his generation, had adopted the Milhaud/Poulenc style. Indeed, in the late 1940s, when Jean-Louis Barrault sent Boulez—at that time his music director—to Sauguet's home to pick up scores, Boulez waited outside on the front doorstep, refusing to enter the house on aesthetic grounds.

But one figure emerged in France during the war who was to change the path of music in Europe—René Leibowitz, a composer and conductor. Almost singlehandedly he revived 12-tone writing in Europe, where it had gone underground during the 1930s and early 1940s when Hitler was determined to destroy modern art. Leibowitz first heard Schoenberg's *Pierrot Lunaire* in 1932, when he was nineteen, and the work made a formidable impression on him: "I hated it but I could not sleep for two weeks. I tried to reconstruct the entire score in my head. Finally I said, 'If this kind of music can be composed, then I must compose it.'" With a small inheritance from his father, Leibowitz went to Vienna to study with Schoenberg. When he arrived, he learned that Schoenberg had moved to Berlin. So he settled for lessons with Anton Webern, Schoenberg's quiet, submissive pupil. Webern taught Leibowitz harmony and counterpoint, but Webern never displaced Schoenberg in Leibowitz's esteem.

After finishing the course, Leibowitz returned to Paris via Berlin, still determined to meet Schoenberg. Armed with a letter of reference from Webern, he introduced himself to the imperious Viennese, then teaching at the Prussian State Academy of the Arts. Schoenberg invited Leibowitz to attend class for six weeks.

On his return to France, Leibowitz studied conducting with Pierre Monteux and played violin in a Paris nightclub in order to make enough money to buy all the Schoenberg scores he could find. It was then he discovered dodecaphony, for Schoenberg had never discussed the technique in class.

To confirm his suspicion that a new system governed the composition of Schoenberg's post-1923 works, Leibowitz consulted Rudolph Kolisch, Schoenberg's brother-in-law and the violinist who premiered many Schoenberg pieces. Kolisch told Leibowitz that when Schoenberg was fifty years old he had evolved a new musical law, a method of composing with twelve tones, each one equal to the other, which he had hoped would displace the old tonal law based on a hierarchical seven-tone scale.

Schoenberg crystallized the rules in 1923. Ten years later he was dismissed from his post at the Prussian State Academy. Forced to flee Berlin because he was Jewish, he first went to Paris, then to Boston, and finally settled in California. During the late 1930s and early '40s his work was rarely performed in the United States and virtually never performed in Europe, where it was branded as decadent. Thus the generation of Leibowitz—and of Boulez and his colleagues—had no opportunity to hear dodecaphonic music.

When World War II broke out, Leibowitz went into hiding in

Vichy, then in an apartment in Paris until the Liberation in 1945. Almost immediately he began to conduct the first postwar performances of Schoenberg in Europe and to record Schoenberg works as well. Friendly with the existentialists Merleau Ponty and Jean-Paul Sartre (Sartre wrote the introduction to his book *L'Artiste et sa Conscience*), Leibowitz became famous and important in Paris. Despite the fact that he, a Polish Jew, had an expatriate passport and therefore had difficulty gaining access to the French government radio, Leibowitz gave performances of the Schoenberg school that were important events among the avant-garde. As Boulanger held on to the reins of the dying neoclassical tradition, Leibowitz was celebrated as the father of the New.

In the fall of 1943, when Boulez first arrived from Provence, he moved into a tiny apartment on rue Beautreillis, near the historic Place des Vosges. In his cluttered, tiny rooms he kept his manuscripts rolled up like papyrus on the floor. In addition to the manuscripts there was a narrow bed, a small desk, an electric heater, and several African masks. Reproductions of Paul Klee were on the walls; the works of Rimbaud, Mallarmé, and James Joyce were on the shelves. Boulez had managed to escape military service because before the Occupation he had been too young to serve, and after the Liberation he was exempt; there were no longer any barracks or camps and those born in 1924 and 1925 were excused.

Free to pursue his metier, he enrolled in the Paris Conservatoire, entering the harmony class of Georges Dandelot in the fall of 1943. There he met Arthur Honegger's niece, who led him to Honegger's wife, Andrée Vaurabourg. She taught counterpoint in a small apartment high up on Montmartre. She recalled him as a remarkable student who "always seemed capable of anything at all." The eight-part counterpoint examples he produced for her still serve as models in her studio.

In the fall of 1944 Boulez entered the advanced harmony class under Olivier Messiaen. Messiaen, one of the most influential composers of his generation, had returned to France in 1942 after having been a prisoner of war. In the early 1940s he was the most important teacher at the Conservatoire. Professors there invariably taught from textbooks; only Messiaen brought music into class, and, what is more, he brought his own newly composed music. Church organist, virtuoso pianist, user of Gregorian melodies, specialist in Asiatic rhythms, fanatical follower of bird songs, Messiaen made a strong impression on his students.

When Boulez entered the advanced harmony class, he had heard only Messiaen's *Variations for Violin and Piano*. Boulez admits he was initially awed, but soon the awe turned to disdain. Later he was harsh on him: "Messiaen never really interested me. His use of certain Indian and Greek rhythms poses a problem—at least to me. It is difficult to retrieve pieces of another civilization in a work. We must invent our own rhythmic vocabulary, following the norms that are our own. Even in my earliest pieces, I was aware of that."

Messiaen recalled Boulez's dramatic shift in attitude: "When he first entered class, he was very nice. But soon he became angry with the whole world. He thought everything was wrong with music. The next year he discovered the serial language and converted to it with immense passion, judging it the only viable grammar."

In class Boulez exhibited extraordinary facility with the piano, playing works he composed at that time. Messiaen not only taught advanced harmony; he also held a seminar in musical analysis at the home of Guy Bernard Delapierre, an Egyptologist and composer of film music with whom he had been held prisoner in France before being interned in a concentration camp in Germany. The class was held outside the Conservatoire because the Conservatoire limited Messiaen's duties to the most traditional harmony lessons and did not confer upon him a professorship in composition. The analysis class was open to exceptional students. There too Boulez shone. He "discovered" Debussy, studied Schoenberg's early works, and produced a dazzling analysis of *The Rite of Spring,* which added considerable information to one Messiaen had produced.

To earn money Boulez played the *ondes martenot,* an electronic keyboard instrument, in a pit orchestra in the Folies Bergères. Messiaen helped him in many ways—even providing him with meals—for Boulez refused to take money from home. "His father," Messiaen recalled, "was very angry when he chose music, and his father was a very severe, very closed man. Today Boulez resembles his father in being exceptionally closed. Even if he is nice and polite there are always hidden things going on. Even if he's smiling, there is more underneath than a smile." But in those days Messiaen could get through to Boulez. After class they would often ride the Metro together. Boulez would say, "Musical aesthetics are being worn out. Music itself will die. Who is there to give it birth?" Messiaen replied, "You will, Pierre."

At the end of the year Boulez earned the Conservatoire's first prize in harmony. Then he moved on to a course in fugue under Simone Plé-Coussade, which he describes as "terrible. After coming from the freedom of Messiaen, I could not stand it. She was unimaginative and the class was dead. That is why I hate all academic teaching. I didn't attend class and received a notice that I would be expelled if I did not change my ways.

I said 'Throw me out immediately and perhaps instead of concerning yourself with attendance you will concern yourself with the more important problem of teaching.' That was what gave rise to the petition I organized that Messiaen be given a full professorship in composition." (That petition did not bear fruit until 1949–50.)

During his early student days Boulez wrote several works of which we have no record today—a sonata for two pianos, a work for *ondes martenot*, and *Oublie Lapide*, a piece for a cappella chorus. The first work which made a mark was the *Trois Psalmodies* for piano, written in 1945. At this time Boulez knew only two early Schoenberg works: *Pierrot Lunaire* and the Three Pieces for Piano, Opus 11. The *Psalmodies* reflected the early Schoenberg style mixed with a little Honegger. Boulez has said, "While I was writing *Trois Psalmodies* I didn't even know of the existence of serial music but I had a distinct sense of the need for it. And yet now I want to forget these pieces were ever written. They have never been published and they never will be—at least not with my consent."

What Boulez calls "serial" in this instance is the serial treatment of pitch or what is generally referred to as dodecaphony. He said he avoids the term "dodecaphony" both because of its "garden of Greek [i.e. old] roots" as well as "its association with academic techniques." But at bottom, I feel, he avoids it because it was Schoenberg's word, and he was interested in carving a movement that would bear his own word for it.

Here is how Boulez said he came upon the serial idea:

> One evening, in 1945, I heard a private performance of Schoenberg's Woodwind Quintet, conducted by René Leibowitz. It was a revelation to me. It obeyed no tonal laws and I found in it a harmonic and contrapuntal richness and a consequent ability to develop, extend, and vary ideas that I had not found anywhere else. I wanted, above all, to know how it was written. Therefore I went to Leibowitz and brought with me other students from Messiaen's harmony class. The first work we analyzed was Webern's Opus 21 Symphony. I was very impressed with this and made copies because the score wasn't available at the time. I felt then the significance of this new language.

So, in 1946, Boulez was still under the influence of both Messiaen and Leibowitz. And Messiaen and Leibowitz represented very different worlds. Messiaen was not only a great composer but also a keyboard virtuoso. Leibowitz could talk analytic rings around Messiaen, who was not very sensitive to pitch or to interval relationships. Messiaen's forte was rhythm and meter.

But the most profound difference between the men can be reduced to national characteristics. Messiaen was part of the French tradition that despised Mahler and Brahms and upheld Debussy against Wagner. Leibowitz was tied to the Austro-German idea. Thus he used to tell his students that Rameau was to Bach what Debussy was to Schoenberg. Stravinsky was the Telemann of the twentieth century. Indeed he saw the then neoclassic Stravinsky, a product of the Franco-Russian milieu, as his archenemy in his quest for a language derived from Schoenberg. And he acted on his beliefs. During the winter of 1945, when Paris was trying to recover from the Occupation, the city began to celebrate Stravinsky, whose music had been branded decadent by the Nazis. One of the first performances included two works Stravinsky had recently composed in the United States—*Danses Concertantes* and *Four Norwegian Moods*. To the surprise of everyone at the Théâtre des Champs-Élysées the pieces were greeted by prolonged booing from a group of Conservatoire students. Leibowitz was the figure behind this demonstration but Boulez was the young man at the center of things. Thus, at that particular moment, Boulez was following Leibowitz's lead. And the message he proclaimed was this: The musical life of the past would not return, neoclassicism was really dead, the future would take an altogether different turn, and he would take over the quest for the Idea.

In 1946 Boulez engaged in a brief, passionate sexual affair, apparently the only one of his life. It was a love-hate relationship so intense and tormented that he has said it could not possibly have gone on. The two joined in a double-suicide pact; Boulez will say nothing more about the affair, not even whether the other person went through with the fatal act. The need for suicide and the release from it proved to be a stimulus of enormous vitality for Boulez. Within the next few years he created a series of wild, courageous works each of which maintained that delicate balance between emotion and intellect. The escape from death—or from the love affair—apparently precipitated a burst of prodigious creativity.

Unable to find words to express his deepest feelings, Boulez, throughout his career, has set poems that do exactly that for him. The first poem he chose after the end of this affair was "Le Visage Nuptial," by René Char. The form of the music adheres very closely to that of the poem. Boulez has said it was Char's "condensation" that drew the poet to him, "a contained violence, not a violence of many gestures. What attracted me to

Char was not, as many have written, his love of nature, his love of Provence, or his deep understanding of men. Rather was it his extraordinary power to gather together in an extremely concise way a whole universe."

Like Boulez's music, Char's poetry is obscure, exceptionally difficult even for a professional to translate. Despite the fact that, in conversation, Boulez emphasized his attraction to Char's technique, he does acknowledge that the violence of the sexual imagery played a role in this particular choice: "It was a strong love poem. It was a good poem for me. It was a meeting with the fancies I was having at that time."

Boulez poured forth works in the mid-'40s. His fecundity at this period confirms Schiller's claim that "genius does not proceed by known principles but by feeling and inspiration."

Le Visage Nuptial was Boulez's first important work with a text, but it was not his first important work. Before beginning it, he had composed the Sonatina for Flute and Piano and the First Piano Sonata.

The Sonatina was commissioned by the flutist Jean-Pierre Rampal, who never played it because it was too extreme for his taste. It is a short work and bursts with musical activity. The flute makes frenetic melodic leaps and rhythmic jolts, giving an impression of uncontrolled hysteria. The First Sonata is also fast and aggressive. The verbal instructions in the score give a clue to the explosive quality of the piece: "très violent," "brusque, incisif, très fort," "plus animé et plus nerveux," and, for the final chord, "très brutal and très sec."

Boulez said that these pieces—both composed in 1946—were strongly influenced by Schoenberg; he was studying with Leibowitz at the time. "What interested me in the Sonatina," he said,

> was the metamorphosis of a single theme, and Schoenberg's Chamber Symphony is a good example of that. But if one didn't know the influence was Schoenberg, one could never have guessed it, for there is absolutely no similarity from a stylistic point of view. The Chamber Symphony is in a post-romantic style that had no effect on me at all.
>
> As for the First Sonata, that was influenced by the first pieces in Schoenberg's Opus 23 as well as the Opus 11 which I had on my piano for a long time. The third piece of Opus 11 introduced me to a style of piano writing that was different from anything I had known. There is a great density of texture and a violence of expression that conveys a kind of delirium.

It is in the First Piano Sonata that Boulez first works with the serial idea. But even here he did not copy Schoenberg. On the first page of the score one finds only the first five notes of the row; the remaining seven do not appear until the first bar of the second page. The series appears, ever after, in two parts—one of five notes and the other seven.

Leibowitz recalled the events of 1946 in a conversation several weeks before his death: "Boulez was one of five or six students from the Conservatoire. He was a regular jack-in-the-box. He was also the most arrogant of all. I thought he wrote too fast, too carelessly, that he threw in too many notes. When he started his First Sonata I told him he knew my address. He should send me the work bit by bit. Then I could help him as he went along. But he brought in the completed manuscript. I didn't like it at all."

With a red pen, Leibowitz began marking up the manuscript, then dedicated to him. Grabbing the score, Boulez fled, shouting at Leibowitz, "Vous êtes de la merde!" Three years later Boulez's publisher Hervé Dugardin asked him if the dedication should remain on the printed score. As Boulez shouted "Non!" he stabbed the manuscript with a letter opener until it was virtually in shreds. Then he and Dugardin sat on the floor and painstakingly glued the pieces together.

Human actions depend on a mixture of motives. Boulez attributes his break with Leibowitz to his irritation with his teacher for his "pedantry" and for "being imprisoned by academic techniques" that he had distilled from Schoenberg's work. Boulez may have been justified, but that could hardly account for such an eruption of rage. So one must consider the deeper possibility that the student could not bear criticism from the teacher to whom he had just given a part of himself, that he was jealous of Leibowitz's eminence as the leader of a movement he would have as his own, that finally Leibowitz was one more father to whom he had been *le fils mal aimé* and against whom he was driven to rail violently.

Boulez's radical break with Leibowitz afforded him the chance to define himself anew, and, during the next few years, he succeeded in organizing a new musical grammar that conferred upon him the unequivocal leadership of the European avant-garde and virtually put Leibowitz out of business. Still he hammered away at Leibowitz, issuing polemical attacks against the man in *Contrepoint* and in *La Nouvelle Revue Française*, France's most prestigious literary magazine.

CHAPTER 20

eibowitz had grown up in the household of Artur Schnabel, the pianist and composer, who had been a member of the early Schoenberg circle. Leibowitz's tie to Schoenberg remained firm throughout his life (he even imitated Schoenberg in his devotion to tennis). In 1947 Leibowitz published *Schoenberg et Son École,* probably the first book on 12-tone music not written in German (German treatises on dodecaphony had appeared in the 1920s). In 1948, he visited Schoenberg in California. Schoenberg, then teaching at USC, told Leibowitz of his great disappointment that, though the war was over, the Germans were still not performing his works.

On his return to Paris in 1948, Leibowitz was invited to conduct and teach at the international school of music in Darmstadt, which had been founded two years before and had focused on European neoclassicism—Stravinsky, Hindemith, and Prokofiev. Leibowitz accepted, but only on the condition that he could conduct a whole Schoenberg program—the Piano Concerto, the Chamber Symphony No. 2, and the Five Orchestral Pieces. Leibowitz delivered eight lectures that summer on the development of music from the turn of the century to the revelation of dodecaphony in 1923. Twenty students attended these talks. None of them had heard this music before, but, by the following summer, Leibowitz claims they knew the literature better than he. Unlike his Conservatoire students, the Germans, with their customary thoroughness, dissected and analyzed the entire repertory. So Leibowitz, steeped in the German tradition, had his first real success with the Germans themselves. During the summer of 1948 he literally opened the doors to the European adoption of dodecaphony.

But by then Boulez had moved onto something new, to the creation of a new musical grammar that would pass over Schoenberg. Boulez found a "new voice in Webern, one that Leibowitz could not possibly understand because he could see no further than the numbers in a tone row." Boulez also discovered rhythmic patterns in Webern that nourished the discoveries he made under Messiaen. "I had discovered elaborate rhythms," he explains, "through both Messiaen and Stravinsky, whereas Webern thought primarily in terms of pitches. The two things had to be unified." Thus Boulez, in his early twenties, was obsessed with the formulation of a theoretical system that would serve composers in the future as tonality had served them in the past. And he appears to have equated the articulation of this system with the definition of himself as a man. *Le Soleil des Eaux,* a powerful and exciting work, manifests a mélange of Asiatic rhythms and Webern. It was composed in 1947–48.

Le Soleil des Eaux was originally a dramatic piece by René Char, which Boulez set to incidental music for a radio performance. In that form the work lasts thirty minutes. It tells of the revolt of fishermen on the Île sur Sorgue against the installation of a factory that poisoned their water and ruined their livelihood. It is the story of the defense of liberty and is thus connected with Char's own struggle against Nazism and with the part he played in the French Resistance.

Boulez's original score was never sung in full because it was much too long. He first conceived it for voice alone; he wanted to provide "incidental music," with the text having clear priority. The interjections had nothing to do with each other; the work was a kind of collage. In 1950 the composer deleted most of the poem, reducing the final work to ten minutes and treating only those segments that held particular meaning for him: "La Complainte du Lézard Amoureux" and "La Sorgue." The political ideology disappeared. Boulez describes the poem this way: "'La Sorgue' deals with human energy. The river comes out completely full grown, like Minerva— abruptly—out of Zeus's head. The river is not obliged to develop; it is already there from the start. There is a big cave, an enormously ebullient source. The Sorgue is the image of strength. It provides a contrast to the first poem which describes the laziness of the country, a country which doesn't have to be busy, as seen through the lizard's eyes."

Le Soleil des Eaux was originally scored for three solo voices and chamber orchestra. In 1958 Boulez made a new version for three soloists, chorus, and full orchestra, and he revised even that in 1965. "La Complainte du Lézard Amoureux" juxtaposes blocks of music in much the manner of Messiaen and Stravinsky, which must have seemed to Boulez an idiom of an earlier and "lazier" time.

Both the words and music of *Le Soleil des Eaux* suggest that Boulez would have preferred to emerge from the womb full grown without the years of immaturity during which he felt impotent against a formidable world. His antipathy to helplessness and passivity (the lizard's love for the goldfinch) and his awe and admiration for the strength of the Sorgue (a river that can rust iron) are themes that recur repeatedly in his conversation. Boulez judges composers on their "strength." He uses the same yardstick in regard to his parents: "They were strong, but we were stronger than they."

Along with *Le Soleil des Eaux*, Boulez completed the Second Piano Sonata in 1948. Compared with the First, all the hesitancy is gone. Boulez knows exactly what he wants—the impression of more violence and more delirium. He also knows how to get what he wants. Boulez still calls the piano "my instrument" and his writing for it was pathbreaking.

Because of the frequency with which this work was performed— it became a tour de force for young pianists—Boulez's Second Sonata was probably the single most important work from which the post-Webern movement took its cues. Here traditional melody disappeared. The harmonic system betrayed nothing of the past. Themes played virtually no role at all.

The work is divided into four movements, three of them savage, one (the second) sweet. Once again the verbal instructions denote the tone: "beaucoup plus rude," "de plus en plus haché et brutal," and even in the lyrical movement, a passage interrupts marked "subito, bref et violent." Underneath the leaping configurations, the work is organized as precisely as a medieval motet. Two rows are used: one governs the first and third movements; the other governs the second and fourth. Boulez's testimonial to form is eloquent: an epilogue at the end of the last movement is based on H C A B, the retrograde of B A C H. Bach's use of his own name in *The Art of the Fugue* provided the inspiration for this choice.

In program notes to the early performances, Boulez noted that "all the counterpoints are equally important; there are no principal parts, no secondary parts." In other words, the work has more in common with the polyphony of the late Gothic motet than with the harmonic-melodic music of the intervening eras.

In addition to the increasingly tight treatment of pitch, Boulez turned his attention to rhythm. He said the great distance between the first and second sonatas can be explained by the fact that there was a transitional work, one that is lost. He adds that when he began the Second Sonata he had "completely broken with the Schoenbergian concept of the series. What interested me was the manipulation of tones in a functional, not thematic way. This can be seen clearly in the first movement; the series of intervals are tied to certain motives that reappear throughout the section. Then I gradually dissolve the intervallic cells to a point where they have only secondary importance in order to call attention to the rhythmic material."

Boulez's Second Sonata appears just as wild as parts of *Le Soleil des Eaux* but here there are no words to suggest the conceptual meaning behind the musical hysteria. The more hidden the meaning the more complex the design. Boulez began to move inward.

In 1948–49 Boulez wrote the *Livre pour Quatuor,* a three-movement work he later revised and orchestrated for strings. It is austere, far more restrained than the works preceding it. That may be due to the use of strings, which cannot convey the violence or excitement of either a keyboard or chorus. But it may also be due to Boulez's increasing interest in Webern. In 1971 Boulez told a Juilliard audience:

> I was attracted by the very small form. What Webern did was very calm, very quiet. It is remarkable to see a face so clearly defined at the beginning of a life. One sees that face in the Five Pieces. Of the five, three are slow, only one is very quick. He had in mind the contrast between them, the order and the symmetry. The middle one is the shortest and fastest.
>
> There Webern's harmony is more complex than simple tonal harmony, more complex than Mahler. The style is still conventional; there are, for instance, still melodic lines. But it's the end of Romanticism. There is an obsession not to repeat. There's a story that Webern, at the end of his life, attended a concert in which a Ravel piece was played. 'Why,' asked Webern, 'does he use so many instruments?'
>
> With Webern, one instrument can summarize the world. In that, his world is comparable to Paul Klee's. Klee rarely painted a big painting. The world of Klee can be contained in a drop of water. One can see as many faces in a drop of water as in a large landscape. With Webern there is this tense, tight, closed vision with a poetic power that is surprising. There is no aggressiveness here.

But by 1975 even Boulez's attitude toward Webern had changed:

> Webern's vocabulary attracted me at the start. I found it very important because it established a grammatic base. But I find that the more Webern went on, the more simple his forms became—too simple, in fact, for my taste. One hearing alone is sufficient to catch the essence of his vocabulary. One does not need a series of readings. It is like a painting by

Mondrian. You see the perfection right away and it is very striking, but when you return to it, there is nothing more to take. That is very different from Cézanne, whose paintings I can look at over and over again because of their complexity, because of the infinite detail in design and texture. In that sense Cézanne can be compared to Berg. More and more I am struck by the complexity in Berg—the number of references to himself, the great intricacy of musical construction, the density of the texture. It is a universe in perpetual motion and one that does not stop turning on itself.

Webern drew Boulez in 1948 not only because of the purity of expression but also because of what Boulez sees in him today: that his voice led towards system, not freedom. And system was what Boulez sought. A Webern work, totally organized as to pitch, consists of the unfolding of the original material. The first movement of the Opus 21 Symphony, which Boulez often analyzes for audiences, is a double canon with a retrograde inversion beginning at midpoint. Such systematization was never true of Schoenberg, who wrote music in which the row was not so readily traceable.

Thus Boulez found the control in Webern that he had never found in Schoenberg, and it helped move him into a totally serial world. On an artistic level, strict serialism expressed itself in a master plan in which the composer calculated everything in advance so that nothing unexpected, untoward, could erupt. On a personal level, it must have represented a herculean effort by Boulez to control all those internal forces within himself.

Control is the recurring theme of Boulez's life, and it fit into the temper of the mid-century. The supremacy of intellect over passion, the triumph of mind over physical instinct, began as early as 1920 with neoclassicism and dodecaphony pulling in the reins on the lavish expressionism of pre–World War I days. Stravinsky's *Oedipus Rex* bore the composer's instructions for no movement on stage. It was as far removed from his *Sacre du Printemps* as Schoenberg's Serenade was from *Die glückliche Hand,* which even specified lighting effects in the score. Structure had become the order of the day after World War I. After World War II it was elevated to a reigning faith.

In the vacuum of religious belief, in the loss of political faith, Boulez fell in love with an idea, and it filled him as Catholicism and Marxism once had. Because Webern's path led towards order, Webern symbolized that idea. Thus Webern became the idol to Boulez that Schoenberg had been to Leibowitz. That made the confrontation clear. That added psychic energy to the aesthetic fight. If Webern, who had been Schoenberg's pupil, could displace his teacher in worldwide renown, then Boulez would crush his teacher, Leibowitz.

Boulez's Second Sonata set the tone, an expression of extraordinary temperament and power in deference to the timid, inhibited Webern. This was high-strung, emotional music, anchored by the most precise of pitch plans. This was Boulez at the moment when he began to turn his violent expression into a *technique* for violent expression, into a technique for all composers to use to crush the life out of Romanticism and Schoenberg.

The system, then, underlying the Second Sonata was Boulez's antidote to passion unleashed, passion out of control. An admirer of Antonin Artaud, author of the Theater of Cruelty, Boulez had, only a short time before, echoed Artaud in an article published in *Polyphonie*: "I believe that music should be collective hysteria and spells, violently of the present time." But the hysteria and spells were to be brought under the tightest possible control and done so in the name of Webern.

In 1948 Boulez was alone. By 1955, many gifted and tough composers would echo Boulez's praises of the quiet, neglected Webern who was overshadowed and bullied by an imposing master.

Thus Boulez led music at mid-century because aesthetic conditions made it possible. But he did it for his own private reasons as well.

To be free to compose Boulez needed money. In 1946, Jean-Louis Barrault and Madeleine Renaud separated themselves from the Comédie Française, established an independent company at the Théâtre Marigny and made plans to stage André Gide's translation of *Hamlet* with incidental music by Honegger. Honegger orchestrated the work for brass, percussion, and *ondes martenot*. To play the electronic keyboard instrument he recommended a counterpoint student who was exceptionally gifted on the instrument, Pierre Boulez. Barrault said that as soon as he met Boulez, he recognized his enormous gifts:

> He was aggressive and possessed by music. He had an extraordinary personality, a combination of rage and tenderness. Although he was only twenty years old I made him music director right away. My wife and I became mother and father to him. We remained that way for more than ten years.
>
> During that time we produced plays with incidental music by Auric, Poulenc, Honegger, Milhaud, Sauguet, and Offenbach, all of which—although Boulez did not like

them—he conducted with extreme vigor and authority. He composed prolifically in those early years. But he didn't write incidental music for us; he arranged and conducted what others wrote. Only in 1955, did he agree to compose for our theater. That was for the *Orestes*; he thought he could join the antique theater with the musical language of serialism.

I remember once, when he first came here, Honegger and Boulez were searching for sounds that could accompany moving stars. Boulez began to joke and improvise at the piano. Soon he was destroying Beethoven and Brahms and all the other classic and romantic composers, both verbally and stylistically. Mme Honegger was there and sighed, 'Poor Boulez! He will have to relive history all by himself.'

Boulez profited from his experience with Barrault. His experience in the pit put him in contact with musicians and their instruments for the first time. But he is quick to deflate any overblown image:

The title "Music Director" sounds much more impressive than the job was. Generally I arranged between ten and twelve minutes of music—mostly fanfares and the like—and an occasional half hour of pantomime. Although it brought me to the theater each night, it left me time to compose during the day. The *Orestes*, the only work I set for Barrault, was an important project musically, because there was an opportunity for a lot of music. I was interested in the Japanese Noh drama at the time and I experimented with that in mind. But the actors were not trained musicians. They could not deliver one simple rhythm. I had to change and simplify so much.

One member of the company reports that Boulez beat the rhythm so violently on her back that she collapsed weeping on the floor. Others say he threw chairs when he lost his temper.

But the Barraults gladly put up with it all. "Behind his savagery, there was an extreme bashfulness, a quivering sensibility, even a secret sentimentality." The surrogate parents loved the son, not only for his great musical talent but also for his special blend of violence and charm.

Boulez always enjoyed polemics, and Paris provided a sympathetic milieu for him with lectures, journals, and an active social and intellectual life. Boulez had been playing *ondes martenot* not only at the Folies-Bergère and at the Barrault theater, but for a variety of theatrical productions. Martenot, its inventor, was grateful for the publicity. To repay Boulez he arranged for a performance of Boulez's First Piano Sonata at his house, with Boulez at the piano, and invited a group of friends that included conductor Roger Desormière, composer Nicolas Nabokov, and composer-critic Virgil Thomson. Afterward Thomson wrote in the *New York Herald Tribune* that Boulez was "the most brilliant, in my opinion, of all the Paris under-25s."

One evening in 1948 Boulez attended a lecture in Paris. Afterwards Pierre Souvchinsky introduced himself to Boulez, who describes Souvchinsky as "the last of the conseillers. He had great scope, a very sharp mind. Souvchinsky brought people in contact with one another."

Souvchinsky, an aesthetician and critic of the contemporary world, had a desire to make "discoveries" and to help these new talents to carve out important careers. An elaborate defender of Stravinsky in the 1930s, he helped draft the *Poetics of Music,* which Stravinsky delivered at Harvard University in 1940–41. But in 1939 Stravinsky moved permanently to the United States. And in the 1940s he appeared to be drying up, devoting his time to the reorchestration of old scores and to unsuccessful attempts to write for Hollywood. This left Souvchinsky hungering for a new talent.

Boulez was the man; and so, immediately after their first meeting, Souvchinsky brought him to Suzanne Tezenas, a charming and cultivated woman. Blond, slender, then in her forties, Tezenas presided over an elegant apartment on rue Octave Feuillet in the fashionable sixteenth arrondissement. The high-ceilinged apartment was crammed with books piled on tables and lining walls, and abstract paintings mounted and stacked behind every piece of furniture. Two great ceiling-to-floor French windows overlooked carefully ordered gardens. A wood-burning fire, large rubber plants, and small Persian rugs over soft brown carpeting added warmth to Tezenas's pink Venetian living room. Her money came from her family's steel mills; she contributed generously to the arts.

For years Tezenas had been the constant companion of the novelist Pierre Drieu la Rochelle, a gifted writer and poet and a major spokesman for French Fascism during the 1930s and early 1940s. Drieu was a leader of France's largest Fascist party, the Parti Populaire Français. During the German occupation he actively collaborated with the Nazis. With the departure of Gide and Malraux from *La Nouvelle Revue Française,* Drieu became its editor. The articles he published in the NRF and in avowedly Fascist journals caused many of his countrymen to accuse him of opportunism and treason. At the end of the war he chose to commit suicide rather than stand trial as a collaborator. After the war Tezenas tried to reenter French society. On Sunday evenings she held salons, one for painters (de Stael and Dubuffet were her favorites) and one for writers. But none of these salons achieved any striking success.

When Souvchinsky brought Boulez to her apartment, Tezenas was drawn to him at once. She said that while Drieu "always seemed an amateur, Boulez was a strict professional, a man completely apart." Still Boulez did possess qualities in common with Drieu: here was an artist, no doubt about that, one with the faith of a true fanatic; here was a man altogether intolerant of any who disagreed with the way he viewed an idea; here was a man, who, like Drieu, relished confrontation and victory. At their first meeting, three years after Drieu's suicide, Boulez played his Second Sonata for her. It was then that Suzanne Tezenas committed herself to the realization of his ideals.

The first of the many Tezenas-Boulez ventures took place in 1949. The evening was devoted not to Boulez himself or to any European avant-garde group but to Boulez's introduction of one American to Paris. John Cage, then thirty-six years old, still virtually unrecognized at home, hoped to take the Old World by storm.

CHAPTER 21

There is a strong anti-intellectual streak in American culture. Nowhere is it more pronounced than in Southern California, where John Cage was born and grew up. It was this anti-intellectualism that threatened to pull the rug out from under Boulez.

As a boy John studied piano with an aunt, and with a woman composer of bird songs; he neither heard nor played music by the great artists of the past. After graduating from Los Angeles High School he entered Pomona College in Claremont, California, but soon dropped out to travel abroad. In Paris Cage worked with an architect. Then he began to paint and compose in response to painters and composers he met in France. Two piano lessons introduced him to Bach. He was then twenty years old. "I was completely stunned by it," he recalls. "It was just plain beautiful."

In 1930 and 1931, Cage traveled extensively: to Capri, Majorca, Madrid, and Berlin. During these years he devised a mathematical system of composition he hoped would endow his works with a precision comparable to that of Bach's. None of these early pieces survives.

"I am the son of an inventor," Cage said. "I had read Henry Cowell's *New Musical Resources* and copied by hand *The Theory of Rhythm.* I had also read Chavez's *Toward a New Music.* Both works gave me the feeling that everything that was possible in music had already happened. So I thought I could never compose socially important music. Only if I could invent something new, then would I be useful to society. But that seemed unlikely then."

In 1933 Cage sent some inventions and sonatas to Henry Cowell, who had invented tone clusters on the piano and once slipped a darning egg between the strings to alter the sound. Cowell suggested Cage study composition with Schoenberg.

In 1934, Schoenberg, then teaching at UCLA, accepted Cage as a private student despite his inability to pay. Schoenberg did this frequently.

All he asked in return was that the student consecrate his life to music. Cage agreed to do that and studied harmony, counterpoint, and analysis for two years. He found Schoenberg "inspiring but discouraging. Schoenberg very quickly discovered that I had no feeling for harmony, and that it would be useless to try to cultivate it. Once, when I wrote a three-and-a-half-measure subject for a fugue, he told me to save it for my first symphony."

During his two years as student of Schoenberg, Cage met and married the daughter of an Alaskan priest, Xenia Kashevaroff. About the same time he began to work—without pay—for Oscar Fischinger, an abstract filmmaker in Hollywood. Fischinger used squares, circles, and triangles in his films. "Fischinger told me," Cage recalled, "that everything in the world has a spirit that can be released through its sound. I was not inclined towards spiritualism but I began to tap everything I saw. I explored everything through its sound. This led to my first percussion orchestra."

In 1937 Cage accepted the post of composer/pianist to a dance class in Seattle, Washington. He raised enough money to buy three hundred percussion instruments and invited American composers to contribute to the then painfully thin percussion repertory. Varèse's *Ionisation*, scored exclusively for percussion, had been performed in New York and California by then—Cage attended the Los Angeles performance—and that work clearly inspired many compositions. Over one hundred pieces were submitted to Cage, who presented concerts of percussion music each year. His press clippings began to accumulate.

Schoenberg had impressed Cage with the value of structure in music. "Schoenberg convinced me," Cage reported, "that music required structure to differentiate parts of a whole. At first, when I worked with Fischinger, I used the serial technique in connection with musical cells which I did not vary at all. Then I began to work with rhythm. Each piece was based on a number of measures having a square root so that the large lengths have the same relation within the whole that the small lengths have within a unit of it. One could then emphasize the structure at the beginning and move into farreaching variations."

In 1938, to accompany a dance, Cage wrote his first piece for prepared piano. "I followed Cowell's example with the darning egg and put nuts and screws in between the strings." In that way he transformed the instrument into a one-man percussion orchestra and obtained a whole new set of sounds.

Cage followed his first prepared piano piece with a number of others, which were played in a small Manhattan studio and reviewed by composer Lou Harrison, who compared one to the music of Webern. Like most Americans in 1944, Cage had never heard any Webern. But because of Harrison's review he made a special effort to track him down. And he loved what he heard.

> I used to go with my hair on end and sit on the edge of my seat. It was so completely different from anything I'd ever heard. Of course he cannot compare to Schoenberg. Schoenberg is so clearly magnificent. Boulez is responsible for the shift to Webern and I think I understand why. Schoenberg's music is traditional. It continues the past magnificently. Whereas Webern seems to break with the past. For he shook the foundation of sound as discourse in favor of sound as sound itself. But in Webem the supremacy of pitch relations remains. And so he was really tied to an earlier time.

For Cage it was Satie who effectively broke with the past. "In Satie," he said, "the structures have to do with time, not pitch. Virgil Thomson introduced me to Satie just at the time I first heard Webern. I connected the two composers in my mind."

But Webern and Satie are worlds apart. Satie was a Dadaist, in a sense a Duchamp. In *Parade,* written for the Diaghilev ballet, he called for a typewriter, a steam whistle, and a rattle in the instrumentation. A full-fledged inventor who looked at music irreverently, Satie was out to destroy art, not preserve it. With his antisentimental stance, his verbal and musical attacks on culture, and his violent assaults on high art, he soon dominated Webern in Cage's head and heart.

In 1946 Cage enrolled in D. T. Suzuki's class in Zen Buddhism at Columbia University and wrote *Sonatas and Interludes,* a seventy-minute work for prepared piano that reflected a new absorption with the East. *Sonatas and Interludes* was first performed at Carnegie Recital Hall in New York and was well received by both the press and private foundations. The National Institute of Arts and Letters presented Cage with an award, and the Guggenheim Foundation gave him a grant to work abroad. In 1949 Cage went to Paris and stayed for six months. He planned to do research on Satie and to look into the European scene. Virgil Thomson, who had been instrumental in securing the Guggenheim for him, suggested he look up Pierre Boulez.

Immediately after moving into his hotel, Cage walked the short distance to 4 rue Beautreillis and left scores, records, and a note for Boulez.

Quickly and enthusiastically, Boulez showed up at his door with the material in his hand. They became friends. Cage found Boulez "stimulating and exciting, always surrounded by interesting people." Boulez found Cage "refreshing, genuine in his search for new material." They saw each other often during the next few months.

Cage enjoyed the Boulez entourage: poet Armand Gatti, a renegade Catholic and later a left-wing dramatist; mathematician-painter Bernard Saby, probably the closest of Boulez's friends, whom Boulez describes as an "expert in Chinese culture, butterflies, and moss"; journalist Pierre Joffroy, who later wrote a book about a Christian S.S. man; and Pierre Souvchinsky, one generation older than the rest. Walking along the Seine, Boulez and Cage exchanged ideas. In each other's rooms they ate and drank. But Boulez never offered any confidences; his friendships were at best tenuous. He explained that he finally broke with Saby "because I found his work uninteresting. There's no reason to continue a friendship after that. To be faithful is just nonsense. I didn't say anything. I just disappeared."

Still, in 1949, Boulez found Cage's work interesting, and Cage did a great deal for Boulez. Thirteen years older and better connected than he, Cage promoted Boulez to Phillippe Heugel and Amphion, two influential music publishers in France. He told them he had an invitation from Henry Cowell, then publisher of New Music Editions in New York, to publish Boulez's scores. Hervé Dugardin of Amphion replied that he had had Boulez's Flute Sonatina and First Piano Sonata on his desk but had not yet made a decision about them. However, he said, this was a "French problem." The next morning Cage brought Boulez to Heugel and Amphion and a deal was made to publish everything Boulez wanted published then. Heugel would publish *Le Visage Nuptial, Le Soleil des Eaux, Livre pour Quatuor*, and the Second Sonata; Amphion, the Sonatina for Flute and Piano and the First Sonata. That evening there was a great celebration; it was the night before Cage was to return to the United States. Souvchinsky brought all his friends together at Gatti's; Cage and Merce Cunningham were there and everyone rejoiced in Boulez's triumph.

On his part Boulez did what he could for Cage. He introduced him to Messiaen who invited him to the Paris Conservatoire to demonstrate the prepared piano in class. He also brought him to Suzanne Tezenas. She, Souvchinsky, and Boulez prepared a guest list of one hundred artists and made plans to present Cage's *Sonatas and Interludes*. The afternoon of the performance, Cage spent three hours carefully inserting objects into the piano that he had chosen for the work. Suzanne Tezenas watched with apprehension as Cage poured cognac into her Bechstein to weaken the glue between the strings so he could move the hammers in a way that would secure the effect he had in mind.

The evening of the performance the living room was jammed. Chairs were set up close together and Cunningham lay stretched out on the floor between the foyer and the living room. Boulez introduced Cage with a careful lecture in which he emphasized that Cage was a Schoenberg pupil and analyzed the rhythmic structure of the work. Whatever innovations Cage brought with him that night, chance operation was not one of them. Cage had not been away from Schoenberg long enough to have lost his ties to structure in art.

Still, there were enough innovations. *Sonatas and Interludes* was probably the first Western work to have been nourished so lavishly by the East. It was also probably the first Western work in which the printed score didn't begin to tell the story. Thirdly, it was probably the first serious work that transformed the generally sacrosanct piano. Over and above everything else, the celebrated invention, the prepared piano, challenged accepted ideas of acoustics and pinpointed the technological impoverishment—in contrast to ideological advance—that characterized music up to mid-century.

The work was also an eloquent reminder of how, in the West, harmony had been cultivated at the expense of rhythm. *Sonatas and Interludes*'s highly structured metrical scheme plus its highly structured distribution of sounds and pauses made Boulez and Cage aesthetic comrades. That Boulez took his cues from Webern while Cage took his cues from Satie should have served as sufficient notice to both that their paths would diverge radically. But neither composer foresaw how radically at that time.

CHAPTER 22

hat Boulez set out to do was "to strip music of its accumulated dirt and give it the structure it had lacked since the Renaissance." He went into it, "with exaltation and fear. It was like Descartes's 'Cogito, ergo sum.' I momentarily suppressed inheritance. I started from the fact that I was thinking and went on to construct a musical language from scratch."

As Boulez constructed serialism "from scratch," Cage constructed chance operation from scratch. The letters they exchanged between 1949 and 1952 reveal the development of their thoughts as each formulated the *idée fixe* of his life. Neither one ever changed his fundamental concept about music.

In 1950 Boulez left for South America with the Barrault company; it was his first trip outside France. Just after he left Paris, a young woman played his Second Piano Sonata at the Salle de l'École Normale de Musique. One of Boulez's friends described the event in a letter to Cage that includes not only his judgment of her performance but an elaborate picture of Parisian musical life and of the hostility that greeted the new language:

> The interpretation, while quite decent, was pitiful. I heard at least 25 times the main passage of this sonata played by Pierre. I assure you it was very different in the hands of this pianist. According to Souvchinsky she took seven minutes longer to play the entire piece than it normally requires. But all this did not warrant in any way the reactions of the audience. From the very first bars, three quarters of the audience smiled with already prepared smiles and shrugging of shoulders. Already in the first movement I felt compelled to call two women utter fools and to threaten another with knocking her block off. The rest of the audience only increased by tenfold the hostility already

rampant. The women—low breed which should be extermi-
nated by using red hot pokers on their stomachs—were
exultant. Sighs of boredom, invitation cards that they
were passing along to each other on which they had put
next to Boulez's name the number ZERO. At one point a
few respectable musicians (and they do exist here and there
in the world) felt the need to shout vehemently and
indignantly, "Have you quite finished your stupid antics?"
(The music being performed then was that of Boulez.)
Fortunately for the performance Max Deutsch demanded
silence in imperative tones and obtained it. The scene ended
with some exaggeratedly heavy applause (provided by a
few of Boulez's friends) and a general lethargy on the part
of a slightly amused audience. I went out without hearing the
rest of the concert, shouting all the coarsest language
I could muster. "It would be necessary to put a bomb in
your vagina before you could ever understand that! You
should all have your balls smashed in! Bunch of bastards
etc. etc." A short while later Joffroy met me, accompanied
by Saby and Souvchinsky. We spent the night going from
one bistro to the next to get rid of some of the bitterness
we felt. We tippled until we were completely drunk. Not
a single music critic in any one of the daily papers thought
it wise to discuss the work. The few who bothered into
it at all were to a one surprised that the public did not boo.
Quite the contrary, they were full of encomiums—as was
the public, moreover, for this poor ass Martinet whose
sorry "fugue" sounded like a song by Edith Piaf. The
whole affair made me ill for two days. Now things have
fallen into perspective and I view it all with more equanimity.
Unfortunately this poor lady must play the Second Sonata
again at the Sorbonne around the end of the month. (If in
the meantime we could at least graft a pair of testicles to
her.) The only felicitous aspect of this story is that
Pierre, having left the day before for South America
(with Barrault and company) did not attend the circus
that accompanied the performance of his piece and the
irremediable mess that was made of his work.

On learning that Boulez was in South America, Cage contacted the

International Institute in Middlebury, Vermont, to arrange for Boulez to give two lectures there. Cage hoped that such an engagement would help Boulez obtain a United States visa. Boulez responded with delight. But he could not obtain a visa in Buenos Aires, so he did not see Cage for another two years.

From South America Boulez wrote Cage that he was orchestrating *Le Visage Nuptial*. "It is easier to reorchestrate an old work while one is constantly changing one's environment than it is to create an entirely new work." But he also began to compose something new. He referred to it to Cage as a "work-in-progress"; otherwise he was guarded about it. "It would be premature for me to talk about it at length. Silence is more prudent and I shall break it only later. I can tell you at any rate that it will not be easily accessible."

On his return to France, Boulez plunged into *Polyphonie X*. Based on the organization of rhythmic cells to which all other elements remain subservient, it displays serial organization of the most relentless kind. Boulez said that the X in the title is neither a letter of the alphabet nor an algebraic symbol. "It is rather a graphic symbol. I called the work *Polyphonie X* because it is based on certain structures which intersect each other in the sense of augmentation and diminution. It is in the series of the rhythmic cells that the main point of the work can be found."

One day while at work on this piece Boulez received a visit from Heinrich Strobel, director of the Southwest German Radio, who had been told to look up the composer in Paris by Marcel Mihalovici, a conservative composer of operas but a man who, Strobel later said, at least understood the merit of Boulez. Like Souvchinsky, Strobel had a nose for talent and had spent his life in the arts. A student of Paul Klee's at the Bauhaus, he moved into music in his early adulthood and contributed to the music journal *Melos*. In Berlin, before the war, Strobel had held radio interviews with Schoenberg, and had published books on Stravinsky, Hindemith, and Debussy, fighting for Hindemith and the neoclassical Stravinsky. He hated Webern and Berg at that time; according to Boulez, he could "not stand the hysterical post-Wagnerian sound."

In Baden-Baden, Strobel became editor of *Melos* and director of the regional radio system as well. In 1945 he combined it with the city's orchestra as the Südwestfunk and engaged Hans Rosbaud as its conductor. In the winter of 1950, when Strobel made his first postwar trip to Paris, he was open to the discovery of a great talent and was certain he had found him when he met Boulez.

Seated at his composition table, Boulez was wrapped in a blanket (the small stove gave little warmth) and surrounded by a number of serial charts. Strobel later wrote:

I was fascinated by this young man with his sharp stare, his very progressive ideas, and a charm that did not fit at all the description I'd been given of this *enfant terrible* of the avant-garde.

P.B. was at work on a score. The notes were so tiny, as tiny as the feet of a fly. About him were pieces of charts that would seem to have more properly belonged to a mathematician. The composition he was writing was *Polyphonie X*. I decided immediately to do it for the first performance of the festival I planned for Donaueschingen, near Baden-Baden, scheduled for October 1951.

Strobel's festival became an annual attraction, providing what was probably the most important marketplace for new music in Europe. All the heads of German radio stations came, composition students came. Recalling the first performance Strobel wrote, "*Polyphonie X* was the greatest scandal I went through after the war. Unfortunately, the press, in writing about the work today, still uses some of the pejorative phrases it used at the premiere. But those who knew anything at all knew that this was a very special work, one that in both structure and color opened completely new paths."

Rosbaud reportedly hated the piece, but it is difficult to determine whether that alone made for what was generally deemed an inadequate performance. Boulez was in London with Barrault, so he was spared the disastrous reception of the work. The audience responded with whistles, hisses, and boos. Still, the specialists celebrated it. Strobel told Souvchinsky, "Boulez is a genius." Souvchinsky replied, "He is a Mozart."

On his return from London, Boulez heard a tape of the Donaueschingen performance and must have concluded that even the most disciplined, professional musicians could not have executed the work with any degree of fidelity. Possibly prompted by the distance between the intention and execution of both his Second Piano Sonata and *Polyphonie X*, Boulez turned to electronics. Theory held that the electronic instrument could do what the performer and conventional instrument could not. Joining the Groupe Recherche de la Radiodiffusion Française, recently founded by Pierre Schaeffer, Boulez produced *Deux Études* for magnetic tape. But his liaison with the center was a stormy one. In a letter to Cage, Boulez wrote that the shouting match between Schaeffer and himself would provide "enough material for a thick portfolio. Schaeffer," he added, "is a bastard."

In 1949, before Boulez began *Polyphonie X*, Messiaen had published his

Quatre Etudes de Rythme of which the second, entitled *Mode de Valeurs et d'Intensités*, was probably the first European composition which extended the serial principle beyond pitch to the other musical elements. The work was organized in this way: a melodic series of thirty-six notes, a rhythmic series of twenty-four durations, a dynamic series of seven attacks, and an additional series of seven intensities. (The work is for piano, therefore timbre does not undergo permutation.) This fourfold determination is then set into three-part canon. Despite the imposition of such mathematical formulas, the *Mode de Valeurs et d'Intensités* is expressive, extroverted music. Messiaen used his formulas in a free and romantic way. After the completion of this work he chose not to pursue the path of total organization.

It was left to Boulez to remove the trimmings, to make music "from scratch," to go, in a sense, bone dry. "This was the zero point of writing," he said. "What I was after was the most impersonal material. Personality had to be involved, of course, in bringing the mechanism into action, but then it could disappear after that. To have the personality not at all involved was a necessity for a while."

Boulez did not merely adopt Messiaen's technique; he complicated it considerably. In place of a rather straightforward method, Boulez developed a most intricate mechanism which appears to have been designed to transmute his private anguish and joy into something distant, universal, and cold. In *Structures* even the smallest aspect of each musical event undergoes a perpetual transformation. Thus each pitch never recurs with the same duration, the same intensity, or the same attack. A staggering multiplicity of combinations occurs. Boulez has said, "Messiaen dealt with modes which were static. Everything was held together from beginning to end. When I took his material, I untied the various characteristics and made them work independently."

Going one step further than the HCAB of the Second Sonata, Boulez planned the work to be an *Art of the Fugue* for the serial language. It was to consist, Boulez said, of three large books covering all aspects of the grammar. Book I, written in 1952, includes three pieces numbered 1a, 1b and 1c. 1a exposes the basic material, which is stated in the opening measures. The four basic constituents remain clearly defined throughout the piece: 1a concentrates on pitch and duration; 1b on differences in attack; 1c superimposes contrasts of dynamics on the other elements. To reduce rehearsal problems Boulez scored the work for two pianos, but he more than compensated for this instrumental limitation by pushing the piano to incredible lengths.

The excitement of the instrumental writing saves the work from being suffocated by its pedagogy. Indeed, Boulez said he sensed the dead end implied in his relentless application of the Idea and therefore inscribed on the first page of Book I a provisional title he took from a painting by Paul Klee: *À la limite du fertile pays* (At the limit of fertile ground).

Perhaps to effect a reconciliation with Messiaen, with whom he had broken in 1948 (Boulez ascribes the break to "the inevitable disenchantment that comes after one has made a tour of someone"), and possibly to compensate Messiaen for having exploited his idea, the younger composer borrowed the row the older one had used for the *Mode de Valeurs et d'Intensités*—a deferential act. "It was a test," he said, "with borrowed material. The piece is based on choice at very important moments; then the structures are generated by the automatism of the numerical relations." In 1952 Boulez and Messiaen collaborated in a performance of *Structures* in Paris. Just before they went on stage Boulez whispered to a friend, "I hope it goes well. I believe in it." The work became a milestone in postwar music.

While in pursuit of total serialism, Boulez wrote intermittently to Cage, alternating trenchant comments about "neoclassic" composers with enthusiastic comments about the Viennese: "In Paris Horenstein will soon perform *Wozzeck* by Berg, a piece which I find more and more remarkable by its complexity, at times undecipherable, resembling the Labyrinth without Ariadne's thread. He will have fifteen orchestra rehearsals and I shall do my best not to miss one. It should be quite an event and I am exultant beyond belief."

But the most important aspect of the correspondence was Boulez's definition of serialism. In 1952 the critical letter arrived. (Because Boulez never dated letters, it is impossible to be more precise as to when.) His minuscule writing covers every millimeter of six sides of tissue-thin pages, articulating the details of the technique, listing the parameters in the following order: frequency, timbre, intensity, and duration. Almost immediately he published an expanded treatment of the letter in an article entitled "Eventuellement" published in *La Revue Musicale*. Tables, graphs, algebraic symbols abound. Boulez writes: "We must expand the means of a technique already discovered: that technique having been, up to now, a destructive object linked, for that very reason, to what it has wanted to destroy [tonality]. Our first determination will be to give it autonomy, and, furthermore, to link rhythmic structures to serial structures by common organizations, which will also include the other characteristics of sound: intensity, mode of attack, timbre. Then to enlarge that morphology into a coalescent rhetoric."

Manuscript copies of this aesthetic treatise were circulated around Paris as though it were a call to arms. This was the basic message: "Anyone who has not felt—I do not say understand—but felt the necessity of the dodecaphonic language is USELESS. For everything he writes will fall short of the imperatives of his time."

What Boulez shared with Cage was the need to destroy the tonal language. But he said that by 1952 he knew serialism would not be Cage's means. Cage's personality and correspondence left no doubt about that.

After returning from Paris in 1949, Cage wrote Sixteen Dances for a small orchestra and Concerto for Prepared Piano and Chamber Orchestra. He composed them both

> as a bridge between the earlier pieces and chance. It was then I began to work with the Magic Square, a square with an uneven number of squares. Boulez had been working with a similar diagram at the time, but he put numbers into the squares whereas I put in aggregates of sounds. They had no relation to harmony. They had no necessary direction. Each was a musical fact, without any implication at all. If one moves in this way one produces a continuity of sound that has nothing to do with harmony and is freed, at the same time, from the imposition of one's own taste.

Shortly after he had developed the Magic Square, Cage learned of an Oriental idea that insured, he thought, the removal of himself from the creative process. One evening in 1950 he attended a performance of Webern's Opus 21 and met composer Morton Feldman and pianist David Tudor. A sort of club formed: Cage, Feldman, Tudor, and a young high school student, Christian Wolff. Just after they met, Wolff brought Cage the two volumes of *I Ching*, the *Book of Changes*, a collection of ancient Chinese oracles translated into English by Richard Wilhelm.

Fascinated by the similarities of the tools in *I Ching* and those of his own work, Cage began to compose the *Music of Changes*. To determine each of his musical moves he would toss a coin. This is how he made the piece: Cage drew twenty-six large charts. To plot a single note, he tossed three coins six times. The results, noted down on paper, would direct him to a particular number in *I Ching* which, in turn, would correspond to a numbered position on the chart. That position would determine only the pitch of the note. The entire procedure would be repeated over and over again to determine the note's duration, timbre, and other elements. Cage applied the principle of the Magic Square to "all," he emphasizes, "the parameters of sound." The *Music of Changes* was to be Cage's *Structures*.

Only in retrospect do *Music of Changes* and *Structures* seem far apart. Indeed, until 1952 each man graciously acknowledged the other. In "Eventuellement" Boulez declared that "Cage's direction is too similar to my own for me not to take note of it." And in *Transformations,* a short-lived art journal emanating from New York, in which articles by Boulez and Cage stood side by side, Boulez articulated a philosophy which implied compatibility between serialism and chance: "We may conceive of musical structure from a dual viewpoint: on the one hand the activities of serial combinations where the structures are generated by the automatism of the numerical relations; on the other, directed and interchangeable combinations where the arbitrary plays a much larger role. The two ways of viewing musical structure can clearly furnish a dialectic and extremely efficacious means of musical development."

CHAPTER 23

In June 1951 Boulez attended a two-week festival of the arts that was being held at the Abbaye de Royaumont just outside Paris. Musicians came from all over Europe. It was there he met Henri Pousseur, the first composer to join his quest for a new and pervasive order in art.

Pousseur was born in 1929 in Malmedy, a small town on the Belgian-German border. He said that as a child he was "fanatic" about Mozart. He heard his first Schoenberg piece when he was ten. It struck him as "something bitter, something sour."

In 1947 Pousseur attended the Liège Conservatoire. When he first arrived, he and his young musical friends clustered around a young teacher, Pierre Froidebise, a specialist in fifteenth- and sixteenth-century organ practice who was interested in contemporary music as well. For his students, Froidebise bought Leibowitz's recently published books on Schoenberg and the 12-tone school.

Pousseur said, "I was thrown by this group when I first came to Liège. I was seduced by the intellectual aspect of new music. I had always been interested in the constructive aspect of music, and when I heard about dodecaphony, it opened my mind and ears."

In 1949 several of his friends went to Paris and met Boulez, who

was not absolutely central then, not like Froidebise was to us. At that time he had written an article for *La Revue Musicale* on the rhythm and athematicism in his Sonatina for Flute and Piano and the article was discussed a good deal. And, because it was the two hundredth anniversary of Bach's death, he was writing an essay for *Contrepoint* in which he defined the role of Webern clearly; his point was that the parallel was not between Bach and Schoenberg—as so often had been claimed by Leibowitz—but that it was between Bach and Webern.

Just after I read that essay I heard Webern for the first time. The occasion was the International Society for Contemporary Music—the year was 1950—and the work was Webern's Second Cantata, the one Boulez discussed in his essay on Bach. It was done divinely. Those intervals were sung with such facility. There was such purity of sound. It was then that I made the distinction in my mind that Schoenberg was expressionistic and Webern was not.

The following June, Froidebise paid Pousseur's expenses for the trip to Paris so that he could attend the festival at the Abbaye. Pousseur showed Boulez his tonal Mass and an earlier 12-tone work, *The Seven Verses of the Pentecost Psalms.* "Boulez put the *Mass* aside right away," Pousseur recalled,

and carefully looked at the other work. We played it together at the piano, four hands. Boulez showed me the technique of intervals. He showed me what to do so it could be correct in the Webernian sense There were several techniques, easy enough to describe: (1) Don't use leading intervals, use a major seventh instead of a leading tone; (2) if you have a note return in another octave, place a chromatic note between, not only in time but in register—so you can rub out the initial note; (3) do not repeat the same interval or the same group of notes in the same way; have the group reversed.

Boulez's objective was to move Pousseur away from the treatment of intervals in a melodic context towards the treatment of intervals in a more structural way. Schoenberg often used minor seconds and sevenths, which would supersede everything else he did and reinforce a tonal base. And even when Schoenberg did not do that, his traditional treatment of rhythm often gave the notes the sound of a baroque score just a little bit out of tune.

To illustrate his lesson, Boulez lent Pousseur the tape of Desormière's performance of *Le Soleil des Eaux* along with the score. He also showed him the score of his Second Piano Sonata and *Polyphonie X.* "I was absolutely fascinated," Pousseur said, "for Boulez helped me to understand that Webern was not an end but a real beginning. By meeting him, all the elements had been put in place. Boulez provided the real center."

During the weeks at the Abbaye de Royaumont, Boulez spoke to Pousseur about Pierre Schaeffer's studio and how he had made his *Deux Études* for magnetic tape. He explained how he had produced permutations of tape. "In criticizing Schaeffer's methods," Pousseur said,

> Boulez showed me exactly what he wanted to do. He wanted to restructure the material so he could have complete control. He wanted to unify the germ, to unify the seed, to have everything grow from one idea, and to apply a very precise, a very structured type of elaboration. The first piece of *Structures* is an example of that, without electronic means, of course. There is one series of numbers in a very automatic scheme. In duration it is very clear. In other words, the scheme of duration is not newly created but derived from the initial pitch row. Everything is based on the principle of permutation. There are no perceptible relations, only statistically derived relations.

Boulez's music at this moment was based on the quantification of pitch and rhythm. It was totally abstract. Boulez's need for an anchor for his imagination was shared by his young colleagues and the compass they chose was that of a large square, filled with boxes numbered from one through twelve, that charted their way through a musical work. But no logical perceptual law, no physical acoustical law connects Duration No. 2 with Pitch or Timbre No. 2, nor Dynamic No. 4 with Pitch or Timbre No. 4. Although the box could allow the composer to permute absolutely anything, the method by which choices were made had virtually nothing to do with the way listeners would perceive a work. The system was totally arithmetical; it seemed, in 1950–51, to be a logical outgrowth of Webern's Opus 21 Symphony.

On July 13, 1951, one month after Boulez's meeting with Pousseur, Arnold Schoenberg died. Reflecting on the death Boulez said:

> Of course I was not especially touched. Schoenberg was to me part of the mystic adoration of Leibowitz. The Leibowitz cult was repulsive to me, as repulsive as the Stravinsky cult. And Leibowitz was a joke. I never forgave his dishonesty. He was serviceable at the beginning, but I began to resent him when I saw how narrow and stupid he

was. His analyses of Schoenberg are an arithmetical count-down. His book is a compilation of Adorno and Willi Reich.

Cult always kills the man at the center. Look how repul-sive Schoenberg became: 'I have discovered a method to save German music.' He opened the field but he closed a lot too. The last third of his life was terribly academic. With Opus 25, his work is not attractive anymore. Opus 31 is a lesson in counterpoint and variation. In it he pursues the aesthetic of Brahms. I don't find it very interesting to go back to Brahms.

During the winter of 1951–52, Boulez wrote Cage that it was necessary to demolish the Schoenberg cult. He said that in Schoenberg the series is only the lowest common denominator and that the real reason for Schoenberg's failure lay in his lack of understanding of the structural, not the thematic, function of the series. He told Cage of an essay that he had written for the English journal, *The Score*. In it he killed Schoenberg and crowned Webern. The title of the piece: "Schoenberg is DEAD!"

It is easy to forget that a certain Webern also labored; to be sure, one never hears this discussed anymore. . . . Perhaps we can see that the series is a logically historical conse-quence, or, depending on what one wishes, a historically logical one. Perhaps, like a certain Webern, one could pursue the sound EVIDENCE by trying to derive the structure from the material. . . .

Perhaps one could generalize the serial principle to the four sound constituents: pitch, duration, intensity and attack, timbre. Perhaps . . . perhaps . . . one could demand from a composer some imagination, a certain dose of asceticism, even a little intelligence, and finally a sensibility that will not be toppled by the smallest breeze.

It has become indispensable to demolish a misunder-standing that is full of ambiguity and contradiction; it is time to neutralize the setback. That correction will not be accom-plished by gratuitous bragging, much less by sanctimonious fatuity, but by rigor free of weakness and compromise. Therefore I do not hesitate to write, not out of any desire to provoke a stupid scandal, but equally without hypocrisy and pointless melancholy: SCHOENBERG IS DEAD.

It is not altogether surprising that a young Frenchman, passionate in his hatred of his personal past and raised in the tradition of annihilating the historic past—Leibowitz's attack on Stravinsky provided an eloquent model for that—should embark on as strong an effort to liquidate Schoenberg as this. What is surprising is his success in recruiting disciples both in and out of France and in maintaining his leadership as long as he did. When he finally was dethroned, it was at the hands of his own "favorite son," the tall, slender German Karlheinz Stockhausen, three years younger than he and a very green composer when the two first met. What Boulez had done to Leibowitz and Schoenberg, Stockhausen would finally do to Boulez.

In January 1952, seven months after Boulez enlisted Pousseur, he met and made a strong impression on Stockhausen, who had come to Paris to study at the Conservatoire. Stockhausen also made a strong impression on Boulez. "I recall the first meeting very well," Boulez said. "I knew no German. Stockhausen knew no French. A friend, Louis Sauger, translated. We gesticulated wildly. I knew immediately that here was someone exceptional. I was right. I came to trust his music more than anything else. We talked about music all the time—in a way I've never talked about it with anyone else."

Stockhausen was born on August 22, 1928, the first child of poor people from a rural background. His father was an elementary school teacher; his mother had three children in the first three years of her marriage. Soon after the last, she began to suffer an extreme depression and was committed to a mental hospital in 1933. She died there eight years later, when Karlheinz was thirteen years old; "officially killed," he claims. Karlheinz's father was killed in battle in Hungary when Karlheinz was only seventeen.

Stockhausen spent much of his early life in a Catholic monastery. He graduated from a gymnasium in 1947 and then attended the State Academy in Cologne. There he studied piano and music education, all the while earning his living playing piano in Cologne bars, serving as accompanist to an amateur operetta theater, and providing background music for a magician's act.

At that time he was familiar with almost every work by Schoenberg, Stravinsky, and Bartók but knew only one piece by Anton Webern—the Five Movements for String Quartet Opus 5. Stockhausen composed two pieces in 1950–51: Three Songs for Alto and Chamber Orchestra and a Sonata for Violin and Piano. The strongest influence on both was Schoenberg.

During the summer of 1951, when dodecaphony was the prevailing aesthetic at Darmstadt, Stockhausen attended the summer school there and met the composer Karel Goeyvaerts who had just completed his studies with Milhaud and begun to study under Messiaen. Goeyvaerts had seen the score of Messiaen's *Mode de Valeurs et d'Intensités* and had taken off from it in much the manner that Boulez had: by writing a rigid, totally serial piece. Indeed Stockhausen subsequently claimed, when he was trying to undermine Boulez, that Goeyvaerts's piece, a Sonata for Two Pianos, which he and Goeyvaerts played in Adorno's composition seminar at Darmstadt, predates Boulez's far more famous *Structures*. But Boulez disclaims any importance to priority in this instance. "Goeyvaerts is an invention of Stockhausen's. He was to me what Hauer was to Schoenberg."

Boulez's depreciation of Goeyvaerts's talent is echoed by other specialists in the field. Still, Stockhausen was young and awed by Goeyvaerts—he named him godfather to his first child—and he followed Goeyvaerts's example by going to Paris in the late winter of 1952 to study under Messiaen. That is when he met Boulez.

Immediately, under the influence of the slightly older and immensely powerful man, Stockhausen made the shift from Schoenberg to Webern and to an extension of the serial principle to areas other than pitch relations. Within a year Stockhausen returned to Cologne and the post-Webern movement took roots in Germany.

And so, for one long intense moment in the early 1950s, Boulez, Pousseur, and Stockhausen were at one in their efforts to establish serialism as a common language and to seduce all those they could to the celebration of Webern.

CHAPTER 24

When John Cage returned to the United States after his 1949 visit to Paris, he did everything he could to promote Boulez in America. But by 1952, after Boulez spent several months in New York, the break between them was irreparable.

When Boulez was traveling with Barrault in South America in 1950 and working on *Polyphonie X* and *Structures* in Paris, Cage was writing articles about him for American music journals and expounding eloquently about his work to private foundations. First he persuaded the League of Composers to program Boulez's Second Sonata with David Tudor as pianist for a concert in December 1950. The *Times* critic was more open-minded than the French critics had been: "The music was scattered all over the keyboard in rapid, surrealist patterns that could hardly be apprehended. Composed in the twelve-tone technique, the work was consistently arhythmic, athematic (in the usual sense), and its sonorities were acerbic."

Thus in the fall of 1952, when Boulez made his first trip to the United States to conduct and play *ondes martenot* for the Renaud-Barrault theater, he came also as an artist in his own right. The way had been paved for him by Cage. Lillian Keisler, widow of the architect and sculptor Frederick Keisler, recalled that "Boulez was the White Knight of the time. I remember a performance of his work at Carl Fischer Hall. All the abstract expressionists came. His name was legendary even among painters. We knew that conventional music had been carried to its limits and that here was a genius, a genius who brought a tidal wave of the new."

The "new" that Boulez brought was still hysterical and passionate; the Second Sonata was played a great deal. But it hovered on the brink of the secretive as well. Virgil Thomson has written that Boulez "loves the deeply calculated," and Boulez was not alone in this.

Perhaps to resist the increasing popularization and, on occasion, the vulgarization of art which had flourished under neoclassicism and socialist realism and had been encouraged by radio and films, perhaps to restore a more intellectually aristocratic elite, many artists—both in Europe and the United States—began to build on the refined, inaccessible language that had its roots earlier in the century. This is not to say that it was the intent of Schoenberg, Kandinsky, or Pound to be as hermetic as they were; it is rather to point out that inaccessibility was certainly a consequence of what each of them did. But those artists who came of age after World War II elevated this secondary consequence to a primary purpose. For Boulez, James Joyce was a critical symbol. He had read *Ulysses* in French, and an exhibit in 1949 at Le Hune bookshop in Paris increased his excitement about Joyce's work. Recalling what drew him to Joyce, Boulez cites the "specificity of technique for each chapter, the fact that technique and story were one. The technique reflected exactly what Joyce meant; it was rich and I had never met it before in a book."

But it was *Finnegans Wake* that overwhelmed the group. In a letter to Cage written in December 1949, a young French poet wrote:

> The advent of *Finnegans Wake* at Pierre's has not yet finished provoking many arguments and discussions. There were several stormy sessions on Rue Beautreillis where the tone of things reached such a high pitch that the vocabulary consisted of several forceful "merdes" which each of the participants flung at each other without any mental reservation concerning the parsimony of the words used.
>
> If by now the heated arguments have abated somewhat, discussions are still frequent on the subject. I must admit, to be completely objective, that after experiencing Joyce in a very serious way my admiration for Faulkner has vanished.

It is possible that technique alone did not draw Boulez to Joyce for the similarities between the two artists transcend technique. Both Boulez and Joyce were raised devout Catholics; both became disenchanted when they were still young. Both were clearly in search of a father, a search that dominated both men's lives. (Leopold Bloom was to Stephen Dedalus what Barrault, Souvchinsky, and Strobel were to Boulez.) Both moved towards revolution in the political arena but neither liked manifestos when drawn up by others. Art alone was the route for Joyce and Boulez. It gave them the stature and dignity they sought. Able to renounce the dogma they had been taught, each cast his own revolution in the most dogmatic of aesthetic terms. Thus Boulez built *Structures* on a medieval-like musical language with its secrets hidden from the public at large. Like *Finnegans Wake*, which inspired numerous "skeleton keys" and "guides," *Structures* inspired musical analyses. That the traditional value of beauty played virtually no role in Boulez's conception is revealed by a passage Boulez wrote to Cage on the eve of his trip to New York: "Soon Monroe Street will see us and hear us. Tell David Tudor, whom I am very eager to know, that he should get some aspirin ready—I am doing as much myself—for *Structures* is not easy to listen to. But since he has worked on your *Music of Changes* (here Boulez makes a diagram excerpting CAGE from CHANGES) I would say he is properly prepared."

When Boulez arrived in New York he moved into Cage's loft on the Lower East Side. Cage's studio had white walls, no "art" on display, and two windows overlooking the East River that he had carved out of the solid wall by himself. A piano dominated the room. There was a studio couch but no chairs. Visitors sat on straw mats on the floor. Cage moved out so that Boulez could move in.

At the first meeting of Cage, Tudor, and Boulez, Tudor played parts of Cage's *Music of Changes* in the Grand Street loft. This was Cage's realization of the Magic Square, in which coin-tossing determined all the elements of every note played. For the first time in many years Cage used the piano without special preparation. He did not abandon, however, his interest in inventing new sounds and called for the instrument to be plucked from the inside as though it were a huge guitar. But he focused his attention on structure through rhythm. "What I did," Cage explained, "was to develop rhythmic structure from a fixed tempo to changes of tempo. I had not yet moved to a renunciation of absolutely all structure."

Tudor played the entire work for Boulez, who appeared genuinely excited by the sounds. But from the start, Tudor adds, "he was unsympathetic to the idea of chance. He responded politely but it was clear that he was more than hostile to the loss of control." The work presented no real surprises to Boulez who had anticipated his response to Cage's method in a letter he wrote to Cage shortly before he left France. In it he declared: "By temperament I cannot toss a coin. . . . Chance must be very well controlled. *Il y a suffisamment d'inconnu.* [There is already enough unknown.]"

Boulez's duties with the Renaud-Barrault theater allowed him to move about a good deal on his own. He dined several times at Virgil Thomson's and met important musicians there. Cage had a Model A Ford—already an antique—and he, Tudor, and Boulez visited friends in Stony Point, New York, and took a trip to Cape Cod to introduce Boulez to M. C.

Richards, who had translated Antonin Artaud in the United States. Boulez also wrote an article of homage to Webern which was published in the *New York Herald Tribune*:

> We are only beginning now to perceive the novelty of the horizons that Webern has opened to us . . . and when we consider the limited number of his works, we are astonished at the importance of his contribution. His work has become the threshold to the music of the future, and its role as such is unfortunately obscured when we think of it in terms of what has been too hastily labeled: "Schoenberg and his disciple."

Boulez gave performances of his own work at Carl Fischer Hall, at the Peabody Conservatory in Baltimore, at a lecture in a course by Henry Cowell entitled "Musical Iconoclasts: 2700 B.C. through 1952 A.D." at the New School in Greenwich Village, and at a Composer's Forum concert at Columbia University's McMillin Theater. Boulez moderated the Columbia event, which was devoted to electronic music from the Schaeffer studio in Paris. Works by Messiaen, Pierre Henry, Andre Hodeir, and Boulez (the *Deux Études* and *Structures*) were played. In discussing the work with the audience, Boulez said that his fundamental purpose was to eliminate from his vocabulary all trace of his musical inheritance in an effort to start from scratch and reconquer, little by little, the various states of composition and arrive at a wholly new synthesis. Despite what he said, there were ghosts in Boulez's world, for he aimed to emulate Webern, who drew on Schoenberg, who drew on Wagner and Brahms.

New York Times reviewer Arthur Berger, the American neoclassic composer stemming from Stravinsky via Aaron Copland, hit Boulez where it hurt most: "Shifts of register occur indiscriminately, without any nuance and textural variety that we find in Anton Webern, of whom Boulez considers himself a disciple." Neoclassicism still had the upper hand in the United States; the avant-garde had made little progress as of 1952, so Berger's comments should be viewed in the context of the establishment's efforts to crush the revolutionaries, as was the case in France. But in his statement, Berger touches on something valid: although Boulez repeatedly claimed he was tied to Webern, his more audible ties in the early years were to Debussy and Messiaen. To say this is not to deny the fact that Boulez's technique was infinitely more complex, even at that stage, than that of either Debussy or Messiaen. It is rather to emphasize that Boulez's attachment to

Webern was more ideational than musical at that moment in his career, for Webern was never drawn to the dense texture or large form that characterize Boulez's early work.

Shortly before Boulez returned to Paris an important concert took place at the Cherry Lane Theater in Greenwich Village. It included Boulez's Second Sonata, Cage's *Music of Changes,* Feldman's *Intersection III,* and Four Pieces for Prepared Piano by Christian Wolff. The tiny playhouse was jammed, with people overflowing onto the stage, into the pit, and lining the back and sides of the house. Ross Parmenter, in *The New York Times,* emphasized the radical nature of Cage's work and the traditional aspects of Boulez: "The Second Sonata was the most conventional piece of the evening . . . at least it did not depart from customary notions about the sort of instrument a piano is."

The review in the *Herald Tribune* was written by Peggy Glanville-Hicks, a neoclassic composer in the tradition of Thomson, her superior on the *Tribune* staff. Although she was in the conservative vein and therefore not partial to Cage, she celebrated him over the European avant-garde:

> In Cage's piece . . . the arrangement of the fragmentary arabesques, the choice of infinitely varied tonal and sound-patch sequences, the contrasted pedal and staccato levels, all went to create the real impression of the real poetry that Cage's scores create.
>
> The Boulez Sonata—to this reviewer—is chaos, organized, stabilized chaos. American composers—be they ever so dissonant and ever so arbitrary—somehow impart an *élan,* a *joie de vivre,* that transcends the unrelenting sounds used. But the European "dissonanters" are deadly deliberate as though maximum acidity was their only aim. To the eye and intellect, the printed page of Boulez presents logic and design, but to the ear, its true arbiter, these are not apparent.

Thus the New York press heralded the split between the music of Boulez and Cage, between the Serialists and the Dadaists, between those who, in spite of polemics, were still moved by tradition and those who did not acknowledge any debt to the past. By the time Boulez returned to Paris the lines were drawn. Boulez and Cage had virtually no contact after that.

Discussing Boulez in the 1970s, Cage recalled what attracted him at the start:

The smile, the energy, the brilliance of the eyes, all of it was electrifying to me. But in New York I saw another side. Once, on our way back from Cape Cod, we ran out of gas. Pierre thought that was inelegant. I also remember a diner in Providence. Pierre was indignant over the service and the food, and I believe that he required us to leave. I was always frightened by his superior taste. He was always uncompromising. Things had to be exactly where they should be. I was still terribly poor. I wanted to make poverty elegant but Pierre was not interested in that. What he wanted was an excellent richness. Everything had to be exactly right, aesthetically right. Once I dropped into my studio unannounced and he was wearing an elegant silk robe.

With Pierre music has to do with ideas. His is a literary point of view. He even speaks of parentheses. All of it has nothing to do with sound. Pierre has the mind of an expert. With that kind of mind you can only deal with the past. You can't be an expert in the unknown. His work is understandable only in relation to the past. He has never said he would annihilate Webern!

Now when I think of the face, I no longer see the electricity. What I find is a look around the eyes, nose, and mouth that is the look of a bad animal, an animal waiting for the kill.

Discussing Cage about the same time, Boulez recalled that what attracted him at the start was Cage's search for new materials.

He was refreshing but not very bright. His freshness came from an absence of knowledge.

There was a progressive divergence between us. Our original ground had nothing to do with technique. It was interesting to find new sounds—those of the *Sonatas and Interludes*—but finally that was not terribly exciting because the same sound always returns in the same way. One needs neutral material "A" to become different in a different context. "A" cannot remain the same through different structures. Cage was interested in pure material. Material was the only thing on which he worked. It was a practical exercise. Today repetition is impossible. There is no escape!"

After the New York visit Boulez stopped corresponding with Cage. Cage was devastated by the turn of events. He could not understand how a difference in ideas could destroy a friendship as close as theirs. But serialism was Boulez's oxygen, and anyone who threatened its success was, in effect, trying to suffocate him.

As a symbolic blow to Boulez, Cage wrote a paragraph about the French being "cold in spirit and lacking in freedom of the mind" which he published in his book *Silence*. But Boulez had struck Cage in a more devastating way even before he made his trip to New York. Writing a few paragraphs for *La Revue Musicale,* which he entitled "Erik Satie: Chien Flasque" ("Erik Satie: Spineless Dog"), he decimated Satie thoroughly. If Webern begat Boulez and Satie begat Cage, then Boulez's aggressive attack on Satie was tantamount to an aggressive attack on Cage.

The bitter feelings between Boulez and Cage produced considerable reverberations. In February 1953 Virgil Thomson wrote in the *Tribune*: "Cage and his associates, through their recent concerts at the Cherry Lane Theater, have got the town quarreling again."

At its heart the quarrel was between the Old and New Worlds, between Europe and the United States, between a serially derived language and virtually no language at all. Thomson describes the manner in which this particular war was waged: "When Europeans organize they produce a real Mafia; when Americans organize they form a club." As soon as Boulez went back to Europe he and Stockhausen became very close. They were in power as the avant-garde and they developed branches in every country. That was the basis for the European organization that turned its back so violently on Cage.

CHAPTER 25

The existence of the Boulez-Stockhausen "Mafia" versus the Cage-Feldman "club" reflected a long-standing suspicion—on all sides—that Europeans were superior to Americans in the production of serious music. Not that music was singled out for this deprecatory treatment. On the contrary, it was part of what Henry James called the "complex fate" of the American imagination struggling against a powerful tendency to hold its historical precursor, Europe, in awe. From the other side, Europeans have often accused American artists of having no technique, soul, or mystery in their work. As early as the 1920s and 1930s, European fans of George Gershwin and Charles Ives are reported to have qualified their admiration by acknowledging that Gershwin and Ives were not "real composers, of course." Gershwin's widespread use of jazz and Ives's unprejudiced approach to all sounds disqualified them from admission to the European community of intellectualized musical and aesthetic ideas.

Many Americans felt that they indeed were inferior. When Nazism forced the exodus to the United States of the major European figures, some Americans privately expressed the hope that the balance of power would shift somewhat. They thought that if they were to study with Schoenberg, dine with Stravinsky, and converse with Bartók, some of the prestige of these great artists would rub off onto them. But nothing of the sort occurred.

This is not to say that American composers failed to prosper during the Depression and Second World War. The rise of Hitler and the start of the war generated an intense distaste for all things German which brought about a sharp decline in the performance of Austro-German works. There was a consequent increase in the performance of American works, not only by large orchestras such as the New York Philharmonic but by smaller organizations as well. The Pro Musica of the Middle and Far West, the New Music Society of San Francisco, and the Pan-American Association of Composers were a few that concentrated on indigenous works. Most famous of all was the League of Composers which had begun before the war and had spawned the Philadelphia Music Society and the Copland-Sessions Modern Music Concerts. In addition to the many chamber groups, two famous conductors leading great orchestras—Serge Koussevitzky, the Boston Symphony and Leopold Stokowski, the Philadelphia Orchestra—systematically championed American art.

But one fact stood out; American music, for the most part, was "derived" music, music that came over a bridge from the Old World. What is commonly referred to as the "first" or 1930s generation of American composers, the one that included Virgil Thomson, William Schuman, Marc Blitzstein, and David Diamond, took its musical cues from Stravinsky, and that tied them all to the French idiom. Such rugged individualists as Charles Ives, Carl Ruggles, and Henry Cowell stood alone throughout their lives. They never enjoyed successful musical careers.

David Diamond was a prolific composer of the 1930s. One of the youngest composers ever to receive a Guggenheim fellowship, his career was in a class by itself. To chart it is to chart the growth and death of neoclassicism in the United States. Diamond's career grew in the 1930s and reached its peak in the 1940s when his works received premieres under Mitropoulos, Rodzinski, Stokowski, and Szell. By the mid-1950s the tide had turned. Looking back, Diamond said, "How did the new group of composers get famous so fast? Not through recognition by the musical public but by foundation grants and university positions."

By the mid-1950s neoclassicism was as dead in the universities of the United States as it was on German radio. And the universities were the sole support of American composers in the post-World War II years. Serious composers had begun to create small, refined worlds of their own that called for the use of the sharpest intellect and closed out those who could not meet these demands. Serialism took hold step by step, not through a revolution such as the one ordered by Boulez, but through a more gradual evolution; for Schoenberg, the original serialist, was living and working here.

As the American serialists increased in power during the 1950s and 1960s, those of their colleagues tied to the tonal syntax found themselves under the oppressive power of the new main-line modernism. Many tonal composers received prestigious positions on prize committees, in philanthropic organizations, and as executives in conservatories. William Schuman, for example, became president of the Juilliard School, then of Lincoln Center. But institutions invariably trail creative life; and by the late 1950s serialism had displaced tonality as the musical grammar of the young artist.

Personal tragedies in this period abound. Marc Blitzstein suffered as

Diamond did. Unable to reconcile his affection for tonality with his desire to be in the vanguard, Blitzstein became increasingly depressed and appears virtually to have precipitated his own murder in Martinique. Others made accommodations: Thomson cultivated a career in music journalism as critic for the *New York Herald Tribune*. Still others attached to the old grammar slowly moved into the new. Roger Sessions composed his first 12-tone work, the Sonata for Solo Violin, in 1953. And Stravinsky's shift to the grammar succeeded in sweeping the rest along. After his *Canticum Sacrum* of 1957, in which he used the entire chromatic scale for the first time, Irving Fine, Arthur Berger, even Copland followed suit. But Stravinsky did not regard with affection those who shifted from the old to the new. No longer interested in disenchanted neoclassicists, he wanted to develop a new set of friends. One man whom he sought was Milton Babbitt, father of serialism in the United States, whom Boulez met at a party in Cage's loft when he was visiting New York in the fall of 1952.

Babbitt and Cage were then America's major postwar avant-gardists; yet each inhabits a separate universe.

Milton Babbitt was the first son of upper-middle-class, well-educated Jews. He grew up in Jackson, Mississippi, where he began to play the violin at eight, learned classical Latin in his early years, and played with his neighbor, writer Eudora Welty. The young boy appeared to be nurtured in the best of all possible worlds. He was spared an education like Cage's, in which Bach and Mozart were unknown, and spared also what Boulez's sister has described as the "atrophying Catholic system" imposed on her brother and herself.

In 1932 Milton's uncle, a film critic, went abroad and returned with some recently published scores. One was a work by Honegger; the other was Schoenberg's Opus 11 Piano Pieces. The Schoenberg attracted the twenty-year-old student and precipitated his decision to make composing his life's work.

During the worst years of the Depression, when most musicians were dependent on the Works Progress Administration, a federally funded project to give artists work, Milton's father was prosperous enough to put his son not only through college but through graduate study as well. After leaving New York University in 1935, Babbitt selected Sessions as his composition teacher. Although Sessions still opposed the 12-tone technique—Babbitt said Schoenberg was considered a musical freak at this time—Sessions's rigorous and intellectual approach drew the younger man to him.

A clue to Sessions's approach to music can be found in his emphasis on the Schenker system of musical analysis. Heinrich Schenker, who died in 1935, had attempted to reveal the organic structure of music by demonstrating that every composition is the elaboration of a simple, harmonic progression that makes for its continuity and coherence. Europeans paid little attention to his work; it was never, for instance, adopted at the Paris Conservatoire. But in the United States the Schenker method was widespread. Babbitt interprets this situation as one that reveals true "intellectual rigor here" and "basic intellectual naiveté abroad." Boulez, on the other hand, depreciates Schenker. "It's analysis for the sake of analysis," he said. "I have no interest in that."

In 1947–48, Babbitt wrote his first important work, *Composition for Four Instruments*. It was first performed in 1948 and published by New Music Editions in 1949. It was a thoroughgoing serial piece, composed not only three years before Boulez's *Structures* but before Messiaen's *Mode de Valeurs et d'Intensités*. But Babbitt disparages concern about being first and adds that he and his French colleagues are so far apart on fundamentals that the fact that it is all "serial" is of no consequence to him.

Neither the Babbitt nor the Messiaen work created the attention that Boulez's piece did. There is something about Boulez's presentation that creates a strong effect, that fixes the notice of serious men upon him. When he is on the way up, attacking those who represent "the law," Boulez generates electricity. The music reflects the man. Thus Boulez's *Structures*, perhaps because of its stridency, turned out to be far more trailblazing than Babbitt's more intellectual and academic work. Still, Babbitt can claim priority for a "serial" work.

Rivalries about priorities are not uncommon. Newton said Leibniz stole the calculus from him and there followed a bitter fight that degraded both Newton and Leibniz. Such quarrels do not imply that the thinkers are thieves; rather they support the multicentricity of important ideas. Like natural selection, arrived at simultaneously and independently by Darwin and Wallace, like dodecaphony, arrived at simultaneously and independently by Schoenberg and Hauer, serialism was an idea whose time had come.

Babbitt's *Composition for Four Instruments* attracted the attention of "new" musicians, of course, and it particularly attracted John Cage. Cage, working on *Sonatas and Interludes,* was delighted to find another maverick, so he analyzed Babbitt's work in *Musical America.* According to Babbitt, what fascinated Cage was the numerology in the piece as well as the hidden nature of the tone row. "It is difficult," Babbitt said, "to find the twelve-note set, which was partially derived from the opening tritone chord, because the clarinet opens with twelve different pitches leading one to expect that these twelve pitches would constitute the row. Cage was also intrigued by the fact that triads appear in the score, for triads had supposedly been legislated out of classical twelve-tone writing."

But Cage's attention to this early Babbitt work was the last manifestation of genuine interest in what his colleague composed. Soon after, Cage embraced chance and that separated him from the American serialists as much as it separated him from Boulez.

Fortunately for Cage, by 1950 he was enjoying considerable support from composers who were more attuned to him than to either Boulez or Babbitt. The year after his Paris visit, when Cage became friendly with Morton Feldman, he delivered a lecture on Feldman's music in Greenwich Village, and began to build his gentle but very firm little club, a club in which Babbitt played no role at all. Babbitt said, "Cage has always referred to me—half-jokingly—as 'America's best academic composer.' The fact is we are really not interested in each other. Cage is totally honest, totally direct, but finally a very naive man. We are mostly embarrassed by each other. I knew we had nothing in common when he published the analysis of my early work."

But while Babbitt knew in the late 1940s that he and Cage lived in separate worlds, he thought he was inhabiting the same universe as Boulez. For one thing, a small publishing house, Boelke-Bomart, which had printed Babbitt's earliest work, had also shown interest in the music of Boulez.

Walter Boelke, an Austrian-Jewish engraver for Schirmer, began his publishing firm in the late 1940s. For musical advice he turned to Kurt List, editor of the music journal *Listen,* who was a composer and a friend of Leibowitz. Because Schirmer had dropped Schoenberg in the early 1940s, List suggested that Boelke publish Schoenberg's current works as well as compositions by Schoenberg's disciples. He asked Leibowitz to submit suitable scores. Leibowitz sent pieces from his composition class that included the First Piano Sonata by Boulez. Although List admired the Boulez score, he found it too long and turned it down. This was one of the pieces Cage persuaded Amphion to publish in France.

Indeed the Cage-Boulez friendship of 1949 was symbolic of the interaction and good feeling that prevailed between Europeans and Americans in the musical avant-garde. Leibowitz, who had spent most of his life in France, was collaborating with the New Music Quartet in New York and was at the same time living in Paris with Ellen Adler, daughter of Stella Adler, director of the Actors Studio in New York. In 1947 Leibowitz and Ellen Adler visited the United States, and Stella Adler gave a party for them. Her apartment was crowded with Europeans and Americans. Leibowitz and

Babbitt played four-hand jazz. There appeared to be no rift between composers at that time.

But by 1952 the good feeling had disappeared. In the summer of that year Babbitt made a trip to Paris. List asked him to get in touch with Boulez to see if Boulez had any more works for him. But Babbitt claims that he could not get hold of Boulez. "By then," he reports, "the lines were so firmly drawn that those who remained loyal to Leibowitz would do absolutely nothing to help Boulez in his career." Babbitt left Europe without seeing Boulez.

Later that year, when Boulez was in New York with the Barrault troupe, Babbitt and Boulez met at a party in Cage's loft. Babbitt recalls the circumstances: "We went into the bedroom and sat on the bed. I showed Boulez my *Composition for Four Instruments*. Boulez was surprised at its ties to Schoenberg. He said: 'I thought you were interested in Webern.' I replied that I was interested in some aspects of Webern and some aspects of Schoenberg but that I really looked to Schoenberg. After all," Babbitt said, "there are so many more levels to Schoenberg, so much more complexity in Schoenberg. I started to talk about combinatoriality and derivation, subjects about which I knew we disagreed but which I thought could have led to an interesting discourse. I don't know whether he did not understand or did not have any interest in what I said. But I do know we never sat down with a score again."

As Leibowitz represented the apex of the European-Schoenberg school, so Babbitt represented the apex of the American-Schoenberg school. Thus Babbitt, in whom Boulez had hoped he would find an ally in carving out a language based on Webern, proved to be no ally at all. Because of what Boulez calls his "academic handling" of the serial idea, Babbitt was almost as removed from Boulez's world as Cage.

Shortly after Boulez left the United States, his essay "Schoenberg is DEAD!" reached New York. The effect was predictable. "George Perle, Leon Kirchner and I were furious," Babbitt said. "That essay was dead wrong. That was what finally separated us from Boulez. We could never forgive him for that." Nor did they. More than twenty years later, when a Boulez retrospective at the Whitney Museum fell on the same date as the Schoenberg centenary concert at Alice Tully Hall, people accused Boulez of setting that date to seduce the already small new-music audience away from Schoenberg across town to Boulez. Tully Hall was empty and the Whitney was jammed.

CHAPTER 26

Less than three months after Schoenberg's death, in July 1951, Stravinsky made his first postwar trip to Europe and scheduled a stop at Baden-Baden. There he listened to the tape of *Polyphonie X* made at its premiere in Donaueschingen. Craft said that it was the "nose-thumbing force of the work that impressed the composer of *The Rite of Spring,* who may have been reminded of his own 1913 premiere, for *Polyphonie X* was at times all but drowned out by the laughter, shouts, hoots, and whistling."

In January and February of 1952, Craft repeatedly played for Stravinsky a recording of Webern's Opus 22 Quartet. Stravinsky showed the powerful effects of that score by composing, in April, the Cantata for soprano, tenor, female chorus, and orchestra in which he used the serial technique for the first time. Thus, Stravinsky began to use a method that gave rise to the kind of music he had claimed to abhor all his life. He was able to do this partly because of Craft's guidance and partly because Schoenberg was, as Boulez wrote, finally "dead!"

In May 1952 Stravinsky attended the Paris concert in which Boulez and Messiaen played *Structures.* According to Craft, Stravinsky was struck by the "arrogance" of the work. Clearly Stravinsky was drawn by the aggression and toughness of the man as reflected in his rocklike, nonflabby art. Stravinsky talked with Heinrich Strobel, who gave him the following picture of the then current musical scene in Europe: Neoclassicism was out; Boulanger, Stravinsky's ardent defender, a spent force. Serialism was in; Boulez, Stravinsky's strident attacker, the man on top. In the fall of 1952. Stravinsky assisted at several rehearsals of *Polyphonie X* in Hollywood and even made an analysis of the score. Then he let it generally be known that he would very much like to meet Boulez, the revolutionary who had publicly set out to do him in.

In the fall of 1952, when Boulez was in New York for the first time, he was invited as a guest along with Stravinsky to dinner at Virgil Thomson's apartment in the Chelsea Hotel. Other musicians also attended. Thomson described the evening: "Everyone there expected trouble because of Boulez's repeated and violent attacks on Stravinsky. That didn't happen. The two hit like comets. They sat together. Shortly after dinner Stravinsky left. Boulez remained for three or four hours in a very excited state. Before leaving, Stravinsky invited Boulez to visit him the next day."

Boulez accepted the invitation. The personal contact between the two composers resulted in a kind of truce. Boulez stopped speaking disrespectfully of Stravinsky, and Stravinsky began to speak eloquently about Boulez. This was natural. Each deeply admired the other's talents and, as Virgil Thomson said, "Stravinsky needed the support of the young, while Boulez was pleased to have Papa's blessing."

Boulez tells this story of the Thomson party:

> Everyone waited for the clash between Stravinsky and me because of my past polemics against him. It didn't occur. As it turned out, Jean Morel was at the party, and I didn't know who he was. There was a discussion of *Carmen*. That is not my favorite opera and I said so. Morel thought I was attacking him because he had conducted it so much at the Met. So he left. People saw that. They were surprised— because they didn't expect trouble with Morel. The trouble they expected was with Stravinsky.
>
> On the contrary, there was no trouble with Stravinsky at all. As far as polemics are concerned, we never discussed them. Polemics are tied to a year or period. To survive musically you must be in touch with your time. The meeting took place soon after Stravinsky composed *The Rake's Progress*. He picked up on Webern at about that time.

Stravinsky's ingestion of the quiet Viennese may have replenished for him the musical oxygen that had begun to run out. In Webern he found a new way to make music that would sustain him for the rest of his life. Thus, in his late sixties and throughout his seventies, Stravinsky composed as prolifically as he did when he was a young man. What aged artist would not be elated to produce such progeny as these.

Elated and grateful. In 1955 Stravinsky acknowledged his debt to the Idea. For *Die Reihe,* an abstruse German journal dedicated to serialism and edited by Stockhausen, he wrote an eloquent tribute to Webern: "The 15 of September, 1945, the day of Anton Webern's death, should be a day of mourning for any receptive musician. We must hail not only this great composer but also a real hero. Doomed to a total failure in a deaf world of ignorance and indifference, he inexorably kept cutting his diamonds, the mines of which he had such a perfect knowledge."

Like Boulez, Stravinsky was drawn to Webern for the hard, clean edges of his music, for the nonrhetorical, nonexpressionistic purity of his art. And, like Boulez, Stravinsky was prepared to deify Webern, particularly if that meant annihilating Schoenberg—for the ghost of the proud Viennese still hovered. Thus Stravinsky and Boulez shared a common purpose, motivated by taste and private need.

In addition, each found much that was agreeable in the other. Stravinsky was "captivated," Craft reports, "by Boulez with his new musical ideas, and an extraordinary intelligence, quickness, and sense of humor." Boulez, in turn, was awed by Stravinsky's life-style and told several friends he would try to emulate it. He had never, he said, seen an artist live so grandly before.

At the end of 1952 Boulez returned to Paris. Although he had not succeeded with Cage and Babbitt, he did have Pousseur and Stockhausen in his camp and was assured of Stravinsky's blessings as well. But almost as soon as he had succeeded in controlling a totally serial world—not only with *Structures* but also through the recruitment of the talented young and old—Boulez began to break away from that world. Indeed, he pinpointed the problem inside serial research from the start: it lay in its rigidity.

When Stockhausen and Boulez first met, the younger man showed the older his first serial piece, *Kontra-Punkte*, a thirteen-minute work. Boulez told him the piece was too rigid, that he should find a way to render it more baroque. He would like to see more density, more vitality in the score. Stockhausen altered the composition so as to suit Boulez and at the same time maintain his artistic independence; he retained the original treatment in alternate sections and embellished the remaining ones in different ways. Thus, the final version of *Kontra-Punkte* was not an expression of rigid serialism in the pristine sense of Boulez's *Structures*. Still, it satisfied the aesthetic requirements of the new syntax: the score contains no repetition, variation, or development, nor was there any apparent contrast in the sense of extended sections that vary in character, mood, or key.

A similar sequence of events took place between Pousseur and Boulez when he showed Boulez an early piece for three pianos tuned in 1/6 tones.

Boulez declared it too mechanical and suggested ways of loosening it up. Pousseur made the suggested changes. Later Pousseur said, "Boulez was ahead of Stockhausen and me at that time."

Indeed the polemics Boulez then engaged in were directed against those who followed his lead too strenuously. "Having been preceded by a generation in part illiterate are we to become a generation of technocrats?" he asked in the essay ". . . Auprès et au loin" published in 1954. Boulez wrote that his generation could now take leave of its predecessors and concern itself with the problems within the serial syntax. He pointed out several seemingly self-evident truths: that all the elements of music are not of equal importance—some, like pitch, can be heard more precisely than others, that because there are twelve notes in the chromatic scale it does not follow that the other parameters should be divided twelve ways, and that some instruments are louder than others. He concluded that the composer's function is to choose among possibilities. It was not only talk. He wrote to Pousseur, "After all this work, I am writing an *oeuvrette*." The *oeuvrette* turned out to be *Le Marteau sans Maître*, his third work based on poetry by René Char, the piece hailed by Stravinsky as the best work Boulez's generation had then produced. In 1955 Boulez told associates, "*Marteau sans Maître* is my *Pierrot Lunaire*."

In *Par volonté et par hasard*, a book of interviews that appeared in 1975, Boulez expostulates about what he set out to do:

> There are three cycles based on three different poems. These three poems produce different pieces. One cycle gives rise to three, the next to two, the last to four. But instead of presenting these pieces one right after the other, I distributed them in such a manner that they would actually penetrate one another. So you see that as early as *Marteau*, I was making an effort to obtain an effect of permeability, to create a dimension different from the closed musical form. The fact that there are not one but several continuities, that the cycles penetrate one another, that the last piece is a microcosm of the whole work, constitutes an important first step towards the effective breaking of traditional musical continuity.

In *Marteau* the notation does not exceed the limits of conventional notation; it is simply more complex. *Marteau* is the first of his post-1948 works that appear to be haunted by elements of the past. It is almost as if

Boulez had to formulate a new syntax before he could relax and draw on some of the music he loved. The length of the pieces and their sequence remind the listener of *Pierrot Lunaire*. The percussive treatment and rhythmic invention recall early Stravinsky. The tenuous balance of sound and silence, the athematicism of the plinking and plonking strings, all this owes a large debt to Webern.

Techniques used in *Polyphonie X* and *Structures* are used again here, no longer as ends in themselves but rather, as Boulez said, "to formulate thoughts." The composer's alterations of tempo, his holding back and thrusting forth of movement, his startling breaks in sound are characteristic of the piece and serve to further Char's message, which is that we are in the grip of a civilization that is marching inexorably towards its doom, independent of the individual. For Boulez the "hammer without a master" appears not only to be civilization in general but an automatized musical system in particular, a "timetable of trains," he has called it, "that never move." As Boulez looked around at his own disciples and at the composers in Darmstadt, he found them being drowned in serial charts. In his essays and *Marteau* he tried to "save" them.

For in contrast to *Structures,* what Boulez was concerned with in *Marteau* was the making of music, not system. Here Boulez introduces a soft resonance that displaces his early pointillistic style. Here Boulez exhibits a complete union of word and sound and does that despite the use of a poem in which each word has a weight and meaning of its own. Here Boulez creates a work of art notable for its delicacy of feeling, for its fineness of musical thought. But the wild, free spirit of the early days is gone. Neither "violent" nor "brutal" appears in this score; there is little more aggressive than "moins lent" or "assez vite." The formidable inhibitions that gave birth to *Structures*, the annihilation of personality that that work suggests, has been transformed to far more artistic purposes in *Marteau*, but the essence of the inhibition remains intact. The personality of Webern has finally triumphed.

Because of Boulez's guarded nature, because of his refusal to reveal personal details, one cannot know what happened in his mid-twenties to move him to distrust his own imagination and invention and invest his faith in theory and system. It may be that nothing in particular occurred. If that is the case, the shift can be attributed partly to a return to his earlier ways, when system and order took precedence over everything else, and partly a result of his newly acquired deified position—articles by and about him were circulating everywhere—in which he felt it necessary not only always to be "right" but also to proclaim a set of commandments to the world, much as Schoenberg had done before him. Boulez's fame threatened to become a kind of death mask.

Whether Boulez's loss of spontaneity was due to personal or cultural factors is not of critical importance in his story. The fact remains that the prodigious invention of *Visage Nuptial,* the Flute Sonatina, *Le Soleil des Eaux,* and the early piano sonatas was replaced in *Polyphonie X* and *Structures* with a tight, closed, hermetic formula. Boulez himself was horrified by the result. He said *Structures* was not "Total but Totalitarian." And he tried to twist and unlock the system with *Marteau.* Here, in contrast to the transparency of *Structures Book I,* the machinery of twelve-note organization is so complex that it is impossible to trace the steps which lead from one pitch to the next.

CHAPTER 27

As Pousseur said, in advocating a freer use of the serial language, Boulez was ahead of both Stockhausen and himself in 1952–53. But if "ahead" is to be interpreted as in the vanguard, then John Cage was ahead of them all.

Inspired in part by Zen teachings, Cage began self-consciously to remove his own will, to remove his own personality from his work. He said *Music of Changes* did not go far enough, for, although he did not choose the progression of sounds—that was dictated by the flipping of coins—he did choose the sounds themselves; and once those sounds were notated on the score the performer was forced into performing what was there. To go a step further, Cage composed the *Imaginary Landscape No. 4* for twelve radios and twenty-four players. Twelve pairs of instrumentalists sit on either side of the podium as though they were string players in a conventional orchestra. One of each pair holds the radio, the other tunes it, and a conductor presides over the action with a score. Thus Cage manipulates a dozen radios according to a precise schedule of durations and dynamics. The experiment was one of combining exactitude and chance.

On an evening late in August 1952, pianist David Tudor walked onto a stage in the "art" community of Woodstock, New York, and bowed, placed a score on the piano, and sat down on a stool. He remained seated, not playing for four minutes and thirty-three seconds. He did not touch the keyboard nor did he produce any other audible sound. The "music" of this piece consists of the collection of background sounds that can be heard during the time that the pianist is seated at the instrument.

Surely this "work" represented no effort on Cage's part to revise or renew any art work of the past. Surely it represented no effort on Cage's part to transform any aspect of his artistic inheritance. Rather it was a strong theatrical gesture designed to obliterate the past, to obliterate everything from Machaut through Boulez. Implicit in this now famous work is the assumption that individual personality should be dissolved, that artistic form should be destroyed, that the formerly self-confident bourgeois listener should distrust all values of beauty and truth. Over and above everything else, *4' and 33"* loudly proclaims to its listeners that "uneventful" time is the best of all possible time and that individual talent is nothing more than a fiction, a fraud that has been perpetrated on the Western world.

Strobel invited Cage and Tudor to the Donaueschingen festival, October 1954, the festival at which *Marteau sans Maître* was scheduled for its premiere. While Cage was in Donaueschingen, Tudor traveled to Cologne where he met Stockhausen for the first time. Stockhausen and Cage had never met. All that Stockhausen knew about Cage was Boulez's abhorrence of his music.

At their first meeting Tudor played Stockhausen Part I and Part IV of Cage's *Music of Changes*, Christian Wolff's *Piece for Prepared Piano*, and Feldman's *Intersection III*. Tudor said Stockhausen "was fascinated by the newness of the sounds and by the variety of keyboard attacks, particularly by the clusters Feldman used. Stockhausen's interest and excitement was obvious. For years he continued with the desire to know the music coming from John Cage and his group."

But other Europeans were not so hospitable. Everywhere Cage and Tudor went they were treated like a couple of clowns. At Donaueschingen the audience was angry and the press outraged. Complaints focused on the "noise." In describing the Cage-Tudor event to Boulez, Strobel characterized it as "poor Dada."

By the time Cage and Tudor arrived in Cologne, Stockhausen had had over a year's experience building up an electronic studio there. After his studies guided by Messiaen in Paris, which had begun in January 1952, he had returned home in May 1953 to work at the West German Radio's electronic studio under the direction of Herbert Eimert. The studio gave the first demonstration of electronic music in Germany. Beyer introduced the word "parameter" into music, borrowing it from mathematics apparently to give weight and dignity to what otherwise would be called an element or dimension. The parameters of a musical tone are its pitch, rhythm, dynamics, articulation, texture, and register, each of which was to be subjected to permutation.

At Cologne the sine tone was the raw material, produced by an electronic generator and then manipulated on tape. In contrast to the tape studios in Paris and New York (the Columbia University music faculty had set up a laboratory on its campus), the one in Cologne concentrated on generating sound electronically.

Thus, when Stockhausen arrived in Cologne in the spring of 1953, he found a large and impressive body of electronic theory that could be allied to the serial principle. With the sine tone one could achieve the precision mandatory in the most complex serial works. "Work and material have the same structure" became the teaching motto at Cologne, distinguishing it from the *musique concrète* of the Paris and New York studios where the emphasis was on sound and texture.

In December 1953, seven months after he had left Paris and one year before he was to meet Cage, Stockhausen invited Boulez and Pousseur to a festival of new music at Cologne in which works were to be played by Eimert, Beyer, and himself. En route Boulez told Pousseur that he did not expect to like what he was going to hear. He said he thought one heard sine tones as single pitches, not as whole sound entities. What he heard confirmed his expectations. He told Stockhausen that "to produce what you have done I would have preferred an orchestra of sine tones that was, at least, manipulated by people. I would even prefer the use of a ring modulator for that would have added considerable richness to the sound." An intense discussion ensued. Boulez dates the beginning of his break with Stockhausen from the end of 1953, just a little more than a year after they had met. "There was always the root of a split," he said. "Stockhausen had a strong ego from the start."

But Stockhausen's initial refusal to loosen the reins of his electronic work did not mean he was generically opposed to loose reins. The impetus to let them fly wide was provided, a year after Boulez's visit, by the arrival of Tudor and Cage in Cologne. Here was an ironic turn of events. By its call for precision, serial music had accelerated the development of electronically generated sound. But almost at the very moment when the electronic medium made that precision a reality, instrumental music became the suitable arm for freeing just about everything.

As egos go, Boulez's, of course, was not weak. But the arrogance he had displayed in the early years of his career became less apparent when he began to receive recognition. And he received it in turn from Barrault, Souvchinsky, Strobel, and Suzanne Tezenas, then from the thoroughgoing professional, Roger Desormière, the first conductor to perform Boulez's work and perhaps the finest French conductor of his generation.

By the early 1950s, Boulez was well known in avant-garde circles throughout Europe. His polemics made him famous among intellectuals outside the arena of modern music. Pianists grappled with his Second

Sonata, and composers paid attention to his most recent verbal utterance. The serial language, which he identified as his own, was on the road to becoming the musical language of the post-Einsteinian age.

Late in 1953, Boulez proclaimed that it was time for his generation "to prove itself with a series of chamber concerts that would serve as a means of communication between the composers of our time and the public that is interested in its time." This was the first occasion on which he indicated any concern about bringing the listener closer to his own musical world.

Boulez persuaded the Barraults to launch a modest series of chamber concerts at the rehearsal studio of the Petit Marigny, a tiny, airless theater with wooden seats. The series soon expanded; it became known as the Domaine Musical. Boulez did virtually everything. He invited the people, determined the repertory, handled the library, collected the patrons' checks, put up the chairs and stands, selected the performers, edited the program notes, and put out one issue of a journal, *The Domaine Musical,* which included essays by Stockhausen, Pousseur, Nono, and himself. His contribution, "Incipit," was an unqualified tribute to Webern. Boulez dropped the journal after the first issue because his work with Barrault, the Domaine, and his own composition did not leave time for such a taxing enterprise. The next year, Universal Edition began to publish *Die Reihe,* a revival of its *Anbruch* of the 1920s; the journal did not appear regularly, only when there was enough material.

During the early years of the Domaine, Boulez did very little conducting, delegating this responsibility to Hermann Scherchen. He said he found very few conductors who were competent in the contemporary repertory and willing to take on the risks involved. Apart from Scherchen there was Hans Rosbaud, whom Boulez invited along with the Südwestfunk orchestra. According to Boulez, these two men were practically the only ones capable, and he adds that what was even more striking was the fact that both were then around sixty years old. "There were no younger men who could assist them besides myself."

In his initial statement of aims, Boulez wrote that he would offer works that played a vital role in the evolution of music, particularly those rarely performed pieces by Stravinsky, Bartók, Varèse, Debussy, the Viennese school ("especially Webern so little known in France where he is practically ignored"), as well as the motets of Machaut and Dufay, the madrigals of Gesualdo, Bach's *Musical Offering,* and pieces by Messiaen, Stockhausen, Nono, Pousseur, Fano, Maderna (Boulez had not yet met Luciano Berio whose work later would be performed often at the Domaine), and Cage, Brown, Wolff, Barraqué, and Phillipot. Even then Boulez presented pieces he did not like, offering them as "documents."

But he concentrated on those compositions he loved. Between 1954 and 1964 the Domaine Musical presented almost sixty percent of the combined works of Schoenberg, Webern, and Berg. Often these works were being played in Paris for the first time. In 1957 Hans Rosbaud conducted the Südwestfunk in the first Paris performance of Berg's Three Pieces for Orchestra Opus 6.

The first program of the Domaine Musical took place on January 13, 1954, and presented Stravinsky's *Renard* (not only because it was composed during Boulez's favorite "pre-neoclassic" period of Stravinsky but also because Barrault could provide the mimes), pieces by Stockhausen and Nono, and Webern's Opus 24 Concerto. Boulez invariably offered long programs. American pianist Paul Jacobs recalled the following incident. In 1954, Jacobs visited the composer on Rue Beautreillis. Boulez handed him a pile of scores and said they were to be played in ten days. "In other words," Jacobs noted, "the program had been listed and scheduled but there was no one to play the pieces. It was an immense program— almost five hours—which included Berg's Lyric Suite, pieces by Webern and Bartók . . . and a number of other compositions as well. There was too much on one program. . . ." Boulez demanded of others as much as he demanded of himself.

The series became fashionable very quickly, attracting both the far-out and the chic. But the cost proved to be prohibitive for the Barraults, who bore the deficit for the first season but could not do it again, offering only their theater rent-free. There was no question of state support; in the early years, the French Radio would not even broadcast a single program. Private funds finally came from Suzanne Tezenas, who made Boulez and the Domaine her primary concern.

Because of the shift in patronage in 1955, the series' name was changed from Les Concerts du Petit-Marigny to the Domaine Musical. Tezenas not only gave money but after each concert gave a lavish reception attended not only by the very wealthy but by painters and writers as well. In a short time she succeeded in inducing members of the *haute bourgeoisie* to become members of the board. Even Nadia Boulanger, Tezenas reports,

> was a little member, right from the beginning. At that time we had so many people against us. Like Sauguet and Marie Blanche de Polignac, whose aunt had presided

over the Stravinsky-Boulanger salon before the war. Yet Boulanger came regularly to the concerts. She would say, "You are occupying yourself with scientific music," but she came, nevertheless.

Almost everyone was against us in those days. Modern music was for Austria, not for France. There is something about French nationalism that makes this so. When we gave *Pierrot Lunaire*, Poulenc and Auric told me that they had heard the premiere in Berlin. Still they would not expose that composition here. Auric was the only French composer, who helped us at the beginning. He was one of the first members of the Domaine Musical.

The antagonism of the Establishment in France only heightened the success of the Domaine, for, as Sir William Glock explained, "There is a snobbish support among the French for contemporary art." Pousseur recalls the atmosphere of the concerts: "The climate was immensely favorable. There was incredible fervor. Soon Boulez had to do the same program twice. The house sat only 200 people, so he did it Saturday night and Sunday afternoon. On Sunday morning he would moderate a round table discussion and those involved in that particular concert would talk about the pieces in that program. In those early years we thought we had found a common language and were together in trying to strengthen it.

"If I were to pinpoint the decision that I think was fatal to Boulez," Pousseur, a Marxist, observed, "it was the involvement of the *haute bourgeoisie*. This seems to have changed his attitude towards musical life. To get money for his cause he started this particular business. Then he found himself very well in the world, very comfortable in the *grand monde*."

By the mid-1950s, Boulez, enemy of the status quo, was king of the musical avant-garde. Writing about him a few years later, Souvchinsky claimed, "There are not many who, between the ages of twenty-two and twenty-six, succeeded not only in making a mark on their art, but in changing its face and even its essence."

CHAPTER 28

Boulez's sister has said, "Pierre has no trouble with women because women are not important to him. He has no trouble with cats and dogs either."

Confronted with information about the early affair that precipitated *Visage Nuptial,* Boulez acknowledged that it took place and that it culminated in a double suicide pact. But he refused to identify the object of his passion or to say anything more than that the person was "neither intellectual nor intelligent." He added that in such matters "only one can be strong; the other weak." Boulez's demand for inequality in bed does not preclude extremely decent behavior with women out of bed. And in fact he maintains such friendships with a few women, friendships that are remarkably free of the intensity and the breaks that generally characterize his relations with men.

To say that Boulez's emotional life has nothing to do with women is not to deny him an emotional life. It is rather to assign his feeling for ideas its due and heroic place. And because ideas have generally been embodied in men, here Boulez is out to conquer and destroy. Between 1945 and 1952 Webern displaced Schoenberg, Leibowitz displaced Messiaen, and Strobel displaced Souvchinsky in his life.

Such intellectual jousting, playing people as though they were pawns in a chess game, appears to be a popular French sport. There is something unique about the lycée discipline that encourages a curious kind of self-denying rigidity coupled with an imaginative rationalization that leaves little room for intimacy and accounts for a good deal in Boulez's temperament and behavior. In any case, if one wants to get anywhere in France—or, for that matter, anywhere—it helps to have a steel-tempered soul. How better to test one's ultimate strength than to insult, attack, and repudiate one's country and then move on?

Boulez's move to Germany took place in cautious, somewhat tentative steps. The summer courses at Darmstadt began to function under Wolfgang

Steinecke in 1946. Although Boulez was by then immersed in Schoenberg and Webern, the German program still clung to Stravinsky, Hindemith, and Prokofiev. Leibowitz arrived in Darmstadt in 1948 and singlehandedly changed all that.

By 1949 dodecaphony was the prevailing aesthetic there. But Boulez did not make the trip until 1952 when he had already premiered *Structures* in Paris and knew the serial language was under control in his hands.

That same year, 1952, Boulez left his French publishers, Heugel and Amphion, and moved to Universal Edition, the Viennese house of Schoenberg, Webern, and Berg. Stockhausen introduced him to Alfred Schlee, director of Universal Edition. Significantly, *Structures* was the first Boulez work Universal Edition printed. It may be that "à la limite du fertile pays," which the composer inscribed on the score, did not imply the end of fertile ground—as Boulez later claimed—but rather the beginning of a new and fruitful grammar.

Although Darmstadt was not physically glamorous—the school took over a tent and a few buildings that had been evacuated by the Seventh Day Adventists—it was bursting with vitality in the mid-1950s. Richard Rodney Bennett, a British student of Boulez, said that "to hear Berio, Stockhausen, the Flute Sonatina by Boulez—you cannot imagine how fantastic that was. Either you were at *the* performance in Darmstadt or you knew you wouldn't hear that masterpiece for a very long time."

Still, Boulez said he had reservations about Darmstadt. Although his works were played there a good deal, and although he appeared sporadically to conduct and lecture, he said he was not often physically present and that he never identified with Darmstadt's activities. The Germans devoured Boulez's serialism as thoroughly as they had devoured Leibowitz's dodecaphony, and Boulez was critical from the start of the obsessive way composers were handling the serial language. According to Pousseur, he was also critical of Steinecke. "As early as 1954 and 1955," Pousseur has said, "Boulez spoke of Darmstadt with disgust. He said it was boring, there were always the same heads, that Steinecke was a fat bear who was never talking, always smiling, that he was nothing more than an organizer who profited from what Boulez, Stockhausen, and I did."

If Boulez complained privately about Darmstadt, he was no more sanguine about France. "The French Establishment," he claimed, "was exactly like it had been before the war. It loved the neoclassical Stravinsky and hated the Viennese school. Only Max Deutsch, a third-rate musician, and Leibowitz, a hanger-on to the Merleau-Ponty group, were promoting the Viennese. I wanted to show you had to promote the Viennese not because you were a 'left-over' but for the right reasons. It was a kind of guerrilla warfare."

While Stockhausen was working in Cologne absorbing the effects of his encounter with Tudor and Cage, Boulez was engaged in guerrilla warfare in Paris, fighting the tradition that pervaded Parisian musical life. His fight against authority did not interfere with his creative work. On the contrary, it appeared to nourish a prolonged ecstasy of creation.

In the mid-1950s, Boulez worked obsessively. He not only did everything for the Domaine Musical, but he continued to publish articles in journals and to serve as music director for Barrault. Still, composition took precedence over everything else. In 1955 Boulez wrote the score for Barrault's *Orestes*, and between October 1954 and April 1955 he completed *Marteau sans Maître,* doubling the note values, which he said were much too small, and adding the ninth and final movement. The first performance of *Marteau* took place in June 1955 at the International Society for Contemporary Music Festival in Baden-Baden, with Hans Rosbaud conducting the Südwestfunk. Boulez conducted a second performance at the Domaine in April 1956.

Throughout this period Boulez remained faithful to the Barraults, although the elitism of French artistic circles decreed that they, being performers, were not in the same league as Souvchinsky, Strobel, and most of Boulez's newer friends. Boulez also remained loyal to Roger Desormière. In 1952 Desormière suffered a stroke that left him paralyzed. During that time Boulez sent scripts to the French Radio in Desormière's name in order that the conductor could collect the fees. He also escorted Desormière to musical events and social evenings—lifting him in and out of cars—to make life as bearable as he could for the stricken man. This side of Boulez—and the Desormière situation is not exceptional—did not reach the public eye. The public saw only the aggressive fighter. Tezenas described Boulez in the 1950s: "He was terribly trenchant then. He attacked everyone who did not see music in the purist way that he did."

Boulez was insulting not only to critics—he attacked them with obscenities to the press—but also to performing musicians. Boulez went to Baden-Baden to supervise the last eight days of rehearsal before the première of *Marteau*. He stood above and behind Rosbaud in the broadcasting box, shouting out every major and minor mistake. It was not as though Rosbaud was delighted to be there. Hired by Strobel for the Südwestfunk, he had conducted the premiere of *Polyphonie X* and genuinely hated the work. Strobel's widow said, "My husband fought Rosbaud every step of the way. He told Rosbaud that Boulez was a genius, that he would be the new

Stravinsky. And he worked on Boulez as well. Strobel told Boulez that to set things right, he should dedicate *Marteau* to Rosbaud."

Strobel's strategy worked. From then until Rosbaud's death, Rosbaud and Boulez cooperated. In any case, Rosbaud was the first conductor after Desormière to perform any of Boulez's music, so the composer was very much in his debt. But Boulez's primary tie was to Strobel. Boulez described Strobel as "rough-edged and peasant-like, not intellectually articulate like Rosbaud, but a man with extraordinary flair. He had an earthy instinct for things that I liked very much. Rosbaud, on the contrary, was a clever man, like a character out of E. T. A. Hoffmann. It was hard to know what he thought."

It is also hard to know what Boulez thought, but there is no doubt that he thought a great deal. In response to which men influenced him, Boulez, without pausing, spills the following names, all of which belong to artists who have rejected tradition in favor of moving into unexplored worlds: "Klee, Kandinsky, Mondrian, Joyce, Char, Michaux, Artaud, Genet, Becket, Messiaen, Webern—of course you know that—Schoenberg, and Stockhausen. Stockhausen had a very strong influence on me."

But Boulez left out the name of Stephane Mallarmé, the poet who died in 1898. In 1952, Boulez told David Tudor that he would write his masterpiece by the time he was thirty and that it would be based on Mallarmé. Boulez hit the target late; he was thirty-four when *Pli Selon Pli* was completed. But it turned out that Mallarmé moved his art a good deal more than by just providing him with words he chose to set.

Mallarmé, born in 1842, was one of the most influential cultural figures in 19th century France. Avant-gardist, translator of the poems of Edgar Allen Poe, forerunner of the Symbolist poets whose innovations with language exerted a powerful impact on modern art, he worked in ways that profoundly influenced Boulez.

Mallarmé believed that writing should aspire to the abstraction of music, that it should create its effects by veiled suggestion rather than by anything more concrete. Conventional syntax, he believed, was expendable. In 1897, the year before he died, Mallarmé published *Un coup de dés jamais n'abolira le hasard* (A Throw of the Dice Will Never Abolish Chance), unpunctuated and unrhymed. Typographical idiosyncrasies played a major role here. This was Mallarmé's last poem. The painter Redon, who illustrated it, viewed the poem as an attack on bourgeois notions of meaning and sense. It was, in sum, a prescient example of much of the art to follow.

Boulez has said he was drawn to Mallarmé because of the "density of his texture, because of the obscurity of his language. I like work that resists easy comprehension." He was also drawn to the open form described in Mallarmé's *Livre*. It provided a model for his own formulation of controlled chance which calls for a freedom for the performer limited, to a greater or lesser degree, by instructions from the composer. Boulez considered this formulation one of his most striking contributions. Even Mallarmé's topography influenced Boulez. Perhaps Boulez left Mallarmé off his list because his debt to him was so great.

Boulez was first attracted to Mallarmé because of the analogy he found between his own solutions to compositional problems and Mallarmé's solutions to poetic problems. Rejecting poetry as a decorative exercise, Mallarmé searched for the deeper structure behind the words, for the essence, the music, behind the poetry. Thus Boulez found parallels between Mallarmé and Webern, both lyric artists, who rejected rhetoric and expressionism; what the phonemes in the French phonological system were to Mallarmé, the intervals derived from the twelve-note scale were to Webern. In "Recherches Maintenant," published in *La Nouvelle Revue Française* in November 1954, Boulez compared Mallarmé's efforts with his own in relation to carving out an *ars poetica* for music:

> These reflections on the composition of the musical work make me hope for a new poetics, a different way of listening. Perhaps it is precisely at this point that music manifests its greatest lag in relation, for example, to poetry. Neither the Mallarmé of the *Coup de dés* nor Joyce was paralleled by anything in the music of his own time. Is it sensible or absurd to use these points of comparison in this way? (If one thinks of what they loved: the one Wagner; the other Italian opera and Irish songs. . . .)
>
> Although I do not want to refer too closely to their investigations, they having dealt with language, to see them as having been marked by a search for a new musical poetics is not illusory.
>
> Even when the most essential contemporary works reject formal classical schemes, they do not really abandon at all a general idea of form which has not varied since the development of tonality. A musical work is made up of a series of separate movements; each of them is homogeneous in both structure and tempo; it is a closed circuit (a characteristic of Occidental musical thought); balance among its different movements is established by a dynamic

distribution of tempos. . . .

For the moment I want to suggest a musical work in which this separation into homogeneous movements will be abandoned in favor of nonhomogeneous distribution of developments. I demand for music the right to parentheses and italics; a notion of discontinuous time, thanks to structures that will be bound together rather than remain divided and airtight; finally a sort of development in which the closed circuit will not be the only solution envisaged.

I want the musical work not to be that series of compartments which one must inevitably visit one after the other. I try to think of it as a domain in which, in some manner, one can choose one's own direction.

That essay was published in November 1954, a month before Stockhausen met David Tudor and John Cage. At this time, Boulez was ahead of his European colleagues in advocating a break from a strict serial syntax locked into otherwise traditional forms. He addressed himself to recapturing the deep meaning that he felt had been lost under a mass of serial charts. Against overrationalization, he sought a more mysterious, more ambiguous way. In his searchings he found an ally in Mallarmé, who had been dead for more than fifty years. Boulez shared with Mallarmé not only a profound respect for structure but, more important, the deep intuition that knowledge, however useful, must be secondary in art.

In 1954 and 1955 Boulez met Stockhausen from time to time in Paris and Cologne. They corresponded sporadically, tackling the pulverizing of classical meter, the other face of the pulverizing of classical tonality. Boulez and Stockhausen shared ideas on "discontinuous time," on tempos controlled by the limits of a player's breath or by the player's ability to articulate rapidly. But along with the exchange of aesthetic ideas, the friendship began to show strain. Pousseur recalled a Domaine concert that took place on April 27, 1955, with the following program:

I. Ionisation (1930) . . . . Edgar Varèse
    pour instruments de percussion
    Pièces pour Piano . . . . .Karlheinz Stockhausen
    (1 reaudit.) Paris
    Marcelle Mercenier, pianiste
    Symphonies . . . . Henri Pousseur (creation)

II. Musique electronique
   avec le concours du studio electronique de la N.W.D.R.
                                                  Cologne

(Director: Herbert Eimert)
Études de: Henri Pousseur, Karlheinz Stockhausen
suivies d'une presentation des moyens de travail employés
au studio électronique

Pousseur said, "Stockhausen and I were like brothers at that time. Both of us were there with our young wives. Boulez, as always, was quite alone. Stockhausen was furious at the printed program. He was furious that we had been lumped together. He expected to be singled out."

Stockhausen didn't express his anger directly to Boulez. It took shape in an increasingly opposing aesthetic commitment derived from the chance procedures of Cage that moved much further than anything Boulez had in mind when he proselytized for some opening up of form. The medium Stockhausen used to effect this shift was the pianist David Tudor, whose every gesture symbolized the aesthetic of "uneventful time." Stockhausen's appropriation of Tudor as his pianist in the late 1950s, drew this from Boulez: "Tudor was an exceptional interpreter, and Stockhausen—like Wagner—had an acute sense for knowing the people who could serve him."

The bond that tied the early serialists together was not merely love of an aesthetic idea but included aggressive energy against the power structure. At first Stockhausen identified with Boulez's goal: the overthrow of tonality. But when Boulez, or the serial language, became a new authority, when the goal of musical revolution had been in good measure achieved, then Stockhausen redirected his hostile energies against Boulez and the idea for which he stood. "In 1953 and 1954," Boulez said, "I put these composers on the map. Then, very quickly, they turned against me."

Boulez's position shifted radically. New allies, new enemies were born; "avant-garde," one must remember, was a military term. The alliance of Boulez and Stockhausen against John Cage was displaced by another less advertised one: Stockhausen and Tudor against Boulez. At the close of their 1954 meeting in Cologne, Stockhausen gave Tudor his Piano Pieces I through V, VII, and VIII for Tudor to perform in New York. And the following month, Tudor programmed them along with Cage's 31' 57" in a recital at Carl Fischer Hall. Stockhausen and Tudor were corresponding then; Stockhausen had virtually perfected his English and the exchange between them grew. During the winter of 1955–56, when Stockhausen was telling colleagues that Boulez was "overrated," that his music was "too homogeneous," that everything Boulez did was "much less interesting than people in general thought," he also chose a more active course to undermine Boulez—and that was to undermine the idea in which he believed. Stockhausen got in touch with Steinecke and persuaded him to invite Tudor to Darmstadt in order to give three seminars there on the music of Cage and his friends.

In May 1956, David Tudor played parts I and IV of the *Music of Changes,* the very work that had precipitated Boulez's break from Cage, in a seminar at Darmstadt attended by Bruno Maderna, Luigi Nono, Stockhausen, and Boulez. After the performance, Stockhausen and Boulez engaged in a fight that, by all counts, lasted at least an hour. Stockhausen fought passionately for the ideas of the work; Boulez fought against them passionately. Tudor has said, "Boulez cared enough about Stockhausen to do everything he could to get Stockhausen to change his mind." But his efforts were unsuccessful.

Earlier Stockhausen had sent Boulez his most recent work, a wind quintet called *Zeitmasse.* In *Zeitmasse* (tempi) Stockhausen applied the new theories of relative rhythm that he and Boulez had so often discussed. Boulez found the piece impressive; later he said it was Stockhausen's best. Despite the bitter fight at Darmstadt, and the world première there of *Zeitmasse* in July 1956, Boulez programmed Stockhausen's new work for the Domaine Musical. But first he prepared an analysis of the piece; then he delivered a meticulous performance on December 15, 1956, and finally he made a noncommercial recording that put *Zeitmasse* on the map.

CHAPTER 29

On July 15, 1956, Tudor played Boulez's Second Sonata at the Domaine and gave the first public performance, with Severino Gazzelloni, of the Flute Sonatina on a program at Darmstadt that included Webern's Six Bagatelles, Schoenberg's Opus 26 Woodwind Quintet, and the world premiere of Stockhausen's *Zeitmasse*. The Flute Sonatina was so successful that he and Gazzelloni had to play it twice. Tudor said, "Many composers were very jealous of Boulez on that day."

During that particular session at Darmstadt, Luciano Berio was in the audience. He recalled the July 1956 concert:

> I was attracted to the Flute Sonatina right away. It took me longer to feel close to *Zeitmasse*. As a work, *Zeitmasse* belongs to the typical Germanic tradition, an idea pushed to its very limits. Immediate contact with the piece can be difficult. I had the impression that it was a tight, coercive piece. The elasticity in meter was absolutely not apparent. In fact *Zeitmasse* had very little impact on me until Boulez conducted it at the Domaine about six months later.

"The problems between Stockhausen and Boulez," Berio has said, "always had to do with ideas. I recall very strong discussions. Usually they had to do with Webern. In fact, Stockhausen wrote an analysis of Webern's Opus 24 Concerto that proved to be an incredibly important moment in modern music."

In this essay, published in *Melos* in 1953, Stockhausen attempted to reveal to composers how Webern had used the serial principle in areas other than pitch relations. Later Boulez said, "Stockhausen found a symmetry of parameters in Webern. All that I discovered in 1946 and 1947. There's a piece by Stockhausen in *Die Reihe* that goes to absurdities in this domain. It deals with the Webern Quartet. Here Stockhausen takes the consequence for the cause. He did it to help him formulate his own ideas."

The tension between Stockhausen and Boulez grew and crystallized into a race between the two men, into a need for setting precedents, for being first. Paul Jacobs, who played piano for the early Domaine concerts and was in close contact with Boulez in the mid-1950s, has described what went on between them at that time: "Stockhausen and Boulez developed a lot of ideas together: tempos controlled by the limits of a player's breath or by his ability to articulate rapidly. But each time Stockhausen got there first. Perhaps the most important idea was that of 'controlled chance.' But even here Stockhausen beat him to it. Boulez began his Third Piano Sonata before Stockhausen began *Klavierstück XI* (the outstanding models of the new principle). Yet Stockhausen's piece was played at Darmstadt first."

Tudor played *Klavierstück XI* at the scheduled concert in New York. But when it was time for him to go to Darmstadt, he experienced a "tightening of the hand and arm muscles" and canceled his trip less than two weeks in advance. Tudor admitted deep disenchantment with the work: "I had the impression when Stockhausen was talking to me about the piece that it would be much freer than it turned out to be. I remember my shock when I found the rhythmic values notated. How frantically I tried to get out of the four walls that the piece represented to me."

So Tudor said no, and as soon as Stockhausen received that message he sent the score by mail to Jacobs in Paris. Stockhausen had met Jacobs only once, in 1955, when Jacobs and Boulez had visited him in Cologne. On that occasion Jacobs played Debussy and Webern and came armed with the reputation of playing the most difficult contemporary music at sight.

As soon as Jacobs received the score he brought it to Boulez, who, according to Jacobs, "was very interested in it. If he felt any anger that Stockhausen had anticipated him with 'controlled chance' or any sense of betrayal that Stockhausen had called upon me, Boulez did not indicate it. But then, one never knows what Boulez thinks or feels. Still, he suggested I go immediately to Darmstadt to have as much time as possible to work with Stockhausen on the score."

Jacobs went to Germany and gave the first European performance of *Klavierstück XI* in the summer of 1957. And the piece created its intended effect; everyone talked about the new performer freedom. But not everyone was equally impressed. Berio said, "I knew right away that there was something superficial, some sheer exhibitionism in this work. I had the sense that Stockhausen had made a philosophical mistake, for whatever connects the various sections is purely arbitrary. There is not enough musical thinking on the inside to justify the openness of form."

When he began to plan *Klavierstück XI*, Stockhausen had shared his ideas with Boulez. Pousseur reported,

> Boulez replied he was against the conception. He had already begun his Third Piano Sonata. He thought of composing several "formants" (or sections) in which the sections would have a certain kind of character and would be divided into various parts. He had in mind a fixed sequence; he referred to the Beethoven Ninth as a model. But when he finished the work he had it flexible. Mallarmé's Le Livre had been published in the interim. It describes a book in which pages could be taken out and read in every possible order. Clearly it affected Boulez very much.

Jacques Sherer's *Sketches of Mallarmé's Le Livre* reveal in great detail Mallarmé's plan for a constantly variable work of art. And that was Boulez's purpose with the Third Sonata. "I have often compared this work with the plan of a city. One does not change its design, one perceives exactly what it is, and there are different ways of going through it. One can choose one's own way through it, but there are certain traffic regulations."

Here is how Boulez's Third Sonata was made: the first section, Antiphonie, consists of pairs of lines that are interchangeable. The next part Boulez composed was Trope, a title he borrowed from the medieval "trope" in which there were melodic interpolations in the *cantus firmus*. But in Boulez's work the "tropes" are not of melodies but of whole complex structures. There are four sections within this "formant" (movement). The sections are Texte, Parenthèse, Glose, and Commentaire—titles borrowed from literary scholarship. The performer may start with any of these sections and Commentaire must be played before or after Glose; otherwise the order is fixed. Texte contrasts subsections in strict rhythm with subsections where the rhythm is left to the performer—as in Stockhausen's *Zeitmasse*. But with Boulez, each of these sections never lasts more than five seconds. In Parenthèse, the strict sections are very slow and the free ones, now longer, have a continuously changing beat.

After Trope, Boulez wrote Constellation-Miroir, the longest formant, which lasts twelve and a half minutes. Constellation-Miroir can be played either forward or backward and was planned as the middle piece. Groups of notes are strewn together on long sheets of thick paper—to withstand the performers' handling—producing what Boulez calls "constellations." There are particular rules of play for the succession of these groups. Taking off from the special typography that Mallarmé used in the *Coup de dés*, which Boulez considers "one of the most important poems in French literature" (Mallarmé's typography changes on each page with the white background being transformed into a kind of stage), Boulez uses green and red ink for staves and musical notes carefully placed on the long, thick, unfolding pages, reminiscent of the form of Mallarmé's *Le Livre*. The order of the fragments is not fixed but is very carefully controlled. Each fragment is followed by another from which the performer can choose between one and four possibilities. The composer indicates the various choices by means of arrows.

Boulez maintained he saw *Le Livre* only after he had completed the work and reported that he was delighted to find that Mallarmé had moved, more than fifty years before, in a direction that he, on his own, was moving then. He added that he and Mallarmé even used the same words; "constellation" was the most striking one. To support his shift toward interchangeable structures, Boulez wrote an essay he entitled "Alea" for the *Nouvelle Revue Française*. It appeared in November 1957. In the first two paragraphs he attacked free-floating chance. Then he sailed into a complex discussion of "how to reconcile composition and chance," giving his recipe for "controlled chance." He concluded with a mock prayer for those who would not temper chance with discipline: "Peace to these angelic creatures; we can be sure they run absolutely no risk of stealing our thunder, since they wouldn't know what to do with it."

Cage was enraged. He said, "After having repeatedly claimed that one could not do what I set out to do, Boulez discovered the Mallarmé *Livre*. It was a chance operation down to the last detail. With me the principle had to be rejected outright; with Mallarmé it suddenly became acceptable to him. Now Boulez was promoting chance, only it had to be his kind of chance."

Cage's rage never abated. For, from the time of Boulez's famous essay, chance music has been widely known as "aleatory music." The most intolerable insult of all was that it was Boulez's erudite word with its esoteric roots (alea is one of a pair of dice) that gave Cage's fresh invention its quasi-official new name.

Several years after Stravinsky's death, Robert Craft wrote in *The New York Review of Books* that "the creative eruption that started with *Firebird* and that seemed to come entirely from within . . . had run its course" with *Pulcinella*, written when the composer was only thirty-six. Craft said that

Stravinsky's acceptance of Diaghilev's commission to rearrange Pergolesi's music for his ballet company "may imply an awareness that he could no longer subsist on his own inner resources."

Virgil Thomson suggests that Boulez followed a similar course which, he said, was not an uncommon one in France. "The strategy to create before thirty," Thomson wrote, "through talent, brains, determination and hard labor a handful of unforgettable works, then to retire into private or public life and wait for an immortality which, when all production is complete, arrives on schedule" is also characteristic, he said, of such figures as Duchamp and Rimbaud.

It is true that in his early twenties Boulez produced powerful and original music. Yet after his early affair and these violent expressive works, Boulez shifted considerably. In *Polyphonie X* and *Structures*, one no longer feels the violent expression alone. And, by the time of *Marteau*, the violence and energy of the artist lie hidden behind a hard and closed shell.

The radical inhibition in Boulez's creative life was accompanied by an increasing withdrawal from personal relationships that echoes his childhood days. Paul Jacobs recalled that when he met Boulez, early in 1954, the composer addressed him with the formal "vous." Jacobs asked Boulez how long one had to know him before being addressed by the familiar "tu." Boulez replied he gave no thought to such things and continued to address Jacobs with "vous."

Other composers note the same shift. Tudor said that after 1952 Boulez refused to discuss ideas, saying that he was saving them for publication. And Babbitt claims he never had a serious conversation with Boulez after the one in Cage's apartment that same year. Boulez's form and facade had become that of the isolated hero, in need of no one and nothing.

That such withdrawal indicated internal trouble and an awareness of his own blockage is suggested by Boulez's statement to Tudor, when he was twenty-seven, that he expected to write his "master work" at thirty. But to say that Boulez anticipated the height of his creative power to be that of a mathematician is not to say he would have preferred it that way. At the concert in the Whitney Museum during the spring of 1974 devoted exclusively to his work, he told the New York audience that it was good to get away from his duties as music director and return, for one evening, "to what is really myself." Boulez revealed repeatedly what he wanted most: to be the best and most advanced composer of his time; to be in power, of course, but with the power emanating from his centrality to the spirit of his age.

In 1955 Boulez's production began to taper off as Stockhausen's began to soar. Boulez worked on *Marteau* for two and a half years, completing it in the spring of 1955. He did not finish his next work, the Third Piano Sonata, until the fall of 1957. During this time, Stockhausen knocked off pieces with incredible rapidity, each of which introduced some new structural concept. As though *Zeitmasse* and the *Klavierstück XI* were not enough, he produced *Gesang der Jünglinge,* the first striking European electronic composition. The piece was played on Cologne Radio in May 1956; Boulez repeated it later that year at a Domaine concert, where he told his listeners to fasten their seat belts, that they would be hearing sounds they had never heard before.

Stockhausen began, in 1955, to develop ideas and materials for *Gruppen,* an aggressive, large-scale work that, according to his own published notes, "initiated the spatial deployment of instrumental music." (The "spatial deployment of instrumental music" was, in fact, initiated by Gabrieli and again by Berlioz long before, and used again more recently by the American composer Henry Brant. Indeed, composers who visited Stockhausen while he was at work on *Gruppen* report that an *American Composers Alliance Bulletin* [1955: volume 4, no. 3] containing Brant's article "The Uses of Antiphonal Distribution and Polyphony of Tempi in Composing" was invariably open on Stockhausen's desk; Brant's own first "music-in-space" work was then two years old.) In *Gruppen* three orchestras surround the listener. Each is under its own conductor. Each plays independently and in different tempos, from time to time meeting in a common rhythm. *Gruppen* was an immediate success.

The new music world was aware of the difference in production between Stockhausen and Boulez. Jacobs has said, "Stockhausen showed an intense energy in regard to composition. It started in 1955 to affect Boulez who was terribly shaken by it." Thomson reported, "Boulez was threatened with sterility early on. Stockhausen, on the contrary, is a faucet; all you have to do is turn him on." Tudor added, "Stockhausen's pieces kept coming all the time, each of them strong, each of them striking. There was Boulez slaving over his desk to complete works that had been in the process for years. Why the slowness? Because his compositional plans are so elaborate, because there is so much concern for system. He knew he couldn't move fast enough. But Boulez is a person capable of assessing himself absolutely accurately. He knew he couldn't succeed through composition anymore."

Of course, it is impossible to know what Boulez knew. Prisoner of his own idea—that being most advanced is being best—he pulled back. "In Stockhausen's good period," he said, "I came to trust his music more than anything else. I felt he could solve all the problems, that it was no longer necessary for me to address myself to them."

Thus Boulez shifted his career, turning from composition to conducting. The shift made it possible for Boulez—and interested listeners everywhere—to hear new scores played with vitality and accuracy. And, as he confessed, the act of conducting "intoxicated" him.

Boulez had begun to conduct with the Barrault company as early as 1946. Boulez's primary duty was to coordinate sounds from the pit very precisely with what was happening on stage. But precision was all that was required, precision applied to works that did not interest him.

In 1955 Boulez began to conduct chamber music at the Domaine. First he tried a quintet by Pousseur, then the Schoenberg Serenade, and in 1956 *Marteau sans Maître*. Also in 1956 he conducted a full orchestra for the first time. On his third South American tour with Barrault, Alejo Carpentier, a Cuban novelist and friend of Barrault, invited Boulez to conduct the Venezuelan Symphony. Boulez said he thought to himself, "To conduct so far from home is not dangerous." The program was scheduled to be Debussy's *Jeux* and *Ibéria*, Stravinsky's Symphonies of Wind Instruments, and Bartók's Music for Strings, Percussion and Celesta. But the parts for the Bartók did not arrive, and Boulez conducted Prokofiev's Classical Symphony instead. He said that he promised himself then that he would never conduct the work again, and he has fulfilled that promise. But the fact that he did conduct—even once—what surely must be the epitome of neoclassic music indicates that Boulez could compromise.

But he was not then in a position to dictate events. Boulez has said of the year 1957: "It was a shaky one financially. I did lectures and two piano concerts with Yvonne Loriod at radio stations in Germany. We performed my own works and pieces by Debussy. I made some recordings, too, but there were not many financial gains. I was aware that I would have to leave Barrault."

In the fall of 1957 Barrault left the Théâtre Marigny and moved to the Palais-Royal. "That meant," Boulez went on, "that Barrault was no longer connected with the Domaine. At that, all he had done for the previous three years was to give us the theater rent-free. The Domaine then moved to the Salle Gaveau. I thought this change in arrangement made it a good moment for me to make a change in my life. So I left Barrault. My interest in him was fading at the time. It had been a good relationship, but you can't stay in one place forever. You can't conduct incidental music for the rest of your life."

Boulez left the company, returning only to help with an occasional premiere and to accompany it to New York that winter.

Just before Easter 1957, Boulez had his first opportunity to conduct his own work outside the Domaine. "Hermann Scherchen was preparing *Visage Nuptial*" at Cologne, Boulez said,

> and he simply did not know the score. He was more or less floundering. There was a crisis between the orchestra and him. I was asked, "Are you strong enough to do it?"
>
> It is a very difficult work for chorus and orchestra. But everything went well. I had no feeling then of embarking on a conducting career. The career took on great proportions without my making any effort. At that time I had a good deal to learn. I had no connection with the performing side of music. I had no idea of how to cope with large forces. It was interesting for me to see the realization from the inside of big instrumental forces. The professional consequences I never foresaw. I made no effort to make a career. I did it only to benefit my composition.

Boulez took over again unexpectedly, eight months later when he was in California with Barrault, and attended a rehearsal of the Monday Evening Concerts at which Robert Craft was preparing *Marteau*. The Monday Evening Concerts, then in their eighteenth consecutive year were under the direction of Lawrence Morton, a friend of Stravinsky's and Craft's.

Morton recalled that Craft simply deferred to Boulez as the composer and, on his own, suggested that Boulez take over the podium. In a published essay in the *Saturday Review,* Craft wrote that Boulez came to Los Angeles precisely to conduct *Marteau*. In any event, Boulez did conduct the piece, and although the musicians responded warmly to him, even presenting him with a pair of cuff links—a gesture Morton characterized as exceptional—*Marteau* earned harsh criticism from the musical press.

On his return to Europe in the spring of 1958, Boulez appeared in Cologne as one of the three conductors of Stockhausen's *Gruppen*. Along with Stockhausen and Maderna, he conducted one of the three orchestras for the premiere. The piece was enormously difficult, and there were moments when Maderna threatened to leave. Finally the three artists conquered the work. Tudor said Stockhausen was immensely pleased with the results. *Gruppen* was played twice.

Speaking of *Gruppen* later, Boulez noted, "It was good, but there were already some compromises, an abstracted jazz that I found very vulgar. Sometimes Stockhausen would blast his way. There was a cheap side showing that I did not like very much. I could see it in *Gesang der Jünglinge* as well. Stockhausen was covering abstract categories with splashy gowns."

The relations between Stockhausen and Boulez were then tense. Pousseur has said that in 1957, in an effort to restore good feelings between them, Stockhausen named Boulez godfather to his third child. The gesture seems to have made professional relations easier, but it cannot have gone far in abating Boulez's fury against the younger man who displaced him in the new music world as he himself had displaced Leibowitz a decade before. Surely there are many men who resent their students' climb to their own status level. But psychoanalyst Jacob Arlow writes that a boy born after the death of an earlier son fantasizes that he murdered his predecessor in the womb. Such a man, Arlow said, is destined to fear retaliation from a younger man and to react in an exaggerated way if it should seem to come.

Whether or not this was true of Boulez, the rage against Stockhausen became increasingly difficult to suppress. Less than a month after the *Gruppen* premiere, Boulez began to work on a commission from Strobel. Following Stockhausen's lead in *Gesang der Jünglinge* and *Gruppen*, he composed a piece for voice, two orchestras, and tape. For his poem he chose one by Henri Michaux, *Poésies pour Pouvoir* (Poems for Power), a title with much meaning for Boulez at a moment when he found himself drawing on Stockhausen's ideas. The poem is one man's curse on another, and is as murderous a set of verses as I have ever read.

Poésies pour Pouvoir received its first and only performance at the Donaueschingen Festival in October 1958. Otto Tomek, then a music director at Cologne Radio, attended: "The piece was exciting. But it required technical facilities that were not available at the time. There was a loud-speaker turning slowly in the room. The result was highly unsatisfactory. At that, it was fortunate the words could not be understood."

Freud, in *The Interpretation of Dreams*, quoted Socrates: "The good man does in his dreams what the wicked one does in actual life." Socrates might have said, "in his dreams and his art." Boulez used poetry to this effect.

Cage attempted to prove that Boulez's interest really was in literature rather than music by citing Boulez's essay of 1954 in which he demanded "italics and parentheses in music." Stockhausen, in an article in *Die Reihe,* illustrated with musical examples how the instruments in *Marteau* served only to "intensify the comprehension of the words" and added that under these conditions "the phonetic properties of speech" cannot be sufficiently exploited for composition. Boulez freely admits his passion for poetry and has said Stockhausen is uncultivated in this realm: "Otherwise he would know better than to write his own texts."

Boulez's sister provided another clue: "My brother is completely closed. The only way to know what he has thought is to read very carefully all the poetry he has set."

Boulez has said that a period in music ended in 1958. "I know it sounds egocentric," he added, "but that period began in 1944." Thus Boulez identifies the birth and apparent death of the serial language with his own endeavors to establish and nourish it.

In 1959 Boulez left France and moved to Germany.

CHAPTER 30

n June 1958 Boulez went to Baden-Baden. He took a room in a hotel next to the Southwest German Radio station and across a lawn from the apartment building where the Strobels lived. Twice a day, at noon and in the evening, Hilda Strobel called out her window to Boulez's balcony to announce that dinner was about to be served.

Hilda Strobel described Boulez: "He was a young man with enormous charm who had something spiritual about him. One could speak on any theme, on literature, the fine arts, anything at all. There was always much joking, many obscenities. He could be as nice as he was aggressive. He thought of us as his parents, perhaps even as his best friends. His parents gave him nothing. At the beginning Pierre hated his father and Pierre had a cruel temperament. He could get as furious at an orchestra as he could get against his father."

Boulez spent two weeks in Baden-Baden that June working on *Poésies pour Pouvoir*. Because he had to complete it for the Donaueschingen Festival in October, he canceled his plans to teach at Darmstadt.

"It was in 1958," Tudor has said, "that Stockhausen surpassed Boulez as a power in Europe." Stockhausen, as Boulez described him in those days, was "very sure, very strong." And he used that certainty, strength, and power to move the musical world into an altogether new realm. When Stockhausen learned of Boulez's cancellation, he persuaded Steinecke to hire Cage in Boulez's place. Elated at the invitation, Cage accepted. "In 1954," Cage explained, "Europeans had taken me as some kind of clown. I thought that my presence at Darmstadt would mean that now I'd be taken seriously."

Cage was right. "If the truth were known," Tudor said, "it was Stockhausen who turned the tide. If ever a question of negation came up, Stockhausen came to our aid."

Stockhausen, in fact, embraced Cage with such fervor that by absorption he all but annihilated him from the musical scene. Appropriating

Cage's interest in Eastern mysticism as well as his notions of performer involvement and chance, Stockhausen continued to pour out work after work. *Refrain* is in a large circle of notation with a plastic strip that can spin. Cage said that many composers at Darmstadt asked him if he would be offended if they were to adopt the ideas on graphism that he had presented to them in 1958. "I made it clear," Cage said, "that none of these ideas belonged to me personally."

And in no time they hardly belonged to him at all. Composer Hans Werner Henze had been at Darmstadt in the early Leibowitz days. But he left in 1954 because of the excesses he then felt in serialism. He described how Stockhausen "embraced" Cage. Henze extended his arms in a wide circle, then brought them together as though to embrace a friend, and finally crushes them tightly against his chest.

To be maintained, power must always be increased, and Stockhausen knew that well. By the end of 1958 he refused to play a role in any program in which works by any other composer were to be included along with his own. Stockhausen demanded exclusive treatment, and generally he received it. And the propagation of the serial syntax was just about the last thing he had in his mind.

Thus Boulez saw his Idea slipping away and he attempted to move along with the tide: *Pli Selon Pli* continues the efforts he made in the Third Sonata to combine improvisatory with fixed elements. But as Messiaen said, "He never had his heart in aleatory work. Whatever he did was with great prudence." The grammar for which Boulez had had such high hopes was being displaced, in his lexicon, by theatrical gimmickry, by anarchic and nihilistic philosophies. Boulez, in 1974, summed it up in one sentence: "Stockhausen, with his hippie, hormonal cure, pedantically revived what was genuine in Cage."

The higher the hopes, the more bitter the disillusion. Death and despair are evident in the hour-long work, *Pli Selon Pli*, all of which was mapped out in 1958–59. The dates of the realizations of specific movements follow: Don, 1961; Improvisation I, 1958–60; Improvisation II, 1958; Improvisation III, 1960; Tombeau, 1959.

The first movement begins with the opening line of the Mallarmé poem "Don du Poème": "Je t'apporte l'enfant d'une nuit d'Idumée" (I bring you the child of an Idumaean night). Wallace Fowlie, a Mallarmé scholar, writes that "from the title we know the gift is a poem but the image signifies it is a dismal birth. The poem is inadequate and the birth is covered with blood. The poem is disinherited as soon as it is created and is thus compared to the child of Edom, which was the country of Esau, the brother disinherited in favor of Jacob." That is surely an accurate metaphor for the way Boulez viewed the birth and savage assault on his Idea.

The end of the last movement declaims the last line of Mallarmé's "Tombeau": "Un peu profond ruisseau calomnié la mort" (A shallow rivulet misrepresented is death). The sonnet which ends with this line suggests that the artist does not die—as ordinary men do—but lives on in some extraordinary way after death. Written to commemorate the first anniversary of the death of Verlaine, Tombeau was composed shortly before Mallarmé's own death. Boulez's choice of it as the only line of text placed at the end of the last movement of a work he had long planned as his "masterwork," suggests that, just as this was the end of Mallarmé's life, so was it the end of his own creative life.

The Mallarmé poems used in their entirety for the intervening movements, Improvisations I, II, III, confirm the despair and sense of death the outer movements evoke.

The first, "Le vierge, le vivace et le bel aujourd'hui" (The virginal, lively and beautiful day) paints a picture of a swan stuck in the ice and unable to fly. The second, "Une dentelle s'abolit" (A piece of lace disappears), is replete with tomblike images: a room without a bed, a mandolin with a hollow inside, each impotent in its effort to give birth. The third, "A la nue accablante tu" (To the overwhelming cloud hushed), concerns the catastrophe of a shipwreck. "The poet imagines," Fowlie writes, "the highest mast, stripped of its sail, sinking last into the water. Something has been abolished. . . . The threatening cloud, pressing low against the water, has followed a storm that has left its mark in some unaccountable way. . . . Some act which is just over must have been tremendous in its spectacle and meaning. Almost nothing of it remains: a low cloud and a bit of foam. The act has descended into its own secret."

Something tremendous had happened to Boulez. He had brought forth a consequent and rigorous grammar that he designed to replace the tonal grammar and to serve his art for hundreds of years. Now almost nothing of it remained.

Boulez took his title, *Pli Selon Pli* (Fold by Fold), from another of Mallarmé's poems in which the poet describes how the dissolving mist gradually reveals the city of Bruges. "In the same way," Boulez wrote in program notes for his recording, "as the five pieces unfold, they reveal, fold by fold, a portrait of Mallarmé." One might add, "and of Boulez, as well."

The Improvisations are set for soprano and chamber ensemble; the ensemble varies from movement to movement but consists, primarily, of percussion instruments. The outer pieces are written for a larger ensemble and produce an orchestral sound. Don is scored for three orchestras. Before 1959, Boulez had set three works by René Char and one poem by Henri Michaux. He explained his shift to Mallarmé:

> I found many sources of inspiration in Char and Michaux, but preoccupation with form was not one of them. Char's interest was in an extremely tight vocabulary; Michaux's in the creation of an original imagery. But syntax itself, the arrangement of words and their cohesion and sonority, was not the obsession of either poet.
>
> What seduced me with Mallarmé was the formal density of his work. Not only is the content extraordinary—for his poems have a very particular mythology—but the French language has never been led further, from the point of view of syntax. I wanted to find a musical equivalent and that is why I chose the strictest forms.
>
> There are various levels of convergence between poetry and music. The simplest is the conveying of the sense of the words. Thus, when Mallarmé speaks of "absence," there is a musical sonority—a sound held for a long time—that can convey this idea. Another point of convergence is the form itself. The sonnet has a very strict form which calls for a certain musical structure. My purpose was to attribute a kind of form to each verse according to the rules of the sonnet itself. There is also numerology here: one structure is based on the number 8 because it is a verse of eight syllables. Gradually these improvisations become analagous with the structure of the sonnet, but in a manner more and more detailed, more and more profound. That is why I call them Improvisations I, II, and III.

Boulez's elaborate discussion of technique in the interview quoted here, which was broadcast on Belgian Radio in 1972, serves to hide from the listener the real "meaning" of the work, which can easily be discovered in the words of the poetry.

Few listeners could pick up Boulez's devices, for the system is impenetrable. Few could even pick up the words, for they are virtually drowned in the music. What the listener will pick up is the dazzling instrumental color: *Pli Selon Pli* is a remarkable work for its instrumental passages of great beauty, for its technique and proportion. The first two Improvisations, commissioned for the concert series *Das neue Werke,* were performed in Hamburg in 1958. The complete five-movement piece received its premiere in 1960 in Cologne under the direction of Boulez. Stravinsky was there. Craft reported that Stravinsky was disappointed, that he thought *Marteau* presaged a "stronger next work." Craft said Stravinsky thought it was "pretty, a piece with no balls." By then the Stravinsky-Boulez alliance had undergone considerable strain. Stravinsky was angry about a disastrous performance of his *Threni* at a Domaine concert, so his judgment may have been spiteful.

In December 1958 Boulez went to Baden-Baden for a second time. He stayed in servants' quarters just above the Strobel apartment and spent Christmas with the Strobels. The following month Boulez signed a contract with the Südwestfunk which, he recalled, "lasted two or three years." So the Germans, who captured him in 1952 through a publication contract with Universal Edition, now had physical possession of him as well through a well-paying composer-in-residence arrangement: "I was to perform my works with them and also conduct some chamber concerts. It provided enough money for me to keep going."

Hilda Strobel found an apartment in the Pension Rubens on which he took a one-year lease. In 1961 he moved into the first floor of Hilda Strobel's dentist's house, a four-story building banked against a hill. And so Boulez took up residence in a town of parks, patisseries, and Marienbad-like hotels, a town which still looks like a little German principality of the nineteenth century. He gave up his quarters in Paris.

A little earlier, owing to Hans Rosbaud's illness, Boulez's conducting career received an unexpected boost. Strobel asked Boulez to fill in for Rosbaud by conducting a performance at the Domaine. "When he saw I did well with that," Boulez said, "he gave me more: the big orchestra."

In July 1959 Rosbaud invited Boulez to lunch and told him he was suffering from cancer of the kidneys. He asked Boulez to substitute for him, conducting in a festival at Aix-en-Provence. Boulez took over Rosbaud's complete program: "*Wozzeck* excerpts, Webern, Pousseur, Hindemith—that awful Concerto for Orchestra."

In October 1959 Rosbaud could not conduct at the Donaueschingen Festival. Boulez again took over the podium. "I was called in on Thursday for Saturday and Sunday and there were five new scores, including Berio's *Alleluiah.* Everyone was enthusiastic; I had saved the festival."

Hilda Strobel recalled:

There was Boulez: small, fat, a real peasant, a peasant from Auvergne. He came as a paysan, without making compliments to the orchestra or paying deference in any way to the audience. At the end there was a tremendous success. Boulez had conducted the *Miraculous Mandarin* and there was total disorder in the orchestra. He had only a few rehearsals and he knew nothing about conducting then. So naturally the Bartók could not have been very good. But Boulez's temperament enchanted the public. People were so taken by his personality that they didn't seem to care how bad the Bartók really was.

From that point on, conducting proliferated in Boulez's life. He said he never "studied" conductors for long periods, that he "observed" Desormière and Hermann Scherchen. After 1955, when he visited Baden-Baden regularly, he said he had the opportunity to watch Rosbaud and pick up some details, "particularly Rosbaud's patience with the musicians when they made mistakes. If musicians make mistakes, it is not because they want to make mistakes, but because there is something they do not understand and it is up to the conductor to help them. How can I describe my development as a conductor? I always had a good ear, could catch mistakes and correct them. But it is true that I gradually became more sensitive to stylistic matters, to phrasing, tempo, balance, timbre, color, and all the rest."

In addition to the Südwestfunk, Rosbaud had been principal conductor of the Concertgebouw Orchestra of Amsterdam. Boulez moved into his place there too. He also began to teach composition and analysis in Basel in 1961. Strobel arranged the appointment through Paul Sacher, general director of the Academy of Music there. Boulez would receive one thousand Swiss francs ($250) in exchange for one or two days' teaching a month. Sacher's wife was the widow of a Swiss pharmaceutical manufacturer. In her youth she had been a friend of Klee and Kandinsky and she had a great collection of abstract expressionist works. She asked Boulez for a sheet of his manuscript. On receiving it she pressed him to accept a fee; when he refused, she gave him a Karmann Ghia instead. Once indifferent to money, Boulez began to taste what it could bring.

Many of Boulez's most impassioned early admirers believe he had given himself up to a vulgar career. But Boulez's student Susan Bradshaw, who was in contact with him during the 1960s, came considerably closer to the truth in suggesting that Boulez's striking change was motivated not by choice but by need: "Stockhausen was such a strong musical personality that Boulez felt driven into a corner. It is ridiculous to feel rivalry but that is clearly what happened. Boulez was conscious of being in Stockhausen's shadow. Boulez's conducting career made it impossible for him to compose. And he probably prefers it this way. Conducting is just reproducing other people's work. It means you never have to reveal yourself."

Messiaen articulated the particular causes that lay behind the shift:

> Immediately after World War II, serial music was everything. Since then there have been many other things: concrète, electronic, aleatory. . . . And some of these have finished already. The eighteen-year-old looks for still another way.
>
> Boulez is very intelligent. He understands the changes and they make him suffer. There are people who go unperturbed through change. Like Bach. Like Richard Strauss—who lived to know Debussy, Wagner, and Stravinsky. But Boulez cannot. This is extremely sad because he is a great composer.

Souvchinsky has said, "Boulez became a conductor because he had a great gift for this. The phenomenon of his genius is complex. He is not in a class with Ravel and Messiaen but with Beethoven, Mozart, Wagner, and Debussy. He stands among the highest categories of creators."

CHAPTER 31

Boulez has said he never "stopped" composing, that he just shifted his energies, that he "fell into" his new career.

I quickly discovered that I was able to conduct without taking any lessons. I think one can learn to conduct only by conducting. People began to offer me engagements and I accepted them. At first I had no intention of conducting "classical music." My aim was to make known what I call the "classics of the modern period." Those were very rarely played. But orchestras always have limited rehearsal time and as contemporary music needs a great deal of rehearsing, it is best to "buy" this time by including in your programs a large proportion of standard pieces which the players already know. So I began conducting Handel and Haydn as well as Schoenberg and Webern. Then the thing began to snowball. There is such a need for conductors today that if you are just a little bit gifted you get sucked into the machinery.

Simultaneously with his initial foray into conducting, Boulez turned to pedagogy. He had begun to teach at Darmstadt in 1956, but these sessions were seminars and did not call for the articulation of an aesthetic creed. In 1960 Boulez presented a series of formal lectures there which were designed to do precisely that. They were published in German in 1963 and translated into English by Richard Rodney Bennett and Susan Bradshaw as *Boulez on Music Today*, published in 1971. Unlike Stravinsky, for whom Souvchinsky wrote the Harvard lectures twenty years before, Boulez asked for no help at all. Souvchinsky has said of Boulez's pedagogy: "What Boulez has done is to make a school, build a base. It remains intact as a kind of academicism. It is a system he follows but passes around. Still, the school stays."

In these talks Boulez made an effort to reverse through words the musical situation he found intolerable. His language was turgid, but one thing is clear: very few escaped his wrath.

Boulez issued his attacks without mentioning a single name. The enemies were there but never identified. Boulez never named names, he explained, because he refused "to make such people martyrs."

In place of all he despised, Boulez advocated a balance of control and chance, of both improvisatory and nonimprovisatory elements, of "being at once both free and disciplined." And through it all he insisted on Webern's paternity, not only for the previous decade, but for future decades as well: "It is obvious that Webern—who emerged very early as the chief landmark in defining our personalities—stands at the center of these explorations."

The lectures were dogmatic and pompous, lacking the grace of his offstage manner. Rather than "I am," he said, "We must." And the musical analyses he offered were meticulous and dry. Bradshaw said, "The explanations are so intricate and detailed; even when challenged he refused to explain them. I believe it was willful secrecy on his part. He showed little interest in the book. He never looked at the copy of the typescript."

Here is Boulez on the second formant, Trope, of his Third Piano Sonata:

> The series is divided into four groups, of four, one, four and three notes respectively, which I will call *a, b, c, d*. Groups *a* and *b/d* are joined isomorphically, the original figure *a* being at the same time inverted and permuted; group *c* consists of two isomorphic figures. Figure *a* is reducible to two generative intervals, the semitone and the fourth, which will create the vertical and horizontal relationships *(E♮–F♮/B♮–F#; E♮–B♮/F♮–F#)*; the connecting intervals are the augmented fourth and the whole tone *(F♮–B♮; F#–E♮)*. In the figure *b/d* obtained by inversion and permutation, the vertical relationships are the augmented fourth and the whole tone *(G#–D♮/C#–E♭)*; the horizontal relationships and the connecting intervals being the semitone and the fourth *(G#–C#/D♮–E♭; D♮–C#/E♭ G#)*. Figure *c* is composed of two isomorphic elements, minor thirds *(G♮–B♭/C♮–A♮)* observing globally the transposition of a whole tone *(G♮–A♮/B♭–C♮)*; but if the notes obtained by inversion are seen in apposition to those of the original figure the relationship of the semitones and the fourth will again be found *(G♮–C♮; B♭–A♮)*.

Finally, the series is composed of two isomorphic figures: *a/bd*, and of a group which itself includes two isomorphic figures: *c*; this last group—which is *divisible—divides* the second isomorphic figure *bd* into two unequal parts: *b (one note, G#)* and *d (three notes: D♮ C#E♭)*. Thus there is, on the

one hand, manifest symmetry within *c* and, on the other hand, concealed symmetry between *a* and the two fragments *b, d*. In addition the intervals which relate the groups to each other are the same as the fundamental intervals of the groups: whole tone, semitone and fourth.

A single series can obey several isomorphic laws. A figure of three notes *(e.g. B♮B♭D♮)* may undergo an augmentation *(E♭C#A♮)* in which all its intervals are doubled, and then appear in a symmetrical, retrograde form *(G#E♮F♮)*; finally, to complete the twelve notes, a figure is added which is irreducible to the principal figure.

What do we notice? Other isomorphic relationships result from this triple succession of three-note isomorphic figures. There are two four-note figures linked by very obvious relationships; these include a pair of intervals *a*, separated by another interval *b*, *a* and *b* being interchanged from the first to the second group. The first pair of intervals, two minor seconds *(B♮–B♭/D♮–E♭)*, is separated by a major

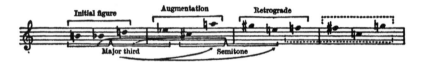

third; the second pair, two major thirds *(C#–A♮/G#–E♮)*, is separated by a minor second *(A♮–G#)*. The minor seconds are inverted in relation to each other (descending and ascending seconds), whereas the major thirds are parallel (descending); moreover, one of the central intervals that act as axes of symmetry is ascending, the other descending. The third four-note figure is irreducible. Once more let us take the same three-note figure; this time it will be augmented, then inverted, and to complete the twelve notes, another irreducible figure will be added to it.

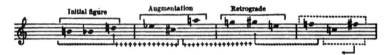

What do we notice now? Two isomorphic figures, each of five notes, the second of which is the retrograde of the first; the last three notes correspond to the first three, by retrogradation *(B♮B♭D♮–G#E♮F♮);* from the pivotal third note, the retrograde is combined with inversion of the intervals *(D♮E♭C#–A♮G♮G#)*. The final figure of two notes *(C♮F#)* is apparently irreducible to the other two. Notice, however, that the interval between the last note of the second figure and the first of these terminal notes is the same as that between the second of these two notes and the first note of the first figure *(F♮–C♮/F#–B♮)*; if the second note *(F#)* is placed at the beginning of the series, we shall have two six-note isomorphic figures. This series will obey two different isomorphisms; the first, partial, forming three figures; the second, total, forming two.

Finally, there are totally asymmetrical series; these occur principally when a limited number of elements is used, because isomorphic elements are almost inevitable, even if only of a single interval or a given proportion, as soon as the number of basic elements increases.

In conclusion, there are three distinct types of serial structure:

— totally symmetrical
— partially symmetrical and asymmetrical
    manifest isomorphic figures
    concealed isomorphic figures
— totally asymmetrical.

Boulez noted, "If I have dwelt at length on the structure of the series itself, it is because it forms the basis of an entire organization of series derived from it."

Thus Boulez's method of making music can be seen as one in which some kind of mathematical equations have displaced human beings as the center of art. Purpose and intention have capitulated to structure and system. Boulez's ties to both can be traced, perhaps, to Catholicism and his rigid early life. But in subscribing to this method he was also in line with many important intellectuals in France for whom structuralism had become an overriding philosophy. Claude Lévi-Strauss has built a creed on the way a myth changes as it moves from one culture to another; he deemphasizes the meaning of the content of the myth. Jean Piaget concentrates on the way a person conceptualizes the world; he never really deals with what the person wants to do with that world.

Lévi-Strauss, Piaget, and their colleagues imply that structures are ultimately logico-algebraic in nature—whether they involve myths, behavior, or interval relationships. Thus the structuralist is oriented towards mathematics and away from the interpretation of life. The most complex of such formulas underlie Trope and every other composition of Boulez's post-1952 career. Still, Boulez derives no satisfaction when someone else discovers the mechanisms at work. Claude Helffer, who has recorded the Third Piano Sonata, said, "In Boulez there is always the aspect of a sphinx. One assumes there is always structure, although he will not talk about it. Once I noted the structure of the tempos in Constellation-Miroir. Boulez was not pleased at all. He feels that what's important are the periods at the end of sentences, not the grammar itself. When I ask him to explain something, he said, 'I don't remember.' He has his own language. He believes: if it's good, I'll use it but it's not important to understand it."

The problem of new music is one of language. Language is a set of propositions to render the world around us concrete. But language is something we must catch on to, not something that can be contrived. As the meaning of life lies outside what can be said, so the meaning of music lies outside any syntax.

Boulez knows this only too well. And he has steadfastly addressed himself to transcending these propositions to see the world both freely and right. Still, the rigor of his approach, with its sparse sensuous contents, may allow him to be great, but not popular. Not popular with the public at large or popular even with the specialists, most of whom, in the early 1960s, were moving onto a suggestive, more symbolic art, in which disciplined intellect played a minimal role.

Boulez never wants to expose himself, not through his handwriting—which is so small it is virtually unreadable—his clothes, his furnishings, or his art. Thus the structuralist approach is exactly suited to his needs. Even his most complex works are not "hidden" enough for him. Boulez said he hates Picasso "because everything is visible," and adds that he does not like to study his own scores "because that is like looking at yourself in the mirror and you can't be pleased with only your own head in the mirror." So, much as Boulez would have loved to be advancing the advance guard, he could not move into their seemingly uninhibited world. He was locked into a demanding and dignified language. Souvchinsky has said, "Boulez's last piece is no different from his early ones. There is nothing contradictory in his work from beginning to end." That Boulez's ideas about composition have not changed from the start of his career is supported by the fact that, in 1963, he gave permission to Editions du Seuil to publish a collection of his essays that had appeared in the *Encyclopédie de la Musique,* published by Fasquelle, and in various journals between 1948 and 1962.

In the early 1960s, Boulez's polemics appeared in Darmstadt through the lectures, in Paris through the published essays, and in New England. In the spring of 1963, Boulez was named Horatio Appleton Lamb Lecturer at Harvard University, where he discoursed on the "Aesthetics of Composing." His opening statement acknowledged his awareness that there were other messages in the air than his own: "My vision is only my wager and, as Baudelaire said, I have the right to be wrong." In class Boulez analyzed *Wozzeck, The Rite of Spring*, and Webern's Opus 21 Symphony. The sessions were open to auditors, but the number who attended decreased with every session. One outside visitor was a journalist on assignment from a nationwide magazine. Her story never materialized, but she left the following comments on file:

> Boulez lived in Adams House. . . . His room was devoid of personal effects. I asked him why the room was so neat. "Because I'm against disorder," he replied. . . .
>
> Boulez was upset by the music floating in all of the windows. "About midnight they all get to Chopin discs." He sighed and waved his hand in a gesture of complete despair. . . .
>
> A graduate student in philosophy showed him around Lexington and Concord. "Boulez is a real tourist type," the student told me. "He's well informed and doesn't like it when people explain things he already knows. Someone asked him today if he knew who Thoreau was. That was a mistake. . . ."
>
> The lectures are not coming off. In class he is very lively and technical. He is fighting his way through the translation and has no time for communicating with the audience because he is so busy with the translation. . . .
>
> I have never worked so hard to get so little information. Or specific quotes. It is very difficult to get him to answer a question although he doesn't answer it in a most pleasant way.

CHAPTER 32

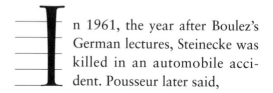n 1961, the year after Boulez's German lectures, Steinecke was killed in an automobile accident. Pousseur later said,

> Steinecke was the man behind things at Darmstadt. He rendered everything possible materially. By 1961 each composer had begun to go off in his own direction. With Steinecke alive, they were still together although their paths had long since gone astray.
>
> During the summer of 1961 each person felt an immense hole. Steinecke was present in his absence. We all went to the cemetery. Boulez had planned to make a speech. He began to speak to the man himself, as though Steinecke were alive and could hear everything he said. He began by saying that we were all there, that we would go on doing what we had done. But almost immediately he began to cry. Then he cried so uncontrollably he had to run away. Everyone was surprised at his reaction. Everyone was surprised at the depth of his feeling.

Everyone was surprised because Boulez's behavior was out of character. Steinecke was a symbol of a time when unanimity of taste and homogeneity of purpose spared music the scattering influence that confused it in the years that followed. Steinecke's reign coincided with a moment when music was concentrated in a single style that genuinely was at one with its time. Several summers before his death, it was clear that serialism was not to be the way. But by the summer of his death it was equally clear that serialism would not be supplanted by a single burgeoning art—like the preclassicism that displaced the high baroque—but rather by a plethora of styles. "In Bach's time," Boulez has said, "there was an accepted language, an accepted convention. It is not at all the same today. There is no longer a complete frame of expression. That is what there was at Darmstadt. That is what is needed again."

When the Darmstadt lectures were published in 1963, Boulez dedicated them to the memory of Steinecke.

"For me," Boulez told an American interviewer in 1963, "the external shock value of music matters little. The work I find really important is the one that has a kind of metaphysical truth, a truth in harmony with its time. An artist must be able to speak for his time in language of both precision and freedom. The trouble with 'beautiful' and 'ugly' as criteria is that they are tied up with superficial pleasure. I know I'm Germanic in this respect because I find sensual pleasure only a rather limited part of music. That is quite un-French, isn't it?"

In 1958 Boulez began *Doubles for Orchestra* on commission from the Südwestfunk. He abandoned it to work on *Pli Selon Pli* but returned to it in 1964, expanding it as *Figures, Doubles, Prisms.* Boulez revised and added to it in 1968 and again later. He conducted the first performance in Brussels in 1964. The work shows the influence of his experience conducting large orchestras. The orchestra is symmetrically grouped: a solo ensemble in the middle of two larger groups. The woodwinds are divided into three groups, the brass into four, the strings into five. The harps, xylophone, vibraphone, celesta, timpani, and percussion are placed individually between these main groups. Boulez said that his writing for strings in this piece was a deliberate gesture in homage to Berg's Violin Concerto.

Here is what Boulez wrote about the title in program notes for the Cleveland Symphony performance in 1966:

> *Figures* refers to simple elements, sharply characterized by dynamics, violence, softness, slowness, and so forth. These elements can be purely harmonic, or more rhythmically oriented, or purely melodic. They are not themes in the conventional way, but "states" of musical being.
>
> *Doubles* has two meanings: the first is that of the eighteenth century word doppelgänger, which means a human double. Thus, in the process of development, each figure may have its double, which is related only to it and no other.
>
> *Prisms* occur when the figures or their doubles refract themselves one through the other. And in this case, one figure

becomes the prism, and the other is refracted through it. By this process the maximum complexity is obtained, and the effect will be comparable to that of a kaleidoscope.

This confusing description dates from 1965. Later Boulez did not tell the public even this much about the making of a work. In response to queries about a new piece, he would generally limit his answer to mentioning the instrumentation and performance time. The manuscript of *Figures, Doubles, Prisms* reveals a dense, contrapuntal texture and a hint of the aggressive style of his earlier years. But here the explosion is under control; no "hysteria" or "spells" anywhere in the score. Otto Tomek, who heard the piece, said, "It is a dramatic work. I would call it 'controlled explosion.' Comparing it to his early pieces is like comparing Schoenberg's orchestral Variations to *Erwartung*."

An effort towards drama and excitement is also evident in *Structures, Book II*, begun in 1958 and completed in 1962. With its organization into chapters and texts, it reaffirms the author's attachment to literature. *Structures, Book II* has more in common with the Third Piano Sonata, composed only a short time before, than it has with *Structures, Book I*, dealing, as it does, with elements of choice as well as with sonorities and continuity. The precise instructions for pedaling (exactly how high to raise the pedal) are consistent with the tiny gradations in dynamics in *Structures, Book II*. Tomek said, "Boulez's late works may not be as explosive as the very early ones, but they do have particularly fine structures. Not big structures, of course, but structures in the most minute details. If you're quiet enough to hear the music, if you can hear the tiny differences, you can discover a whole world of invention."

Defining his aims of the 1960s, when he was not composing as prolifically as at other times, Boulez said the period began in 1958 when he wrote *Poésies pour Pouvoir*: "I was concerned with reconciling opposing elements. I wanted to bring electronic and orchestral sounds together. I was also working with small and large groups, with improvisation and nonimprovisation." The balance between control and aleatory procedures occupied his attention in *Structures, Book II*. The sections called "texts," within rigorously defined limits, are open to various choices in the manner of the Third Piano Sonata. Boulez and Yvonne Loriod gave the first performance in Donaueschingen in October 1962. In a program note Boulez asked, "Is a musical work conceivable only in one precise and organized direction? Must one treat it as a kind of novel in which events move in one direction alone?"

Obviously still inspired by Mallarmé's *Le Livre*, Boulez attempted, in his own words, "to break completely the closed form." But he refused to share responsibility with the performer. In a 1964 interview in *The Times* of London, Boulez deprecated the performer's ability to participate in the creative process. "I have no confidence in the imagination of performers," he said. "The performer's head is full of formulas drawn from the music he plays. If he had the necessary invention, he would be a composer himself."

Boulez's harsh attitude towards interpreters separated him from the prevailing aesthetic and caused bitter feelings among many performers with whom he worked, particularly those playing supposedly aleatory works. Susan Bradshaw said, "The Mallarmé contains certain freedoms but no freedom. It's 'Play it as you like as long as you play it my way.'" "Richard Rodney Bennett said much the same: "The second Mallarmé *Improvisation* seemed a beautiful, free piece. In the pauses I did pretty things under another conductor. That was not so when I played it under Boulez. He snaps the whip. Then you do it. The performance gets tension and vitality, but not the vitality from being happy."

In 1963, after completing his Harvard lectures, Boulez went to Los Angeles to conduct *Improvisations I* and *II* for the Monday Evening Concert. The program also included *Structures, Book II*. To please Boulez, Morton not only programmed his most recent works and gave the *Improvisations* all the rehearsal time Boulez wished, but he also devoted half of the concert to a tribute to Mallarmé by including the Debussy and Ravel Mallarmé settings. An ardent Boulez fan, Morton, between 1952 and 1973, presented nineteen performances of Boulez works in his Monday Evening Concert series.

Boulez decided to give the world premiere of his next work, *Éclat*, at a joint concert of the Monday Evening series and the University of Southern California in March 1965. He worked on the score until the day of its premiere. The date of the concert coincided with his fortieth birthday, and Morton gave a party for him. The Stravinskys and Craft were there. All the old wounds appeared to be healed. The early attacks on neo-classicism belonged to the past. As with *Marteau sans Maître*, *Éclat* moved Stravinsky to pay tribute to Boulez. In *Themes and Episodes*, written when Stravinsky was still checking Craft's attributions to him, Stravinsky is quoted:

> Boulez's *Éclat* for piano and chamber ensemble is another small masterpiece and one which introduces a new technique of time control. The score does not list the conductor's part

along with those of the other performers, yet it is composed just as any of the instrumental parts are composed, and is, in fact, the most interesting of all, so much so that for the moment one fails to see any conductor being able to perform it half so well as Maître Boulez himself. Indeed, to watch him conduct it as I recently did, is an experience inseparable from the music itself. What a sense of timing he has! The score contains only verbal directions for tempo ("très vif," "plus modéré," "très longtemps," etc.) and is therefore at the opposite pole to mechanically geared pieces such as my Variations. Every event is controlled by cue, ordinal in most places but aleatory in others. The aleatoric idea is not new— each player stands by cocked and ready to play his group of notes, his turn determined by the flick of Maître Boulez's fingers—but the effect is attractive. . . . *Éclat* is not only creative music, but creative conducting as well, which is unique.

The eight-minute score, published later that year in a photocopy of Boulez's manuscript, contains more music than that played at its first performance. Boulez continued to add to the work. In 1974, at a Boulez retrospective in New York, the composer conducted and talked about *Éclat*:

Western music always seemed moved by gestures from here to there. It is never static. We in the Western world are always running, even in the slow movements. That is because we consider music part of our aesthetic life, not part of our ethical life. I became fascinated by the different conception of listening to music from the East.

I had been acquainted with Eastern music since 1946. But sometimes it is a long time before an acquaintance becomes an influence inside of you. The big thing in *Éclat* is time. There is no meter. You will see I do not beat. Sometimes I leave the sound by itself. The sound never dies in the same way twice. I decide at the last minute what I will give as cues. The performer waits and waits. Then. Here it comes. It takes time to listen to this very complex sound that is progressively dying. In this work conducting is no longer something that has nothing to do with sound [much laughter from the audience]. I mean, of course, there's always balance and all that in conducting. But here sound is part of the structure and the form. In *Éclat* the conductor controls the sound.

In *Éclat* the conductor virtually takes over the role of the composer, for he gives the cues that determine the form at each performance. The performer can play his sections in any order once the conductor gives the cue, but it is the timing that takes precedence over everything else.

Boulez said that he chose the name *Éclat* for its ambiguity. "First, 'éclat' means fragment, and the first *Éclat* was a very short piece. Second it can mean éclat-explosive—a kind of burst or sudden shattering. Finally it suggests reflected light, reflections that are very fleeting. Any of these meanings can apply equally well to the poetic expression of the piece."

Boulez's need to exercise control was thwarted partly because of the accident that placed him in Baden-Baden when Stockhausen was asserting himself in Cologne. In the area which the Südwestfunk reached from Baden-Baden, eighty percent of the population lived in rural communities. Cologne Radio, on the other hand, reached a highly urban group. Because taxes support the radio system, Cologne enjoyed a large subsidy.

German Radio virtually created new music in Europe, the directors competing for the biggest and the best. Strobel had initiated the reorganization of the system, taking over the Südwestfunk after the war. The West German Radio at Cologne followed. Eimert brought the electronic studio to life when Stockhausen was still a young man. Then Hamburg, Munich, Bremen, Berlin, Stuttgart, and other cities followed suit. They sponsored concerts in their studios placing a high premium on first performances.

It should not be supposed that the German people at large looked with favor on this activity. New music was programmed only after eleven at night when most were asleep. Boulez emphasized, in fact, that "for the general audiences, neither Stockhausen nor I were the subjects of glory. Rather were we an embarrassment."

But there was no new music anywhere else in Germany. Not in public concerts, not in the universities (as in the United States), not as accompaniment to plays (as in France). So the focus of attention was radio, and Cologne was Number One. At Cologne there were big performances, made possible by a big orchestra and chorus, which became the most important ensemble of modern music in Europe. It toured the big cities, dwarfing the activities in Baden-Baden.

Cologne had a star to match its resources. By 1957, Stockhausen began to exert a strong influence, and in the late 1950s and throughout the sixties the influence was an aleatory one. Tudor characterized his movement as one "towards freedom and opening out." Musicians began to regard Stockhausen with the fear and awe an earlier generation had reserved for Schoenberg. And Stockhausen felt he was entitled to such deference. Once a devout Catholic, Stockhausen dropped his ties to structure and God at the same time. He left his wife and their four children and married a painter and produced more progeny. Then he built a splendid house in the suburbs of Cologne and expected both women and all the children to live with him. Despite the domestic chaos, his work moved on. Pousseur has said, "After 1961, after the death of Steinecke, Cologne became the mainspring of contemporary music with Stockhausen the primary animator." Boulez comments that even Strobel turned: "At first Strobel thought Stockhausen was too close to kitsch. Then he became his strong defender." Hilda Strobel told why: "What Stockhausen does is not démodé. It is true he can be very close to kitsch. That is because he is not frightened by these sentiments. He feels, 'It's in me; it must be free.' "

Stockhausen heeded Cage's admonition of 1958 to go still further in following Cage's lead. In 1960 Cage presented *Theater Piece 1960* in Greenwich Village; it consisted of a series of incoherent "happenings" and featured several performers, including David Tudor. In 1961 Stockhausen presented *Originale* in Cologne; it consisted of a series of incoherent "happenings" and featured several performers, including David Tudor. Stockhausen also went further towards indeterminacy in his purely "musical" works. In *Carré* (1959–60), scored for eighty players (four orchestras) and sixty-four singers (four choruses), the tones do not matter. What matters is the density. Thus the choice of tones is left to the performers themselves. About *Carré* Stockhausen wrote, "You can confidently stop listening for a moment if you cannot or do not want to go on listening; for each moment stands on its own. . . ." His comment recalls the description of *Music of Changes* by Cage which he articulated again at Darmstadt in 1958: "The aggregates of sound have no necessary direction. Each is a musical fact, without any implication at all."

To say Stockhausen adopted Cage's philosophy is not to suggest Cage was delighted with the results. Cage said, "Stockhausen's work resembles Morton Feldman's more than it does mine. In Feldman there is a concern with different registers. I have never had such a concern. A good deal of Karlheinz sounds like mezzo-forte Feldman. A little louder, but unsurprising."

As for Stockhausen's acknowledgment of his debt to Cage, that was never to be forthcoming. According to Otto Tomek, who served Stockhausen at Cologne throughout the 1960s: "Cage had a tremendous influence on Stockhausen. But Stockhausen always refused to confess this. Sometimes he would say, 'One has to help Cage. He is such a big man.' Then he would turn around and be very hard: 'Let's do nothing. It's not music at all.' "

In fact, by the 1960s, when the revolution against old music appeared almost to have been won—Cologne Radio had begun broadcasting new music in prime evening time—the danger lay in the new composers' annihilating each other. Fratricide, not patricide, became the order of the day. Wolfgang Becker, who replaced Tomek at Cologne, characterized the situation then: "It's like the antagonism of one big company to another. Each composer wants to take the whole market."

CHAPTER 33

Boulez did not go into conducting "to take the whole market." That aim crystallized somewhat later when he decided, he said, that he had a "missionary job to change the organizations, to change the threshold of our period," to lead large audiences up to but not beyond the language he loved.

But at the beginning his aim was more modest. Lawrence Morton has said,

> Boulez told me long ago how concerned he was about the poor performances he had heard in his young professional days of the music of the Viennese, Bartók, Stravinsky, etc. How could conductors ever be expected to do his own music decently if they still didn't know how to conduct the classics of the twentieth century? And I remember my first visit to Cleveland in the late 1960s: he commented then that even at this late date he had found errors in Debussy scores that had so far escaped conductors everywhere. So his first impulse towards professional conducting was stimulated by the need for accuracy in the twentieth-century classics, and I feel he must have been encouraged in this by the two people with whom he surely must have discussed the problem: Strobel and Rosbaud.

Between 1960 and 1963 it was on-the-job training for Boulez. Many who played under him at the beginning say they would never have predicted he would go far. Several support Hilda Strobel's description of the chaotic performance of Bartók's *Miraculous Mandarin*. Some believe that Boulez neither liked nor admired that work.

But why should anyone expect Boulez—who was out to "kill the musical past," out to erase repetition and contrast from his own and his colleagues' musical scores—to suddenly do an about-face and find those attributes admirable ones? In addition to problems of phrasing and drama, Boulez's early performance of the *Eroica* was sloppy. Wolfgang Becker was there and said that although it did have the clear structure for which Boulez is known today, it was "not at all note-perfect." Boulez did not then have the precision and control he sought.

In those years he concentrated on his conducting technique, avoiding the baton which he calls a "crochet de manchot [the one-armed man's hook] that keeps you from expressing yourself with your fingers." Boulez's use of his fingers and thumb as against his arms and body in conducting seems analogous to his use of tiny gradations in dynamics and durations as against big structure in his own music. Boulez has a marvelous ear, a remarkable sense of rhythmic exactitude. But what separates him from the other major conductors is the precision of his digital gestures, immeasurably useful in the intricate twentieth-century scores he loves. Boulez indicates time and rhythm with the forefinger and thumb of his right hand. The left is rarely used to imitate the right. It is as though the "ethics" that legislates against the repetition of a "theme" in composition also legislates against the left hand imitating the right. Instead he raises or lowers the left hand steadily with his fingers extended rigidly to indicate an increase or decrease in volume.

After moving to Germany, Boulez went to Paris to conduct four or five of the Domaine's five or six concerts a year. While there he stayed with his parents, who then lived on Boulevard Raspail. Although the family's favorite newspaper was *Le Figaro,* whose music critic at that time attacked Boulez not only for his revolutionary music but for his character and personality, the bitterness between generations had diminished: Boulez's contract with the Südwestfunk convinced the father that his son had done well. In fact, not only he but his son-in-law, Jack Chevalier, were members of the board of directors of the Domaine Musical.

While in Germany, Boulez has said, he did not miss France. "I always felt very good there, never alien in Germany. I am very adaptable, not like the French in this way. The French generally adapt poorly out of their own country. I find this attitude unbearable. There was always great anger in France when I spoke of Germany."

In January 1963, Boulez conducted the Orchestre National in a fiftieth anniversary performance of *The Rite of Spring.* It took place in the Théâtre des Champs-Elysées where he had staged an anti-Stravinsky revolt twenty years before. The piece was recorded; Boulez also recorded, with the same orchestra, Stravinsky's *Les Noces* and *Renard.*These were his first commercial recordings.

In 1962, Georges Auric, one of the original supporters of the Domaine Musical, was appointed director of the Paris Opéra. To stage something of a coup d'état, Auric invited Boulez to preside over a new production of *Wozzeck,* an opera Boulez had regarded with awe from his earliest composing days. Boulez insisted on thirty rehearsals—instead of the usual three or four—and he got them. He also insisted on a performance in the original German, which appears to be an even more outrageous demand, for it had been only twenty-three years since Parisians had watched Nazis strut in their streets. But the fact is that as early as 1950 a German company did Wagner at the Paris Opéra to packed houses and with no protests. So Boulez's German *Wozzeck* should not be interpreted—as has often been the case—as his personal triumph over the resistance of his countrymen.

Boulez at the Paris Opéra proved a tremendous success. After the first performance the musicians rose to applaud him. The man who felt himself the much maligned son, both by his family and by France, made his first impressive move towards a triumphant return home.

Having flirted with Germany, and having received a diploma from France, Boulez was ready to move on to England. The invitation was extended by William Glock who, like Auric, was an early Boulez supporter and the man who commissioned the essay that proclaimed the dogmatic "Schoenberg is dead!" In 1952 Glock was director of the Bryanston and Dartington Summer Schools, where he brought in such advanced and not yet well known figures to teach as Stefan Wolpe, Luciano Berio, Elliott Carter, and Luigi Nono. Glock had been a pupil of Artur Schnabel, the pianist in Schoenberg's early Viennese circle and the man in whose home René Leibowitz grew up. The "new music" circle in Europe was small, but it was intelligent and exerted great influence.

Boulez had begun to think about conducting even when composition seemed to fill his life. In 1954 he started to send Glock regular bulletins from the Domaine Musical, emphasizing those performances he would conduct himself. In 1956 Boulez visited London with Barrault. Glock was then director of the International Musicians Club, an association of musicians from all over the world. During that visit Glock invited the Domaine Musical with Boulez at the helm to give a concert in London the following year. Boulez agreed. He conducted *Zeitmasse,* Webern's Opus 24 Concerto, Nono's *Polyphonie,* and his own *Marteau sans Maître,* all works which met his standards as difficult and demanding.

By 1959 Glock was Controller of Music, the highest musical post at the BBC and a man deeply committed to new music. English critic Andrew Porter writes that Glock "singlehandedly changed the concert life of London by making the music of our time central to the BBC Symphony's concert series, to the Proms (that enormous 'festival' of orchestral music which for weeks fills the Albert Hall, and over the air reaches a wider audience still), to the countless concerts and chamber and solo recitals promoted by the BBC both in public halls and studios, to the broadcast relays of new works up and down the country, to recordings and relays from abroad and to the broadcast talks about music and the printed commentary and discussion appearing in the BBC's publications. . . ."

Glock invited Boulez to be guest conductor of the BBC in 1964. "Boulez brought a tiny list," Glock recalled, "not more than twenty works. We gave a whole series in Festival Hall of twentieth-century programs. I was tremendously impressed by the way Boulez rehearsed. The concerts were so fresh, so entirely new for everyone. Many people wrote and told me that. He gave the orchestra a beautiful sound, not velvety, but delicate and disciplined."

Between 1963, when he had twenty pieces in his repertory, and 1969, Boulez rose to be music director of the BBC and the New York Philharmonic orchestras. In between he appeared throughout Europe at the head of such orchestras as the Orchestre National, the Lamoureux, the Paris Conservatoire, the Concertgebouw, the Berlin Philharmonic, the Vienna Philharmonic, the New Philharmonia, and the London Symphony. Boulez's rise as conductor was therefore as meteoric as his rise as a composer had been. Alfred Schlee, director of Universal Edition, said, "Boulez is a musician above all. What else is there to say?" Lawrence Morton said a little more: "Boulez is 95 percent musician. The other five percent is worrying about his diet and taking long walks."

But while rising in his conducting career, composition still seemed to determine his moves. Those who have had Boulez as a guest report that the light never goes out in his room until after 3:00 A.M. His decision to record with Columbia instead of E.M.I. was determined, he has said, by Columbia's offer to record his own works. And his move to replace Michel de Koos, the manager he had inherited from Hans Rosbaud, with Howard Hartog of Ingpen and Williams was stimulated by Hartog's efforts to bring the Südwestfunk to Edinburgh for a full-scale Boulez festival. Hartog's efforts did not succeed at that time. But his plan materialized in 1965 when Edinburgh mounted the largest retrospective of Boulez's work that had until then been presented, with Boulez conducting *Marteau sans Maître* and *Pli Selon Pli* in Hamburg.

An eloquent testimonial to the fact that conducting never displaced composing in Boulez's esteem is his absence of difficulties with other conductors. Like women, conductors are not important to him. On the other hand, the troubles with Stravinsky grew. Stravinsky was, after the death of Schoenberg, universally recognized as the greatest living composer. True, his serial works were rarely played, but there was a tacit acceptance of the fact that the genius who had composed *The Rite of Spring* was at work on something too difficult to understand. There was, therefore, little speculation—as there had been at one time—about the Master drying up.

So the competition, the war, broke out again. It did so with the performance of *Threni* in November 1959 at the Domaine Musical. In Boulez's view this was what went on:

> Craft had prepared *Threni* and Stravinsky was to conduct. The disaster came from two directions. The singers had not been chosen by me but by an agent in charge of the Aix-en-Provence festival. They were absolutely awful. I, myself, with Stravinsky, did the piano rehearsals. I quickly knew the worth of the singers. Four or six could not manage their parts. Rehearsing at the piano, I told Stravinsky that he should be stronger with them. But Stravinsky was fatherly and supported them. He refused to be strong. And he was not a good conductor; he was a terribly lousy conductor. I was in the middle of the choir myself, giving cues. I told him, "We will have a catastrophe." We did. The admiration the singers had for him could not compensate for the minimum of clarity. And the orchestra had been ill-prepared by Craft. The reason *Agon* had gone so well two years before was that Rosbaud had prepared the Südwestfunk thoroughly.

Craft has said that Boulez had given his assurance that he would rehearse *Threni* himself and that he was unable to fulfill his promise because he was finishing a piece for Donaueschingen. "In consequence," Craft wrote, "*Threni* was so badly sung and played that it was received with jeers by the audience. And when, at the end of the performance, Boulez tried to maneuver Stravinsky into taking a bow, the humiliated composer curtly refused, swearing that he would never conduct in Paris again, a promise that he kept."

Craft said Boulez added insult to injury by offering *Rencontres avec Pierre Boulez,* a new book by "Stravinsky's archenemy" Antoine Golea, for sale in the lobby. "On all counts," Craft went on, "the Paris *Threni* was a disaster and the true cause of the rift between Stravinsky and Boulez."

Still, the friendship picked up again. The Stravinskys and Craft celebrated Boulez's fortieth birthday at Lawrence Morton's house and Stravinsky (as we saw) wrote generously about *Éclat* in *Themes and Episodes,* published in 1966. But another incident occurred in 1967 that proved to be the last. In a film directed by Richard Leacock and distributed over network television, Stravinsky is shown looking at his own *Les Noces.* Boulez is looking at the piece with him. Boulez notes that at the end there is one bar's rest too much. Stravinsky, in his eighties, appears confused. Then he concedes that the score is wrong. As the scene closes Stravinsky seems to be muttering something in Russian.

Boulez said that the actual incident occurred before the filming, that Rolf Liebermann, the director of the Hamburg Opera, was present as Leacock was following the Stravinsky entourage around in California, and that Liebermann suggested they restage the incident for the cameras. Boulez said Stravinsky was not disconcerted about that, and even added that he would sign his name to the effect that Boulez discovered this particular error.

But Craft has said that the television incident coupled with an interview that followed soon after in which Boulez referred to Stravinsky as being "Webern-influenced"—Stravinsky did not want to appear influenced by anyone at that late date—convinced Stravinsky that Boulez was two-faced and made him resolve never again to have anything to do with him. Boulez thought Craft was the instigator of the trouble, and that too is possible. In any case the bitterness persisted beyond the grave. In a "conversation" published just after Stravinsky's death in *The New York Review of Books,* Craft quoted the aged and very ill composer in an attack on Boulez. Boulez shot back in a "commemorative" article on Stravinsky for the *Saturday Review,* in which he took Stravinsky severely to task for his reliance on old music. It was not as harsh as "Schoenberg is dead!" but Boulez was older and more controlled then. "I am no longer wild on the outside," Boulez said in 1973, "because I found that useless to me. But I am still just as wild on the inside."

In the 1960s, Boulez was still somewhat wild on the outside, and his pattern of testing authority, of seeing just how far he could go in undermining or insulting Stravinsky and still retain his affection, was also the pattern he followed in regard to France. Regarding Boulez's relations with his country, his sister explains, "If my brother seems antinationalistic, it is because he was not recognized in France. He is uncompromising. The only meaningful thing to him is quality and he feels he was not recognized in France. He was truly *le fils mal aimé.*"

The most flagrant example of Boulez's fight with France occurred in 1964 when André Malraux, Minister of Cultural Affairs and a famed novelist and art critic, established a commission to investigate the "deficiencies" in French musical life. Malraux did not know Boulez well. He had come to Domaine concerts only twice. But Gaeton Picon, director of the Department of Arts and Letters and a longtime Boulez fan, introduced the composer to E. J. Biazini, an official under Malraux. Biazini, according to Boulez's account, told Boulez that he was the only one who could help them. Boulez responded by sending Malraux a long letter full of suggestions. One suggestion was to divide all of Paris's five orchestras into two large and flexible groups, one managed by the State, the other by the city. The plan threatened many who made their living through the established system, and Boulez displayed his idea of diplomacy by becoming honorary president of the musicians' union in order to persuade them to agree to his plans.

It was all to no avail. Malraux named Marcel Landowski, a neo-Romantic composer, to the office of musical director of the ministry. Boulez protested with a vitriolic essay published in *Le Nouvel Observateur* which began, "André Malraux has just made a decision concerning music in France which I find unthoughtful, irresponsible, and inconsistent." Then he canceled all engagements with the Orchestre National, forbade the newly formed Orchestre de Paris to play his music, cut off his connection with the Domaine Musical, and publicly announced that he would never again live in Paris where music was in the hands of incompetent men.

Some journalists attributed Boulez's failure with Malraux to the efforts of André Jolivet and Henri Sauguet, neoclassic composers and long-standing enemies of Boulez. But Suzanne Tezenas offered a still more reasonable explanation: she said it was the Comtesse de Fels, Marcel Proust's niece and the powerful patroness of a Proust salon, who maneuvered Landowski into a position where he could beat Boulez for the post under Malraux.

Boulez's periodic efforts to return to France as the one in control is an important contrapuntal theme to the main motive of his ambitious thrust to make his ideas prevail. After London, Cleveland seemed right. In 1964, George Szell went through Baden-Baden and called Boulez. Szell had heard about his conducting through the Concertgebouw and engaged him as a guest for March 1965. Boulez said he learned to conduct the classics in Cleveland. Szell, whose conducting was lean and lucid, became progressively more enthusiastic about Boulez. The next year Szell heard about Boulez's troubles with Malraux. "He knew," Boulez said, "that I had given up all my French engagements and that I would be free in 1967. He thought I had a good attitude about Malraux and invited me to conduct again, this time for a four-week engagement in 1967. A four-week engagement is unusual."

Carlos Moseley, then managing director of the New York Philharmonic, had engaged Boulez for a guest appearance in the spring of 1969. Moseley notes that the Philharmonic has a tradition of hiring composer-conductors that extends from Tchaikovsky to Gustav Mahler. After Boulez's Cleveland performance, Moseley met with him to plan programs for a second guest appearance in 1971. "I think," Boulez said, "he more or less began to consider me as head of the Philharmonic then."

Moseley confirmed this. But that information did not get through to Sir William Glock, who engaged Boulez for long periods as a guest conductor with the BBC orchestra. After conducting the BBC in three concerts at Carnegie Hall in 1965, Boulez took the British orchestra on tour with an exclusively twentieth-century program: Schoenberg's Opus 16, Webern's Opus 6, Debussy's *Images,* excerpts from *Wozzeck,* the Berg *Altenberg Lieder,* and his own recently composed *Figures, Doubles, Prisms.* In 1967 Boulez brought the BBC and much of that same program, adding his own *Éclat,* to Czechoslovakia, Poland, and Russia, countries that had not been exposed to contemporary music.

Glock recalled Boulez's early days with the orchestra: "Up to 1967," he said, "the concerts were really revelations. Boulez was still conducting a repertory every note of which meant a great deal to him. During the spring of 1968, the BBC was on the lookout for a new chief conductor; Colin Davis was preparing to leave. I told my bosses at the BBC that Boulez was the only man for the job. He was then conducting the Hague Orchestra at Scheveningen. My plan was to invite him for a three-year term beginning in 1971. I flew to Holland and we went for a seven-mile very fast walk on the beach. He said one thing which typifies his orderly and planning mind: 'I'll do it if you stay on.' He didn't want to be a new boy with a new man. I was nearing sixty; in the BBC when you are sixty they can say 'thank you very much' and let you go."

But the BBC did not let Glock go, and the plan was made for Boulez to spend two five-month sessions a year in London. Glock said that he had a "slight unease, even then, that this was not using Boulez in the best way. I always wanted him to get on with composition."

Olivier Messiaen, Boulez's composition teacher in the early 1940s, with Suzanne Tezenas, who created a salon in Paris around Boulez. It was in her fashionable apartment in the 16th arrondissement that John Cage poured cognac into her Bechstein while preparing for a performance of his Sonatas and Interludes.

COURTESY OLIVIER MESSIAEN

John Cage, the American composer, working on his Sonatas and Interludes for Prepared Piano, *1947. Cage and Boulez became close colleagues when they met in Paris in 1949. By 1952 their paths had diverged.*   FRANK DRIGGS COLLECTION

Cage's prepared piano. Cage said that he always left a piano in better condition than when he found it.   FRANK DRIGGS COLLECTION

Hans Werner Henze, who, along with Stockhausen, was one of the two most important composers in Germany after World War II. In the early 1950s, Henze wrote 12-tone music but in 1955 he turned his back on the serial idea. FRANK DRIGGS COLLECTION

In 1977 Karlheinz Stockhausen embarked on the composition of a seven-evening cycle of operas collectively called Licht. *The composer told me he had composed one formula and that seven sections of that formula would expand to become seven parts of the whole. He continues work on this project.* CLIVE ALBA/KARLHEINZ STOCKHAUSEN VERLAG

The undisputed father of serialism in the United States, Milton Babbitt is eloquent proof that the American vernacular—jazz and popular song—lies at the heart of virtually all American music; Babbitt is an expert in this arena. Here he is, at ten, with saxophone in Jackson, Mississippi. COURTESY MILTON BABBITT

Here is Babbitt c. 1959 with his then favorite electronic instrument, the RCA Synthesizer, housed at the Columbia-Princeton Electronic Music Center.

FRANK DRIGGS COLLECTION

Stravinsky conducting in the 1960s with Robert Craft, who played a major role in the composer's life and work. COURTESY ROBERT CRAFT

Roger Sessions and Mario Davidovsky, both winners of the Pulitzer Prize, at a Composers Conference, early 1970s, Vermont. Sessions died in 1985.   CLEMENS KALISCHER

Dimitri Mitropoulos (left) conducting Gunther Schuller's Symphony for Brass and Percussion *at a recording session for Columbia Records in the late 1950s. On the same disc, produced by George Avakian (second from left), Schuller (third from left) conducts modern jazz artists John Lewis, J.J. Johnson and Jimmy Giuffre.* DON HUNSTEIN

Leon Kirchner combined live performers with electonic means in his String Quartet No. 3. It earned him a Pulitzer Prize in 1967. In a reply to my interview in which Boulez attacked American composers, Kirchner, in a mock interview published in the Sunday Times, *attacked Boulez's attack.* JOHN GOLDMAN

Luciano Berio delivered the Charles Eliot Norton Lectures at Harvard in 1993–94. Previous speakers in this series include T.S. Eliot, Stravinsky, Bernstein, and Boulez. Berio's two most recent operas are Outis *(La Scala, 1996) and* Cronaca del Luogo *(Salzberg Festival, 1999).*

PETER SCHRAMEK/EUROPEAN-AMERICAN MUSIC ARCHIVE

Charles Wuorinen, the youngest composer ever to win the Pulitzer Prize in Composition, and a recipient of the MacArthur ("genius") Award, at the ruins at Ben Shean, Israel, in 1997. HOWARD STOKAR

Boulez, Andrew Gerzso and Tod Machover in London, 1982, preparing for a performance of Rèpons, *Boulez's most important composition of the Ircam years.* © MALCOLM CROWTHERS

Boulez c. 1966, conducting without a baton. In the 1990s, at a conductor's workshop at Carnegie Hall, Boulez told students "my fingers are ten batons." Boulez started to conduct late in his career, primarily because so few conductors were capable of handling his kind of music. Today he is recognized as one of the greatest living conductors. COURTESY OF DON HUNSTEIN, COLUMBIA RECORDS

Augusta Read Thomas and Pierre Boulez at Symphony Center, Chicago, November 27, 1998. Boulez and the Chicago Symphony presented Orbital Beacons, *the second occasion on which the conductor and that orchestra gave Thomas a world premiere.*   DAN REST

lthough conducting never displaced composition in Boulez's mind, it certainly began to occupy the greater part of his time. In 1969, Boulez was scheduled not only to conduct *Pelléas et Mélisande* at Covent Garden and to fulfill his guest commitment with both the BBC and New York Philharmonic orchestras, but he also engaged himself for the demanding position of principal guest conductor of the Cleveland Orchestra, where he was to concentrate on the contemporary repertory—which, with the exception of Berg, held very little interest for George Szell.

"Inevitably," Lawrence Morton said, "this kind of career earned him a good income. I think Boulez has enjoyed having money—after all, he had known intimately the lack of it. I never saw but I heard accounts of his quarters on Rue Beautreillis where he lacked a good many of the essentials of genuine comfort. But I think that with him money has been less a motivation than a reward. Surely no one has worked harder for it."

Boulez's greatly augmented income made it possible for him to rent the entire Baden-Baden house and to decorate it as he wished. He selected austere furnishings, in harmony with his favorite period of Webern and Klee, and asked the former wife of the late pianist Geza Anda (she was also an interior decorator) to arrange the pieces for him. The outside of the house, turn-of-the-century Wilhelm II, successfully disguised its Bauhaus interior. Mies van der Rohe's Barcelona chairs made for an airy, antiseptic look. No memorabilia were permissible in a Bauhaus world. Not a photograph, not a newspaper was visible. Richard Rodney Bennett described it as a house which would not allow a love letter anywhere.

In addition to chairs, couches, and tables on pale carpeting, the living room contained a television set that enabled the viewer to see four programs at one time, and a leather and marble bar—not a gratuitous piece of furniture, for Boulez could drink an extraordinary amount without suffering any diminishment of his wits. An evening meal might include several cocktails, the better part of a bottle of wine, a cognac, and two or three scotches.

On the walls were paintings by Miró and Klee; Giacometti's drawings of Webern and Stravinsky hung in his study. His desk appeared as if never used; 4 x 6 cards on which he composed stood stacked next to a container of sharpened colored pencils. In a larger library were the complete works of Haydn, a gift from Universal Edition; a Steinway grand piano, a gift from the Südwestfunk; and a framed letter from Debussy to Varèse, a gift from Varèse's widow, Louise. One had the impression that Boulez bought nothing, that he just accepted whatever was given to him, not because he was frugal—he gave his nieces very costly wedding trips to Egypt, Greece, and Turkey, and he invariably picked up dinner checks no matter how expensive the party—but because it required too much time and trouble, too much of an expenditure of taste, to make a purchase of anything at all. Impersonality oozed out of every pore of this large house; about a dozen seemingly identical dark suits hung in his closet.

As a conductor, Boulez not only made enough money to live exactly as he wished, but he was then in a celebrated enough position to dispense with writing his own polemics, for journalists were delighted to interview him. The first of the news-making interviews was published in the German weekly magazine *Der Spiegel* in September 1967. Boulez accused Liebermann, director of the Hamburg State Opera, of having hoodwinked the public into believing that he had transformed his traditional opera house into a center for genuine music drama. As was usual with his public pronouncements—a far cry from his exceptionally courteous personal manner—Boulez's tone was abusive in the extreme. He said *Wozzeck* and *Lulu* were the last operas worth mentioning (thus putting the knife deep into Stravinsky's back); that Hans Werner Henze was like de Gaulle: "Whatever rubbish he puts out he still thinks he is King" (thus insulting both socialist Henze and de Gaulle); and that Liebermann had "institutionalized his own bourgeois tastes as director for the Hamburg Opera." He also attacked the Paris Opéra as a house "full of dust and dung. . . a place where only tourists go, because it is part of the circuit, like the Folies-Bergère and the Invalides."

Jean Vilar, director of the Paris Opéra, called on Boulez to collaborate with dancer-choreographer Maurice Béjart in a thoroughgoing reform of the Opéra.

By May 1968, Boulez and Béjart had their reforms ready. The Opéra-Comique, the company's second house, was to be closed for good. The Opéra would give nothing but concert performances for one year. The orchestras and choruses of both houses would be amalgamated and their standards raised. When the Opéra reopened, it would offer a more limited but more substantial repertory. Workshops in music and drama would flourish. An entirely new theater would be built, suited to the needs of the late twentieth century. Finally, the most striking reform of all: Boulez, who had written Verdi off as "dum de dum, nothing more," would be music director of the Paris Opéra.

Boulez said of this apparent paradox: "The general object was to deal with music among other things. It was to have been called the 'Center for Music and Theater.' It would have involved exploring many possibilities concerning theater, dance, music, and the rest. It was in the making of these plans that I started to think in different terms, in terms of changing the threshold of the music of our time through rearranging the musical life of an important city."

But the month that the plan was ready was also the month of the tumultuous political events of May 1968. De Gaulle issued a call to his supporters to resist the revolutionary situation. Vilar, a man of the Left, refused to resist it and resigned. Glock learned Boulez's most recent French project had collapsed and offered him the BBC orchestra in its place.

Boulez's London appointment was announced in January 1969. It would seem to have given him everything he wanted. Apart from providing a decent salary, the BBC post carried the assurance that he would be under no great time pressure and that he could try to do in London what had been aborted through the political events in Paris. "Being part of as vast an official organization as this meant no tight budget problems," Boulez said. "Of course the orchestra has a budget, but those in the administration understand that you have to lose money if you want to provide a genuine cultural life."

It was during that same month, January 1969, after reading of Boulez's tour of the United States, that I suggested an interview for *The New York Times*. My editor accepted the suggestion on the basis of Boulez's appearance as a conductor. As a composer he would not then have passed the *Times*'s test: a New York performance of a news-making work. It is true that older established composers often make it on less than that. I interviewed Benjamin Britten when he came to New York to do nothing more than accompany Peter Pears at the piano, and I interviewed Elliott Carter to celebrate his sixtieth birthday. But in 1969, at the age of forty-four, Boulez's entrée into the Sunday *Times* was as a guest conductor who had established himself as a leading composer abroad.

Hurok Attractions had arranged a Monday lunch at Boston's Ritz-Carlton Hotel. The day before the appointment, the East Coast was blanketed under a fierce blizzard. I called Boulez in Boston to arrange another date. We settled on a day later in the week. No intermediary was involved. No member of the Hurok firm, no officer of a public relations business, no secretary, no disciple or friend. I was struck by the spartan simplicity of the man. Now I think that "formidable isolation" seems a more appropriate description than simplicity.

The *Times* headlined the interview, "A Fighter from Way Back."

In 1945, when he was 20, Pierre Boulez led a group booing a performance of Igor Stravinsky's "Four Norwegian Moods" at the Théâtre des Champs-Élysées in Paris. "I was not attacking Stravinsky," he explained recently over lunch in Boston's Ritz-Carlton, "but the Establishment, which considered him the God, the Idol, the Only Truth. I did it to draw attention to Schoenberg, whose influence was still limited to Vienna and Berlin." A few years later, when 12-tone writing was accepted by the avant-garde, Boulez attacked Schoenberg to bring attention to Webern. And sure enough, post-Webern serialism dominated the 1950's and early 60's.

Boulez played a crucial role in shifting the balance of musical power from Stravinsky and Stravinsky's American disciples, trained in Paris under Nadia Boulanger, back to the Austro-German domain, where it had prevailed from Bach through Wagner. In 1959, he even left France and moved permanently to Baden-Baden: "Germany was the most exciting country for contemporary music."

Boulez won the significant battles. Stravinsky, in a famous about-face, adopted the serial technique and hailed Boulez as the best composer of his generation. And after Boulez conducted at Bayreuth, a German critic wrote that he could teach the Germans how to handle Wagner. Today the 43-year-old composer-conductor is in demand all over the world. I spoke to him just after he served as guest conductor for the Boston Symphony Orchestra and before he left for Chicago, his last engagement before New York. Thursday Boulez starts a month-long assignment here conducting the New York Philharmonic.

Dressed with the same attention to unusual combinations of color that characterizes his musical work—a dark blue shirt under a brown tweed jacket, with a subtly hued plaid tie—Boulez was restrained for about half an hour. He ate red snapper, drank German beer, and spoke politely about his parents and his teachers. When I mentioned an American composer whose work he dislikes, Boulez suddenly came to life, launching a virtuoso attack on various facets of U.S. music.

Electronic music: "This same frenzy for technology began in Europe about 1953. By 1958 it had all died down. The idea of electronics as the big future of music is just an American trick of fashion. Next year they'll discover the viola da gamba. Playing Bach on the computer doesn't interest me at all because it's artistically irrelevant. All this indicates a simplistic way of thinking—an appallingly low level of thinking."

As for "Perspectives of New Music," an avant-garde journal published by the Princeton University Press: "'Perspectives' is similar to 'Die Reihe,' begun in Germany about 1953. Its writers think they are great scientists. They are not. I know great scientists and they possess invention and imagination. Composers who publish in this journal never discuss important questions of choice and decision. They write only about putting different things together. This is not an esthetic point of view. It's what I call a 'cashier's point of view.'"

New Image of Sound, the Hunter College concert series at which Boulez appeared last week as composer, conductor and performer, is, says he, "the best series in New York. It is just like the Domaine Musical, which I began in Paris about 1953—the same kind of programming, the same six concerts a season."

But after a second beer, Boulez relaxed and described how he views the gulf that separates the American composer from his European colleague: "There should be no antagonism between the American and European composer. I am always fighting the nationalistic point of view. Americans are jealous—I'm not sure if that's the right word—thinking the Europeans are taking attention away from them. The Americans do operate under a severe handicap, of course; they have no strong personalities in the field. If they were strong enough to establish their personality on the world, they would see that no national favoritism exists.

"After World War II, Europeans were thirsty for all America's creative products—Faulkner, Cummings, Jackson Pollock. Europeans bought, almost without discrimination, anything Steinbeck or Dos Passos wrote. But for an American artist to be exported to Germany he has to be better than the German product. They have no one in America as good as Hans Werner Henze, and that is not setting your sights very high. A composer the stature of Stockhausen they have not."

Boulez diagnosed what he feels is the American malady: "European music is not connected with the university. There is no ivory castle for us. But here, university people and practical musicians ignore each other. It's a very unhealthy state of affairs.

"I do not like this pedantic approach. I do not like scholars who bring only Death to music. The university situation is incestuous. It is one big marriage in which the progeny deteriorates, like the progeny of old and noble families. The university musician is in a self-made ghetto, and what is worse, he likes it there."

I mentioned some American university composers who deny the role of self-expression in new music. Boulez said: "They do so because they are not expressive. It is a type of dialectic I find very childish. Not that I consider expressivity to be the final goal of music. The goal of music is far richer than that. But university composers have no mystery, and music must give a sense of mystery.

"This endlessly, hopelessly academic work reminds me of the Conservatoire. There is no difference between this music and an eight-part counterpoint study. Composers must start with a strong technique, but a technique is just the beginning; it is the means and not the end.

"I have no confidence in those who think they know their goals. You discover your goal as you come upon it. It's out there in front of you; you discover it each day."

Commenting on the unhealthy situation separating intellectual composers from practical musicians, Boulez prescribed his own specific treatment: "An intellectual must use intellectual power to change things not directly related to intellectual affairs. When I compose, I have Debussy,

Stravinsky and Berg in my background. For an audience to listen to my compositions, it must have the same background as that. So I conduct early twentieth-century music to prepare people to listen to more advanced pieces. The fact of conducting is not exciting to me. I'm not super-happy to conduct a large orchestra. But I feel compelled to bring new creative aspects of music to the whole of musical life everywhere. To go into the crowd without losing my integrity, that is what I want to do.

"It is useless only to complain about the 'degraded' audience. That is why I conduct. In Boston I played Debussy's 'Jeux,' which this orchestra played the last time about 10 years ago, and the infrequently heard 'Three Orchestral Pieces,' by Berg. The job of a conductor is to bring an audience to realize it's as important to hear Berg as to hear Mahler."

Boulez does not think that the United States is beyond all hope. But, he feels, salvation will be difficult. "It must lie with an American who is both intellect and practical musician. What is needed in America is a musical John Kennedy. As long as you have no Kennedy in music, you have no future of music in America."

I mentioned Leonard Bernstein as both intellect and musician. Boulez replied: "Bernstein was not there at the right time. When he arrived at the New York Philharmonic, it was too soon for this activity. Then too, such a figure must be personally involved in the advanced creative thinking of the time. You can't introduce a new work to the orchestra, apologizing for it at the same time."

Boulez denied rumors that anyone had ever approached him with the suggestion he take over Bernstein's present job: "But if anyone had, I could not have considered it. The circumstances of directing the New York Philharmonic are such that you are the prisoner of a frame. I am not American enough to be such a prisoner. Nor do I know enough about New York's musical life to bring about the necessary changes. To change bad habits, one must know them well."

Boulez says that—as director—he would require a much larger orchestra, between 150 and 160 musicians, who would play two different kinds of programs. Boulez would do a conservative series featuring big-name soloists as well as a series of avant-garde concerts. "The same musicians," he says, "should be able to do both. A culture center moves in many directions. The money you make with the 'museum' series you must invest in performing new pieces."

In 1971 Boulez will curtail his extensive traveling to settle not in Germany but in London, where he'll take over as permanent conductor of the BBC Symphony Orchestra: "London is the model of my conception of contemporary musical life with the BBC's regular repertory including many twentieth-century works. Today London plays the role of Berlin in the twenties—not only in music but in everything. And with Berlin all cut up, there's no city the size of London left in Germany."

London also offers a swingier life as well as a big prestigious job. With Sir Thomas Beecham dead, Boulez will rule the city's music while Von Karajan is alive and well in Berlin.

The interview enraged America's university composers—there were demands for "equal time" in the *Times*. But it did not appear to enrage anybody else, and when Boulez came to New York and conducted those twentieth-century "classics" which he was then conducting better than anyone in the world, he received only accolades from the press. It is true that many people walked out, particularly the women of the Friday matinees, but the critics were unanimous in their praise. *New York Times* critic Harold Schonberg raved.

The Philharmonic's board of directors was ready to act right away. The late David Keiser, a literate amateur musician who had studied at Harvard and Juilliard in his youth, was chairman of the orchestra's Music Policy Committee. Keiser was also chairman of the board of the Juilliard School and a member of the board of directors of Lincoln Center.

Keiser reported the background of the Boulez decision:

In 1967 and 1968, Szell was enthusiastic about Boulez. I went to Cleveland to hear him conduct. I was impressed. He first conducted our orchestra in March 1969. After the first concert I said to my wife, "That is our new music director." You really cannot make such a decision until you hear a man conduct our own orchestra in our own hall. That first concert I was very favorably impressed with him. After the second I knew for sure.

Then Carlos Moseley and I talked about appointing Boulez. On April 1, after Boulez had conducted several weeks of programs, Alice Tully gave a luncheon for him. About twenty people were there, among them members of the Music Policy Committee. Boulez was charming and likable, as he always is. After lunch we held a meeting. We decided we wanted him as music director. We checked with those absent and all agreed. Carlos called Boulez to tell him we wanted to meet with him right away. We met at 7 o'clock at the bar of the Essex House where he was staying. Although he had vast commitments he did not say No. Both Carlos and I knew then he would say Yes. The Music Policy Committee presented their recommendation to the board which accepted it unanimously.

It was clear Boulez was the right man for the job. There were a few old men—Szell, Steinberg, Stokowski—but such a person would come in for not more than two years and also men of that age would find the burden of music director far too onerous. There were, of course, some young men— like Mehta and Ozawa—but they were not old enough for the job. They did not have enough experience.

As far as all this "revolution" is concerned, the press has gone much too far with it. To be sure, Boulez let us know from the start that he would not be interested in taking over a standard repertoire and continuing to do only standard things. He wanted to do concerts in Greenwich Village and to lecture on new music. He thought this would be the scene in which he could do all of that.

Boulez reported that when he received the call from Moseley, he anticipated it was due to a snag in the programming for his guest appearance in 1970–71. He said that when the two men arrived and Moseley asked, "How would you like to be music director of the New York Philharmonic?" he first thought that because this was April 1, this must have been an April Fool's joke. It took him more than a few seconds to comprehend that it was a genuine, serious offer.

Boulez returned to London to discuss the matter with Glock who, understandably, was horrified. Glock had planned to have Boulez for ten months a year; in addition he had reservations about Boulez in New York:

> The BBC had a background for doing contemporary work. It seemed so much more suitable for Boulez than New York. Why did he want to do both? I shall never quite know that. He loves New York. Partly he hoped to influence musical attitudes in these two super-cities. I thought, then and now, that it would have been more fruitful for him to concentrate his efforts in London. When we spoke in April, he appeared to agree with me. I went off for a holiday in France thinking that the threat had been averted. But when I returned Boulez said the New York problem had come up again.

Indeed it had hardly gone away. In May, Boulez flew to New York to confer with Moseley. Boulez and Moseley agreed on a plan: Boulez would give the orchestra one week of tour and seven weeks in New York during the 1971–72 season. After that the year would be divided in three parts: four months in London, four months in New York, four months for composing in Baden-Baden. Szell, then serving as music advisor and senior guest conductor of the New York Philharmonic, would continue to handle the bulk of the traditional repertory, allowing Boulez to concentrate on the works he does best. (Szell died on July 30, 1970, a year before Boulez assumed the directorship.)

Glock was not pleased with the proposed schedule. "Being chief conductor," he said, "is quite different from being a guest. One must choose players, sack players, and all the rest. But in late May Boulez reiterated he wanted to do all that so I had to accept him on his own terms." On June 1, 1969, less than six months after his appointment with the BBC was made public, Boulez's post at the New York Philharmonic was announced.

When the news broke, Boulez's father was ill in the hospital with cancer. Leon Boulez died two months later. Jeanne Chevalier said that the Philharmonic appointment brought her father "the greatest joy of his life." Boulez could not be found by reporters on that day for comment. The *Times* front-page story asked why Boulez had gone back on the stand he took in the *Times* interview several weeks before.

CHAPTER 35

In March 1971, Boulez and I met in Cleveland, where he was conducting a Varèse program, to discuss a book about him. At the concert Boulez first talked about "Varèse, the man," then about *Arcana, Ionisation,* and *Poéme Électronique.* Interspersed with his precise discussions, replete with diagrams, were the performances of the pieces. At the end he opened the floor to questions. The audience was attentive and polite. After the concert many went to the home of Mr. and Mrs. Robert Frankel in suburban Cleveland to celebrate Boulez's forty-sixth birthday.

Boulez's party was extravagant, but it was not entertainment à la Tezenas. A blown-up photograph of Carol Frankel and Boulez was mounted in the Frankels' living room. Handprinted posters proclaimed: "Schoenberg loves Boulez," "Webern loves Boulez," "It's Bartók's birthday too but he couldn't make it." Drinks flowed. The food was generous. Hotpants had just come into fashion, and several of the women were wearing them. The Frankels and their guests called Boulez "Pierre," and, as the women left, most of them kissed him affectionately.

The morning after the party I met with Boulez in Cleveland's Severance Hall. I outlined my purpose in regard to the book. Boulez agreed to cooperate and to waive all approval rights. He said he would be in New York in a few weeks for his second guest engagement with the Philharmonic—he was not to take over as music director until September—and that I could begin to go to work then.

The schedule for his guest appearance in 1970–71 included five long programs with the orchestra, one concert for the New and Newer Music series at Alice Tully Hall, one concert for the Chamber Music Society of Lincoln Center at Alice Tully Hall, one article commemorating Stravinsky's death for the *Saturday Review,* and recordings of Berlioz's overture to *Beatrice and Benedict,* Debussy's *3 Nocturnes* and *Printemps,* and Ravel's *Tombeau de Couperin.* The New York press celebrated Boulez;

his image was that of the disciplined revolutionary who would stop at nothing until he had converted New York. *Newsweek*'s cover story was "Boulez to the Attack."

For the first week of concerts, Boulez programmed Webern's *Passacaglia,* Schoenberg's *Verklärte Nacht,* Berg's *Altenberg Lieder,* Seven Early Songs, and Three Orchestral Pieces. For some, the concerts proved to be "the revelations" that Glock said they were for Londoners a few years before. For others, that proved not to be the case; those listeners left the house in droves. Harold Schonberg criticized them in his review of Boulez's first concert that spring: "There was nothing very problematic about the program . . . which consisted of early works by the three [modern Viennese] composers. That meant late romanticism and early expressionism. Nevertheless, a good part of the audience fled the last half of the program as though sirens warning of an atomic attack had been set off." Schonberg concluded his review: "The performance was tremendous. Mr. Boulez created the kind of music unity that only a musician immersed in the style could do. The music, which can sound spasmodic and febrile, went with the logic and power of a Beethoven symphony. Is any living conductor superior in this repertory? One doubts it."

For the second week of concerts, Boulez conducted scenes from Berlioz's *Beatrice and Benedict,* Messiaen's *Oiseaux Exotiques,* Varèse's *Ionisation,* and Ravel's *Tombeau de Couperin.* New Yorkers can be a docile lot. Exhorted by Schonberg to remain in their seats, most of them did exactly that. But the Furies were unleashed afterwards. One woman lashed out at me about Boulez: "That was the most dreadful concert I ever heard. What are those bongo bongo drums doing in Philharmonic Hall? When I listen to music, I am put in another world. I sit with my needlepoint, listening to Mozart, and I am in another world. But with tonight's music I am in Hell. The board of directors will have something to say about this kind of programming."

Other listeners could not tolerate the predominantly modern diet. No Schubert, no Beethoven was in Boulez's programs at that time. Management received many letters of protest, and, for the first time in memory, the perennially sold-out Philharmonic took out ads offering subscriptions for the approaching season. Still, critics continued to rebuke the audience. In a May 1971 issue of *New York* magazine Alan Rich wrote, "If the Thursday night fogies—to say nothing of the dear Friday ladies—find this programming not to their tastes, it is because their tastes have been coddled far too long."

The reaction to the New and Newer Music concert moved as predictably in the other direction. The first rehearsal gave a sense of the rapport that prevailed. Boulez was conducting an outstanding group of performers from the Juilliard School in Schoenberg's Septet, Stravinsky's *Pribaoutki* and *Berceuses du Chat,* and his own *Marteau sans Maître.* He sat on a stool and appeared relaxed. He worked carefully, taking each of the players separately and then in combination with one another. During the break he bought a Coke from the machine and behaved the way he does when he is around friends: he was cordial, responsive, convivial, good-humored, and had inexhaustible patience with those working with him. The rehearsal lasted more than three hours, and at the end the players wanted to stay for more. The performance was splendid; the audience enthralled.

After Boulez left New York at the end of May, I wrote an article about him for *The New York Times.* My purpose was to contribute some degree of humanity to his generally austere image and at the same time make clear that Boulez was intransigent in his demands. The major theme of the piece was this: if he did not get his way with programming, if he could not "supply a model of musical life as I conceive it, a musical life that is part of genuine culture," if he did not find a responsive audience for the major works of the twentieth century, he would leave. Such an action would recall one that had happened more than fifty years before: when Varèse, in 1919, founded the New Symphony Orchestra in New York to bring new music to those "eager to listen and learn." Three pairs of concerts were scheduled, but Varèse conducted only the first. After the initial performance the orchestra's board notified him that he would have to compromise on the programming. Varèse refused and lost the post to Artur Bodansky who took over with the traditional repertory.

Here is the text of the article I wrote on Boulez for *The New York Times*:

> Pierre Boulez is finally making the New York scene, but he is traveling light. He rents no apartment, subletting a different one each time he is here, and though he will take over as musical director at the New York Philharmonic in September, he avoids all the props of today's American musical life. With no manager, press agent, secretary, maid or wife—without even a telephone answering service—the 46-year-old French musician lives simply and alone. He says that his aim as musical director of the Philharmonic is "to supply a model of musical life as I conceive it, a musical life that is part of genuine culture—not a kind of second-rate enjoyment."

What he's trying to accomplish with his style, with his pace, and especially with his programming may be hard for Philharmonic audiences to take, and many subscribers have written to the management demanding a return to Beethoven and Brahms. If Boulez cannot find a responsive audience for the major works of the twentieth century, he says simply: "I will leave."

His output is formidable; between March 15 and May 15 when he returned to Europe, Boulez conducted more than 60 different works in Cleveland and New York. The musicians performed most of them for the first time. On Monday of his fourth week in New York we met for lunch. I asked how things were going for him.

"Intensely," he replied.

The night before he had conducted the Chamber Society in Mozart, Berg and Schoenberg at Alice Tully Hall. That morning he had rehearsed the next Philharmonic program which included "The Miraculous Mandarin" and the rarely performed Schoenberg Opus 22 Songs. Later, at 7:30, he conducted the last performance of the Stravinsky Memorial program. Boulez never chooses the easy way out: "Pulcinella" and the "Requiem Canticles" were new to the men and he could have simplified his work by using the 1947 version of "Petrushka," the one they know. But he chose the 1911 original. Not all of these are among his favorite works, but Boulez programmed them because he thinks they should be heard.

This refusal to impose his taste on others is consistent with a general sense of mission. During his stay in New York, he rarely was diverted from his work. He attended no films, shows, galleries, or large parties. Here is a typical Boulez day, pieced together by observation and conversation. It is April 27, a Tuesday, traditionally a day off for the orchestra:

In an apartment overlooking Central Park West, Boulez awakens early—about 5 o'clock. Without breakfast, he begins to work. Generally he spends these early hours composing, but this morning he finishes an article on Stravinsky commissioned by the Saturday Review. Stravinsky's recent death does not stop Boulez from criticizing him for using quotations of old music. He concludes with a plea for amnesia in composers. (Later he takes off from Stravinsky's use of the past. "Creators," he says, "must look straight ahead. It is not enough to deface the Mona Lisa because that does not kill the Mona Lisa. All the art of the past must be destroyed.")

At 8:30 he showers. Then he takes calls. Totally unconcerned with fashion—with no trademark like Bernstein's cape, Ozawa's bell bottoms or Stockhausen's pony tail—he puts on blue suit, white shirt and dark tie and walks a few blocks to Philharmonic Hall to make his first record with the orchestra: the overture to Berlioz's "Beatrice and Benedict" and Ravel's "Tombeau de Couperin." Still without breakfast, he steps onto the podium at exactly 10 o'clock. He takes off his watch, places it on the music stand, takes off his jacket, hangs it by the collar on the podium rail, and said good morning to the men.

From the sound booth, producer Andrew Kazdin said: "This is the overture to 'Beatrice and Benedict.' Take one." Prefacing each direction with "May I take, please, from bar . . ." Boulez works until 12:50, thirty minutes into overtime, when the telephone next to the podium rings. Kazdin said: "I'm afraid I'll have to stop now." Not yet satisfied with the Ravel, Boulez answers—with intensity— "Please don't." Two minutes pass. Even the usually restless musicians remain still. Then Kazdin gives him the go-ahead. About 1:10 Boulez brings down both his arms (he never uses a baton), puts on watch and jacket and rushes backstage to hear the replay. He and I had a one o'clock appointment. As I wait in the wings for him, the musicians file out. Several discuss the overtime; it means $47.50 for each of the 57 men who played the Ravel.

Boulez is laughing as he leaves the sound booth. Obviously he likes what he heard. On seeing me, he remembers our date and puts his hand to his head in a gesture of shock. It's 1:35; he meets with Columbia Records at 2. "Let's go to La Crêpe," he said. "It's faster than The Ginger Man." As we run down the steps (Boulez never walks), he compares himself to Sisyphus: "I push the rock up and it comes down again."

At La Crêpe he talks of the audience's reaction to his first program of Schoenberg, Webern and Berg. "Can you imagine how it feels to see more empty seats each time you come back out on stage?" I ask if it feels bad enough to persuade him to compromise with the audience's taste.

"A free society," Boulez says, "is not very different from a state society. In one case you are dictated to by subscribers, in another case by the government. I know some subscribers have complained that there is too much modern music in next year's programs. But there is very little and I'll reduce it no further. A few days ago I was at a friend's house for dinner and the guests said they had never been able to buy Philharmonic subscriptions. I told them to buy them now. I'm hoping for a younger audience—by that I mean people in their forties." Boulez adds that he'll leave the bulk of the conventional repertory to guest conductors: "I see no reason why I should conduct Brahms when there are others who do it better."

In front of La Crêpe, he says he loves New York. I ask how he knows because he never seems to go anywhere. "That's true," he answers, "but the streets are enough." Crossing 66th Street, he extends his left hand, bringing an oncoming automobile to a halt. "I love to do that," he beams. "It works—most of the time." After the 2 o'clock conference with Columbia Records—in which scheduling and promotion are discussed for an hour—he leaves the Board Room for the Green Room of Philharmonic Hall. There he coaches the soloists for "Pulcinella" from the piano until after 5. Then back to the apartment to rest.

During his five weeks in New York, Boulez spent only three full evenings with friends. This Tuesday was not one of them. At 7, in a rehearsal room at Juilliard, he works with student performers on his own "Marteau sans Maître," part of the New and Newer Music program for that Sunday night. It's the only concert in either Cleveland or New York in which Boulez programmed a work of his own. Later he explains he wants no one to say he is using his position to promote his own work. During the break, he talks informally with the performers about Schoenberg's Opus 29 Septet. At 10:15, friends from Cleveland—

with whom he stays when he is there—join him for supper at Le Poulailler.

Boulez drives everyone as he drives himself. And, on occasion things break down. Two important instruments dropped out of the last bars of the Requiem Canticles during the Thursday night performance. When the conductor spoke to the players during intermission, one said that his mind went blank. This is not hard to understand. Boulez says he needs 20 hours of rehearsal for the kind of programs he conducted this spring. He gets only 10. The problem of time hangs over everything. All his politeness—the pleases, thank yous, I beg your pardons—cannot conceal the time-pressure he feels. He has suggested a rehearsal storage plan: if one program requires only seven hours' work, can we have 13 for the next? The union said no.

What he does at rehearsal is to clean everything up. The musicians played under guest conductors for two years and that is death to discipline. Bernstein had a whole other way: concerned mostly with sweep and thrust, he allowed the instruments a great deal of leeway. But precision claims top priority for Boulez. He'll say to a violinist, "Your rhythm is wrong," and then work with him until his rhythm is right, while the other men shift restlessly in their seats. He concerns himself with balance, not only the balance within one section so that the one horn doesn't stand out over the rest, but balance among the various sections. Above all, he works for correct intonation. During the course of an orchestral passage, Boulez stops: "Third trumpet, your E flat is too sharp." Then he thrusts his right arm out in front of him and brings down his thumb, ever so slowly, until the instrument hits the exact pitch. To close the issue, he whistles it. The performance that results is crystal clear.

This approach to conducting works miracles for twentieth-century music; Louise Varèse, widow of composer Edgard Varèse, told me that Boulez brought out the lyric poetry of her husband's "Ionisation" as no other conductor has ever done. The approach does not always work as well for older music; the sensuous aspects of a melodic line can get lost in Boulez's excessive attention to detail.

Still, at this juncture, there are only two roads for the orchestra to take: it can remain a museum for the presentation of old work, or it can bring to life the music of this century. If Boulez cannot transform the New York Philharmonic into an instrument of "genuine culture," there is little likelihood that anybody can.

The Sunday editor, Seymour Peck, indicated his skepticism regarding Boulez's success in New York with a question mark at the end of his title: "Bringing 'em Back to Life?"

CHAPTER 36

Boulez's success in New York is measurable not in terms of curtain calls or sold-out houses but in terms of programming alone. Boulez reiterated to the press that if the Philharmonic had wished to proceed as it had in the past, it would have hired a music director who conducted the standard repertory better than he did. "It is obvious," he said repeatedly, "that the management in New York wants something new."

Indeed, in London, since 1964, Boulez had been doing something new. Between his conversation with Sir William Glock in 1963, when he had twenty pieces in his repertory, and the end of 1972 when Glock retired from the BBC, Boulez conducted 187 pieces with the orchestra, the great majority of them twentieth-century works. On occasion he did intersperse traditional pieces, but he never did much of that. Glock explains: "There are composers with whom Boulez cannot get deeply involved. What Beethoven has to offer him is very little. He speaks with passion about Bach's Chorale Preludes but I cannot imagine him conducting the St. Matthew Passion, or, for that matter, the B Minor Mass. I cannot imagine Liszt by Boulez.

"We had a marvelous time planning concerts together," Glock recalled. "Planning programs became like a game of tennis. I would come with suggestions. He would not want what wouldn't fit. I always tried to make a start so he wouldn't be faced with a blank page. A good program is like a work of art. It's made of works that not only fit but genuinely enhance each other as well. Boulez had the instinct for what was a positive program and what was not. I remember suggesting *Éclat* and Berlioz's *Symphonie Fantastique*. At first he just stared in stunned silence. Then he said, "It's really not so bad. It's a program to show off orchestral virtuosity."

"Boulez is a theorist," Glock went on. "He likes patterns. Concert life is not one good concert after another to him. I'm always looking for the next good thing. He's out to establish attitudes. His approach is more methodical, more intellectual. I was against this idea of a season of people or a season of, say 'Cantatas, beginning with Buxtehude.' I could not do it. It was too systematic for me. I was never enamored of titles and the like and on that subject we disagreed.

"But in the main we worked very well together. Boulez's main idea was to break down divisions in audiences themselves. The BBC began to take big risks there. Of course I had my bosses at the BBC, the heads of the administration there. But these men were always my allies; the BBC had a background of doing contemporary work."

The New York Philharmonic had no comparable background, and it depends on the box office, so the orchestra entered Boulez's arena somewhat tentatively. Boulez's first season focused on Berg and Liszt—Liszt, a professed enemy during Boulez's youth, and the composer whom Glock could not imagine Boulez conducting. Indeed, during the first season, Boulez himself conducted not only many major works by Liszt, but also works by Mahler, Schubert, Schumann, and Mozart. Boulez's appointment, then, was less a tribute to the management's faith in the twentieth-century repertory in which Boulez believed, than to the age and personality factors noted by Keiser as well as to one other exceptionally important fact: the anti-bourgeois attitudes associated with the modernist movement in art had, by the late 1960s, been adopted by the middle class itself. As distinguished professors deferred to impassioned rebels in blue jeans, so the oldest and one of the greatest orchestras in the country elevated to its own helm the most articulate enemy of traditional music in the world.

When Boulez arrived in New York in September 1971, he read an advertisement in the morning's *Times* that the first two weeks of concerts were sold out and that information pleased him a great deal.

The opening, a benefit, was a festive occasion. Boulez conducted Wagner's *Faust Overture*, Berlioz's *Royal Hunt* and *Storm* from *The Trojans*, Liszt's *Totentanz* for piano and orchestra, Debussy's *Prelude to the Afternoon of a Faun*, and Stravinsky's *Rite of Spring*, surely a program to warm the hearts of the most traditional audience. During the intermission one gentleman, in a red moiré jacket, said he had decided against subscribing this year "because this guy is supposed to be very far-out." Another commented that "Boulez is in the same camp as Szell, but Szell's academic ways are saved by a certain uniqueness of style that saves it from the lack of incandescence we feel here tonight." His companion asked: "Is Boulez Jewish?" "Heavens, no," he replied. "I think he must be the son of a Swiss watchmaker."

After the last piece on the program, *The Rite of Spring,* the house was filled with thunderous applause. The Green Room overflowed the way it had with Bernstein. Mayor Lindsay was on hand, posing for photographs along with Goddard Lieberson—president of Columbia Records—and Felicia Bernstein. Parties were very much in the air.

The next evening Boulez telephoned me to confirm an appointment and also to talk about the opening concert. He said the orchestra had worked so well, had sounded so well, and that his rapport with the men was so good. I asked whose party he attended afterwards. He replied: "Carlos and I dined at Poulailler alone."

The glitter and glamour were for the occasion, not for Boulez. By then he had emitted the unmistakable sign of compulsive isolation that the astute hostesses of New York picked up.

It seemed only right and proper that Boulez's milieu in the United States would not be the social whirl but rather his avant-garde concerts in Greenwich Village. It was at these "Prospective Encounters," held in one of the Shakespeare Festival's complex of theaters, that Boulez was to present contemporary works. And it was to the first of these concerts that *Life, Time, Newsweek,* and network TV sent its reporters and camera crews. On the ride downtown in the Philharmonic car, someone remarked on the ugliness of the abstract sculpture in Cooper Square. Boulez said, "It's better than the generals on horseback all over France."

The Encounters had been heralded as informal affairs, with people free to come and go as they chose, with conversation among participants and listeners, with performances repeated as the audience wished. At 7:15 Joseph Papp, founder of the New York Shakespeare Festival, appeared to introduce Boulez. Papp wore boots and a long suede jacket. Boulez's concession to informality was a blue turtleneck shirt under his dark business suit, the same blue turtleneck shirt he was to wear to each of the Encounters that year.

Boulez came to center stage—it was a theater in the round—and described in a clear and staccato delivery exactly how the evening's program would proceed. He said he hoped to bring the two worlds together, that people from the Village would go up to the Philharmonic and that people from the Philharmonic would come down to the Village. He said the programming for the series was guided by conversations with composers in New York and that the first year would be exclusively American.

Because of the attention that the press and public had focused on the first of the Village concerts, the programming for it was critical. Boulez chose Mario Davidovsky's *Synchronisms No. 6* for piano and electronic instruments—a ten-minute work for piano and tape, and Charles Wuorinen's *The Politics of Harmony*—a forty-minute work with musicians from the Philharmonic and members of the American Mime Theater. Davidovsky and Wuorinen were logical choices: both were members of the Columbia University music department and the Columbia-Princeton Electronic Music Center, probably the most powerful base for composers in the United States. In addition, Wuorinen had recently been awarded the 1970 Pulitzer Prize in composition.

By the time Paul Jacobs, the pianist of Boulez's early Paris days who was then official pianist for the New York Philharmonic, appeared on stage, the house, seating 350, was packed. Every pillow on the floor was taken, "regular" subscribers were sitting on benches, and the press section overflowed. Jacobs was to play the Davidovsky, synchronizing his part with the prepared tape. Boulez explained that Davidovsky was not there because he had hurt his back while moving one of the speakers into place. Boulez quipped that the electronic medium is filled with such unforeseeable dangers.

Jacobs played the piece, then described several sound patterns to the audience. After his exposition, he played it again. Boulez asked for questions from the audience. A man asked if the work were happy or sad. Jacobs replied he found it "engaging." The man said he didn't like it at all and found Jacobs's comment pretty low-key. Boulez stepped in. He said he found the mood contemplative and that, in fact, he liked it very much. Then he invited Wuorinen to say a few words about Davidovsky's piece.

Wuorinen began by dissociating himself from Davidovsky. He said Davidovsky liked to "manipulate substances" whereas he preferred to "work with pitch relationships." As it came out it was a put-down of Davidovsky. At the same time it was useful to make clear that the medium does not dictate the syntax, that a piece for conventional instruments by Wuorinen is more like a computer piece by Wuorinen than it is like a piece for conventional instruments by Davidovsky. Whatever the means, Wuorinen considers pitch the most important aspect of music while Davidovsky concentrates on texture, on sound per se.

There was a twenty-minute break. I walked down from my seat in the bleachers (for that is how the house was set up) and conversed with Wuorinen, who was angry. He said that in our society, it is a question of "either-or," that if an evening is to be informal, "an inappropriate intimacy ensues." He objected, he spelled out, to Boulez's light jokes. Julius Baker, the orchestra's first desk flutist—who was on hand to play the Wuorinen work—said he was sorry he had not brought his eight-year-old son because "the boy loves the kinds of sounds Davidovsky makes." Robert Miller, a pianist specializing in the contemporary repertory who had given the world premiere of Davidovsky's piece, reported that Davidovsky's bad back was caused by learning that the Philharmonic, which had devoted so many hours to rehearsing Wuorinen's piece, would not replace the small piano in the house with an appropriate concert-size grand. Composer Stanley Silverman noted that Wuorinen had put down Davidovsky and that he himself worked like Davidovsky. Silverman said he was distressed and would like to go home but added that if he did, everyone would see him leave. That was a problem of performance in the round.

Teresa Sterne, then director of Nonesuch Records, a company with an excellent history regarding new music, was livid with rage. She said Boulez was on "a big ego trip," that two-thirds of the audience were professional musicians and what the hell is he doing talking to them as though they were kids. Someone noted that not everyone there was professional: What about the man who asked if the piece was happy or sad? Sterne replied, "My God, that was Earl Price of Columbia Records. He was just pulling Boulez's leg." She added that the avant-garde in New York had been knocking themselves out with such concerts for years and then Boulez walked in and capitalized on it all.

The hall was unbearably hot. Harold Schonberg took off his jacket. Wuorinen walked on to center stage to discuss his own much longer work. He spoke of the ancient Chinese tale on which his piece was based, and he described, in detail, the calligraphy on the backdrops that were to act as sets which were not yet before the audience.

The tedium of the piece, set for three voices and chamber instruments, was not relieved by the mimes. But the audience was more imprisoned than any audience uptown. Those who tried to leave were impeded by a door that would not open easily. People pushed and scuffled around in embarrassment with the audience's eyes riveted on them as they tried to make their escape. Afterwards, when the discussion began, there was a mass exodus. Boulez asked Wuorinen to talk about the compositional principles of the work. Wuorinen said he didn't want to "bore" anyone. Someone asked him if it were 12-tone. Wuorinen replied, "It is at least that."

After the second break, poet Richard Howard, librettist for the Wuorinen work, talked with Wuorinen and Boulez on stage. Howard said there was generally a fifty-year span between the creation and appreciation of a good work. Boulez said it was not necessarily so, that *The Rite of Spring* was popular immediately and that Schoenberg's *Erwartung* was not. Both, Boulez said, are good works, so obviously there is no rule. Howard continued to plug obscurantism, ignoring Boulez's statements and insisting that if an artist works quietly he will have to wait fifty years for recognition.

In his review of the concert, Harold Schonberg wrote: "The Davidovsky was a rather conventional arrangement of serialized synthesized tape. At least it was clear and direct. The Wuorinen was one of those academic post-serial drags, completely amelodic, awkwardly set for three voices." In his Sunday essay, Schonberg went on: "The Wuorinen work ran some dismal forty minutes with the singers maltreating the English language in extended twelve-tone syllabic extensions, with the usual academic kind of organization, with a 1960s kind of athematicism, with virtually no personality, without a trace of charm." In commenting on the final discussion, Schonberg wrote, "It did not seem to occur to anybody that if a work of art has not established itself in fifty years, it conceivably, just conceivably, might be the fault of the work of art and not the public."

The next morning a member of the Columbia-Princeton group called and asked me what I had thought of the concert. I said the Wuorinen was not one of my favorite Wuorinen pieces. He said it was probably the worst Wuorinen had composed and accused Boulez of selecting it to show American music in the worst possible light.

When I asked Boulez why he had chosen *The Politics of Harmony,* he said it was because he believed the use of mimes would prove attractive to the audience.

In September 1972, when Boulez was on tour with the New York Philharmonic in Bloomington, Indiana, Dean Wilfred Bain of the Indiana University's School of Music hosted a picnic. A student orchestra was there. Bain asked Boulez to conduct the fourth movement of Tchaikovsky's Fourth. Boulez shook his head. Later Bain made the request again. Again Boulez shook his head.

A large canvas was mounted and the dean invited everyone to paint on it. The first person he addressed was Boulez. Boulez said he did not want to dirty his fingers. Bain said it was only watercolor. Boulez smiled. A half hour later Bain reappeared. By now the canvas was filled with color and must have been, in Boulez's eyes, "a mess." Boulez was such a creative person, Bain said. It would mean so much to the university if he would add his personal touch. Boulez smiled again. At the end of the party Bain returned. "Look how beautiful the painting is now. Surely you will grace it with a stroke or two." Boulez smiled at Bain for the last time: "It is far too beautiful for me to spoil."

CHAPTER 37

n New York Boulez established the Rug Concerts, with carpets replacing the seats on the first floor of Avery Fisher Hall. Held after the end of the season, ticket prices were strikingly low in order to attract the young. During one of these concerts, when the chamber ensemble Tashi was playing Messiaen's *Quartet for the End of Time*, Boulez sat next to me in the audience. After the cello movement I whispered, "It is such romantic music." He replied, "It is much less than that."

If Boulez despised the Messiaen quartet, what, then, does he love? He never uses the word love (except to describe his feeling for yogurt), but if I were to assess what he does love, I would include pre-1925 Schoenberg and Stravinsky, Webern, Berg, some Debussy, and some Berlioz. He probably merely likes Varèse and some works by Bartók, Ravel, Messiaen, Carter, Stockhausen, Vinko Globokar, and Berio. George Crumb, who enjoyed considerable success both in the United States and Europe, he found "cheap—a kind of entropy of serialism."

He gave stiff performances of the classic and romantic repertory. After his performance of Schumann's Rhenish Symphony, Harold Schonberg wrote in *The New York Times*, "There was no tenderness . . . a brainy orchestral technician at work." Boulez remarked to Milburn that Schonberg was wrong: "I conducted the Schumann freely," he said.

The audience responded accordingly. After a Boulez performance of *Sacre du Printemps* or *La Mer*, where melody did not play the most significant role, the Green Room used to be crowded with fans. After Mozart, Mendelssohn, Schubert, or Haydn, the Green Room was empty; people did not know what to say. (By Boulez's fifth season, the Green Room was empty even for *Sacre du Printemps*. That was partly because of Boulez's personal style in greeting his visitors, and partly because his initial enthusiasm had dampened and he rarely brought to life even works he admired.)

Columbia Records, which recorded Boulez and also had the New York Philharmonic as its major contract orchestra, seemed to share the public assessment. Columbia recorded only what was being performed so it didn't have to pay for rehearsal time. When Boulez began to conduct more and more Mendelssohn and less and less of the twentieth-century repertory, Columbia reduced its recording of him and the New York Philharmonic. In fact, when, in 1975, Boulez recorded the monumental twentieth-century works *Gurrelieder* and *Moses und Aron,* it was not with the New York Philharmonic, because that orchestra had never played them, but with the BBC Symphony.

Boulez began his recording career with CBS-UK in January 1966. Ken Glancy, then chief of the English division, made the deal with Boulez's manager, Howard Hartog. The contract allowed Boulez to record whichever of his own works he wished.

Initially, Columbia did not rule out Boulez and the traditional repertory, but no one in London had heard him conduct it. Then, late in 1966, when Otto Klemperer fell ill, Boulez substituted for him in a Beethoven cycle at Festival Hall. Columbia recorded his Beethoven Fifth. Glancy, a first-rate musician, characterized the performance as "eccentric; it sounds a little like Mahler," and Columbia could not sell that record. Years later, when Boulez conducted the New York Philharmonic in the Seventh and Ninth symphonies, Columbia did not change its estimate of Boulez's compressed, asensual Beethoven.

Boulez's first project at Columbia was one that was important to him: the complete works of Webern. Columbia had produced a Webern album under the direction of Robert Craft, but Boulez wanted to do one of his own. Boulez began discovering undiscovered Webern and also started to compose an essay about Webern that would be included in the package.

Although he said in the 1970s, "Webern thirty years later is a historical quantity, solidified lava, no longer something directly vital to me," he regarded the essay seriously enough to have worked on it off and on for more than nine years.

Between 1969 and the mid-1970s, when Boulez changed his contract to Columbia New York, he had recorded about twenty-five albums, several with the Cleveland Orchestra and London Symphony but most with the New York Philharmonic. The ones that sold well were very good indeed. The sales of his *Sacre du Printemps* with the Cleveland Orchestra far exceeded any executive's expectations. The complete *Petrushka, The Miraculous Mandarin, Valses Nobles et Sentimentales* all sold very well. Of his own works, he recorded *Marteau sans Maître, Livre pour Cordes, Pli Selon Pli* and his Piano Sonatas No. 1 and No. 2 and two movements of No. 3. Apart from the sonatas, which were played by the American pianist Charles Rosen, all were performed by European groups.

For Columbia Records, all of this amounted to little more than prestige. Only five percent of the record industry's output in the United States at that time was made up of the classical repertory, and only a small fraction of that was contemporary music. The pieces that continued to sell best were *Scheherazade,* the *1812 Overture, Boléro,* and the Beethoven symphonies. Therefore it could not be said that Columbia hired Boulez as a potential gold mine. It hired him because he was "a bright star on the musical horizon, the great new figure to come out of nowhere," as one Columbia executive put it to me. But because of the skyrocketing costs, Columbia was reluctant to record anything but the most certified twentieth-century works. And when, in 1974, Boulez said he wanted to record Mahler, Columbia turned him down.

Because of Columbia's selectivity regarding Boulez, the conductor left a great legacy with those works he did record. *Gurrelieder* and *Moses und Aron* are extraordinary achievements, both in power of conception and refinement of execution. The same can be said of virtually all Boulez recordings of twentieth-century music as well as the French repertory.

One man working at Columbia when Boulez arrived in New York was David Kleger, a soft-spoken, low-key publicity agent. Kleger liked Boulez and concentrated on publicizing his records. Because Hurok was then Boulez's American agent, Kleger called to ask if he could work for Boulez for nothing. The Hurok office, delighted, agreed.

Then in a budget squeeze, Columbia fired many of its staff, including Kleger. At the same time Boulez was called by the Internal Revenue Service for his first audit. He was in Cleveland at the time and Hurok did not send anyone to help. Angry, and no longer in need of management now that he had the Philharmonic post, Boulez left the Hurok establishment. It was then that Kleger approached Boulez to see if he could handle his publicity on a private basis. Boulez agreed.

Kleger was uncritical, intensely loyal, even adoring of Boulez. But there was still another reason Boulez agreed to Kleger's offer. By then he must have been aware that the publicity issued by the New York Philharmonic and the publicity on which he himself had always thrived were at cross-purposes. The Philharmonic wished to present Boulez as a man for all seasons, as a great conductor of a great orchestra. They were determined not to present him as a composer possessed with a demanding language that most of their subscribers neither wanted nor understood. So Boulez went along with Kleger, probably believing it would offer him the chance to control his own image as "revolutionary."

One of Kleger's early coups was to put Boulez on the Dick Cavett Show. Boulez was enthusiastic. I counseled against it, saying what I believed to be true: that few serious people can benefit from this kind of exposure. I cut out an article from the *Times* magazine in which the Yale drama professor Robert Brustein claimed substantially the same thing. I showed it to Boulez who made little of it. He said he would have complete control, that he would probably appear with Joseph Papp and no one else for the two hours, and that he was therefore assured of a dignified milieu.

On the afternoon of the taping, in February 1972, Boulez flew in from Cleveland, arriving at the studio in the late afternoon. But that morning the Philharmonic press department got wind of the plans for the first time, so when Boulez stepped out of the car, Moseley and Milburn were waiting for him. Moseley drew his lips back, imitating a smile, and instructed Boulez not to say anything revolutionary on the air.

At the studio Papp was nowhere to be seen. While Boulez waited backstage for an hour and a half, Cavett talked to Leonard Frey, Sada Thompson, and Chuck McCann, all show-business personalities. McCann did a funny vacuum cleaner salesman routine. Boulez was scheduled last. That meant he would appear well after midnight, in the graveyard slot reserved for intellectuals. Cavett began by introducing Boulez as a controversial figure who had caused many subscribers to cancel tickets. Boulez replied, "That is melodramatic. Not so many people canceled tickets." Cavett asked Boulez about the story I reported in the *Times* interview that he had booed Stravinsky in 1945. Boulez replied that other students were booing too and that he was not out to attack Stravinsky but to bring attention to those composers who had been overlooked. Cavett must have been disappointed. His researchers had presented him with the picture of a rebel, and here, instead, was a company man. He told the audience about Boulez's perfect pitch and asked someone in the band to blow a note. Boulez answered correctly; it was a G-sharp. Then Cavett informed the audience that Boulez could simultaneously conduct two different beats with each hand. Again Boulez obliged. The audience applauded, as it had with McCann. Cavett asked Boulez what was happening in new music, particularly in regard to John Cage. Here Boulez's congenial manner disappeared: "Cage is not new anymore," he said.

At 7:10 Boulez left the theater and at 7:30 stepped onto the podium in black tie. I entered the hall and saw Joe Roddy, a former senior editor of *Look* magazine. Roddy had been to the Cavett show and viewed Boulez's appearance as a "fall from grace." He was certain Moseley had compelled him to do it. When I told him this was not true, Roddy groaned, "The virus is the cancer of ambition."

Roddy speculated about Boulez's future in New York. He thought the Philharmonic had made a bold move in taking on Boulez and that it could not back down from it now. He predicted Boulez would be hired for another few years. Neither Roddy nor I knew at that time that Boulez already had signed a second three-year contract in December 1971. Throughout the spring, summer, and fall of 1972 Boulez told me he would not return to New York unless his demands were met. But they were not met, if indeed they had been made. Howard Hartog told me of the second contract in June 1972. Frank Milburn told me about it on November 1. Yet the news was not announced until November 5, the morning after Nixon's landslide. The election news dominated everything else. It is hard not to conclude that the Philharmonic postponed the announcement for ten months and finally chose the day that it did to stave off the negative reaction it anticipated if the news were to be given prominence. By that time the majority of Philharmonic subscribers were turned off by Boulez. They want someone who will reach out to them not only with programming but with a personality that suggests there is a dialogue between them and him.

Roddy's negative reaction to Boulez's appearance on the Cavett show reveals the trouble Boulez had with interviews while he was in New York. As he made his way up the ladder—whether as composer or conductor— Boulez's bold attacks on powerful people brought him attention and respect, particularly among the intellectuals. But it is easier to attack Malraux in print than it is to handle a face-to-face interview, particularly if one is set on hiding many things. One of Boulez's least successful interviews was at the opening of John Gruen's series, "The Art of the Live Interview," held at the New School for Social Research in Greenwich Village. Several hundred people were there.

Gruen asked what it meant to be music director of the New York Philharmonic. Boulez spoke of the complexities of the post. He said he had to consider guest conductors and guest soloists, what each of them wished to do and how he could integrate their wishes with his theme of the year. He said he had to balance instrumental and vocal music, all the different historical periods, deal with the even and odd subscription series, and then, when he was told a work cost too much, had to substitute another and still maintain all the balances. Boulez spoke of the internal life of the orchestra: of musicians retiring who had to be replaced, of the competition between first desk men, of the preaudition committees and the final auditions—when he and members of the section in question agreed on which of the players to select.

As soon as Boulez stopped for a breath, Gruen popped the big question: "What were you like as a little boy?"

> BOULEZ: "All little boys are practically the same. The boy you were does not imply the man you are."
> GRUEN: "Well, anyway. What kind of little boy were you?"
> BOULEZ: "I don't remember."

Boulez refused to give the name of the town where he was born. He spoke only of its provincial quality.

Gruen pressed for details; Boulez answered, this time angrily: "You know by now I am not inclined to give my biography point by point. All I will say is this: I played an instrument and sang in the choir. Neither my family nor my environment was musical. In middle-class families, girls and boys have piano lessons. So by chance I was confronted by the sound of the piano. The most important things need no explanation. It is just a seed."

> GRUEN: "Do you know you are known as a cold conductor? What do you do when a composer writes 'con amore' in a score?"

Boulez ignored the second question: "There is a kind of legend that I am just caring for structure. I think the form is the feeling and that the feeling expresses itself through the form. Composers work through conceptions. You have to navigate a long work. In *Parsifal* you can't just begin and follow the fancy of the moment. Wagner spent four years writing it. It's not fair to the composer or the score just to follow one's fancy. There's more freedom in knowing than in not knowing."

After the interview someone in the audience asked Boulez what he thought of Copland and Bernstein. Boulez said he would not answer the question because he doesn't like to influence people's reactions. Another asked how he stood politically: "I am personally against making my opinions known, or using the public person to influence things. I prefer to be discreet about this."

The next morning I telephoned Gruen to ask for a transcript of the interview. He said he could not give me one because he hoped to publish all his interviews at a later date. (This accounts for the above quotations being only approximations of what was said.) Gruen complained that his opening event was a dismal failure: "Boulez turned the interview into a lecture. His not answering was unbelievable. He didn't even talk to me on the way downtown in the taxi. He is so noncommittal. Did you ever find out anything about his sex life?"

The answer to that question then and now is no.

Like Kleger, I did what I could to give Boulez the chance to tell the people of this country who he really was. Barbara Walters, then a host on NBC's *Today Show*, had been my closest friend in the last two years of high school and we had kept in touch. Would she, I asked, interview Boulez? Barbara told me to give her a few questions because she was no expert in the new music field. Boulez answered them in his characteristic, uninflected, impersonal way. Barbara sighed: "Well," she said. "You certainly don't have the panache of Leonard Bernstein." Boulez replied: "The time for panache is over."

Both of them were correct.

CHAPTER 38

A few incidents in New York reveal a lot about the relationship between Boulez and America.

Just after Boulez began his tenure, I ran into an old friend, the conductor Alfred Wallenstein. I told him I was writing a book about Boulez. He attacked the programs of Boulez's first year, mainly its extravagant dosage of Liszt.

"And do you know the reason," Wallenstein went on, "for all of this Liszt? It's because Harold Schonberg wrote at least three columns complaining about the neglect of Liszt and saying some hero should devote a whole year to him. That's the reason—and the only one. It's not because Liszt deserves it. And it's not because Boulez loves Liszt. He has attacked him all his life."

Whatever Wallenstein's motivation, his perception of events seemed right, despite Schonberg's repeated assertions that he has no power at all.

When Boulez conducted Berg's Three Pieces for Orchestra, he needed a second trombone because the regular man was ill. He himself picked up the telephone and called John Swallow, on the music faculty of Yale. Swallow was moved by Boulez's personal call; that is a rare gesture for a conductor. But what he wished for more than anything else was a personal word of gratitude after the performance—and he was never to receive that. Instead Boulez sent the orchestra's personnel manager, Jimmy Chambers, to Swallow with the message that in general he did well enough but that he missed the entry at bar such and such. Swallow was hurt and furious.

Boulez's display of his ability to spot the smallest musical error is considered by a number of the players to be his most reprehensible trait. Many musicians complain Boulez takes precious time from the rehearsal to point out mistakes and to have the men make corrections in their scores, rather than note them silently and instruct the librarian to make them later—as other conductors generally do.

Boulez himself is not impervious to criticism and, indeed, often tries to give the critic what the critic wants. Unlike many composers and conductors, he admits he reads reviews. When a feature article appears, he goes through it without interruption, as he did at the start of his American career, when *Newsweek* came out with a highly complimentary cover story. It happened again eighteen months later when *The New Yorker* ran a scholarly profile. It happened again when the magazine section of the Sunday *New York Times* ran a particularly damaging essay, attacking Boulez's coldness not only in personal relations but also in his handling of the traditional repertory. That weekend Boulez was conducting Brahms's A Major Serenade. I did not attend, but Roddy did. He called me to say Boulez was moving all over the stage, swinging and swaying as he never did before. "It was painful to watch," Roddy said, "like a woman faking an orgasm."

When I asked Moseley to cite Boulez's most striking personal trait, he said "his practicality." I would agree with Moseley on that. Boulez was practical in signing a second contract only three months after he began the first. He was practical in agreeing to tone down his advanced stand when he saw people leaving the house in droves. And he was practical in building a research institute in France while maintaining his power and income in the United States. But his strong practical bent can be seen in smaller ways. One evening at Poulailler, then Boulez's favorite New York restaurant, Daniel Barenboim, who had just played under Boulez at Juilliard, complained to Boulez about his changing the uniform of conductor and soloist from white tie and tails to black tie. He said the buttoned-up jacket interfered with his freedom of movement. Boulez said he made the change so that he could go straight to a restaurant without changing his clothes. He said it with charm but he was serious. Barenboim told Boulez, also with a laugh, that he exhibited an "elitist" attitude.

Boulez had little success with either the super-chic or the bourgeoisie. Amy Greene ran the beauty shop at Henri Bendel, one of the most fashionable stores in New York and was a friend of the Leonard Bernsteins. One afternoon when I was in her shop, she told me she had attended a performance of Bernstein's *Mass*. She said it was the most religious experience of her life and added that this was no mean compliment because she had been brought up in a convent. She said she had not been to the Philharmonic since Bernstein left because she heard that "nothing good was going on there." Then she laughed: "Anyway, where's the melody?" A woman from Long Island was trying eye shadow: "I dropped my subscription," she said, "because my husband is tired at the end of the day and he just wants to listen to music he likes."

Boulez had greater success with many serious students of music. Susan Sommer, a Columbia University-trained musicologist and a librarian in the research music division of the Lincoln Center Library, told me Boulez used the library all the time. "It's so gratifying to have one's work applied in this way. Boulez is continually searching out old music: the difficult, inaccessible scores. And I love to go to his concerts. I hear things in the music I never heard before."

When there is adequate rehearsal time, what one hears are the results of Boulez's uncanny ear and the technique he uses to get each note sounding right. But it is never because he is swept away. Several days after conducting Carter's Concerto for Orchestra at the Juilliard School, he met Peter Mennin, the school's president. Carter was there. Mennin had not been to the concert and he asked Boulez how it went. Boulez shrugged his shoulders in response. Carter was disconcerted by this and later asked me why Boulez had behaved this way. I put the question to Boulez who said, "Everyone is always asking me how everything went. How is it to go? It went, that's all." I asked if he could recall a performance that did more than that, that took off in an unusual and incandescent way. He thought for a moment and said no.

During his first two years as music director, Boulez held annual "composer conferences." He invited a number of New York-based composers and asked their advice on what pieces to perform at the Prospective Encounters in Greenwich Village. Most of them objected to the entire project; they thought their works should not be relegated to a series in the Village but be given wide attention at Lincoln Center itself. Nevertheless, those invited to the conference generally went. One was Lukas Foss, the Berlin-born composer-conductor who came to the United States in 1937 and composed then in the "neoclassical" style Boulez hated. In the 1960s Foss turned "radical," writing music that involved both theater and chance, again an idiom that was anathema to Boulez. Foss was the conductor of the Buffalo Philharmonic from 1963 until 1970. Later he became musical advisor and conductor of the Brooklyn Philharmonic and the Kol Israel Orchestra in Jerusalem.

Foss spoke to me after the first of the composer conferences:

> It was nothing more than a public relations maneuver, only the maneuver did not work. Frederick Rzewski said he heard the Village concerts were costly. Boulez asked him where he heard that. Rzewski said he didn't remember. Boulez mocked him: "I don't remember. I don't find that answer very interesting."

Boulez graded the answers as they came in. "That's a good point." "That doesn't interest me." "That is nonsense." "That is idiotic." He was like a party boss with his stooges only there were not many stooges there, only a few composers who do not yet know who they are.

Boulez's only concern is with power. He lost the leadership of the avant-garde more than ten years ago to Stockhausen. Now others have moved in. With the need for power, where was he to go? So he chose to be a conductor. He is a wonderful musician, a wonderful intelligence. It's a pity there's no humanity there. Does he have sex? I think not. When men have no sex, they go after power in this big, obsessive way.

Stanley Silverman, an admirer of Boulez, reported that at the end of the meeting there was an explosion between Foss and Boulez. Foss asked Boulez why he put Americans in a small chamber series instead of presenting them in the big house. Boulez snapped, "And succeed the way you did in Buffalo?" Silverman laughed at the incident. "They are all the same." he said. "Foss did exactly in Buffalo what Boulez is doing in New York. He gave prominence to Henze and Penderecki and put Americans out in left field. It doesn't matter whether the music director is German or French. They're foreign, so Americans will get the raw end."

Boulez failed in terms of his own promise of "revolution." Certainly he infused the New York Philharmonic with more contemporary music than it had known before he came, and more contemporary music than it knew after he was gone. Pitted against performances by a powerful conductor like Szell or a popular conductor like Bernstein, Boulez's performances of contemporary scores remained among the best one could get anywhere. It was precisely because he was capable of doing them impeccably that American composers became angry when he gave them less than that. Davidovsky was unhappy with a small piano; Babbitt thought his instruments were not placed in the right way; Peter Lieberson found his work underrehearsed. Inevitably some accused him of malicious intent.

And they appeared to be on firm ground, for Americans were hardly heard in the big house during Boulez's early years in New York. Even the most recognized received short shrift; Boulez did not program a Copland work until his third season, and first-generation Americans less famous than Copland were virtually ignored until the Bicentennial, Boulez's fifth season in

New York, and then they often were not conducted by Boulez. Diamond was one who had been the victim of neglect.

"When Boulez first came to New York," Diamond reports, "Moseley and Bernstein sat down with me and went through my orchestral scores. They decided I should send Boulez my Sixth Symphony and my *Elegy in Memory of Maurice Ravel*. They thought these pieces in particular would hold some interest for him. I am certain he never opened them. He is intransigent in his musical views. He will not play a score with octave doublings. That is why he has never programmed Sessions." (Sessions was performed later during the Bicentennial.)

A year after this conversation, Boulez was programming American scores that contained far greater heresies to him than octave doublings. That was because he did not care any more and was moved by political pragmatism alone.

Such stories suggest Boulez is a monster. But he is not a monster at all. In fact, in day-to-day relationships, he is an extremely decent man—never greedy, vulgar, or phony in any way. A mass of contradictions, Boulez is a man who can ignore David Diamond when he sends scores, but cables birthday greetings to a secretary an ocean away; who, because he detests "rituals," would not attend his nieces' weddings, but paid for their expensive honeymoons; who almost never compliments a soloist, but drives two hours in the snow to visit a Philharmonic musician recovering from a heart attack. Alternately aggressive and timid, alternately bold and vulnerable, Boulez can seem a bullying egomaniac to his composer-colleagues, but to others he can appear a generous man: shy, charming, eager to be loved, just somehow incapable of expressing any warmth.

On January 5, 1973, the Chamber Music Society of Lincoln Center played Boulez's *explosante-fixe*, his first major composition after becoming music director in New York. During its preparation, Boulez was nervous—a state reserved only for his own creative work. The piece is quiet, unsensational, and the audience responded with polite applause. Schonberg wrote a respectful review. *Explosante-fixe* was to be recorded later that week, but, after the performance, Boulez apparently wasn't satisfied and canceled the recording date.

Scored for vibraphone, harp, violin, flute, clarinet, trumpet, and a number of complicated devices including a giant new electronic instrument, the Halaphone, the work was supposed to have lasted eighteen minutes. But in its first performance it lasted much longer than that. The new instrument—named for its inventor, Peter Haller—was said to have been capable of projecting sounds in various directions and at various speeds. It is reported to have cost Alice Tully $5,000 to bring it to the United States from Germany.

The Chamber Music Society, then led by Charles Wadsworth, consisted of first-rate, experienced soloists. For the Boulez premiere, none was given his part until the last minute. After that the parts were changed constantly. Boulez invariably works up to the deadline, then revises what he has done.

I attended the first rehearsal. Boulez was concentrating on the exceptional performer, Paula Robison, because the flute plays the most prominent role. "It must be very quick. Can we do it again?" Robison had just been handed a completely revised score, replete with musical notes, and she asked if she could look it over first at home. "Do it," Boulez said, "just for the character of it."

Boulez stood to the right and just over Robison. He would have breathed for her if he could. "Very *knopf*," he said, "*knopf . . . knopf . . .*" Then he found the English equivalent. "Tight . . . tight . . . tighter," he went on. Robison was overcome with anxiety. She punctuated her performance with a series of sighs, gees, and oh-yeses. She was on the verge of tears. Boulez then reminded her that her part opened the work so her performance had to be "really brilliant."

Then Boulez moved on to the others, working with each player individually. After the opening flute solo, the flutist signals the next instrument when it is to enter. Instruments pile up in this way until the texture is very thick. Then there is a diminution until the flute remains alone. There is no freedom in duration or pitch. Whatever freedom there is lies in the length of the sequences; there are moments when rests can be introduced at will.

Boulez began to work again with the now thoroughly upset Miss Robison. "It must be very uneven," he said, beating in an uneven way. It had to be precise in its unevenness. Robison's eyes were filled with tears. "The notes come so fast one upon the other," she wept. Boulez laughed with false cheerfulness. "The point is to be irregular," he explained. "The point of the piece is to be free."

Before the Friday afternoon concerts, a lecture series was offered to members of the audience. On September 26, 1975, the start of Boulez's fifth season, he dropped in to introduce the speaker for the day and to give a short talk himself.

He spoke of his experience with Japanese calligraphy. He said that when he was visiting Japan he was struck by the beauty of the characters. But to gain understanding of their meaning he needed someone to translate for him. Boulez mentioned that he wished he knew Japanese so that the perception of the beauty and the understanding of the words would come to him simultaneously.

Then he paraphrased a letter of Diderot, the eighteenth-century encyclopedist, to illustrate his point that in art there is first darkness, then understanding, then one enters darkness again "because finally you do not know why you like a work." He concluded: "To reach darkness after understanding is better—I think—than to be in darkness before understanding."

Boulez's assets and liabilities remained intact in his shift from composer to conductor. His talent and energy served him as much as his rational intellect served him little. Again his ambition interfered, but it was his personality that caused the deepest trouble. Boulez's inability to engage in a genuine dialogue with whatever is different from himself—whether people or earlier musical periods—seemed to be the flaw that pulled him down.

CHAPTER 39

uring the reception that followed a concert in Indianapolis in 1972, one young woman asked Boulez why the press represented him as a revolutionary figure when he conducted traditional concerts such as the one he had just done: Berlioz, Haydn, Schumann, and Ravel. Boulez laughed. The woman waited. Boulez smiled. Then the woman moved away. Later I repeated her question to him. He answered, "How many people would have bought tickets tonight if we had programmed contemporary music?"

The incontrovertible fact is this: Within the arena of programming, Boulez deferred to that bourgeois society he had only recently announced he would ignore. He did not leave as he threatened to do, but he retreated from his progressive stand in regard to large audiences, concentrating his efforts on those isolated "special events"—the Prospective Encounters, Mini-Festivals, Informal Evenings and Rug Concerts—which added up to little more than a dozen contemporary evenings a year as against one hundred and twenty predominantly conservative evenings peppered with the twentieth-century repertory. If Boulez had persisted in his original aim, he undoubtedly would have brought the organization down with him. He and Moseley appear to have agreed on just how far the audience would move.

Moseley preferred to remain behind the scenes. But foundation executives generally agree that he was a "genius" in arts administration. Moseley began his affiliation with the New York Philharmonic in 1955 as director of press and public relations. He worked his way up through various managerial posts until, in 1970, he became the first full-time professional president of the orchestra. His obligation to the Philharmonic took precedence over a dedication to any musical "style" or "idea." The Philharmonic was one of the first orchestras to offer full-time employment to its musicians.

His gentlemanly manner covered a will of steel. In confrontations between Moseley and Boulez, Moseley generally prevailed. When Moseley learned that Boulez was to appear on the Dick Cavett show, an event not planned by his own press department, he instructed him to steer clear of any revolutionary talk. Boulez deferred. When Moseley learned that Boulez had agreed to conduct the benefit concert for the orchestra's striking musicians, he conferred with Boulez and a retraction followed. (Boulez gave $1,000 to the musicians' fund and attended the concert conducted by Leon Barzin.) On both occasions Boulez deferred to Moseley, and he appears to have deferred to Moseley on the programming as well.

During the 1974–75 season, Boulez acknowledged that he admired less than thirty-five percent of the works he was conducting—and that included not only the traditional but the contemporary repertory. During that year Boulez presented Wuorinen, Carter, George Crumb, and Jacob Druckman (all certified by having won the Pulitzer Prize); Peter Mennin, president of the Juilliard School; Carman Moore, a Juilliard-trained black composer; and Peter Lieberson, who, among other things, was the son of the man who was then president of Columbia Records, the company that recorded the New York Philharmonic. And he left unopened on his shelves the bulk of the scores that continued to pour in. Being music director of the New York Philharmonic clearly did not bring to Boulez whatever it was he had hoped it would bring. But rather than ask, "How do I get out of it?" he seemed only to ask, "How do I get through it?"

As president, Moseley served as liaison between the music director and the board of directors. "Boulez never fought the board," Moseley said. "It is true he had a great desire to bridge the gap between what the mass of people were used to hearing and the contemporary composer. But he is a practical man. He is practical enough to be guided by the subscribers' response."

Boulez reported on the programming sessions:

> I propose a theme and then we meet. Part of the problem is with guest conductors. Often those who will accept the programs are not big attractions, while those who are big attractions will not accept the programs. I was aware myself that the important thing is not to do too much, for then the people will not come and the organization will be in jeopardy. If you bring down the number of subscribers then you cannot go any further. The point is to attract a number of people and do something of what you want at the same time. It is true that in London I did more British music than I have done American music here. But that is because

I played much more contemporary music in London and could do that because of the subsidized BBC.

Perhaps to compensate for the retrogression, Boulez began to spend long hours in the library digging up difficult, rarely performed "older" pieces. During the 1972–73 season, the Haydn works he performed were rarely heard symphonies as well as the *Theresien* and *Harmonie* masses, and the opera *L'Incontro Improviso*. In a Sunday essay entitled "It's Fun For Boulez—But . . ." Harold Schonberg wrote that he thought many listeners would miss the works they knew and loved. The essay precipitated a phone call from Moseley to Boulez (then conducting in Cleveland) which was followed by a meeting between Moseley, Milburn, and Boulez as soon as Boulez arrived in New York. Then Moseley spoke to Schonberg. "I told him," Moseley reported, "that the Philharmonic was really doing what he had always wanted it to do: avoiding the war-horses and introducing unfamiliar pieces. The reaction to Harold's article was that some were furious with him but others were furious with the Philharmonic."

Many who worked under Moseley reported that he was "hypersensitive" to the press, which he has described as "irresponsible." Moseley said, "The press kept at this business of the Philharmonic doing a courageous thing, getting rid of an old audience for a new one. The people read a good deal about Boulez, 'The Great Iconoclast,' and were prejudiced prior to the time to judge. Many held onto their seats but did not attend in a display of protest. Others left the house before the unfamiliar work was performed."

But Moseley was wrong to blame the press; the reporters were merely loudspeakers for Boulez's ideas. The trouble lay not in newspaper accounts or in magazine articles but in the twentieth-century music of Boulez's early programs. During his first official season, subscriber mail poured in against Berg, and when, in October 1971, Michael Gielen conducted a program of Strauss's *Metamorphosen*, Nono's *Canti di vita e d'amore* and Berg's *Lulu* Suite, very few people remained until the end. Boulez said that in his early concerts in New York, when he was conducting much twentieth-century music, he had the fantasy of locking all the doors so the audience would be forced to remain and listen. He said he could not understand why people would not stay even if made uncomfortable by what they were to hear.

But Boulez could not lock the doors, and his programs became not only less remarkable in terms of rarely heard old pieces; they even began to include "war-horses." The 1973–74 audience heard Beethoven's Symphonies Nos. 3 and 5, Schumann's Symphonies Nos. 1 and 2, Mendelssohn's

Reformation Symphony, Mahler's and Bruckner's Symphony No. 1, Debussy's *La Mer,* and Sibelius's Symphony No. 2. All over the United States, orchestras continued to move in the same vein they had moved in before Boulez's arrival in New York. Orchestras like the Chicago Symphony, with a tradition of exploring new fields that went back to Frederick Stock at the turn of the century, continued to move ahead. But the bulk of the orchestras remained firmly entrenched in the traditional repertory. On September 24, 1972, music editor Raymond Ericson wrote in *The New York Times*: "Browsing through the orchestras' schedules does not provide any surprises or suggest any strong trends. The repertory remains the same, with the same works as the symphonies of Bruckner and Mahler more firmly established than ever before. Beethoven cycles or festivals have not disappeared by any means."

One would expect Boulez to have felt despair at what can only be described as the failure of his mission in New York and the consequent failure of his larger mission to change the whole direction of American musical life. But Boulez is a very private man, and just as no one in Europe, in the late 1950s, suggests any anguish could be sensed within him then, so no one in New York, in the mid-1970s, could have detected any anguish in his demeanor. One evening after dinner in 1973, Boulez complained about his recent weight gain. Elliott Carter noted that that was odd, that conducting modern music should guard against that. Boulez laughed. "What gave you the idea I conduct modern music?" he asked. It is impossible to know with Boulez whether indifference or bitterness lay behind that gaiety.

It is a fact that the "wildness" Boulez said persists on his inside was kept under check. An uncaring attitude permeated every move in the mechanics of his daily life. Renting an apartment in New York for the first time in the fall of 1974, Boulez asked his Cleveland friends, the Frankels, to decorate it for him, noting only that the furniture should be "modern." This was a far cry from the care he took with his Baden-Baden house where he chose each piece of furniture himself, seeking professional guidance only in arranging it. The Frankels worked with Bloomingdale's, a department store in Manhattan, and in one day put together chairs, lamps, clocks, rugs, tables, glassware, china, and sheets.

Boulez's indifference extends to clothes. Wherever he is taken he will buy everything he needs. Record executive Ken Glancy brought Boulez to Harrod's in London where he chose a complete wardrobe. When that wore out, the Frankels brought him to a store in Cleveland and he chose a complete wardrobe there. To "select" means to commit oneself as to one's likes and dislikes, and Boulez virtually never did that during his tenure in the United States. To christen his New York apartment he gave a party for his "American friends": the Frankels, six officials of the New York Philharmonic, two secretaries, and my then husband and me, all people who had sought him out or are connected with him through professional affairs.

Boulez's avoidance of choices extended to advice he gave me concerning this book. I told him that for every incident in his life there were as many stories as there were participants. Rarely did other people's narratives coincide with his own. Not whimsically, Boulez suggested that I take my cue from Mallarmé: for each event have a fixed first and last page and place all the variations in between. The idea that statements must be so ambiguous that they shift in relation to one another, that there is really no true meaning of a text, is not, of course, peculiar to Mallarmé. But surely it receives one of its most eloquent confirmations from him.

Mallarmé was one of the first artists who self-consciously appropriated elements belonging to science into art. In the *Sketches of Mallarmé's Le Livre* published in 1957, the Symbolist poet wrote of the "scientific relationships" expressible in numbers which he hoped his own work would embody. "Everything in the cosmos," he added, "exists in order to emerge as a Book, a book, perhaps, in several volumes, but, in fact, only one, which everyone has tried to write, the geniuses included, namely the orphic explanation of the earth." Surely Mallarmé's efforts to bring the panoply of science into art, as well as Boulez's own inclinations, play a role in the evolution of his Institut de Recherche et de Coordination Acoustique/Musique (Ircam) that opened in 1977.

It was during Boulez's fallow period—between 1958 and 1968—that he conceived of a tangible way to incorporate science, or more accurately, technology, into the framework of art. During the winter of 1966, the Max Planck Society in Germany asked him to think about a theoretical basis for a Max Planck Institute of Music. Boulez said,

> I had many meetings with scientists and artists. I found these meetings exceptionally interesting and began to work on a theoretical project that was to have been subsidized by Volkswagen. But then there was an economic recession and the institute did not come to pass. There was considerable hostility towards it. Some scientists were unhappy about spending the money for a musical institute while the music departments of the German schools were equally unhappy about a scientific approach to music. For the first time

I thought of the necessity of such a research center to solve many problems. I said so in an interview in *Le Monde* in late 1969. The interview was published in early 1970 and was read by Pompidou who contacted me.

Boulez organized his career the way Napoleon organized a campaign, and, like Napoleon, he never published his plan. More than a year and a half before he took over the directorship of the New York Philharmonic, Boulez was planning what he would do if his aims with the orchestra did not work out. About the same time, Boulez began to compose again. He said he was brought back to composition by Stockhausen's *Momente* because that piece was so "bad." Stockhausen completed it a year after the release of *Sgt. Pepper*—what one writer has called the "flower-child movement's anthem." As the Beatles appropriated techniques from the musical avant-garde, so Stockhausen, in this work, appropriated much of the manner and message of rock music.

Momente opens with a resounding strike on a gong and a soprano's piercing invitation to "listen to the moments, to the music of love." Bizarrely dressed hippies stream through the theater as they sing, shout, mutter, giggle, clap their hands, and stamp their feet. "*Momente* brought me strongly back to composition," Boulez said, "because it was the cheapest thing Stockhausen had done." As Stockhausen's "good period" had moved Boulez away from composition, Stockhausen's "bad period" moved him back in. For Boulez, Stockhausen's submission to the vulgar and popular undermined the essence of "music" in music.

Boulez then composed *Domaines* for clarinet, which he had begun in 1962; *Multiples,* which he composed in 1970 as an extension of *Éclat,* written in 1965; *Cummings ist der Dichter,* composed in 1970 but inspired by Cage's introduction to him of Cummings's poetry in 1952; *explosante-fixe,* begun in the summer of 1971; *Memoriales,* a commission for the BBC Symphony based on the material of *explosante-fixe* with, in Boulez's words, "lots of brass, percussion, and winds in a number of independent groups all tingling like different clocks." *Rituel* is the opening of that series of pieces.

Although many of these compositions had been performed, far fewer had been published. Boulez sent manuscripts in but advised publisher Alfred Schlee not to go ahead with them because he was continually revising and adding. What he was doing may be compared to Mallarmé's *Le Livre*: a great work, composed in fragments, that will one day be pulled together. But Glock quoted a Boulez letter: "How the years are passing! So many ideas unfulfilled and unrealized and life is passing so quickly."

Boulez explained his ways in precise terms: "I think quickly, but it takes a long time for my thoughts to ripen. I am a long-wave reactor. I don't meet things easily, but I don't forget them easily."

Here is the way *explosante-fixe* ripened: *Tempo* magazine, a British music journal, asked Boulez and a number of other composers to write a piece in memory of Stravinsky. The request was for some sort of canon. "Well, if you have to write a canon," Boulez said, "you can do that. Like Bach. And all the other composers did that. But I thought about mixing echoing and canonic writing. You can't have a plain canon in the twentieth century.

I began to think about the work in August 1971, soon after receiving the commission. That month I visited a castle in Scotland that had once belonged to the Duchess of Argyll. The woman who invited me was an Austrian who lived in France, and she had with her a son who was not very oriented; he did not know what he was to do with his life. Since then he committed suicide. The young man played the flute as an amateur and he improvised in this empty eighteenth-century castle. It was quite impressive. I had the idea then of the work beginning with a flute solo.

The notes were to provide the basic idea, a kind of ground music. Then I wrote a simple text [Boulez followed two pages of musical notes with six pages of verbal instructions] indicating how to make it more complex. My student, Heinz Holliger, realized the piece but his realization was not sufficient. I wanted one much more refined from this matrix. When I did it myself, I did it in a very complex way, with a definitive form, far too complex to improvise. I have rewritten some parts twice, others three times.

Boulez took his title from *Nadja*, by André Breton. "The line," Boulez said, "was 'la beauté will be explosante-fixe or it will not be.' It was a beautiful poetic image which remained within me—independently floating."

As "Poems for Power" revealed a good deal about Boulez in the late 1950s, so "fixed explosion" said much about the man during his polite and orderly tenure in New York.

Boulez admired the world of Paul Klee because "one can see as many faces in a drop of water as in a large landscape." So the world of Boulez is contained in the smallest segment of his music, in which notes are juggled in the most dexterous and complex way. The movement from C-sharp to D in one voice is echoed by D to C-sharp in another, while a rhythmic group of three followed by two in one part comes on the heels of two followed by three in another. In 1965, in Los Angeles, Boulez discovered 4 x 6 cards with staves on them and began composing on them. These small cards enabled Boulez to work out his tiny refinements and then transcribe the final fragments onto the score.

Boulez did it with language and spoken sounds too. Carol Frankel reported that at a diner in Cleveland a jukebox repeatedly blared out a pop record. Finally Boulez asked what it was. She replied, "James Taylor, a smash hit." Boulez said, "You mean it's mass shit." Again, before he was to tour with the orchestra, Boulez picked up a book on oral-genitalism that Carol Frankel had received earlier. She told him he could not travel with that, that it would not be right for him to be seen with it. Taking the dust jacket off my book *The New Music: the Sense behind the Sound,* Boulez put it on the oral-genital tome and said the subtitle would be "the Sound behind the Scents."

Such intellectual punning might be expected of a brilliant multilingual person, and to say that Boulez delighted in it is not to suggest he completely rejected accidents. Many musicians have wondered why Boulez used the German title *Cummings ist der Dichter* for a work based on an English-language poem. Here is the answer: "I was commissioned to write a piece for the festival at Ulm. I couldn't find a title for the work when they asked me what to print on the program. In a letter in German—my German was not very good at that time—I wrote: 'I have not chosen a title yet, but what I can tell you is this: Cummings is the poet.' A reply came from a German secretary who had misunderstood my letter: 'As for your new work, *Cummings ist der Dichter. . . .*' I found that mistake so wonderful that I thought, well, then, that's a title given by the gods."

CHAPTER 40

Within a year, between the summers of 1969 and 1970, four men who had been important to Boulez died: his father, Adorno, Strobel, and Szell. Reflecting on this series of deaths, Boulez said,

It was a strange configuration. Strobel and I heard about the death of Adorno at the end of July 1969, and Strobel asked me to write a memorial essay for his journal, *Melos*. He came to see me August 15, just after his afternoon nap. That must have made it between 3:30 and 4 o'clock. We worked heavily until 7:30 or 8. Then a phone call came that my father had died. I was working on a memorial for one man when news came to me of my father's death. I knew he was dying, so it was not a complete surprise. But it was a surprise nevertheless.

Just exactly one year after, as soon as I returned from a trip to Mexico, I learned of Szell's illness. He died during a concert I was conducting with the Cleveland Orchestra. Szell had exactly the illness my father did.

While in Cleveland I heard that Strobel fainted. I knew he must have had some sort of heart attack. I called the Strobels and said I would be home. On the way I stopped at Bayreuth to conduct *Parsifal*. While there I had a call that Strobel had died.

All of these men were more or less father-figures to me. At one point in your life, you must face the disappointment of such losses and become a father-figure yourself. Of course the loss of Strobel and my father touched me more than that of Adorno and Szell. I met Adorno fleetingly around 1954 and was in close contact with him later in Darmstadt. In the '60s he came to Baden-Baden regularly, but my relationship with him was primarily intellectual. Szell I knew very well but not to the point, of course, of my father or, for that matter, Strobel, whom I had known since 1951 and had been on a day-to-day basis with since 1958.

Boulez's shift from son to father was not accompanied by the lessening of tensions between brothers. One by one the old friendships ruptured. Pousseur, Boulez's first follower into the serial world, has described their estrangement engendered by his own return to tonality:

> In the late 1950s, many of us felt the need for stronger means of characterization. We needed harmony, which was so charged with significance. All the years I had been composing without harmony, I had been playing and listening to harmonic music. The point was to use harmony again but in a still richer, more effective way. I started to work on a piece, *Faust*, with a libretto by Michel Butor. It took seven years to compose.
>
> I began to work on *Faust* in 1961. Boulez planned to do it at the Domaine in 1963. But he became more upset as he saw it. He pulled out of the commitment in 1963. After that we saw each other very little. In the late 1960s I wrote a work, *Crossed Colors*, based on the Negro spiritual "We shall overcome." Boulez conducted it, not only in Europe, but with the New York Philharmonic in 1971. After that performance I gave him an article I had written about Stravinsky in which I discussed Stravinsky's harmonies— being based on polarities as they were. In it I quoted Boulez on Stravinsky but did it in a warm, friendly way. Naturally I quoted the areas in which we did not agree. After that Boulez sent me a letter. He said that for a long time we had had little to say to each other and added, "Now that you have discovered *Agon*, there is nothing left. Perhaps soon you'll discover Hindemith. You wrote *We shall overcome*; I prefer *Burn Baby Burn*." Boulez's point was that I was trying to conciliate old and new, black and white, while he preferred to burn everything.

Boulez was never, even in his earliest years, profoundly attached to Pousseur. But the same cannot be said of Stockhausen; yet even here the relationship exploded into a bitter battle culminating around the performance of Stockhausen's *Mixtur*, a piece in which instrumental sounds are transformed by electronic means. Boulez conducted it at the Round House in London in January 1972. Here is Boulez in 1974 on what happened then:

> Stockhausen was supposed to take care of all the electronics. He said he needed twelve, not six rehearsals. But the piece did not require twelve rehearsals. Stockhausen said he did not want to come to London to supervise the planning of this work. My interpretation of this is that he did not want to be confronted with me on this particular piece. But that may be a psychological excuse on my part: Stockhausen prefers to surround himself with subordinates. He likes feudal relationships.
>
> So I said to him, "If you do not want to come, how are we to realize this piece?" In reply he sent inadequate, unprofessional, pontificating acolytes. One of them told the percussionist how to scratch a tam-tam. This kind of pontificating I do not need. The clan of Stockhausen was very hostile. Those in charge of the ring modulators were never on time. I said, "If you want to do it, do it; if you don't, I don't care." This was reported to Stockhausen by his Mafia. Then he and I talked. I said to Stockhausen, "I can talk with you but not with those on a low level with the Lord."
>
> After it was over, he told me he heard the work did not receive a good performance. I said it was not a good work in the first place. We have not spoken since then.

As for Boulez's fight with American composers, it did not abate. In the spring of 1970, when Boulez was to conduct a contemporary music festival at Lawrence Morton's Ojai concerts, he programmed nineteen twentieth-century works, not one of which was by an American. A group of composers, very different from each other but related, to some degree, to the ideas of Cage—Morton Feldman, La Monte Young, and Frederick Rzewski were among them—wrote a letter to Morton attacking the situation. Morton was upset about it and spoke to Boulez, who waved his hand in a gesture of unconcern. And unconcern was what he felt. Boulez said he took no advice from Babbitt, Sessions, Wuorinen, Rzewski, and others he invited to "composers' conferences" to help determine the repertory at his Village concerts in New York, because "everyone was bringing in his own little circle." As for the correspondence in the Ojai episode, Boulez interpreted the letter writers' silence since then to the fact that "they know they cannot compete with me."

In the fall of 1974, at the start of his second contract in New York, Boulez was as contemptuous of American composers—apart from Carter—as he had been more than five years before: "I have not come across a big talent in this country, not even a controversial talent. Here the big disappointment was for me to find no center of interest in New York. There are the academic people on one side. On the other there are those who experiment but are really nothing more than amateurs. They are just playing in the kitchen and there is a great lack of professionalism there."

As for Cage, Boulez's early benefactor, he was not to benefit from Boulez's presence in New York. In 1971, at a composers' conference, Rzewski said, "Next year is John Cage's sixtieth birthday. How do you plan to celebrate it?"

Boulez replied, "I shall send him a cake."

Boulez was not alone in suffering from motives that appear less than generous in spirit and heart. Competition pervades every aspect of contemporary life, and music is no exception. The bitterest fights in university music departments revolve around which professor's book will be used as the "official" text. And instrumentalists in the New York Philharmonic were well aware of the enmity that existed between two extraordinarily talented first-desk men, one of whom sucked on his reed and chatted with his colleagues whenever the other performed a solo. If such meanness characterizes relations between professors of music and performing musicians, why should it not have characterized relations between Wuorinen and Davidovsky, Feldman and Cage, Stockhausen and Boulez, and Boulez and new music at large? To many listeners, each of these couplings appear to share each other's basic approach to art. But on close investigation one finds competition causing bitterness, and in the end such bitterness changes the character of art. For if we live in an age marked by cynicism and rancor, an age in which there are virtually no heroes, would it not follow that art would reflect this and work its will by affirming it?

In *Le Monde Cassé* (The Broken World), by Gabriel Marcel, the heroine asks:

Don't you feel sometimes that we are living . . . if you can call it living . . . in a broken world? Yes, broken like a watch. The mainspring has stopped working. Just to look at it, nothing has changed. Everything is in place. But put the watch to your ear, and you don't hear any ticking. You know what I'm talking about, the world, what we call the world, the world of human creatures .. . it seems to me it must have had a heart at one time, but today you would say that the heart had stopped beating.

In an essay, "The Mystery of Being," Marcel quotes that speech and writes:

A broken world? . . . We must be careful here. Certainly it would be rash to put one's finger on some epoch in history where the unity of the world was something directly felt by man in general. But could we feel the division of this world today, or could some of us at least feel it so strongly, if we had not within us, I will not say the memory of such a united world, but at least the nostalgia of it.

In 1943, Boulez told Messiaen, "Musical aesthetics are being worn, out," and asked, "Who is there to give it life?" Messiaen replied, "You will, Pierre." Boulez was eighteen at that time. At twenty he discovered the serial idea and has addressed virtually all his actions since then toward using that particular grammar in the service of giving music a new and long life. At first he did it through composing and theory. But that did not work out as he planned. Then he conducted a repertory that he hoped would bring large audiences up to the music of its own time. But once again that did not work. At the end of the Ives Mini-Festival in the fall of 1974, *Times* reviewer Allen Hughes wrote that Boulez was "far and away the most interesting and creative music director in the world." Few would take exception to that. But what Hughes did not say is this: that on all but the last of the evenings, the one on which the Ives Fourth Symphony was played, Avery Fisher Hall was far from full, and that, on the final evening, when the house was brimming with life, it was because the "best seats" were widely advertised at $2 apiece. I asked many people why they were there; none of them replied, to hear Charles Ives. Moseley knew this only too well. Despite the enormous effort that went into this piece, which calls for vast orchestral forces and their mastering massive rhythmic complexities, he did not program it for any regular subscription audience.

The denouement was that after three years of backbreaking work, of performing new scores that neither he nor the orchestra had played before—there were ten such scores for the Ives Festival alone which took place on five consecutive days—large audiences for new music were not to be found. New Yorkers were no different in this respect from audiences for the BBC Symphony or the Cleveland Orchestra. In reply to whether Boulez's presence in London made a significant difference in musical habits there, Sir William Glock said, "It must have made a difference to composers who heard crucial works for the first time. But if you ask me if it has changed the habits of people going to Festival Hall, I would have to say no."

As for the Cleveland Orchestra, when Boulez was conducting his special repertory there in large doses after Szell's death—he conducted thirteen weeks during the 1970–71 season—subscriptions dropped disastrously. One might attribute the loss of ticket sales to regrets caused by the death of the much-beloved Szell. But the brochure for 1974–75 revealed something more, a rejection of what Boulez had introduced: "The season presents a colorful array of world-renowned conductors and dazzling soloists. Familiar favorites and major masterpieces highlight this popular season. . . . Maazel will conduct fourteen subscription programs featuring the music of Rachmaninov, Brahms, Chopin, Liszt, Berlioz, Mendelssohn, and Debussy, plus programs devoted to the music of Mozart, Beethoven, and Elgar." A look at the programs themselves reveals not one work by Schoenberg, not one by Webern, not one, for that matter, by Boulez.

In the fall of 1974, Boulez said he found it disappointing that the two conductors then being considered to replace him at the New York Philharmonic were Daniel Barenboim and Zubin Mehta. "They are both open-minded," Boulez said, "but neither is committed to contemporary music. I wish the board would choose someone to build on what I began."

Boulez still believed in the language he began to carve out in 1945. "It is," he said, "as viable as I thought it was in the 1950s. It must go through this process. Even if Schoenberg at the 'Rugs' was not so successful, eighteen hundred people came. And that is twice the size of Alice Tully Hall."

Boulez's "Rug Concerts" took place during one week in June. The tickets were cheaper and the programming more contemporary than at any other time of the year. The concerts were widely attended and enthusiastically received by a youthful and attentive audience. Boulez interpreted this to indicate that he has succeeded in his mission among the young.

But the size and response of these audiences did not necessarily signify a new and potentially paying public for contemporary music. It seems more likely, in fact, that many of these young people responded to the publicity centered on Boulez as a revolutionary figure (the very publicity that Philharmonic officials abhorred), and attended as an act of soldarity coupled with air conditioning and an invitation to sit on the floor.

CHAPTER 41

Theodor Adorno viewed the progressive materialism in society as the archenemy of what he considered to be the only legitimate twentieth-century musical language. In *The Philosophy of Modern Music,* written in the 1940s, Adorno deplored the decline of dodecaphony during those predominantly neo-tonal years. He viewed dodecaphony as an underground language struggling for life in a society in which gross and vulgar values prevail. "The liberation of modern painting from objectivity," he wrote, "which was to art the break that tonality was to music, was determined by the defensive against the mechanized art commodity—above all, photography. . . . Because the monopolistic means of distributing music stood almost entirely at the disposal of artistic trash and compromised cultural values, and catered to the socially determined predisposition of the listener, radical music was forced into complete isolation during the final stages of industrialism."

But Boulez, whose thinking often parallels that of Adorno, took "radical music" out of isolation and plunged it into the New York marketplace. Initially he had considerable help from the press. *Life, Time, Newsweek* celebrated him, not for the traditional values that Moseley and Keiser would have had them celebrate, but for Boulez's particular principles as well as his obsession for realizing them.

Still, those compositional principles posed problems. One evening during Boulez's early tenure in New York, Harold Schonberg commented to me that he could not hear a "cancrizans," a melody that reads backward, from right to left. I wonder how many can hear a cancrizans, except perhaps at that pivotal point at which the row turns back on itself. But if one cannot hear a cancrizans, or the manipulation of intervals within a complex fabric, what is there within a work to hold it together in one's mind, to give a sense of closure to the listener?

There are two fundamentally different approaches to listening to music, as there are to perceiving any art. One is immediately accessible, the other more difficult to apprehend, requiring labor, intelligence and experience. Both can be present in the same work. In Huck Finn's world, Shakespeare was performed throughout the small towns of the South. Coincidentally, in the North, Beethoven symphonies opened each of the three concerts that marked the New York Philharmonic's first year, 1842. Shakespeare was played in the South and Beethoven in the North because that art would enhance people's lives, would bring them enjoyment and delight. To say *King Lear* and the Beethoven Fifth can be approached on a simple level is not to deny complexity within them. It is rather to emphasize that Shakespeare and Beethoven provide enough pleasure at a first encounter to induce the audience to come back for more.

Neurophysiological evidence suggests that there are two separate modes of viewing phenomena that are related to these two approaches to art. One is holistic: the observer grasps the structure, the shape of the whole. The other is linear-analytic: the observer discerns the "atoms," the substructures of the work. The two are not mutually exclusive. Once the viewer or listener grasps the full shape, he is free to return and absorb the complexity of detail. What separates contemporary "serious" music from the great art of the past is its refusal to give the listener form that is immediately graspable. It is so heavily weighted with detail that it does not encourage the listener to return

Thus the problem of this music "reaching" audiences appears to lie outside the crude values of Adorno's materialistic society, and outside Boulez's revolutionary programs; rather it lies in neurophysiology. A century ago the English neurologist, John Hulings Jackson, wrote that these ways of viewing phenomena were related specifically to brain function, and more specifically to the two sides of the brain. Work undertaken at Columbia University in the early 1970s seemed to indicate that the left brain deals with linear-analytic functions, and the right brain with holistic functions. Experiments reported by Thomas G. Bever and Robert J. Chiarello in the August 9, 1974 issue of *Science* revealed that music specialists—and they are not even dealing with a new language here—hear with the left brain which governs perceptions of the right ear, rather than with the right brain which governs perceptions of the left ear, and which is how the majority of people hear music:

> Confirming the results of previous studies, the musically naive subjects have a left ear superiority for melody recognition. However, the subjects who are musically sophisticated

have a right ear superiority. Our interpretation is that musically sophisticated subjects can organize a melodic sequence in terms of the internal relations of its components. . . Dominance of the left hemisphere for such analytic functions would explain the dominance of the right ear for melody recognition in experienced listeners: as their capacity for musical analysis increases, the left hemisphere becomes increasingly involved in the processing of music. This raises the possibility that being musically sophisticated has real neurological concomitants permitting the utilization of a different strategy of musical apprehension that calls on left hemisphere functions.

These observations lead one to conclude that the inaccessibility of "revolutionary" music makes that music physically discomfiting to the unspecialized listener who is searching for form, without which he is lost. The most skillful manipulation of atomistic details cannot compensate for the holistic void.

If the "linear-analytic" approach does not necessarily make for what we now think of as great art, neither does the "holistic" approach. It is a fact that a good deal of twentieth-century music which displays the most apparently articulated forms has fallen by the cultural wayside. In October 1974, Harold Schonberg devoted a Sunday essay to recalling the ferment in American music during the 1930s and 1940s. He mentioned "Copland, Harris, Piston, Schuman, Barber, Shapero, Berger, Smit, Haieff, Fine, Cilkowitz, Virgil Thomson, Randall Thompson, Hanson, Sessions, Creston, Chandler, Cowell, Cage, Diamond, Dello Joio, Mennin, Hovhaness . . . one can go on and on," Schonberg writes. "Very few had any staying power."

Schonberg attributes the problem to the fact that great music is a function of personality and that there have been no great personalities in composition in recent times. But if that is the case, then one must ask why. And if one asks why, there is only one answer: that this time is different from almost all other times, that we are in the midst of a historical impasse, that a certain kind of cultural synthesis is dead, and with it the high art of our tradition is dead.

In the 1970s, those in the new music market in Europe reported that there were no composers on the horizon. Gilbert Amy, who took over Boulez's post at the Domaine Musical in 1967, disbanded the Domaine in 1971. He did it, he said, because audiences wanted first performances and he could not come up with any decent ones. At Universal Edition, Alfred Schlee reported that he knew "no young artists who are anything but derivative of the now middle-aged ones." Otto Tomek, who had to come up with pieces for the annual Donaueschingen Festival, said that he found himself in extreme difficulty: "Everyone said they want to hear from the young. In 1972 I did what they asked. I planned a program of only new and young composers and it was more dreadful than anything you can imagine. The concerts were dead. Every style was represented and each program terribly received. I can't ever do that again. But the fact is there is no style today."

In the United States, where men are more optimistic than in Europe, and where considerably more money is involved, those in charge speak warmly about the young. But little I have heard supports what they say. Lawrence Morton, after he retired from the Monday Evening Concerts and was free to speak, said:

> The great men of the century were the Viennese, Stravinsky, and Bartók. They have not had any real successors. The closest two are Stockhausen and Boulez. Stockhausen seems to have gone off the deep end. Boulez's works are open-ended; we cannot know them complete.
>
> I go to all the concerts today. The composers are mostly anonymous. Certain idiomatic expressions from Stockhausen and Boulez are repeated everywhere. I don't hear anything that said to me, 'This is the way John Smith composes.'

In the preface to *The Waning of the Middle Ages*, Johan Huizinga writes: "In history, as in nature, birth and death are equally balanced. The decay of overripe forms of civilization is as suggestive a spectacle as the growth of new ones. And it occasionally happens that a period in which one had, hitherto, been mainly looking for the coming of the birth of new things, suddenly reveals itself as an epoch of fading and decay."

CHAPTER 42

In March 1970, eighteen months before taking over as music director of the New York Philharmonic, Boulez was conducting the Cleveland Orchestra in Montreal. The University of Montreal took advantage of his presence to invite him to a long and serious interview in front of an audience of academicians and composers. Boulez's remarks were recorded on tape and published in *Les Cahiers Canadiens de Musique*. Because, in this interview, he touched on matters of great importance to him, it is useful to quote (in my translation) at least a small portion of what he said. What comes across in the twenty transcribed pages is Boulez's analytic, penetrating mind and his repudiation of naturalism and representation in favor of science and technology.

Touching on how the Institut de Recherche et de Coordination Acoustique/Musique would cope with the limitations he found in the present musical situation, Boulez said:

> There are some instruments which should be transformed because we still have instruments that were made for the eighteenth and nineteenth centuries. . . . We are still using half-tone scales because there are no instruments suited to other scales. If you want to write music built on one-quarter or one-third tone scales, there is absolutely nothing available now. . . . We must have a period of research to deal with the transformation of such instruments and for composition and electronics as well. . . .
>
> Another example: the sociology of concerts. We would make sociological studies about different audiences: how to organize a concert hall differently, how to affect an audience [comment toucher un public]. . . . (In this last phrase lies the

underlying theme of Boulez, his obsession with making the serial principle work.)

On musical analysis:

We have been prepared for a basic analysis of music, specifically in regard to the Viennese school. Don't forget that the Viennese school and specifically Webern was a sort of very narrow and rigorous transition [une espèce de passage extrêmement étroit et rigoureux] in which each sound was settled by a very decisive logic, and there were not two solutions but only one for each problem. Of course it is very easy to analyze this type of thing, because there is one solution at any given time, and since the principles are very easy, the solutions are very easy. What is more important—and here analysis is almost nonexistent—are the dialectics of composition. . . the processes, how a composer, through such a system, has started his thought. . . . What you have to analyze is not the way you have reached formal structures, nor the way you have reached given musical objects: what is interesting is the analysis of the relationships between those musical objects, between those formal structures and the contents of the composer's mind. . . .

Because if you husk only the vocabulary [si vous arrivez a décortiquer uniquement le vocabulaire], you will fall into mannerism. . . . What you must do is look at the "way of creativity" of the composer in a very deep way. . . . What is interesting is the connection between the events. . . . When I analyzed *Wozzeck* or *Gruppen* or a Mallarmé poem, I did not go into the vocabulary. I would leave it to the students to discover certain details in the vocabulary or style. But I would throw light right away upon the structural form and the reason for it.

On structuralism in music:

When I say music is nonsignifying, I mean it does not transmit information. . . . For example, language can give mere information. "We are here today." OK, it is information. It is not very important. What is important is that the information was given. On the other hand, if I read a poem by René Char or Michaux, it is not the information that is important, but the structure of the language, which is just as responsible as the message itself. What I mean is that music does not have to "say. . . ."

On mathematics and music:

I studied mathematics because I had a gift for it. But musical gift is not necessarily related to mathematical gift. You can have one or both. . . . I tell you frankly that I have a great deal of respect for the "pure" mathematicians. They are the ones with the widest imaginations. They often have entities which are very hard to seize or even understand and they manipulate them with great liberty and inventive capacity.

There is a sort of perpetual game between the scientific substratum and the emotional content. We are now in a period in which we perceive more the functional, structural, and mathematical aspects of music. Generally speaking, we use in music much simpler terms than in mathematics, and we are much behind, since all the mathematical notions used in music are at least one century old in mathematics. . . .

Asked how he planned to persuade New York subscribers into some understanding of new music, Boulez replied,

By exciting the curiosity of the snobs. And I am not against it, I must say. I did it in Paris and it worked very well. To start, you always find two hundred fanatics. They are very easy to find, too easy sometimes. What is important is to raise the number. If you have a few, people will think, "I must go there. I should know about it." I have witnessed cases of people who came out of mere curiosity because they thought, "I've heard about it. I think I must go and see what it is. I don't want to seem backward." And finally, gradually, these people came.

At the conclusion of the interview, Boulez acknowledged he would be conducting pieces in New York that he had previously characterized as "caramel custards":

When I speak of "flans au caramel" I am speaking of the way people see that music, which is very different from the music itself. If you asked them to analyze what they are listening to, most of the time it reminds them of their youth. . . . It is like a reflex of Pavlov: when they hear the music they loved at twenty, they remember the years when their hormones were more active. And finally there are a lot of people who doze, who come to doze, and remember the time they did not doze so much.

This is not the way I personally view classical music. . . . I think, in fact, that with this music you must go beyond memory and see at all times how it was made and if it brings anything new. What is interesting when you face the so-called masterpieces is not to see them as stiff things in the past, but to see their potential for the present. . . . It is the same thing as when you clean a painting. Before we used to look at paintings through a good coat of dirt and we would say, "Look at this chiaroscuro. How beautiful!" Then, when we looked at it closely, we could see there was some red, and it did not go at all with the idea we had of it. What is important in the masterpiece is to take away the dirt.

Boulez did take away the dirt. Under his direction the orchestra became a reflection of himself: a lucid, clean and gleaming instrument. Robert Craft has described Boulez as the "professional musician's conductor. He knows instruments better than the others, can tell the cimbalon player how to restring his box of wires to facilitate complexities, or show the violist a more effective fingering for a harmonic. Second, he is most fastidious about articulation. Third, he has the keenest ear for balance in the equilibrating of the various components of an orchestra. Finally, he draws the most refined colors from the orchestra. It follows that his performances are clean, clear, intelligent, and supremely controlled."

Boulez's performances are indeed clean, clear, intelligent, and supremely controlled, for Boulez has a composer's ear for structure and a unique conducting technique that illuminates virtually everything in a score. But many concertgoers who listen to old music conducted by Boulez miss the genuine pleasure they associate with it. Harold Schonberg, who at first wrote only positively about Boulez, found his performances of nineteenth-century work "inhibited." The retards were minimal, the phrasing stiff. Harriet Johnson of the *New York Post,* also a fan of Boulez's earlier days in New

York, wrote in the fall of 1974 of his performances of Handel's *Water Music* and Schumann's Symphony No. 1. "These joyous works were played but not really interpreted. They were not played with style. The result was prosaic."

The musicians talked of Boulez's seeming obsession with intonation. When he first came to the orchestra, Boulez found a sloppy ensemble, made so by bad habits under Mitropoulos and Bernstein. Boulez said, "Trumpet, you're sharp" and "Viola, you're flat," and the musicians regarded him with awe. But in time many complained that under Boulez there was virtually nothing but precision. One member of the orchestra's governing committee reported that Boulez "requires only that we play the right notes at the right time. He asks for no sweat, blood, guts, or tone quality. He is very fair to players; he doesn't insult or humiliate them, but there is no robustness in the sound, never any dance feeling in the dances, never any joy in making music."

Boulez steadfastly refused to participate in personnel decisions, referring such problems to management. The raise in salary of a first-desk man was not, by his own choice, influenced by him. The men, therefore, found no tangible rewards in doing their very best work for him.

Nor did many find less tangible rewards. Boulez never complimented them, never saluted anyone for a job well done. His invitation for a soloist to take a bow was, at best, speedy and awkward, and most resigned themselves to a simple, quick nod. In this respect he treated them as he treated himself. He said he cannot imagine why anyone would need outside approval to know if he had performed his part well.

Boulez's isolation and indifference grew on the job. He showed little interest in a repertory as favored by him as the French. Even performances of Debussy began to suffer. Some musicians called his *Iberia* "Siberia," and spoke freely to the journalist who wrote the *New York Times Magazine* story on Boulez. The article was entitled "The Iceman Conducteth."

Nobody is made of ice, but Boulez certainly strove to give that impression. In his Canadian interview, he used the word "beautiful" only once and then in a context of irony. Immediacy didn't enter the picture at all. Criteria used in the evaluation of art for the past 500 years are not part of Boulez's lexicon. This formidable mind, at one time open to passion and feeling, able to produce one work after another, has closed himself off from the outer and inner worlds in a manner that is both self-protective and at one with his age. Boulez has always claimed that Stravinsky wrote his greatest works before he was thirty, and now others are making the same claim about Boulez. That Stravinsky should have invested his faith in quotation and Boulez in system—rather than in invention and imagination—said something imprecise about each of the men. But it said something far more precise about this painful era, this period between the natural scientific synthesis and "high art" and a new synthesis and a new art.

I quoted Boulez saying, "It is not enough to draw a moustache on the Mona Lisa because that does not kill the Mona Lisa. All the art of the past must be destroyed." The need to destroy past art has been almost a banal slogan in France since the last decade of the nineteenth century. But it is difficult to destroy past art, particularly at a time when listeners are exposed to it as never before through live programming, their own record collections, and radio stations' record collections. If a businessman harried by events of the day or a scientist in awe of accumulating data can find the order and significance in a work of art that he cannot find in the stock market or in the ever expanding universe, why would he seek out music in which he could not find his way? The de-emphasis of meaning in music and the celebration of system and structure may be inevitable in a scientific period devoid of belief. But it leaves man without a shadow of a spiritual base.

The fact is that the modern world has not yet evolved an idea that works for both its listeners and practitioners. Because listeners derive nourishment from a certain kind of art does not mean artists can or should deliver it to them.

That Boulez did not go as far in the path of artistic abolition as many who have followed Cage's powerful lead does not make him any the less central or striving in this amelodic, arhythmic dance of death. Rather it underscores the fact that Boulez was brought up in a severely Jesuit household and educated in the strict tradition of the lycée, and that heritage confirmed in this way throughout the first fifteen years of a boy's life may cause a striking reaction but is not easily erased from his character. Cage, on the other hand, is American. He did not hear Bach until he was twenty years old. Discussing the exceptionally fertile field for post-Cageians in the United States, Pousseur concluded his conversation with me: "We, in Europe, are much more bound to cultural precedents. We are living in the soil, the very place, where all this richness was fertilized. You live where the Indians lived."

CHAPTER 43

I arrived at Boulez's sister's house at St. Michel de l'Observatoire in the French Alps in August 1973 to attend the last session of a six-day Ircam seminar. Boulez, also staying with Jeanne Chevalier, had invited architects, technicians, musicologists, and composers from at least six countries to the twelfth-century abbey, an appropriate setting, for, in the Middle Ages, music was an intellectual discipline taught along with mathematics in the universities. The abbey was one hour's drive from Boulez's house. As we drove, Boulez said the major point of the Institute was that "every individual must be free. That is not a moral point of view. It is a vital point of view. Stockhausen imposes himself so completely on the Cologne project that no one else has a chance to breathe. I have goals but I allow for a give and take. The Institute has become much richer than originally planned." Ircam had the money to match Boulez's goals. The funds that poured into the electronic studio at Cologne from its inception to the mid-1970s do not match one year's budget for the Paris Institute.

The meetings were held in a modern wing of the abbey. There were about twenty participants. The plan was to conduct the sessions in English, but as Boulez began his opening address, he decided suddenly to deliver his in French. Other Europeans followed his lead.

The first five days were occupied with strenuous nine-hour sessions during which participants read prepared papers. The title of the treatise delivered by Knut Wiggen, director of the electronic studio of the Swedish Radio, gives a clue to the tone of the conference: "Views on the interaction of our time and space conception and the technical basis for composing computer music." On the sixth and last day Boulez tackled less theoretical issues: division of courses into computer programming, acoustics, and basic electronics; recruiting those trained in linguistics; research into sociology of concerts based on Adorno's views; the number and type of publications;

whether to give three or four concerts a year or group them together in one week of such events.

In the afternoon, pedagogy was discussed. Plans were made for the organization of the teaching of Fortran (a computer language), cross-correlation techniques, cybernetics, and pattern recognition. Several of the participants expressed the idea that one could not begin to teach until the computers and equipment arrived. Boulez disagreed: "One must teach the theory first, for unless one understands the theory, one's invention is inhibited. I think if you know something first, you will be much better equipped. I like to have a coherent piece of information. Otherwise I pick up this and that and do not have a solid tool. To project something strongly, you must know it. If you go to a technician and say 'do it,' he will be filled with contempt for you. And he will do just anything. Then we stand in the position of the blind and deaf, and in that position you cannot go very far."

In the afternoon, Boulez asked for comments that could be recorded by Mme Brigitte Marger, the Institute's press representative, and included in a brochure for foundations and friends. Boulez said he thought the emphasis should be that using science in art does not bring music into the arena of inhuman affairs but rather provides tools the composers need. Babbitt said the Institute would have difficulty attracting scientists. "Mathematicians look down on physicists," he said.

> And physicists look down on composers. The problem is how to confront an attitude that music does not belong in universities but in girls' finishing schools and that exhausts its cognitive content. At Princeton and Harvard one never finds scientists at contemporary music concerts. Scientists think we take ourselves too seriously; they are equally contemptuous of music and technology. Look at Noam Chomsky. To him music is folk dancing, not Schoenberg. Robert Oppenheimer thought of composers as talented children.

Boulez agreed with Babbitt, noting that Werner Heisenberg had "torpedoed" his Max Planck Institute. But he quickly returned to dictating what was to be included in the brochure:

> We must have a new point of view. We must have communication between all of these corners which have remained separate in the hands of specialists. It is necessary to have a team to do research. The Bauhaus is the only

model I can think of. The Bauhaus changed absolutely everything. We are still living off the ideas which were explored systematically by a small group of people in an institute where only this type of research was done. Ircam will provide a "chair," a type of thinking, a point of view. For now we find ourselves in a situation where one finds if one uses different intervals or wants different timbres, certain pieces cannot be performed. That can't be very healthy.

Vinko Globokar interrupted: "I don't want to go on record saying the situation is sick."

Boulez: "I didn't say it was sick. I said I want more. I want all the possibilities."

Globokar: "Ah you. Not me."

Boulez: "O.K., then, me. I'm not satisfied. I find I'm against a brick wall I have to push." Boulez slammed his right fist into his left hand.

Boulez's nature is composed of irreconcilable, unharmonized dichotomies. His puritanism fights his violence. His desire to be loved fights the idea that one should not seek love. Women who have become infatuated with Boulez have confided to me that when they have embraced him in a spontaneous and effusive gesture, he will flush and remain in high spirits for some time. But he never reciprocates that gesture or indicates he wants it done again. Similarly, at the Rug Concerts, when Boulez received bravos and extraordinary applause, he took the next piece at an exaggerated speed, so intoxicated was he by the extreme heat of the response. Yet he never lingered on stage to enjoy or encourage the audience's applause.

Boulez's behavior suggests that he believes man must be a selfless seeker devoted to truth, without any desires of his own. Yet in defining the "most recent period in the history of art" in 1975, he limited it to the one "between 1945 and 1958," the period when he feels that he alone led the way, and thus he reveals his very deep wish to be recognized as the originator of all that was significant and good. Only after some pressure on my part did he push the period back to 1910 and concede some priority to Arnold Schoenberg.

Beset by these warring elements, Boulez attempts to resolve them through his art. His extreme asceticism, his heroic devotion to everyday work, is in opposition to imagination and expression, which may lie too close to passion for him to bear. Boulez programmed every instant of every day and posted the schedule in the orchestra's office so that secretaries could make appointments for him from early morning until midnight. He did not allow an unscheduled five minutes which might permit him to get close to himself. Boulez said, "I am neither reflective nor introspective. I prefer to act."

The condition in which large portions of oneself are inaccessible has been characterized ad infinitum as an "alienated" one and the ultimate condition of modern man. No one represents that condition more eloquently than Boulez, who covers any frustration or rage with the most elegant and gracious manners. Only rarely do these feelings come to the surface.

A person so alienated, so divided, must attempt to restore wholeness with what he has at hand. At first Boulez tried system and it worked for a while. But then composers turned against him. After that he made a tentative approach to chance. But immediately he controlled that chance. Then through the direction of two major orchestras—the BBC and the New York Philharmonic—he tried to convert Europe and the United States to his way. But the world did not go along with him.

In 1974 Boulez decided not to seek or consider an orchestral engagement after 1977, the end of his second contract in New York. He regarded the period of the 1970s as an "exceptional" one in his life and planned to return to "what is more myself" through his work at the Paris Institute. There he would invest all his cognitive and creative passions in an effort to restore both his own sense of wholeness as well as the era's sense of wholeness. For today's music appears to know no way of integrating the past into the present—neoclassicism and collage pieces did not work—and without a past the era is cut off from itself. If your father's a horse, then you are a horse. And if conditions don't allow you to know you are a horse, then the ground dissolves underneath your feet. Boulez's hatred of the past is analogous to his horror of repetition in music; he even cuts the repeats in Mozart. For him music must continue to move on, always leaving the past behind it. This presents a problem for the listener, for whom repetition provides audible articulation and structure.

Boulez's "past" was the music of Schoenberg; he virtually ingested Schoenberg and only after he had eaten him up was he able to separate himself completely from him. That "Schoenberg is dead!" is the title of an essay in which Boulez celebrates a system ultimately based on dodecaphony reveals how crucial Schoenberg was to him.

If the new language he had built from Schoenberg's had matured gently—as tonality certainly did—and if the times had been such to allow for such gentle maturing instead of rewarding a new gimmick a year, then the next generation of composers would have had something to ingest, to move on from or at least attack. But art—during the last third of the twentieth century—is moved by *Time* and television. Each composer was forced to make something new every time he wrote a piece and that was a large burden to bear; and so composers produced far less than in former times. As early as 1918, in a letter to William Carlos Williams, Wallace Stevens wrote, ". . . to fidget with points of view leads always to new beginnings and incessant new beginnings lead to sterility."

To say the period is bad for composers is not to damn the composers at all. Rather it is to emphasize the gravity of the historical impasse, the bewilderment of a period that did not crystallize its own synthesis, nor come up with a predominating style for a new generation to absorb or rail against. It is precisely to bring into being such a style that Boulez invested his faith and reason in sociology, anthropology, and computer technology. With Ircam he strove for the flowering of a new art which he said he would try not to control, but which, he hoped in the deepest possible way, will be based on the art that he himself built by composing directly from his own time.

The struggle Boulez lost in New York he had lost in Darmstadt more than a decade before. In 1977 he returned to France with an international staff of musicians and scientists who probably appreciated him more for what he was than for what he was able to give—which is, in general, what Americans appreciate.

Ircam is a limb of the great cultural center planned by Georges Pompidou on a site called Beaubourg. The Centre Pompidou opened in 1976 and includes France's gallery of modern art, a center of industrial design, a reference library, a variety of eating places, a film theater, games, and exhibitions. Boulez's institute is the only musical constituent; it is located in a subterranean building half a mile to the north of Notre Dame.

Ircam has always been financially independent of the Ministry of Cultural Affairs and enjoys the status of an independent foundation. This frees it from much red tape and, at the same time, enables it to accept whatever money is offered from the outside while receiving a generous subsidy from the State. The building alone cost $12 million. There are laboratories, studios, administrative offices. The main area has movable walls that could be tuned to any acoustical conditions and adapted to any kind of music. It serves for public demonstrations, concerts and research. Boulez told me he composes at night, "when there is no visual distraction, not even a bird," and that, as well as acoustical considerations, may have played a role in putting the institute under ground: it is as free from sensory stimuli as it could possibly be.

At the start, Boulez's administrators included Luciano Berio, in charge of electronics; Vinko Globokar, in charge of "instruments and voice"; Jean Claude Risset, in charge of computers; Gerald Bennett, coordinator of the other three; Jean-Pierre Armand, technical coordinator; and Michel Decoust, in charge of pedagogy. Nicholas Snowman was artistic administrator, Max Mathews scientific consultant.

Of course there have been many electronic studios, but none as big and powerful as this. Boulez has said that studios—like the one in Cologne— are in a "primitive state" because they lack the necessary funds. On the other hand, he found that research centers of American industry, such as the one at Bell Labs, treated music as a hobby, for they make their resources available to musicians only at night or during vacation periods.

As early as 1975, two years before Ircam was scheduled to open, Boulez's plans captured the imagination of some of the press. London music critic Peter Heyworth wrote that if Ircam fulfills Boulez's ambitions, "it will be a milestone in the history of Western music as crucial as the advent of the airplane has been in the field of transport. Ircam will probably succeed in pushing out the frontiers of sound as drastically as the great explorers of the Renaissance succeeded in expanding man's knowledge of the Earth."

CHAPTER 44

Earlier I quoted Boulez: "If it were necessary for me to find a profound motive. . . it would be the search for anonymity. Perhaps I can explain it best by an old Chinese story: a painter drew a landscape so beautifully that he entered the picture and disappeared. For me that is the definition of a great work—a landscape painted so well that the artist disappears into it."

In December, 1980, four years after the publication of the first edition of *Boulez,* I wrote my last article on the composer-conductor for *The New York Times.* The occasion was the United States premiere of *Notations,* a large orchestral work dominated by strings and percussion based on a collection of piano pieces Boulez had composed in the early 1940s. By the time of the performance, Boulez had been active at Ircam for three years. The aspect most innovative to the public was that everything in the hall was in the round: the orchestra placed itself in the center, the audience surrounded the orchestra and the soloists were around the audience. In the *Times* article, I charted the development of Boulez's interest in combining science and art from the 1960s, when the Max Planck Institute had asked for his help in formulating such a plan. Economic problems intervened, but in 1970, Boulez's ideas were set into motion when Georges Pompidou, then the President of France, invited him to organize Ircam as a branch of the then new Centre Pompidou in Paris.

In a statement for Ircam written in the mid-1970s, Boulez noted: "The effort will be collective or it will not be at all. No individual, however gifted, could produce a solution to all the problems posed by the present evolution of musical expression. . . .What is absolutely necessary is that we should move forward towards global generalized solutions."

Boulez's quest for anonymity has paradoxically led him to become the most powerful musician in France since Jean-Baptiste Lully, the court composer who died in 1687. Boulez's anointment is a direct consequence of the service he performed for his country. Throughout the 1950s, 1960s, and 1970s, France had no musical culture that could compare to that of Germany or the United States. Once Ircam received the state's support and generated the resources it came to have, it attracted talented people from all over the world. Boulez was recognized as *the* international musician and France was the center of musical thought. An adroit politician, Boulez has maintained close relations with all the political leaders of France over the last twenty years. François Mitterand was the only one with whom he had trouble and that was over Mitterand's handling of the Bastille Opera. But from Pompidou to Valéry Giscard d'Estaing and even through Mitterand to Jacques Chirac, whose term runs until 2002, the checks have kept pouring in.

To say this is not to suggest the path was smooth. At the beginning, there were ferocious attacks from diverse quarters. Directors of the Lyon and Bordeaux opera houses were outraged over what they considered to be inappropriate moneys from the national budget going to Boulez's computer music center. On May 13, 1996, *The New York Times* reported that between Ircam and the Ensemble InterContemporain, a group of instrumentalists under Boulez's aegis founded in 1977, the two Boulez-run facilities are "drawing $11.1 million in subsidies this year."

In addition to the outcry from directors of opera houses and orchestras both in Paris and the provinces, some of Boulez's composing colleagues were angered. Full-page pieces appeared in *Le Matin*. One was written by Iannis Xenakis, the Greek avant-garde composer, and another by Jean-Claude Eloy, who had studied with Boulez in Basle. On occasion, composer criticism led to constructive changes. Luciano Berio, head of the electro-acoustic department, distrusted the usefulness of computers and brought into Ircam Giuseppi de Giugno, an Italian scientist, who invented the 4X machine, which made possible the sound Berio had in mind with the precision Boulez demanded.

The American composer Tod Machover, a younger man than any of those already mentioned, had been recommended to Boulez by Elliott Carter and joined Ircam in 1978. First he was a composer-in-residence, then director of musical research. In 1996, Machover characterized the late 1970s and early 1980s to me: "Boulez was the person everyone attacked. He was the biggest evil. Then *Répons* happened. *Le Monde* called it a 'triumph' on its front page. Suddenly everything changed. Boulez was great."

Répons, like so many of Boulez's works, emerged in stages. The first performance took place in Donaueschingen, October 18, 1981. The second was held in London's Royal Horticultural Hall on September 6, 1982. The third occurred in September 1984, in Metz, and was repeated the following month in Paris. Along with a 24-piece ensemble, Boulez placed his soloists in various places around the hall playing two pianos, cimbalon, xylophone, harp, glockenspiel, vibraphone, and synthesizer. The star of the event was the 4X computer which played a formidable role in a new system that collects sounds and transforms those that would otherwise linger and die.

In April 1999, Deutsche Grammophon distributed the first CD containing *Répons* throughout the United States. Also on the same disc is *Dialogue de l'ombre double,* which Boulez composed for Berio's 60th birthday, celebrated in Florence in 1985.

Andrew Gerzso, a principal figure at Ircam, wrote the *Notes,* which report that the three different versions of *Répons* last 17, 35, and 45 minutes respectively. Boulez has said, though not in these notes, that he intends to expand the work to fill an entire evening. *Dialogue de l'ombre double,* an immensely attractive piece, a strikingly assertive clarinet solo, is the result of such an expansion.

Commissioned by the Southwest German Radio, *Répons* is dedicated to Alfred Schlee, director of Universal Edition, and contains a hidden reference to Paul Sacher, probably the 20th century's most progressive patron of music, an admirer, in particular, of Stravinsky and Boulez. The letters SACHER form the basis for the harmonic material that underlies the structure of the work.

The title "Répons" refers back to Gregorian chant, most specifically the practice of a solo singer alternating with a choir. "In this . . . form," the *Notes* instruct, "one finds some of the musical ideas which occur throughout Boulez's work: the taking of a simple musical idea and making it proliferate, the alternation between solo and collective playing, and his movement of sound in space."

Tod Machover's most recent opera, *Resurrection,* a combination of technology and a wide variety of musical styles, received its world premiere at the Houston Opera in April, 1999. Two months earlier, Machover described for me how he remembered the first performance of *Répons*:

> I was closely involved in the genesis of this work, so
> I remember well the intensity of technological development,
> the freshness of the music as it emerged, the incredible atten-
> tion to detail in rehearsal of soloists and ensembles (so
> seldom the case with "electronic" music), and the overbearing

pressure on Boulez and Ircam to produce a hit. This hot-house atmosphere reached its peak at the October1981 Donaueschingen premiere, when lightning zapped all the local power during the premiere just before the entrance of soloists and electronics, wiping out our then delicate computers. Boulez gracefully—and in total darkness— offered an "intermission before the performance" to the audience, and we hustled to revive our machines. Miraculously the lights did come back on, the piece started again, the musicians and machines all sprang back to life, and this masterpiece—which in my view it is—unfolded in all its mystery and majesty to overwhelm the who's who audience of European music critics, composers, and aficionados.

My own favorite version of *Répons* has always been this first one, a gem of remarkable proportions and haunting power. Here Boulez merges many opposites: filigreed ornamentation with purposeful harmony, the electrifying computer-enhanced soloists with the subtlety and punch of the accompanying chamber ensemble, propulsive forward motion with moments of shimmering stasis, and the brand-new hybrid—really invented by Boulez in this piece— of instrumental virtuosity with computerized extension. Perhaps most significant of all is the way that *Répons*— especially in its original version—so perfectly blends Boulez's invigorating invention and ever-unfolding melodic proliferation with an extremely satisfying sense of formal proportion and completeness: its four movements bring the listener through a compacted journey of orchestral bravura, the astonishing juxtaposition of soloists, electronics, and ensemble (first antiphonally and then in a whirlwind of cascading layers), and finally to a sublimely beautiful passage of murmuring tremolos where all forces seem to merge and contribute to a slow and shattering crescendo before ending on a quiet, tentative fermata. In *Répons* Boulez convincingly introduces us to a completely new world, but is also unafraid to leave us asking questions about where it—and all of us— will eventually go.

Boulez creates "works-in-progress," investing his energy and attention on lit-tle cells which grow organically. This process can go on indefinitely.

Throughout the 1980s, revised versions appeared of *Le Visage Nuptial, Improvisations sur Mallarmé*, and *Cummings ist der Dichter*. Notations, as noted, also comes from an earlier work; in a December 1998 interview, Boulez said he was just completing it. And the later compositions, such as *Dialogue de l'ombre double*, had their origins in material that first appeared in Domaines and so on. With what ordinarily would be called Opus 1 sometimes following Opus 4, it is not easy to determine the chronology of Boulez's works.

One can speculate that the constant reworking of material comes from Boulez's belief that form is a psychological journey and from his consequent abhorrence of closure, a work with a beginning, middle and end, an attitude that has its echo in his dislike of the "spatial limitations of a swimming pool." But one can also consider what Messiaen had said to me: "Boulez se doute." A few years ago Universal Edition told Mario di Bonaventura, former director of publications at G. Schirmer and a conductor with strong sympathies for the post-Schoenberg language, that it had informed Boulez his scores were bound with care and being kept in atmospherically perfect conditions. Executives asked the composer what to do with them. In German he is reported to have said: "I don't give a crap."

If Boulez doesn't treat his hand-written scores as icons, or even care to get his music into print, he does seem to care a great deal about putting it on discs. And here he has succeeded. Not only did DG record *explosante-fixe* in 1978 but they also redid it in another version that took years to complete. Boulez is far more fortunate than any of his composing colleagues whose works are generally ignored by the big record companies. In March 1994, Peter Gelb, President of Sony Classical USA, told a convention in San Francisco he believed "a handful of Hollywood composers are writing original, artistically challenging music" and cited the best-selling records of the time, all of which were tied to film soundtracks: *Schindler's List, Shadowlands* and *The Piano*.

What Gelb was really saying is manifestly true: such important composers as Boulez, Stockhausen, Berio, Babbitt, Carter and Wuorinen are not creating commercially viable music whose sales can compete with Hollywood scores. Yet, in 1989, after Deutsche Grammophon's attention to *explosante-fixe*, Boulez signed an exclusive contract with the company. The big seduction for Boulez must have been Deutsche Grammophon's commitment to his own work.

It was a wise trade-off for DG, because Boulez, who still claims not to be a professional conductor, is, of course, one of the most remarkable conductors of our day. On April 16, 1995, Alex Ross, now music critic for

The New Yorker and then a music critic for *The New York Times,* wrote: "With the passing of Karajan and Bernstein, Boulez seems to have become, against all odds, the last true maestro."

In February 1992, *Opera* magazine published an interview with Boulez conducted by Andrew Clements: "You have to define yourself in life," Boulez said.

> I'm not a professional conductor, so I conduct what interests me the most. It could have been different at a certain point in my career, but the death of Wieland Wagner certainly changed that. At that time [the mid-1960s] I was not attached to an orchestra. I was conducting in Germany and had just started with the BBC. Wieland and I had quite a list of projects—we had done *Parsifal* at Bayreuth—but he was already sick and I worked with an assistant. Then we did *Wozzeck* in Frankfurt in 1966, which was his last production. I asked him to direct *Pélleas* at Covent Garden in 1969 and we'd planned *Salomé, Elektra* and *Boris.* Had he lived I would have gone on in that direction and done much less orchestral conducting.

But Wieland Wagner did die and Boulez transferred his focus from opera to the BBC and New York Philharmonic orchestras. Opera, however, remained on his mind. In 1976, the year before he left the New York Philharmonic, he conducted *The Ring* at Bayreuth. A centenary production staged by Patrice Chereau, it turned out to be immensely controversial. Costumed as 19th century can-can dancers, the Rhinemaidens cavorted under a contemporary hydroelectric dam and Wotan prevailed over an elegant drawing room. But Boulez's interpretation triumphed over any complaints against the production. Aspects of the score that had never been clear before emerged with stunning clarity. The leitmotifs were there to elucidate the score and text but were never underlined in such a way that they would cheapen the whole.

In 1979 Boulez conducted the world premiere of Berg's complete *Lulu.* Then after a long break during which he put into motion his ideas concerning Ircam and the Ensemble InterContemporain, he returned to opera in 1992, realizing his earlier desire to conduct *Pélleas.* The staging for the Debussy opera was by Peter Stein whose *Peer Gynt* Boulez had seen on German television. *Pélleas* received its first performance in Cardiff, then went on to other performances in England. At the Netherlands Opera,

Boulez opened the fall season of 1995 with Schoenberg's *Moses und Aron,* also staged by Stein and a coproduction of the Salzburg Festival.

On the podium, Boulez is a model of discipline and restraint. There are no histrionics. There is no apparent drama. Everything goes on inside his brain. During the 1970s, he told me he would choose to go on living even if he lost all his body parts but his head.

In the *Opera* interview with Clements, Boulez said: "I haven't given up all my ideas of writing an opera—I've still some years in front of me. I just think it's difficult, that's all. I worked with Jean Genet on a project for a long time, but Genet was . . . always saying the same things—'I'm old. I haven't written for a long time. . . .' I was trying to encourage him. I pushed him, but it was very difficult and in the final years he lived a lot of time in Morocco, always changing hotels, and it was very difficult to keep in touch. He wrote quite a lot of the scenario; but I cannot use it. I think it's too sketchy."

After Genet's death, Boulez turned to Heiner Müller, an East German director and author who died unexpectedly. After this Boulez appeared reluctant to identify another collaborator. But he has acknowledged that he is looking into the work of Edward Bond, a British playwright and the librettist for *We Come to the River,* an opera by the neoromantic composer Hans Werner Henze. It calls for 126 characters and three separate orchestras and deals with the Pinochet regime in Chile.

People often change their minds during the course of their careers. But Boulez's shifts are particularly striking because of the passion with which he articulates what he believes at any given moment. In one of his earliest interviews, he calls for the blowing up of all opera houses. Contrast that with the opera conducting he has done in the last thirty years and with the possibility of writing an opera of his own.

Even more paradoxical than this shift is Boulez's total reversal on electronic music. In my first interview with him, published in *The New York Times* in March 1969, I asked him about America's involvement with the medium. "The same frenzy," Boulez replied, "began in Europe in 1953. By 1958 it had all died down. The idea of electronics as the big future of music is just an American trick of fashion. Next year they'll discover the viola da gamba."

Considering the use Boulez began to make only a few years later of all that Americans had accomplished in the electronic field, these words take on a particularly egregious tone. In the 1970s, Boulez visited Stanford University, Bell Labs, MIT and the California Institute of the Arts, then the computer music center in the United States. And once Ircam was in motion, he invited the computer-using Americans Max Matthews, John Chowning, David Wessel, Tod Machover and others to Paris. Americans were as generous to him then as John Cage had been in the 1950s when he was instrumental in having Boulez's works published.

The area that changes the least is Boulez's preferences for artists. During the concerts celebrating his seventieth birthday, there were debates, master classes, and composer-meets-the-public sessions. Key subjects dealt with Boulez and the artists and poets of his younger days—Klee, Kandinsky, Mallarmé, Char and Cummings—and they are the artists he says he still favors today. Similarly his musical repertory in the orchestral literature has undergone little change. By the time he was 21, Boulez's tastes had been set and the intervening decades have witnessed little alteration. As he did at the start of his conducting career, Boulez still conducts works he considers classics—Stravinsky, Webern and Berg, those in the French school from Messiaen to Ravel, and the two composers he believes are the source for everything important that happened in the twentieth century—Schoenberg and Debussy. He also conducts the same contemporaries—Berio, Ligeti and Carter. Carter is the only American he has championed, probably because Carter was never part of the academic establishment and therefore was not guilty of the musical crimes Boulez unjustly believes were committed by all of its composers.

To say this is not to imply Boulez ignores younger artists. Colleagues describe Phillippe Manoury, not yet 50, as his "spiritual son," and Marc-André Dalbavie, still under 40 and a gifted protegé, agrees. Dalbavie, whose works have been conducted and recorded by Boulez, was recently named the Cleveland Orchestra's composer in residence, and will take a similar position in France with the Orchestre de Paris in 2001. He has composed a celebratory work for Boulez's 75th birthday, which Boulez will conduct at the time with the Cleveland Orchestra. To emphasize that he is in no way an echo of Boulez, Dalbavie says, "My line is Debussy, Messaien, Berio and Ligeti and the more recent spectral music, very far from the post-serialism connected to Boulez." As for the 4X machine, "That is a grandfather machine, a machine for the museum now obsolete." Dalbavie emphasizes that he creates a new sound world, totally dependent on the space in which his music will be heard.

Boulez selects only a few orchestras with which to record—Chicago, Cleveland, the Vienna and Berlin Philharmonics. That—and his approach to repertoire—concentrating on those works in which he believes—not only results in magnificent performances—just listen to his Ravel Piano Concertos with Krystian Zimmerman—but in numerous prestigious recording prizes. By the end of 1998 his discs included Bartók's *Bluebeard's Castle,* Schoenberg's *Pierrot Lunaire,* and Bruckner's Eighth Symphony with the Vienna Philharmonic. Under the title *Boulez Conducts Boulez,* he has recorded the following works: *explosante-fixe, Notations, Structures for Two Pianos, Book II*—all with the Ensemble InterContemporain. In the spring of 1999, there was *Répons,* probably Boulez's most carefully conceived and brilliantly executed performance of the last quarter century.

The most startling choice that Boulez has made in recent years is his decision to record Scriabin. In July 1999 Deutsche Grammophon released *The Poem of Ecstasy, Prometheus: The Poem of Fire,* and the Piano Concerto with the Chicago Symphony and Anatol Ugorski, soloist. Bernard Holland, chief music critic of *The New York Times,* wrote: "Music of sensual extravagance is subjected to minute examinaation and emerges even more sensual and extravagant than before."

Another surprising addition to his repertory are the Mahler symphonies—the Sixth with Vienna, the Seventh with Cleveland and the Ninth with Chicago. The performances are, of course, crystal clear. But they also reveal the remarkable degree with which he puts himself between Mahler and the listener. Boulez projects his own identity so effectively that these recordings emphasize his own qualities—rigor, precision and intellect—and deemphasize the gargantuan psychological catharsis that many Mahler lovers seek.

In March 1995, Boulez told Stephen Plaistow of *Gramophone* magazine, which named him Artist of the Year, why he came to Mahler late. There is not one word in the reported conversation such as "beautiful," "moving" or "profound." Boulez says he came to Mahler late because he was a historical link:

> It is true that I did not discover Mahler when I was young. During the war his music was not performed because he was a Jew. After the Liberation and until 1958, when I left France, the only works I heard were *Das Lied von der Erde* and the Fourth Symphony. Two pieces and that was it. In Germany, in Baden-Baden, I discovered Mahler through Hans Rosbaud. He did the Ninth Symphony which I did not know at all. Later, I began to conduct Mahler in London

with the BBC Symphony—the Fifth Symphony. By then I had come to know the music of Mahler in a sort of backward trajectory, backwards from Berg. I had conducted Mahler's Three Orchestral Pieces Opus 6 quite early but I didn't relate them. Mahler was the missing link! The origin of Berg's inspiration is so often in Mahler, and now I can't conceive musical history without that link.

A historical bias pervades Boulez's choices. Sir William Glock spoke of this to me when we discussed Boulez's reasons for placing particular works on the same program that Glock would find surprising if considered from an aesthetic point of view.

If Boulez approaches his choice of repertory as a historian, promulgating only those works which "advanced" the musical language, he approaches the act of conducting as a technician. Still the result can be surprising in the beauty that is often conveyed. On March 13, 1993, Bernard Holland reported on a two-day workshop at Carnegie Hall under the aegis of Boulez, who was holding a master class for four young conductors.

Describing how Boulez went about making the musicians aware of the physical impact of their gestures on the members of an orchestra, Holland wrote: "Using no baton ('My fingers are ten batons,' he explained) Mr. Boulez demonstrated the efficient outward flick of the fingers for sharp, pointed attacks, the scooping flat of the hands for broader ones, the use of downward arc motions to express heavy accents, the dangers of subdividing beats (when flow is needed) and the necessity for subdividing them (when musicians must be prepared for tempo changes)."

Holland continued with this kind of detail, then concluded: "If all this sounds dispassionate, uncomfortably scientific, there was Thursday's concert, which had at its end the most sensuous, beautifully balanced—and to use a word Boulez would shy from—transcendent performance of *La Mer* this critic has heard. . . . Erudition, precision and rationality are not necessarily the refrigerants of musical performance they sometimes seem. . . the science of beauty, entrusted to reverent pragmatism, conveys in its unspoken way all the fancy words Mr. Boulez's workshop never used."

In addition to the Mahler cycle, Boulez is rerecording much of his old repertory with Deutsche Grammophon. At the same time Sony Classical has been reissuing the recordings he made in the 1960s and 1970s as part of a comprehensive Boulez edition. When, in the *Gramophone* interview, Plaistow asked Boulez why he was rerecording works he had done before Boulez said,

I suppose because I am older. I compare recordings to photographs. I have photographs of what I did 25 years ago and I would like pictures of what I do now. During those years I have acquired a lot of experience with the orchestral literature, and of conducting; and you know, in a paradoxical way, you become more spontaneous when you know more, when you know better; earlier on, when you know less, you're thinking all the time of what you're supposed to do, what you want to do, and how to do it. With experience, you have more spontaneity, more direct contact. You don't jump into something blind, of course not, but I would say it's a different balance, a question of doing less thinking and more acting. You just do it. For me, that's the big difference.

Machover says that after *Répons*, there were several "flip-flops." The negative reaction that had characterized the response to Ircam in its early years resurfaced in the 1990s. In his book *The Comedy of Culture*, Michel Schneider, in charge of music at the French Ministry of Culture from 1988 to 1991, attacked Boulez as a composer with no talent and proclaimed that one had to "choose between Boulez and music." This was written in 1992, the year after Schneider left his post under Jack Lang, then minister of culture.

Enraged, Boulez insisted Schneider appear with him on *Bouillon de Culture*, a popular cultural television talk show. Boulez brought with him Jack Lang, then still minister of culture, who sat between the two men. Boulez acted much as he had almost half a century before when the sight of Leibowitz's markings on his First Piano Sonata provoked him to tear up his manuscript. "Boulez has an enormous temper," Machover says. "He still gets very angry at anyone who attacks him."

Tearing into Schneider in front of an immense television audience, Boulez dismissed him as "incompetent."

A few years later, *Requiem for the Avant-Garde* by Benoit Duteurtre, novelist and music publisher, appeared. Here the author denounced the large subsidies given by the French government to what he called "musical research." Duteurtre wrote that musical analysis had replaced music in France and that audiences were expected to endure painful, complex, dissonant compositions as though they were sermons being delivered from the pulpit of a church.

In *Le Monde*, the critic Anne Rey came to Boulez's defense, with a scathing column on Duteurtre. She compared him to Robert Faurisson, the French historian who denies the Holocaust. The analogy may have seemed apt because undermining Boulez, the only living French musician with international renown, appears tantamount to undermining the nation.

Responding to Rey's vicious character attack, Duteurtre wrote a letter to *Le Monde*. *Le Monde* refused to publish it. But the matter did not stop there; Duteurtre brought the matter to court, which forced the paper to publish Duteurtre's response.

Not only was Boulez's public standing in a state of flux through the 1980s and 1990s; so was the state of technology. "At the beginning," Boulez told John Rockwell in 1993, "when things were less complicated, we were in charge of both hardware and software. We tried to sell it, but we couldn't. French industry does not know how to sell its products. The factory with which we had our relationship did not do its job. Later the hardware became more difficult to produce, and unnecessary. Now we buy the hardware, but we still make our own software."

Rockwell added: "In part, the emphasis on software reflects the rapid evolution of the computer hardware business, which has produced more powerful machines that cost and weigh less. This new flexibility allows composers, supplied with software geared to their specific needs, to work at home, using Ircam more as a technical information center than as their sole source of equipment."

But the flexibility of the new technology is not the only reason some composers might prefer to work at home. The book *Realizing Culture: Ircam, Boulez, and the Institutionalization of the Musical Avant-Garde* by Georgina Born offers some insights:

> Privately divided among themselves, Ircam music intellectuals colluded in putting down outside composers. . . . Tutors, for example, maintained a flow of mocking comments on the progress of visitors' pieces. Sitting down to a musicians' meeting, the group joked about the recent Ircam premiere of a major outside composer whom they considered to have produced a musique concrète-like piece, despite having access to the advanced technology of the 4X. Laughing, they ridiculed the premiere as boring and the composer for his omnipotent pretensions. . . .
>
> Visiting composers were commonly seen by Ircam music intellectuals as willing victims of the commission process, inexperienced with the technology and therefore impotent to produce good pieces and utterly dependent on their tutor as

a "nurse." A tutor mused that the visiting composer he was assisting was being very quick. "He's turning it out by the meter, and as soon as he's finished he says 'OK, now can I have a job at Ircam??!!' at which, again, all in the room fell about laughing with derision at this composer's naive audacity."

When Boulez spoke to Rockwell in 1993, he had retired as hands-on director of both Ircam and the Ensemble, leaving people with low profiles in charge. (The pieces commissioned by Ircam are performed by the Ensemble InterContemporain.) Laurent Bayle succeeded him at Ircam and David Robertson, an American with experience in Europe, with the Ensemble. "Many people," he told Rockwell, "are prejudiced against me. People would decide in advance they didn't want to collaborate with Ircam. Laurent Bayle has a different kind of personality. He can make contact with people who don't like me." But the quest for anonymity had not yet been achieved. Machover told me that the tutors, now called "assistants," keep the star system intact. The stars are not the dazzling performing virtuosos with whom the traditional concert audiences are familiar. Rather they are the music-intellectuals most literate in Ircam's electronic technology.

In the same manner that he prepared to take over Ircam while conducting the BBC and New York Philharmonic orchestras, Boulez developed a new project, the Cité de la Musique, as he was withdrawing from his visibility at the Institut. Located in the 19th arrondissement, a blue-collar neighborhood, the Cité is a $120 million property of angular glass and concrete. Part of the large La Villette Park, it contains a music museum and a modular performance hall.

Once a desolate neighborhood filled with slaughter houses, under Pompidou, the land was planned to become the largest slaughter house in the world. But something went wrong: the conveyor belts designed to move the animals were incapable of turning corners.

Giscard d'Estaing, a minister in Pompidou's cabinet, began to convert the area by overseeing the creation of a science museum. Then Boulez set about making his new home. He uses its location in a working-class neighborhood and its genesis as a slaughter house against the charges of elitism that have hounded him throughout his career. In a conversation published by DG in 1998, Boulez said, "In the Cité de la Musique . . . I am pleading for the building of a media center with many recordings, video, connections to the Internet, and connections to the museums of music and of science."

Boulez has always been more interested in building than in sustaining what has been built. He has never returned to conduct the New York Philharmonic, although management has invited him. With a few other American orchestras, he continues to instill admiration and some affection which the musicians show in their playing. Relations with three orchestras—Cleveland, Chicago and Los Angeles—go back to the late 1960s. Boulez's collaboration with Daniel Barenboim in Chicago must be gratifying to both men. Initially involved with the modern Bastille Opera, they had to abandon plans they had made when Barenboim resigned. Mitterand appointed Pierre Bergé, a political supporter and president of the Yves Saint Laurent fashion house, as the head of the new Opera.

As for the Los Angeles Philharmonic: some of his most memorable performances have taken place in Ojai, California. In June 1996, Boulez was back with the orchestra celebrating the Ojai Festival's fiftieth birthday. One work he conducted was the Mahler Fifth. Holland reviewed it for the *Times*. "When it asked for self-indulgence, players filled in the emotive blanks that their beloved conductor had pointedly passed over. Mahler's music complains about life and Boulez is too dignified to go along."

Over and above these American engagements, Boulez's apppointment as Carnegie Hall's chair in composition for the 1999–2000 season may justifiably be viewed as vindication for his work in the United States. In November, 1999, and March, 2000, Boulez will conduct performances of twentieth century masterpieces as well as premieres of commissioned pieces performed by the London Symphony Orchestra and the Ensemble InterContemporain, and devote an evening to answering questions posed by a music specialist before an audience at Carnegie's Weill Hall.

Boulez still occupies his house in Baden-Baden (which he recently purchased); one in St. Michel de l'Observatoire, on property he shares with his sister; an apartment in Paris; and now a house in Orléans, one hour from Paris, which had belonged to his father. What with his continuing composition, working with the Ensemble InterContemporain at the Cité de la Musique, conducting those orchestras he chooses to conduct, and maintaining decent relations with friends and workers, he appears healthy and cheerful. Whatever personal differences there have been between those composers who initially headed Ircam departments and himself, Boulez does not seem to be diminished in any way.

AFTERWORD

In the very month these lines are written, *Gramophone* magazine is preparing an essay, "American Chromatic: Charles Wuorinen reaffirms the vitality of American modernism," for a special issue: *Gramophone Explorations 4*. Wuorinen begins by emphasizing this century's debt to Schoenberg, much as he did in the preface to this book. "What Schoenberg discovered has grown and flowered so enormously and variously that today there are as many varieties of his musical descendants as there are individual composers. For the truth is that even those who reject his legacy are, in their very rejection, acknowledging their debt to him. For the rest of us, writing music without the frame he first established would be inconceivable. It would be as if we said, 'Enough of this curved space-time nonsense! Let's go back to a comfy flat earth.'"

At the end of the essay, Wuorinen writes that

> . . . in the United States there has always been a double stream of composition: on the one hand the reactionary/populist, and on the other the progressive. Which one seems ascendant is really just the result of which at any moment receives the most journalistic attention. In recent years the reactionary/populist side of composition has received the blessing of music journalists and many institutions have followed the lead of these arbiters. But it is important to remember that the great stream of widely—and wildly— diverse music continues without regard to journalistic fashion, and that what humanity will ultimately come to value may very well not be what is in fashion today.

During the late 1960s and through the 1970s, I interviewed many progressive composers for the music pages of the Sunday *New York Times*. To say this is not to suggest the *Times* favored the advanced aesthetic. Nothing could be further from the truth. But the Arts & Leisure section operated under a separate aegis and permitted me to make the choices I did. Aaron Copland wrote a letter to the paper which appeared on April 27, 1972, accusing me of "gratuitous musical politics." He was reacting to a review I had written of a biography of Varèse. In it I claimed the International Composers Guild of the 1920s, which was led by Varèse, presented more advanced music than the League of Composers, in which Copland played a major role. I would not call this musical politics but a statement of fact.

The title *To Boulez and Beyond: Music in Europe Since The Rite of Spring* indicates that this book's pages do not include a full discussion of twentieth-century American composers. This omission distorts the picture, for there have not only been important composers in the United States who took their cues from the first generation of twentieth-century Europeans—Schoenberg, Stravinsky, Varèse—but also younger Americans who either worked along parallel lines to, or even anticipated major moves made by, Boulez and Stockhausen. To cite three examples: Babbitt composed a serial work before the first such work composed by Boulez, and Brant and Cage generated ideas that were appropriated by Stockhausen, often to the most minor detail.

But there are also Americans who made great contributions to the path of serious music in this century not by setting any particular precedent, but through the high quality of their music. Here are some of them:

Roger Sessions was born in New York in 1896 and spent the ten years preceding World War II living in Europe. In an interview just before the Juilliard School's presentation of his opera, *Montezuma*, Sessions told me it was in Berlin that he met Schoenberg and Stravinsky, "the two best musicians I have ever known." When Sessions's ties to Schoenberg became obvious, he suffered the consequences. Milton Babbitt, who studied composition with Sessions in the late 1930s, told me his teacher was considered a "musical freak." Throughout his life, Sessions's aesthetic convictions remained intact. He never displayed even the most remote connection to other Americans of his generation such as George Gershwin, Henry Cowell, or the Aaron Copland of *Billy the Kid* and *El Salon Mexico*, this despite the fact that less than a decade before these famous Copland works, the two men led the Copland-Sessions Concerts in New York.

Born in Berlin in 1902, Stefan Wolpe studied with Webern in Vienna. With the rise of Nazism, he moved to Palestine and taught theory at the Jerusalem Conservatory. In 1938 Wolpe emigrated to the United States and attracted a large body of students, some of whom achieved great success. They admired him, most particularly, for the poetry he managed to infuse in the new, still unfamiliar language.

Elliott Carter, born in New York in 1908, claims his music stems from such eccentric Americans as Charles Ives and Carl Ruggles. It is true he never used 12-tone means, and that he derived a mode of continuity—he calls it metric modulation—that remains his own. But the total chromaticism pervading his music suggests he has absorbed Schoenberg's language. Now 94, Carter completed a 40-minute piece that the Berlin Opera will present in the fall of 1999. The composer chose the subject, and Paul Griffiths, a music critic for the *Times*, wrote the libretto. "What Next?" centers on a family that gets in an automobile accident on the way to a wedding, and the internecine battles that ensue. Carter says it was inspired by a Jacques Tati film; Griffiths adds that the accident is a metaphor for the breakdown in communication within this family. "What Next?" may, in its entirety, be a metaphor for the life in music Carter looks back on today.

Milton Babbitt, who appears frequently in this book, was born in Philadelphia in 1916. In 1932 he saw his first Schoenberg scores. Total commitment followed. Babbitt says that when he is on an airplane, and someone asks him who he is, he replies "Arnold Schoenberg." Nobody has ever expressed surprise. On November 15, 1998, James Levine and the Metropolitan Opera Orchestra presented Babbitt's new piano concerto (his second) in a magnificent performance at Carnegie Hall. The work exhibits the infinitely complex structure combined with a luminous texture that has always defined Babbitt's music.

Although he has been a musician from his youngest days, Leon Kirchner, born in Brooklyn in 1919, majored in zoology at Los Angeles City College. While there he heard Schoenberg's *Pierrot Lunaire,* and he says that this changed his life. Kirchner transferred to the University of California at Los Angeles, where Schoenberg was teaching. He told me that although Schoenberg made statements he did not then understand, later he often found himself saying, "So that is what he meant." At 80, still nourished by Schoenberg, Kirchner makes music that is lyrical and rhapsodic.

The youngest American in this group is Gunther Schuller, born in New York in 1925. At the start of his professional life, he played horn with the New York Philharmonic, principal horn with the Cincinnati Orchestra, and then became a member of the Metropolitan Opera Orchestra. Schuller's compositional language stems from Schoenberg but what separates him from other serious composers of his generation is his longtime fascination with jazz. Modern jazz pioneer Miles Davis was a close friend; Schuller played in one of his groups. Schuller's two-volume history of jazz was said to be the "definitive" work by *The New York Times*.

Schuller was not the first musician to combine the worlds of serious music and some aspect of the American vernacular. Stravinsky did it in the second decade of the century. In the 1920s and 1930s, George Gershwin infused jazz into his concert works. In 1939 John Hammond, a producer at Columbia Records, recorded classical pianist Walter Gieseking and the Budapest Quartet, as well as Benny Goodman, Count Basie and James P. Johnson.

In 1947 George Avakian became director of popular albums and the international division. At his own expense, Avakian recorded composers John Cage and Alan Hovhannes. He also produced Gunther Schuller's recording debut as composer and conductor. On one disk, Avakian included Dimitri Mitropoulos conducting Schuller's *Symphony for Brass and Percussion* with Schuller on horn, as well as Schuller's conducting modern jazz artists John Lewis, J.J. Johnson and Jimmy Giuffre.

In 1957 Schuller was among those who introduced "third-stream" music, a combination of classical forms with the improvisational elements of jazz. Because of this innovation, he may be the most obvious link to those younger composers whose tools are a mix of the chromaticism of Schoenberg and the chromaticism of post-1940s jazz.

Earlier I noted that the Juilliard School estimates that there are between 20,000 and 40,000 Americans who consider themselves composers of classical music. The enormity of that figure suggests a lot of people doing a lot of different things.

I spoke to one of them, Thomas Langner. Langner, 75, is a retired psychiatric epidemiologist who joined a computer seminar—the New York Macintosh Users Group—to learn how to use the Mac to compose music. The program he now uses, Finale, translates any note Langner types to any staff for any instrument. He types his notes onto the screen, then uses the keyboard to indicate their duration. Langner writes tonal music. He likes, he says, a long melodic line—but with enough dissonance to render it "almost 20th century." Composing is now the main focus of his life.

Considering the fact that many sophisticated people who are not music professionals are serious in their efforts to compose, and considering the factionalism that exists among the music professionals themselves, a comprehensive survey is not feasible for the purposes of *To Boulez and Beyond*. Therefore, at the risk of angering those who have rejected the path that I have described here, I decided to talk to two 35-year-old composers—Augusta Read Thomas and Anthony Cornicello—whom Wuorinen said deserved special attention in his *Gramophone* article. This may appear prejudiced and arbitrary to the reader but because it is Wuorinen whose remarks I chose as the frame for this book, I think it an appropriate selection.

Thomas has enjoyed remarkable recognition for a composer still under 40. In 1996 Boulez conducted her *Words of the Sea* with the Chicago Symphony; in 1997 the Boston Symphony, under Seiji Ozawa, played her *Chansons* for cello and orchestra, commissioned by Mstislav Rostropovich; in 1998 Boulez gave the world premiere of *Orbital Beacons,* again with the Chicago Symphony. *Aurora,* one of several works commissioned by the Berlin Philharmonic, will be performed in June 2000 with Daniel Barenboim as conductor and pianist.

Cornicello, with less powerful establishment recognition, has received many fellowships and awards and is currently writing a song cycle for Phyllis Bryn Julson. I talked with both him and Thomas, and learned their musical roots lie as firmly in Schoenberg's compositional grammar as do the roots of those older Americans described above. Thomas heard *Verklärte Nacht* at St. Paul's School in Concord, New Hampshire. It impressed her. Then she heard the same composer's post-1907 work and determined that this would be her path: "My favorite pieces were Schoenberg's solo piano works. I always loved math. I got 99 percent in every math class. It was natural for me to start thinking the way Schoenberg was thinking."

Cornicello heard Schoenberg's Opus 19 played by a classmate in his Long Island high school. "I thought," he told me, "'this is unbelievable.' I went over that score again and again. I knew 'this isn't tonal but it certainly makes sense.'"

Thomas identifies her other major influences as Debussy, early and late Stravinsky, and Pierre Boulez. She adds, "I'm not your average American: no Disneyland, no McDonald's, no pop." But she is quick to stress her profound connection to jazz: "What interests me is its immediacy. I played trumpet for fifteen years. My beliefs are informed by a lifetime playing jazz. In addition to its being vivid and passion-filled, jazz attracts me because of its chromaticism."

Cornicello, who studied composition with Wuorinen for three years, speaks of jazz's significance to him: "Dave Brubeck had a huge impact. My uncle studied with Lenny Tristano. I played piano in jazz groups all over Long Island. Bill Evans and Miles Davis interested me. They used extended harmonies similar to those of Alban Berg." (Jazz's influence is not limited to

Americans. Luca Francesconi, for example, now 43 years old, juggles jazz-like material with sounds reminiscent of Luciano Berio.)

Electronic technology appears not to play a major role in the thinking of either Thomas or Cornicello. It was I who brought the subject to their attention. "I have so much to learn even limiting myself to acoustic music," Thomas answered. "I love the violin, I love the cello, I love the clarinet." Cornicello attended a week-long seminar at Ircam during the summer of 1998 and said he was impressed with the technology of *Répons*. He added that what he himself likes most is having "a performer attached to a computer. That way the performer becomes really powerful."

As for father figures, Cornicello says, "Boulez was very influential. Wuorinen was a huge influence. But people are moving away from models. There is no towering giant out there."

When asked to characterize his own personal stamp, Cornicello commented that he never thinks about that: "What I want to create is 'character', whether it is a waltz or a concerto. It is the character of the piece that interests me."

In the post-World War II period, Boulez and his colleagues were able to look to a few father figures, such as Schoenberg, Webern, Stravinsky, and Varèse. There is no comparable group of leaders now from which young composers can take their aesthetic cues. Oddly it appears to be an abundance of music, not a deficiency, that lies behind this change. The sheer quantity of music being written today defies even the most ardent listener. While Sony Classical has cut back its commitment to new music, smaller companies have stepped in and the volume of commercial recordings has increased astonishingly, especially with the arrival of the compact disc.

At the end of the 1973 seminar devoted to establishing the principles of Ircam, Boulez said that the public should be taught that bringing science into art does not bring art into the realm of inhuman affairs, but provides composers with the tools they need. One fact is certain: in Boulez's view, science plays a central role in the future of music.

If, as the story in this book suggests, there are no titans in music today, we should ask what is happening in science, the other half of Boulez's Ircam equation.

John Horgan, in *The End of Science: Facing the Limits of Knowledge in the Twilight of the Scientific Age*, argued in 1996 that the best and most exciting discoveries are in the past, that the big truths about the universe and our place in it have been mapped out, and that "further research may yield no more great revelations or revolutions but only incremental diminishing returns." It is an old thesis that has emerged throughout history and perhaps before, but it may have some validity this time around.

Palestrina, Monteverdi, Bach, Mozart, Brahms, Wagner, and Schoenberg may be to music what gravity, the theory of relativity, quantum mechanics, the deciphering of the laws of heredity, and the structure of DNA are to science.

They are behind us.

There may be no more great men or new fundamental ideas. But inevitably there will be social and aesthetic consequences from what has been discovered in the twentieth century that are unimaginable today.

INDEX

Abbaye de Royaumont, 185, 186, 187
Academy of Music (Basel), 239
Actors Studio, 202
Adès, Thomas, *Powder Her Face*, xvi
Adler, Ellen, 202
Adler, Guido, 58
Adler, Oscar, 8–9
Adler, Stella, 202–203
Adorno, Theodor W., 19, 149, 188, 190, 326, 327, 334, 343
  The Philosophy of Modern Music, 333
Aeolian Hall, 126
Afanasiev, Aleksandr Nikolayevich, 87–88
Alice Tully Hall, 203, 290, 293, 331
Alshvang, Arnold, 102
American Academy of Arts and Letters, 53
American Ballet Company, 104
American Composers Alliance Bulletin, 229
American Mime Theater, 301
Amphion, 175, 202, 217
Amy, Gilbert, 335
Anda, Geza, 280
Anderson, Hans Christian, 77
Ansermet, Ernest, 66, 90, 91
Ansonia Hotel, 48
Antheil, George, 72–73
Argyll, Duchess of, 324
Arlow, Jacob, 232
Armand, Jean-Pierre, 348
Arnold Schoenberg Library of Modern Music, 39
Artaud, Antonin, 168, 194, 219
The Arts, 98
Asafiev, Boris, 101, 102
ASCAP, 51
Atonality. See Schoenberg, Arnold
Auden, W. H., 106, 107, 110
Auric, Georges, 155, 168, 215, 258

Austrian radio, 63
Avakian, George, *273*, 366
Avery Fisher Hall, 304, 330

Babbitt, Milton, xvi, 20, 112–113, 200–203, 206, 228, 269, 270, 314, 329, 344, 353, 364, 365
  Composition for Four Instruments, 201–202, 203
  Second Piano Concerto, 365
Bach, David Joseph, 11
Bach, J. S., 46, 98, 99, 112, 146, 160, 172, 185–186, 200, 240, 248–249, 283, 284, 324, 342, 369
  Art of the Fugue, 43, 93, 165, 181
  B Minor Mass, 298
  Chorale Preludes, 298
  E-flat Major Organ Prelude and Fugue, 43
  Missae Parodiae, 91
  Musical Offering, 213
  St. Matthew Passion, 298
Bain, Wilfred, 303
Baker, Julius, 301–302
Bakst, Léon, 80, 90
Balakirev, Mili, 70
Balanchine, George, 80, 104, 114
Ballet Russe, 29, 80, 81, 82, 84, 89, 90, 92, 93, 174
Barber, Samuel, 335
Barenboim, Daniel, 312, 331, 362, 367
Barnum and Bailey, 67, 105
Barraqué, Jean, 214
Barrault, Jean-Louis, 155, 168–169, 170, 177, 178, 180, 191, 192, 193, 203, 212, 213, 214, 218, 230–231, 258
Barrault, Madeleine, 168, 169, 213, 214, 218

Bartók, Béla, 52, 77, 100, 105, 112, 140, *142*, 189, 198, 213, 214, 256, 290, 304, 336
  Bluebeard's Castle, 357
  Concerto for Orchestra, 142
  Miraculous Mandarin, 239, 256, 293, 305
  Music for Strings, Percussion and Celesta, 230
Barzin, Leon, 319
Basie, Count, 366
Bastille Opera, 350, 362
Baudelaire, Charles, 75, 247
Bauhaus, 46–47, 179, 280, 344–345
Bayle, Laurent, 361
Bayreuth Festival, 118, 283, 326, 354
BBC. *See* Boulez, Pierre, and BBC
The Beatles, *Sgt. Pepper*, 323
Becker, Wolfgang, 255, 257
Beckett, Samuel, 219
Beecham, Sir Thomas, 287
Beethoven, Ludwig van, 2–3, 7, 10, 11, 20, 46, 65, 74, 76, 100, 148, 169, 240, 291, 293, 298, 305, 306, 321, 331, 334
  Eroica, 257
  Fifth Symphony, 305, 320, 334
  Ninth Symphony, 3, 226, 305
  Seventh Symphony, 305
  String Quartet in F Major, Opus 135, 2
  Third Symphony, 320
Béjart, Maurice, 281–282
Bekker, Paul, 94
Belgian Radio, 237
Bell Telephone Laboratories, 127, 348, 355
Bennett, Gerald, 348

Bennett, Richard Rodney, 217, 241, 251, 280
Benois, Alexander, 80, 82, 90
Berenson, Bernard, *The Passionate Sightseer*, 1
Berg, Alban, xvi, 3, 17, 19, 35, 36, 39, 56, 61, 67, 104, 107, 124, *134*, 135, 149, 167, 179, 214, 217, 280, 286, 293, 295, 299, 304, 320, 356, 358, 367
    Altenberg Lieder, 263, 291
    Chamber Concerto, 124
    Lulu, 281, 320, 354
    Lyric Suite, 214
    Seven Early Songs, 291
    Three Pieces for Orchestra Opus 6, 214, 286, 291, 311
    Wozzeck, 42, 134, 182, 238, 247, 258, 263, 281, 338, 354
Bergé, Pierre, 362
Berger, Arthur, 103, 194, 200, 335
Berio, Luciano, 213–214, 217, 224, 225–226, 258, 275, 304, 348, 350, 353, 356
    Alleluiah, 238
    Cronaca del Luogo, 275
    Outis, 275
Berlin Academy, 121
Berlin Opera, 365
Berlin Philharmonic, 41, 43, 139, 259, 356, 367
Berlioz, Hector, 19, 153, 229, 304, 318, 331
    Beatrice and Benedict, 290, 291, 294
    Requiem, 123
    Symphonie Fantastique, 298
    The Trojans, 299
Bernstein, Elmer, 143
Bernstein, Felicia, 300, 312
Bernstein, Leonard, 103, 146–147, 275, 286, 294, 296, 300, 309, 310, 312, 314, 315, 341, 354
    Mass, 312
Bernstein, Martin, 48–49
Bever, Thomas G., 334–335
Biazini, E. J., 262
Bizet, Georges, 75
    Carmen, 205
Blaue Reiter, 21
Bliss, Robert, 104
Blitzstein, Marc, 42, 50, 56, 103, 199–200

Bloch, Ernest, 48
Bloomingdale's, 321
Bodansky, Artur, 292
Boelke-Bomart, 202
Boelke, Walter, 202
Bohm, Adolf, 80
Bolzoni, Giovanni, 119
Bond, Edward, 355
Book of Changes, 183
Boosey & Hawkes, 106
Bordeaux Opera, 350
Born, Georgina, *Realizing Culture: Ircam, Boulez, and the Institutionalization of the Musical Avant Garde*, 360–361
Borodin, Alexander, 70, 73, 74
Boston Symphony Orchestra, 142, 199, 283, 286, 367
Bouillon de Culture, 359
Boulanger, Nadia, 52, 99, 103, 106–107, 126, 155, 157, 204, 214–215, 283
Boulez, Jeanne. *See* Chevalier, Jeanne Boulez
Boulez, Léon, 150, 151, 152, 153, 154, 158, 234, 257, 289, 326–327, 362
Boulez, Marcelle, 150, 153, 234, 257
Boulez, Pierre, xvii, 56–57, 62, 63, 135, 146–147, 148–154, 155–162, 163–171, 172–176, 177–184, 185–190, 191–197, 198–203, 204–209, 210–215, 216–223, 224–233, 234–240, 241–247, 248–255, 256–263, 264, 265, 274, 275, 277, 278, 279, 280–289, 290–297, 298–303, 304–310, 311–317, 318–325, 326–332, 333–336, 337–342, 343–348, 349–362, 364, 367, 368
    and BBC, 259, 263, 280, 282, 287, 289, 298–299, 305, 320, 323, 331, 346, 354, 358, 361
    birth of, 150
    as Carnegie Hall's chair in composition, 362
    and Cité de la Musique, 361–362, 362
    and Cleveland Orchestra, 249–250, 256, 262–263, 280, 293, 295, 305, 326, 331, 337, 356, 362

    and Domaine Musical, 213–215, 218, 221–222, 223, 224, 225, 229, 230, 231, 238, 257, 258, 260, 262, 284, 335
    early conducting by, 230–232, 238–239, 240, 241, 251, 252–253, 256–259, 262–263
    family of, 149, 150–152, 153, 154, 158, 234, 257, 281, 289, 315, 326–327, 343
    homes of, 280–281, 321, 362
    as Horatio Appleton Lamb Lecturer, 247
    interviews with, in *Par volonté et par hasard* (Celestin Deliege), 207
    and Ircam, 277, 322, 337–338, 343–345, 347–348, 349, 350, 352, 354, 356, 359, 360–361, 362, 368
    and Los Angeles Philharmonic, 231, 251, 362
    and New York Philharmonic, 146, 228, 259, 263, 280, 283, 286–289, 290–297, 298, 299–300, 301, 302, 303, 304–310, 311–317, 318–321, 323, 327, 329, 330–332, 337, 339–341, 346, 354, 361, 362
    and Prospective Encounters, 300–303, 313–315, 318
    and Rug Concerts, 304, 318, 331–332, 345
    sexual affair of, 160, 228
    solitude of, 146, 222, 228, 283, 292, 300, 341, 346
    works of
        "Alea," 227
        ". . . Auprès et au loin," 207
        Boulez Conducts Boulez, 357
        Boulez on Music Today, 241
        Cummings ist der Dichter, 323, 325, 353
        Deux Études, 180, 187, 194
        Dialogue de l'ombre double, 351, 353
        Domaines, 323, 353

Doubles for Orchestra, 249
Éclat, 251–253, 263, 298, 323
"Eventuellement," 182–183, 184
explosante-fixe, 315–316, 323, 324, 353, 357
Figures, Doubles, Prisms, 249–250, 263
First Piano Sonata, 161–162, 165, 170, 175, 202, 209, 306, 359
Improvisations I, 251, 353
Improvisations II, 251
Le Marteau sans Maître, 207–208, 209, 211, 218, 219, 228, 229, 230, 231, 233, 238, 251, 258, 260, 292, 295, 305
Le Soleil des Eaux, 164–165, 166, 175, 186, 209
Le Visage Nuptial, 161, 175, 179, 209, 216, 231, 353
Livre pour Cordes, 305
Livre pour Quatuor, 166, 175
Memoriales, 323
Multiples, 323
Notations, 349, 357
Orestes, 169, 218
Oublie Lapide, 159
Pli Selon Pli, 219, 235–238, 249, 260, 305
Poésies pour Pouvoir, 232, 234, 250, 324
Polyphonie X, 179, 180, 186, 191, 204, 208, 209, 218, 228
"Recherches Maintenant," 220–221
Répons, 277, 350–352, 357, 359, 368
Second Piano Sonata, 165–166, 168, 175, 177–178, 180, 181, 186, 191, 195, 209, 212–213, 224, 306
Sonatina for Flute and Piano, 161, 175, 185, 209, 217, 224

Structures, 181–182, 183–184, 187, 190, 191, 192–193, 194, 201, 204, 206, 208, 209, 217, 228, 250
Structures, Book II, 250, 251, 357
Third Piano Sonata, 225, 226–227, 229, 235, 242–245, 246, 250, 306
Trois Psalmodies, 159
Boulez, Pierre (original), 151
Boulez, Roger, 151
Bradshaw, Susan, 239–240, 241, 242, 251
Brahms, Johannes, xvii, 1, 2, 3, 7, 11, 12, 17, 46, 59, 111, 149, 160, 169, 188, 194, 293, 331, 369
A Major Serenade, 312
Brant, Henry, 229, 364
Braque, Georges, 80
Brecht, Bertolt, Three Penny Opera, 44
Breton, André, Nadja, 324
British Museum, 92
Britten, Benjamin, 282
Brooklyn Philharmonic, 313
Brubeck, Dave, 367
Bruckner, Anton, 2, 11, 16
Eighth Symphony, 357
Symphony No. 1, 321
Brustein, Robert, 307
Bryanston Summer School, 258
Budapest Quartet, 366
Buffalo Philharmonic, 313
Busoni, Ferruccio, 41, 93–94, 130
Fantasia Contrapuntistica, 93
Sketch of a New Aesthetic of Music, 121, 130
Butor, Michel, 327
Buxtehude, Dietrich, 299
Byron, George Gordon, Lord, 19, 51

Café Griensteidl, 11
Café Landtmann, 11
Cage, John, 115, 140, 171, 172–176, 177, 178–179, 180, 182, 183, 188, 191, 192, 193–194, 195–197, 200, 201–202, 203, 206, 210–211, 212, 214, 218, 221, 222, 223, 227, 228, 232–233, 234–235, 254–255, 264, 265, 266, 307, 323, 328, 329, 335, 342, 356, 364, 366

Concerto for Prepared Piano and Chamber Orchestra, 183
Imaginary Landscape No. 4, 210
Magic Square, 183
Music of Changes, 183–184, 193, 195, 210, 211, 223, 254
piano of, 266
Silence, 197
Sixteen Dances, 183
Sonatas and Interludes, 174, 175–176, 196, 201, 264, 265
Theater Piece 1960, 254
31' 57", 222
Cage, Xenia Kashevaroff, 173
California Institute of the Arts, 355–356
Carl Fischer Hall, 191, 194, 222
Carnegie Hall, 105, 128, 174, 263, 278, 358, 362, 365
Carpentier, Alejo, 230
Carter, Elliott, 258, 282, 304, 313, 319, 321, 329, 350, 353, 356, 365
Concerto for Orchestra, 313
"What Next?," 365
Casella, Alfredo, 5, 39, 43, 96, 124
Casino de Paris, 85
Catherine II, Empress of Russia, 69
Cavett, Dick, 307–308, 319
CBS-UK, 305
Centre Pompidou, 347, 349
Cézanne, Paul, 167
Chabrier, Emmanuel, 75
Chaliapin, Feodor Ivanovich, 80, 153
Chamber Art Society, 107
Chamber Music Society, 290, 293, 315, 316
Chambers, Jimmy, 311
Char, René, 160–161, 164, 207, 208, 219, 237, 339, 356
Charpentier, Gustave, 120
Chausson, Ernest, 120
Chautauqua, 48
Chávez, Carlos, 124
Toward a New Music, 172
Chelsea Hotel, 205
Chereau, Patrice, 354
Cherry Lane Theater, 195, 197
Chevalier, Jack, 257
Chevalier, Jeanne Boulez, 151, 152, 153, 216, 289, 343
Chiarello, Robert J., 334–335

Chicago Art Institute, 106
Chicago Symphony Orchestra, 104, 279, 321, 356, 357, 362, 367
Chirac, Jacques, 350
Chomsky, Noam, 344
Chopin, Frédéric, 77, 152, 247, 331
    Nocturne in A-flat, 77
    Valse Brillante in E-flat, 77
Choralionsaal, 122
Chowning, John, 356
Christian Science Monitor, 123–124, 125, 126
Cimarosa, Domenico, *Astuzie Femminili*, 92
Cincinnati Orchestra, 365
Cité de la Musique, 361, 362
Clarke, Edward, 26
Clementi, Muzio, 98
Clements, Andrew, 354, 355
Cleveland Orchestra, 356
    and Boulez. *See* Boulez, Pierre, and Cleveland Orchestra
Cocteau, Jean, 92, 98, 100, 109
Coleridge, Samuel Taylor, 107
Cologne Radio, 50–51, 229, 232, 253, 255
Columbia-Princeton Electronic Music Center, 270, 301, 303
Columbia Records, 259, 273, 294, 295, 300, 302, 305–306, 319
Columbia University, xvi, 174, 194, 211, 270, 301, 303, 313, 334
Comédie Française, 168
Composers Conferences, 272, 313, 329
Composer's Forum, 194
Concertgebouw Orchestra, 239, 259, 262
Contrepoint, 162, 185–186
Coolidge, Elizabeth Sprague, 43, 100
Copland, Aaron, 99, 100, 103, *141*, 194, 199, 200, 309, 314, 335, 364
    Billy the Kid, 364
    El Salon Mexico, 364
    Piano Fantasy, 141
Copland-Sessions Concerts, 364
Cornicello, Anthony, 367–368
Covent Garden, 280, 354
Cowell, Henry, 42, 51, 52, 127, *140*, 172, 173, 175, 194, 199, 335, 364
    New Musical Resources, 172
    The Theory of Rhythm, 172

Craft, Robert, 17, 59, 67, 69, 84, 96, 97, 107–108, 111, 113, 114, 204, 206, 227–228, 231, 238, 251, 260–261, *271*, 305, 340
    Bravo Stravinsky, 115
    Expositions and Developments, 78
Creston, Paul, 335
Crumb, George, 304, 319
Cui, César, 70
Cummings, E. E., 285, 323, 325, 353, 356
Cunningham, Merce, 175, 176

Daily Mail, 108
Dalbavie, Marc-André, 356
Dandelot, Georges, 157
Dansk Aarbog for Musikforskning, 37
Dargomizhsky, Aleksandr, 73
Darmstadt, 163, 189–190, 208, 216–217, 223, 224, 225, 234, 235, 241, 247, 248, 249, 254, 347
Dartington Summer School, 258
Darwin, Charles, 151, 201
Das neue Werke, 238
Davidovsky, Mario, 272, 301, 302, 314, 329
    Synchronisms, 300–301, 302, 303
Davis, Colin, 263
Davis, Miles, 366, 367
de Bonaventura, Mario, 353
Debussy, Claude, 22, 36, 76, 78–79, 80, 81, 87, 90, 96, 118–119, 120, 121, 148, 149, 153, 158, 160, 179, 194, 213, 225, 230, 240, 251, 256, 281, 285–286, 304, 331, 356, 367
    Ibéria, 230, 341
    Images, 263
    Jeux, 29, 230, 286
    La Cathédrale Engloutie, 119
    La Mer, 304, 321, 358
    Pelléas et Mélisande, 14, 78, 79, 118, 120, 280, 354
    Prelude to the Afternoon of a Faun, 299
    Printemps, 290
    3 Nocturnes, 290
de Chirico, Giorgio, 80
Decoust, Michel, 348
de Falla, Manuel, 80
Degas, Edgar, 65
de Gaulle, Charles, 281, 282

de Giugno, Giuseppi, 350
Dehmel, Richard, 12, 30
    Zwei Menschen, 12–13
de Koos, Michael, 259
Delapierre, Guy Bernard, 158
Delibes, Léo
    Coppélia, 75
    Lakmé, 75
de Pulszka, Romola, 90
de Polignac, Marie Blanche, 155, 214–215
Der Spiegel, 281
Descartes, René, 177
de Schloetzer, Boris, 65
Desormière, Roger, 170, 186, 212, 218, 219, 239
de Stael, Nicolas, 171
Deutsch, Max, 178, 217
Deutsche Grammophon (DG), 351, 353, 357, 358, 361
Diaghilev, Serge, 66, 70–71, 77–78, 79, 80–83, 90, 91, 98, 101, 102, 107, 228
    Astuzie Femminili, 92
    The Firebird, 77–78, 80–81, 82, 83
    The Good-Humored Ladies, 92, 93
    Les Noces, 98
    Les Sylphides, 77
    Petrushka, 80, 81–83
    Pulcinella, 66, 92–93
    The Rite of Spring, 80, 83–85, 93
    The Sleeping Beauty, 96
Diaghilev Ballet. *See* Ballet Russe
Diamond, David, 51, 199, 200, 315, 335
    Elegy in Memory of Maurice Ravel, 315
    Sixth Symphony, 315
Dick Cavett Show, 307–308, 319
Diderot, Denis, 317
Die Musikblätter des Anbruch, 7, 213
Die Reihe, 57, 205–206, 213, 225, 233, 284
d'Indy, Vincent, 119, 120
Domaine Musical. *See* Boulez, Pierre, and Domaine Musical
The Domaine Musical, 213
The Dominant, 99
Donaueschingen Festival, 113, 180, 204, 211, 232, 234, 238–239, 250, 336, 351, 352
Dos Passos, John, 285
Downes, Olin, 126

Drieu la Rochelle, Pierre, 170–171
Druckman, Jacob, 319
Dubuffet, Jean, 171
Duchamp, Marcel, 174
Dufay, Guillaume, 213
Dufy, Raoul, 113
Dugardin, Hervé, 162, 175
Dukas, Paul, 101, 120
Dushkin, Samuel, 102
Duteurtre, Benoit, 360
    Requiem for the Avant-Garde, 359

Eastman School of Music, 103–104
École Normale, 103
Édition Russe de Musique, 106
Editions du Seuil, 247
Eimert, Herbert, 211, 212, 222, 253
Einstein, Albert, 50, 118, 154, 213
Eisler, Hanns, 5, 43–44
Electronic music. *See* Varèse, Edgard
Elgar, Sir Edward, 331
Eliot, T. S., 92, 114
Eloy, Jean-Claude, 350
E.M.I., 259
Encounters. *See* Prospective Encounters
Encyclopédie de la Musique, 247
Ensemble InterContemporain, 350, 354, 357, 361, 362
Ericson, Raymond, 321
Erikson, Erik, 154
Essex House, 288
Evans, Bill, 367

Fall, Leo, 13
Fano, Guido Alberto, 213
Fasquelle, 247
Faulkner, William, 192, 285
Faurisson, Robert, 359
Feldman, Morton, 143, 183, 198, 202, 254, 328, 329
    Intersection III, 195, 211
Fels, Comtesse de, 262
Festival Hall, 259, 305, 331
Fine, Irving, 103, 200, 335
Fischinger, Oscar, 173
Fletcher, Harvey, 127
Fokine, Michel, 80, 82
Folies Bergère, 158, 170, 281
Fontainebleau, 99
Foss, Lukas, 313–314
Fowlie, Wallace, 235–236
Francesconi, Luca, 368
Frankel, Carol, 290, 321, 325
Frankel, Robert, 290, 321

French Radio, 214, 218
Freud, Sigmund, 10, 53–54, 150
    The Interpretation of Dreams, 232
Frey, Leonard, 307
Fried, Oscar, 26
Froidebise, Pierre, 185, 186
Furstenberg, Prince Max Egon zu, 113
Furtwängler, Wilhelm, 41, 43

Gabrieli, Giovanni, 229
Gatti, Armand, 175
Gazzelloni, Severino, 224
Gelb, Peter, 353
Genet, Jean, 219, 355
George, Stefan, 18
    Das Buch der hängenden Gärten, 20
Gerhard, Roberto, 42
German Radio, 199, 253
Gershwin, George, 48, 51, 198, 364, 366
Gerstl, Richard, 19–20, 38
Gerzso, Andrew, 277, 351
Gesualdo, Carlo, 213
Giacometti, Alberto, 281
Gide, André, 170
    Hamlet (translation), 168
    "Hymn to Demeter," 101
Gielen, Michael, 320
Gieseking, Walter, 366
Gilbert and Sullivan, 13
Gimbel, Adam, 124
The Ginger Man, 294
Giraud, Albert, 27
Giscard d'Estaing, Valéry, 350, 361
Giuffre, Jimmy, *273*, 366
Glancy, Ken, 305, 321
Glanville-Hicks, Peggy, 195
Glass, Philip, xvi
Glazounov, Aleksandr Konstantinovich, 74, 76, 77
Glinka, Mikhail Ivanovich, 68, 69, 73, 96
    A Life for the Tsar, 69, 74
    Russlan and Ludmilla, 68
Globokar, Vinko, 304, 345, 348
Glock, Sir William, 215, 258, 259, 263, 282, 288–289, 291, 298–299, 323, 331, 358
Gluck, Christoph Willibald, 3
Goehr, Rudolph, 42
Goehr, Walter, 42, *133*
Goethe, Johann Wolfgang von, 19, 60
Goeyvaerts, Karel, 190
    Sonata for Two Pianos, 190

Golea, Antoine, *Recontres avec Pierre Boulez*, 261
Goncharova, Natalia, 80
Goodman, Benny, 366
Goossens, Eugene, 125
Gounod, Charles, 75
Gramophone, 357–359, 363, 367
Gramophone Explorations 4, 363
Greene, Amy, 312
Greenwich Village Theater, 124
Greissle, Felix, 10
Grieg, Edvard, 69
    Peer Gynt, 354
Griffiths, Paul, 365
Gris, Juan, 80
Gronostay, Walter, 42
Group Recherche de la Radiodiffusion Française, 180
Gruen, John, "The Art of the Live Interview," 308–310
G. Schirmer. *See* Schirmer
Guggenheim Foundation, 51–52, 128, 174, 199

The Hague Orchestra, 263
Haieff, Alexei, 335
Haller, Peter, 315–316
Hamburg Opera, 261, 281
Hammond, John, 366
Handel, George Frederick, 241
    Water Music, 341
Hannenheim, Norbert von, 42
Hanslick, Eduard, 2
Hanson, Howard, 335
Harris, Roy, 335
Harrison, Lou, 51, 173–174
Harrod's, 321
Hartog, Howard, 259–260, 305, 308
Harvard, 79, 86, 103, 104, 108, 170, 241, 247, 251, 275, 287, 344
Hauer, Josef, 32–35, 36, 37, 60, 95, 190, 201, 241
Hauser, Arnold, 8
Haydn, Franz Josef, 10, 74, 98, 105, 281, 304, 318, 320
    Harmonie, 320
    L'Incontro Improviso, 320
    Theresien, 320
Heisenberg, Werner, 344
Helffer, Claude, 246
Heller, Hugo, 21
Helmholtz, Hermann, *Physiology of Sounds*, 120
Henri Bendel, 312
Henry, Pierre, 194
Henze, Hans Werner, 235, 267, 281, 285, 314

We Come to the River, 355
Herman, Woody, 105, *138*
Hertzka, Emil, 21
Heugel, Phillippe, 175, 217
Heyworth, Peter, 348
Hindemith, Paul, 40, 43, 44, 48, 52, 100, *139*, 163, 179, 217, 327
    Concerto for Orchestra, 238
    Neues vom Tage, 44
Hitler, Adolf, 63, 156, 198
Hodeir, Andre, 194
Hoffman, E. T. A., 219
Hofmannsthal, Hugo von, 12, 121
Hogarth, William, *The Rake's Progress*, 106
Holland, Bernard, 357, 358, 362
Holliger, Heinz, 324
Holmes, Mrs. Christian, 124
Honegger, Arthur, 124, 155, 157, 159, 168, 169, 200
Honegger, Mme, 168
Horenstein, Jascha, 182
Horgan, John, *The End of Science: Facing the Limits of Knowledge in the Scientific Age*, 368–369
Houston Opera, 351
Hovhaness, Alan, 335, 366
Howard, Richard, 302–303
Huizinga, Johan, *The Waning of the Middle Ages*, 336
Hunter College, 284
Hurok Attractions, 282, 283, 306
Huxley, Aldous, 106, 114

I Ching, 183
Imperial Opera, 68, 73
Indiana University's School of Music, 303
Informal Evenings, 318
Ingpen and Williams, 259
Institut de France, 101
Institut de Recherche et de Coordination Acoustique/Musique. *See* Boulez, Pierre, and Ircam
Institut Victor de la Prade, 151
International Composers Guild, 124, 126–127, 364
International Institute, 179
International Musicians Club, 258
International Society for Contemporary Music, 41, 98, 112, 186, 218
Invalides, 281

Ircam, Boulez and. *See* Boulez, Pierre, and Ircam
Isaac, Heinrich, *Choralis Constantinus*, 58
ISCM Festival, 112
Israel Festival Committee, 114
Ives, Charles, 127, 198, 199, 330–331, 365
    Fourth Symphony, 330–331
Ives Mini-Festival, 330–331

Jackson, John Hulings, 334
Jacobs, Paul, 214, 225, 228, 301
Jacobsen, Jens Peter, 13
Jalowitz, Heinrich, 17, 51
James, Henry, 198
Janácek, Leos, xvi
Jane Eyre, 105
Jerusalem Conservatory, 364
Joffroy, Pierre, 175, 178
Johnson, Harriet, 340–341
Johnson, James P., 366
Johnson, J. J., *273*, 366
Joio, Dello, 335
Jolivet, André, 262
Jorgenson, 81
Josquin des Prez, *Missa l'homme armé*, 113
Joyce, James, 92, 155, 157, 192, 219, 220
    Finnegans Wake, 192, 193
    Ulysses, 192
Juilliard School, xvii, 48, 49, 166, 199, 287, 292, 295, 312, 313, 319, 364, 366
Julson, Phyllis Bryn, 367

Kafka, Franz, 155
Kalafaty, Vassily, 74, 75
Kallman, Chester, 106
Kandinsky, Wassily, 20, 21–22, 46, 47, 155, 192, 219, 239, 356
    On the Spiritual in Art, 22
Kant, Immanuel, 120
Karajan, Herbert von, 287, 354
Karsavina, Tamara, 80, 81, 82
Kazdin, Andrew, 294
Keiser, David, 287–288, 299, 333
Keisler, Frederick, 191
Keisler, Lillian, 191
Keller, Hans, 7, 108
Kennedy, John F., 114, 286
Kirchner, Leon, 203, 274, 365
    String Quartet No. 3, 274
Kireievsky, Ivan, 87–88
Kirstein, Lincoln, 104
Klee, Paul, 92, 155, 157, 166, 179, 182, 219, 239, 280, 281, 324, 356

Kleger, David, 306–307, 310
Kleiber, Erich, 42
Klemperer, Otto, 49, 205
Kokoschka, Oskar, 20
Kolisch, Rudolf, 38, 52, 63, 156
Kolisch Quartet, 43
Kol Israel Orchestra, 313
Koussevitsky, Natalie, 83
Koussevitzky, Serge, 83, 98, 100, 142, 146, 199
Krasner, Leopold, 50
Krenek, Ernst, 9, 44, 51, 56
    Jonny Spielt Auf, 44

La Crêpe, 294, 295
Laderman, Ezra, 143
Lalo, Édouard, 120
Lamoureux, 259
Landowski, Marcel, 262
Lang, Jack, 359
Langner, Thomas, 366
Lanner, Joseph
    Opus 200, 82
    Tanze, Opus 165, 82
    La Nouvelle Revue Française, 162, 170, 220–221, 227
    La Revue Musicale, 98, 109, 182, 185, 197
Larionov, Mikhail, 80
Lautner, Lois, 56
Leacock, Richard, 109, 261
League of Composers, 99, 126, 191, 199, 364
Le Figaro, 85, 127, 257
Lehar, Franz, 13
Le Hune, 192
Leibniz, Gottfried Wilhelm von, 201
Leibowitz, René, 12, 51, 156–157, 159, 160, 161, 162, 163, 167, 168, 185, 186, 187–188, 189, 202–203, 216, 217, 232, 258, 359
    L'Artiste et sa Conscience, 157
    Schoenberg et Son École, 163
Leichentritt, Hugo, 25
Le Matin, 350
Le Monde, 350, 359, 360
Le Nouvel Observateur, 262
Leonin, 119
Le Poulailler, 296, 300, 312
Les Cahiers Canadiens de Musique, 337–340
Les Concerts du Petit-Marigny, 214
Levant, Oscar, 49
Levine, James, 365

Lévi-Strauss, Claude, 245–246
Lewis, John, 273, 366
Liadov, Anatol, 77
Library of Congress, 51
Liebermann, Rolf, 261, 281
Lieberson, Goddard, 300
Lieberson, Peter, 314, 319
Liège Conservatoire, 185
Lifar, Serge, 80
Life, 300, 333
Ligeti, Gyorgi, 356
Liliencron, Detlov von, 12
Lincoln Center, 199, 287, 290, 313, 315
Lincoln Center Library, 313
Lindsay, John, 300
Listen, 202
The Listener, 31–32
List, Kurt, 51, 202, 203
Liszt, Franz, 91, 298, 299, 311, 331
Totentanz, 299
Liszt Foundation, 14
London Symphony, 259, 305, 362
Look, 307
Lopokouva, Lydia, 80
Loriod, Yvonne, 230, 250
Los Angeles City College, 365
Los Angeles Philharmonic, 49, 231, 251, 362
Lully, Jean-Baptiste, 349–350
Lyon Conservatoire, 153
Lyon Opera, 350

Maazel, Lorin, 331
Macaulay, Thomas Babington, *History of England*, xvi
Machaut, Guillaume de, 210, 213
Machover, Tod, 277, 350–351, 356, 359, 361
Resurrection, 351
Maderna, Bruno, 213, 223, 231–232
Maegaard, Jan, 37, 39
Maeterlinck, Maurice, 26
Pelléas et Mélisande, 14
Mahler (Werfel), Alma, 7, 16, 19, 23, 51
Mahler, Gustav, 7, 10, 13, 15–16, 17, 18, 19, 22–23, 26, 35, 36, 46, 59, 61, 63, 131, 149, 160, 166, 263, 299, 305, 306, 321, 357–358
Das Lied von der Erde, 357
Fifth Symphony, 17, 358, 362
First Symphony, 17, 18, 321
Fourth Symphony, 17, 357

F-sharp Minor Quartet, 18
Kindertotenlieder, 16
Ninth Symphony, 357
Seventh Symphony, 357
Sixth Symphony, 13, 357
Three Orchestral Pieces, Opus 6, 358
Malipiero, G. F., 39
Malkin Conservatory of Music, 48
Mallarmé, Stephane, 62, 65, 157, 219–221, 251, 322, 323, 338, 353, 356
Le Livre, 220, 226, 227, 251, 322, 323
poems of, in *Pli Selon Pli*, 235–237
Un coup de dés jamais n'abolira le hasard, 219, 220, 227
Malraux, André, 170, 262, 263, 308
Mann, Thomas, 7, 51
Manoury, Phillippe, 356
Marcel, Gabriel
Le Monde Cassé, 329–330
"The Mystery of Being," 330
Marcello, Benedetto, 91
Marger, Brigitte, 344
Marinetti, Filippo Tommaso, 82
Maryinsky Theater, 74
Massenet, Jules, 121
Massine, Léonide, 80, 93
Matthews, Max, 348, 356
Max Planck Institute of Music, 322–323, 344, 349
Max Planck Society, 322
McCann, Chuck, 307
McMillin Theater, 194
Mehta, Zubin, 288, 331
Melos, 41, 179, 326
Mendelssohn, Felix, 305, 331
Piano Concerto, 74
Reformation Symphony, 320–321
Mennin, Peter, 313, 319, 335
Mercenier, Marcelle, 221
Messiaen, Olivier, 146, 155, 157–158, 159–160, 164, 175, 180–181, 182, 190, 194, 204, 211, 213, 216, 219, 235, 240, 264, 304, 330, 353, 356
Mode de Valeurs et d'Intensités, 181, 182, 190, 201
Oiseaux Exotiques, 291
Quartet for the End of Time, 304

Quatre Études de Rythme, 181
Variations for Violin and Piano, 157–158
Metropolitan Opera, 90, 99, 104, 205, 365
Michaux, Henri, 219, 237, 339
Poésies pour Pouvoir, 232
Michel, Michel Georges, 98
Michigan Quarterly Review, 56
Mies van der Rohe, Ludwig, 280
Mihalovici, Marcel, 179
Milburn, Frank, 304, 307, 308, 320
Milhaud, Darius, 44, 51, 80, 124, 155, 168, 190
Miller, Robert, 302
Mini-Festivals, 318, 330–331
Mir Isskustva, 80
Miró, Joan, 281
MIT, 355
Mitropoulos, Dimitri, 199, 273, 341, 366
Mitterand, François, 350, 362
Mitusov, Stepan, 77
Modern Music, 51, 56, 65, 66, 100, 126–127
Modern Music Concerts, 199
Moldenhauer, Hans, 61, 63
Monday Evening Concerts, 231, 251, 336
Mondrian, Piet, 155, 167, 219
Monteux, Pierre, 82, 85, 86, 137, 156
Monteverdi, Claudio, 369
The Moon Is Down, 105
Moore, Carman, 319
Morel, Jean, 205
Morton, Lawrence, 231, 251, 256, 259, 261, 280, 328, 336
Moseley, Carlos, 263, 288, 289, 300, 307, 308, 312, 315, 318–319, 320, 330, 333
Moses, 154
Moussorgsky, Modest, 70, 73, 80
Boris Godunov, 80, 152, 153, 354
Mozart, Wolfgang Amadeus, xvii, 3, 10, 46, 74, 90, 98, 105, 118, 180, 185, 200, 240, 291, 293, 299, 304, 331, 346, 369
Cosi fan Tutte, 106
Muck, Karl, 121
Müller, Heiner, 355

Musical Advance, 125
Musical America, 91, 201
Musical Courier, 128
The Musical Quarterly, 51, 126

Nabokov, Nicolas, 170
Nachod, Hans, 10
Naples Conservatory, 92
Napoleon, 10, 323
National Institute of Arts and Letters, 174
The Nationalist Five, 70, 74, 96
National Music, 45–46
NBC, 114, 310
Neoclassicism. *See* Stravinsky, Igor
The Netherlands Opera, 354–355
New and Newer Music, 290, 291–292, 295
New Image of Sound, 284
Newlin, Dika, 15
Newman, Arnold, *Bravo Stravinsky*, 115
New Music Editions, 175, 201
New Music Quartet, 202
New Music Society, 198
New Philharmonia, 259
New School, 194, 308
Newsweek, 68, 149, 291, 300, 312, 333
New Symphony Orchestra, 123, 292
Newton, Isaac, 154, 201
New York, xvii, 291
New York City Ballet, 113
The New Yorker, 312, 354
New York Herald Tribune, 88, 125, 126, 170, 194, 195, 197, 200
New York Macintosh Users Group, 366
New York Philharmonic, 198
and Boulez. *See* Boulez, Pierre, and New York Philharmonic
New York Post, 340–341
The New York Review of Books, 115, 227–228, 261
New York Shakespeare Festival, 300
The New York Times, 126, 149, 191, 194, 195, 274, 282–286, 289, 292–297, 299, 304, 307, 312, 321, 341, 349, 350, 354, 355, 357, 362, 363–364, 365, 366

New York University, 48–49, 200
Nietzsche, Friedrich, 1
Nijinska, Bronislawa, 80
Nijinsky, Vaslav, 80, 82, 84–85, 90, 95, 137
Nixon, Richard, 308
Nonesuch Records, 302
Nono, Luigi, 213, 214, 223, 258
  Canti di vita e d'amore, 320
  Polyphonie, 258
Novembergruppe, 41

Oak Ridge, 127
The Observer (London), 66, 92, 116
Offenbach, Jacques, *Tales of Hoffman*, 75, 168
Ojai Festival, 328, 362
Opera, 354, 355
Opéra-Comique, 281–282
Oppenheimer, Robert, 344
Orchestre de Paris, 262, 356
Orchestre National, 257, 259, 262
Ouelette, Fernand, 119–120
Ozawa, Seiji, 288, 294, 367

Palais-Royal, 230
Palestrina, Giovanni, 369
Pan-American Association of Composers, 127, 198
Pappenheim, Marie, 25
Papp, Joseph, 300, 307
Paracelsus, Phillipus, *Hermetic Astronomy*, 126
Paris Conservatoire, 120, 146, 157, 158, 160, 162, 163, 175, 189, 201, 259, 285
Paris Exposition, 120
Paris Opera, 77, 81, 96, 97, 258, 281–282
Parmenter, Ross, 195
Pavlov, Ivan Petrovich, 340
Pavlova, Anna, 80, 81
Peabody Conservatory, 194
Pears, Peter, 282
Peck, Seymour, 297
Penderecki, Krzysztof, 314
Pennebaker, D. A., 109
Pensionnat St. Louis, 152
Pension Rubens, 238
Pergolesi, Giovanni, 91, 92, 107, 228
Perle, George, 14, 45, 203
Perotin, 119
Perpessa, Charilaos, 42
Perrin, Maurice, 103
"Perspectives of New Music," 284
Peters, xvii, 24

Petit Marigny, 213, 214
Peyser, Joan, *The New Music: the Sense behind the Sound*, 325
Pfitzner, Hans, 36
Philadelphia Music Society, 199
Philadelphia Orchestra, 50, 199
Piaf, Edith, 178
Piaget, Jean, 246
The Piano, 353
Picasso, Pablo, 80, 92–93, 98, 246
Picon, Gaeton, 262
Pinochet, Augusto, 355
Piston, Walter, 103, 335
Plaistow, Stephen, 357–359
Planck, Max, 322, 344, 349
Plé-Coussade, Simone, 158–159
Poe, Edgar Allan, 219
Pokrovsky, Ivan, 74–75
Polignac, Princesse de, 98
Pollock, Jackson, 285
Polyhymnia, 11
Polyphonie, 168
Pompidou, Georges, 347, 349, 361
Ponty, Merleau, 157, 217
Porter, Quincy, 48
Porter, Andrew, 259
Poulenc, Francis, 80, 124, 155, 168
Pound, Ezra, 192
Pousseur, Henri, 185–187, 189, 190, 206–207, 210, 212, 213, 215, 217, 221–222, 222, 226, 230, 232, 238, 248, 254, 327–328, 342
  Crossed Colors, 327
  Faust, 327
  Mass, 186
  The Seven Verses of the Pentecost Psalms, 186
  Symphonies, 221
Praetorius, *Capriccio for Piano and Orchestra*, 100
Price, Earl, 302
Princeton, xvi, 118, 270, 301, 303, 344
Princeton University Press, 284
Prokofiev, Sergei, 80, 163, 217
  Classical Symphony, 230
Proms, BBC, 259
Pro Musica, 198
Prospective Encounters, 300–303, 313–315, 318
Proust, Marcel, 262
  À la recherche du temps perdu, 28–29
Prussian State Academy of the Arts, 41, 46, 156
Puccini, Giacomo, 106

Pushkin, Aleksandr
  Sergeyevich, 68, 70, 76
  Little House in Kolomna,
  96
Rachmaninov, Sergei, 331
Rameau, Jean Philippe, 153,
  160
Rampal, Jean-Pierre, 161
Ramuz, Charles Ferdinand, 91,
  95
Rankl, Karl, 31
Ravel, Maurice, 48, 76, 78, 80,
  95, 121, 166, 240, 251,
  304, 315, 318, 356
  Boléro, 306
  Piano Concertos, 357
  Tombeau de Couperin, 95,
  290, 291, 294
  *Valses Nobles et
  Sentimentales*, 305
Redon, Odilon, 219
Reger, Max, 11, 36, 46
Reich, Willi, 188
Reis, Claire, 126
Renaud-Barrault theater,
  191, 193
Respighi, Ottorino, 92
Revueltas, Silvestre, 124
Rey, Anne, 359, 360
Rich, Alan, 291
Richards, M. C., 193–194
Riegger, Wallingford, 124, 127
Rieti, Vittorio, 32, 80
Rilke, Rainer Maria, 29
  "Vorgefühl," 29, 86
Rimbaud, Arthur, 157
Rimsky-Korsakov, Andrey, 81
Rimsky-Korsakov, Mme,
  76–77
Rimsky-Korsakov, Nikolai,
  67, 70, 71, 73, 74, 75–
  77, 78, 80, 81, 90, 108,
  115, *132*
  Le Coq d'Or, 81
  Scheherazade, 306
Ringling Brothers, 67, 105
Risset, Jean Claude, 348
Ritz-Carlton (Boston), 283
Robison, Paula, 316
Rockwell, John, 360, 361
Roddy, Joe, 307–308, 312
Rodriguez, José, 5
Rodzinski, Artur, 199
Roerich, Nicolas, 83
Rolland, Romaine, 121
Rosbaud, Hans, 179, 180,
  213, 214, 218–219,
  238, 239, 256, 259, 260,
  357
Rosé, Arnold, 15, 16
Rosen, Charles, 306
Rosenfeld, Paul, 123, 125

Ross, Alex, 353–354
Rostropovich, Mstislav, 367
Rouault, Georges, 80
Round House, 328
Royal Albert Hall, 259
Royal Horticultural Hall, 351
Rubinstein, Anton, 70, 74
Rubinstein, Artur, 91
Rubinstein, Ida, 100, 101
Rudhyar, Dane, 8
Rufer, Josef, 38, 42
Rug Concerts, 304, 318,
  331–332, 345
Ruggles, Carl, 124, 199, 365
Russian Ballet. *See* Ballet Russe
Russian Five. *See* The
  Nationalist Five
Russischer Musik Berlag, 83
Rzewski, Frederick, 313, 328,
  329

Saal, Hubert, 149
Saby, Bernard, 175, 178
Sacher, Paul, 106, 239, 351
Saint Cecilia Academy, 39
St. Paul's School, 367
Saint-Saëns, Charles-Camille,
  120
Salle de l'École Normale de
  Musique, 177–178
Salle Gaveau, 230
Salonblatt, 2
Salzburg Festival, 355
Salzedo, Carlos, 124, 127
Sanborn, Pitts, 126–127
Sartre, Jean-Paul, 157
Satie, Erik, 32, 67, 78, 80, 95,
  97, 124, 155, 174, 197
  Parade, 92, 174
  Socrate, 95
Saturday Review, 148, 231,
  261, 290, 293–294
Sauguet, Henri, 155, 168, 214,
  262
Scarlatti, Alessandro, 98
  *The Good-Humored
  Ladies*, 92, 93
Schacht, Peter, 42
Schaeffer, Pierre, 180, 187,
  194
Schenker, Heinrich, 200–201
Scherchen, Hermann, 40, 41,
  50, 213, 231, 239
Schiller, Johann von, 161
Schindler's List, 353
Schirmer, 36, 49, 202, 353
Schlee, Alfred, 217, 259, 323,
  335–336, 351
Schmid, Erich, 42
Schmitt, Florent, 78, 80, 84,
  101
Schnabel, Artur, 51, 163, 258

Schneider, Michel, *The
  Comedy of Culture*, 359
Schoenberg, Arnold, xvi, xvii,
  1–9, 10–18, 19–29,
  30–39, 40–47, 48–55,
  56–64, 65–66, 67, 71,
  77, 81, 83, 84, 86, 87,
  89, 92, 93, 95, 98, 100,
  104, 107, 108–109, 111,
  112, 117, 121, 123, 124,
  125, 129, 130, 131, *133*,
  134, 135, 139, 149, 156,
  157,158, 160, 161, 162,
  163, 165, 167, 168, 172,
  173, 174, 176, 179,185–
  186, 189, 190, 192, 194,
  198, 199, 201, 202, 203,
  206, 214, 216, 217, 219,
  241, 254, 258, 283, 290,
  293, 295, 304, 331, 344,
  345, 346, 353, 356, 363,
  364, 365, 367, 368, 369
  and American Academy of
  Arts and Letters, 53
  birth of, 8, 20
  death of, 9, 20, 108, 111,
  113, 187–189,
  203, 204, 260, 261, 346
  family of, 8, 9, 10, 11, 13,
  14, 15, 17, 19, 20,
  38, 44, 46, 48, 49, 52
  and Gerstl, 19–20
  and Judaism, 9, 10, 11,
  46–47
  paintings of, 20–21
  at Prussian State Academy
  of the Arts, 41, 42, 46
  and Society for Private
  Musical Performances,
  35–36, 41
  works of
  *Accompaniment to a
  Film Scene*, Opus 34,
  45
  Chamber Symphony,
  6, 9, 16, 17, 18,
  58–59, 161
  Chamber Symphony No.
  2, 163
  *Das Buch der hängenden
  Gärten*, 7, 20
  Die glückliche Hand, 7,
  25–26, 27, 30, 167
  Die Jakobsleiter,
  6, 30–31, 37, 38,
  52, 54
  Erwartung, 7, 25, 250,
  302
  Five Orchestral Pieces,
  Opus 16, xvii,
  23–25, 26, 39, 59,
  163, 263

Five Piano Pieces, Opus 23, 37, 38, 45, 161
Georgelieder, Opus 15, 20, 59
Gurrelieder, 5, 7, 13–14, 15, 26, 305, 306
"Herzgewächse", Opus 20, 26–27
Kol Nidre, 51
Modern Psalms, 6, 54
Moses und Aron, 6, 47, 52, 54–55, 65, 305, 306, 355
Ode to Napoleon, 51
Opus 1, 2 and 3 Lieder, 11–12
Orchestral Songs, Opus 22, 28, 29, 293
Pelleas und Melisande, 5, 7, 14–15, 16, 26, 48, 58, 122
Piano Concerto, 163
Piano Pieces, Opus 11, 23, 24, 25, 27, 45, 59, 159, 161, 200
Pierrot Lunaire, 7, 27–28, 30, 86, 109, 122, 124, 156, 159, 207, 208, 215, 357, 365
Satires for Mixed Chorus, Opus 28, 42
Septet, Opus 29, 292, 295
Serenade, Opus 24, 37, 38, 167, 230
Six Little Piano Pieces, Opus 19, 26, 59, 367
Six Pieces for Male Chorus, 45
String Quartet No. 1, Opus 7, 16, 17, 131
String Quartet No. 2, Opus 10, 17, 18, 19, 59, 118
String Quartet No. 3, Opus 30, 43
String Quartet No. 4, Opus 37, 51
String Trio, Opus 45, 5, 7, 52–53
Structural Functions of Harmony, 52
Style and Idea, 7, 52
Suite, Opus 29, 43
Suite for Piano, Opus 25, 37, 38–39, 188
Suite in G Major, 49, 50
A Survivor from Warsaw, 54

Theory of Harmony (Harmonielehre), 22–23, 34
Three Pieces for Orchestra, 59
Three Satires, 98–99
Variations, Opus 31, 43, 44, 188, 250
Variations on a Recitative for Organ, 51
Verklärte Nacht, 7, 12–13, 14, 15, 16, 30, 58, 291, 367
Violin Concerto, Opus 36, 50–51, 111
Von Heute auf Morgen, 44
"Vorgefühl," 86
Woodwind Quintet, Opus 26, 39, 159, 224
Schoenberg, George, 8, 17, 19
Schoenberg, Gertrude, 8, 14, 15, 19
Schoenberg, Gertrude Kolisch, 9, 38, 44, 46, 48–49, 52
Schoenberg, Mathilde, 13, 15, 19, 38
Schoenberg, Pauline Nachod, 10, 11
Schoenberg, Roland (Lawrence Adam), 8
Schoenberg, Ronald, 8
Schoenberg, Samuel, 10, 11
Schola Cantorum, 120
Schonberg, Harold, 287, 291, 302, 303, 304, 315, 320, 333, 340
Schubert, Franz, 10, 20, 46, 74, 76, 291, 299, 304
Schuller, Gunther, *273*, 365–366
Symphony for Brass and Percussion, 273, 366
Schuman, William, 199, 335
Schumann, Robert, 7, 20, 74, 299, 318
Rhenish Symphony, 304
Symphony No. 1, 320, 341
Symphony No. 2, 320
Science, 334–335
The Score, 188
Scriabin, Aleksandr, 22, 36, 73
Piano Concerto, 357
The Poem of Ecstasy, 357
Prometheus: The Poem of Fire, 357
Searchinger, César, 36, 44
Serialism. *See* Boulez, Pierre
Sessions, Roger, 50, 51, 100, 199, 200–201, 272, 315,

329, 335, 364
Montezuma, 364
Sonata for Solo Violin, 200
Severance Hall, 290
Shadowlands, 353
Shakespeare, William, 112
Hamlet, 168
King Lear, 334
Shakespeare Festival, 300
Shapero, Harold, 103, 335
Shapey, Ralph, 143
Sherer, Jacques, *Sketches of Mallarmé's Le Livre*, 226, 321
Shostakovich, Dmitri, *141*
Sibelius, Jean, Symphony no. 2, 321
Silverman, Stanley, 302, 314
Sinding, Christian, 69
Sitwell, Sir Osbert, 83
Skalkottas, Niko, 42
Slonimsky, Nicolas, 4, 37, 127, 128
Smetana, Bedrich, 69
Smit, Leo, 335
Snowman, Nicholas, 348
Socrates, 232
Sommer, Susan, 313
Song of Bernadette, 105
Sony Classical USA, 353, 368
Southwest German Radio, 179, 234, 351
Souvchinsky, Pierre, 170, 171, 175, 177, 178, 179, 180, 192, 212, 215, 216, 218, 241, 247
Sovietskaya Muzyka, 101–102
The Special Schoenberg Birthday Book, 39, 40
Stanford University, 355
Stassov, Vladimir, 96
State Academy (Cologne), 189
Stein, Erwin, 17, 61
Stein, Peter, 354, 355
Steinbeck, John, 105, 285
Steinberg, William, 288
Steinecke, Wolfgang, 216–217, 223, 234, 248, 249, 254
Stella, Joseph, 124
Sterne, Teresa, 302
Sterne Conservatory, 14
Steuermann, Eduard, 26, 51, 63, *133*
Stiedry, Fritz, 51
Stock, Frederick, 321
Stockhausen, Karlheinz, 115, 188–189, 197, 198, 206, 207, 210, 211, 212, 213, 214, 217, 218, 219, 221, 222–223, 224–225, 229–230, 231–232, 233, 234–235, 240, 253–255,

267, 268, 294, 304, 314,
328, 329, 336, 343, 353
Carré, 254
Gesang der Jünglinge, 229,
232
Gruppen, 229, 231–232
Klavierstück XI, 225–226,
229
Kontra-Punkte, 206
Licht, 268
Mixtur, 328
Momente, 323
Originale, 254
Pièces pour Piano, 221, 222
Refrain, 235
Sonata for Violin and
Piano, 189
Three Songs for Alto and
Chamber Orchestra, 189
Zeitmasse, 223, 224, 226,
229, 258
Stokowski, Leopold, 50, 99,
126, 127, 199, 288
Stransky, Josef, 3, 121–122
Strauss, Richard, 2, 11, 12, 14,
23, 36, 45, 46,
76, 121, 146, 240
Der Rosenkavalier, 23
Elektra, 23, 354
Metamorphosen, 320
Salome, 23, 354
Sinfonia Domestica, 16
Stravinsky, Anna
Kholodovsky, 72–73, 90,
104
Stravinsky, Catherine
Nossenko, 76, 95, 104, 105
Stravinsky, Feodor Ignatievich,
72, 73, 90
Stravinsky, Igor, xvii, 3, 23,
36, 44, 52, 57, 65–71,
72–79, 80–86, 87–94,
95–102, 103–110,
111–116, 117, 122, 124,
126, 129, 132, 137, 138,
148, 155, 160, 163, 164,
170, 179, 187, 189, 198,
199, 200, 204–206, 207,
213, 215, 217, 219,
227–228, 231, 238, 240,
256, 260–261, 271, 275,
281, 283, 286, 290, 293,
304, 307, 324, 327, 336,
341–342, 351, 356, 364,
366, 367, 368
birth of, 72
and Charles Eliot Norton
professorship, 104
death of, 261, 293–294
family of, 67, 68, 72–74,
76, 88, 90, 95, 104, 105,
106–107, 108, 115, 251

illness of, 105, 261
works of
Agon, 113, 260, 327
Apollon Musagète, 100,
101, 104, 106
Autobiography, xvii, 65,
66, 67, 68, 70–71,
87, 89, 92–93, 102,
104, 108
Barnum and Bailey
polka, 67, 105
Cantata for Soprano,
Tenor, Female
Chorus and
Orchestra, 111–112
Canticum Sacrum,
112–113, 200
Capriccio for Piano and
Orchestra, 100
The Card Party, 104,
105
Concerto for Piano and
Wind Instruments,
98
Concerto in D, 106
Danses Concertantes,
160
Dialogues, 86, 95, 97
Double Canon, 113
Dumbarton Oaks, 104,
105
Duo Concertante, 102
Ebony Concerto, 105,
138
Elegy for JFK, 114
Epitaphium für das
Grabmal des Prinzen
Max Egon zu
Furstenberg, 113
Expositions and
Developments,
78, 84, 96
Faun and Shepherdess,
Opus 2, 76
The Firebird, 77–78,
80–81, 82, 83, 105,
132, 227
Fireworks, 77
The Flood, 114
Four Norwegian Moods,
105, 160, 283
Histoire du Soldat, 83,
89, 91
In Memoriam Dylan
Thomas, 112
Introitus for T. S. Eliot,
114
Jane Eyre, 105
Jeu de Cartes. See The
Card Party
"L'Avertissement," 99

Le Baiser de la Fée, 68,
100, 104, 106
Le Roi des Étoiles, 87
Le Sacre du Printemps.
See The Rite of
Spring
Les Berceuses du Chat,
88, 89, 91, 292
Les Noces, 88, 89, 98,
99, 124, 258, 261
Mass, 111
Mavra, 68, 96
Memories and
Commentaries, 72
The Moon Is Down, 105
Movements for Piano
and Orchestra, 113
The Nightingale, 77, 91,
99, 106, 112
Octuor, 39, 68, 95,
96–97, 98, 106
Ode, 105
Oedipus Rex, 95,
100–101, 106,
109–110, 113, 167
Orpheus, 111
The Owl and the
Pussycat, 115
Perséphone, 77, 100,
101, 102, 106, 114
Petrushka, 27, 80,
81–83, 84, 86, 91,
96, 97, 99, 106,
132, 293, 305
Piano Rag-Music, 91,
138
Piano Sonata, 76, 98
Poetics of Music, 67,
108, 170
Pribaoutki, 88, 90, 91,
292
Pulcinella, 66, 92–93,
106, 227, 293, 295
Ragtime, 66, 91, 92, 138
The Rake's Progress,
106–107, 108, 110,
111, 205
Renard, 88, 89, 91, 214,
258
Requiem Canticles, 115,
293, 296
Ringling Brothers polka,
67, 105
The Rite of Spring, xvii,
29, 65, 72, 80, 81,
83–86, 87, 88, 89,
93, 96, 97, 98, 99,
112, 122, 132, 137,
148, 158, 167, 204,
247, 257, 260, 299,
300, 302, 304, 305
Scherzo à la Russe, 105

Scherzo Fantastique, 77
Septet, 112
Serenade in A, 67, 100
*A Sermon, a Narrative
and a Prayer,*
113–114
Sonata, 112
Song of Bernadette, 105
Study for Pianola, 88
"Summer Moon," 105
*Symphonies of Wind
Instruments,* 96,
106, 107, 230
Symphony in C, 104–105
Symphony in E-flat, 76
Symphony in Three
Movements,
105–106
Symphony of Psalms,
100, 101, 106, 110
Themes and Episodes,
109–110, 251–252,
261
Three Easy Pieces for
Piano Duet, 90
Three Japanese Lyrics
for Soprano and
Piano, 87
Three Pieces for String
Quartet, 89
*Three Songs from William
Shakespeare,* 112
*Threni: Id Est
Lamentationes
Jeremiae
Prophetae,* 113, 238,
260–261
Variations, 114, 252
Violin Concerto, 102
Stravinsky, Vera de Bosset,
68, 95, 104, 106–107,
108, 115, 251, 261
Strindberg, August, *Jacob
Wrestling,* 30
Strobel, Heinrich, 179–180,
192, 204, 211, 212, 216,
218–219, 232, 238, 253,
254, 256, 326–327
Strobel, Hilda, 218–219, 234,
238–239, 254, 256, 326
Stuckenschmidt, H. H., 38, 52
Sudeikine, Serge, 95
Sudeikine, Vera. *See*
Stravinsky, Vera de Bosset
Südwestfunk, 179, 213, 214,
218, 238, 239, 249, 253,
257, 259, 281
Suzuki, D. T., 174
Swallow, John, 311
Swedish Radio, 343
Symphony Center, 279

Szell, George, 199, 262–263,
280, 287, 288, 289, 299,
314, 326, 327, 331

Tanglewood, 103
Tashi, 304
Tati, Jacques, 365
Taylor, Deems, 126
Taylor, James, 325
Tchaikovsky, Peter Ilich,
67–68, 71, 73, 74, 96,
100, 149, 263
1812 Overture, 306
Pathetic Symphony, 68
Sleeping Beauty, 67–68, 74,
96
Tempo, 51, 324
Tezenas, Suzanne, 170–171,
175–176, 212, 214–215,
218, 262, 264, 290
Théâtre des Champs Élysées,
84, 160, 257, 283
Théâtre Marigny, 168, 230
Theremin, Leon, 128
Thomas, Augusta Read, 279,
367, 368
Aurora, 367
Chansons, 367
Orbital Beacons, 279, 367
Words of the Sea, 367
Thomas, Dylan, 112
Thompson, Randall, 335
Thompson, Sada, 307
Thomson, Virgil, 78, 103, 107,
170, 174, 191, 193, 195,
197, 199, 200, 205, 228,
229, 335
Time, 149, 300, 333, 347
The Times (London),
25, 96, 251
Tin Pan Alley, 105
Today Show, 310
Tomek, Otto, 232, 250,
254–255, 336
Tommasini, Vincenzo, 92
Tristano, Lenny, 367
Tudor, David, 143, 183, 191,
193–194, 210, 211, 212,
218, 219, 221, 222, 223,
224, 225, 228, 229, 232,
234, 254
Tully, Alice, 203, 288, 290,
293, 331
Tureck, Rosalyn, 51
12-tone technique. *See*
Schoenberg, Arnold
Tyron, Winthrop,
123–124, 126

Ugorski, Anatol, 357
Union of Art and Culture, 26

Union of Creative Musicians,
16
Union of Soviet Composers,
101–102
Universal Edition, 38, 39, 213,
217, 238, 259, 281,
335–336, 351, 353
University of California at Los
Angeles, 50, 51, 52,
172–173, 365
University of Chicago, 15
University of Lyon, 152
University of Montreal, 337
University of Southern
California, 50, 163, 251
University of Vienna, 10, 58
Utrillo, Maurice, 80

Vallin, Ninon, 153
Vanity Fair, 97
Varèse, Edgard, 50, 51,
117–122, 123–129,
130, 144, 145, 204, 213,
281, 290, 292, 364, 368
birth of, 117
death of, 129
family of, 119–120, 121,
122, 123, 124, 128,
129, 281, 296
and International
Composers Guild, 124,
126–127
and New Symphony
Orchestra, 123
and Pan-American
Association of
Composers, 127
and Premiere Bourse
Artistique de la Ville de
Paris, 121
works of
Amériques, 117,
123–124, 126
Arcana, 126, 128, 290
Bourgogne, 121–122
Déserts, 118, 124, 145
Ecuatorial, 128
Espace, 127
Hyperprism, 124, 125
Intégrales, 124, 126
Ionisation, 127–128,
173, 221, 290, 291,
296
L'Astronome, 127
Octandre, 124, 125
Offrandes, 124–125
Poéme Électronique, 290
Varèse, Henri, 118–119
Varèse, Louise Norton, 119,
121, 122, 123, 124, 128,
129, 281, 296

Varèse, Suzanne Bing, 121
Vaurabourg, Andrée, 157
Venezuelan Symphony, 230
Verdi, Giuseppe, 106, 149, 282
   Aida, 153
   The Damnation of Faust,
     153
Verlaine, Paul, 236
Vienna Court Opera, 10
Vienna Philharmonic, 11, *136*,
   259, 356, 357
Viertel, Bertold, 30
Vilar, Jean, 281, 282
Vivaldi, Antonio, 91
Vlad, Roman, 91–92

Wadsworth, Charles, 316
Wagner, Richard, 1–3, 13, 46,
   57, 67, 76, 78, 79, 82,
   96, 97, 109, 118, 149,
   160, 179, 194, 220, 222,
   240, 258, 283, 369
   Faust Overture, 299
   Gesamtkunstwerk, 3, 79,
     96, 118
   Parsifal, 309, 326, 354
   The Ring, 354
   *Synthesis of the Arts. See
     Gesamtkunstwerk*
   Tristan und Isolde,
     3, 11, 19
Wagner, Wieland, 354
Wallace, Alfred Russel, 201
Wallenstein, Alfred, 52, 311
Walter, Bruno, 16
Walter, Fred, 42
Walters, Barbara, 310
Warburg, Edward, 104
Weber, Carl Maria von, 3, 100
Webern, Anton, xvii, 4–5, 17,
   23, 35, 36, 39, 50,
   56–64, 67, 87, 92, 95,
   104, 107, 109, 111, 113,
   114, 117, 119, 124, *135*,
   136, 149, 156, 163–164,
   165, 166–168, 173–174,
   179, 185–186, 188, 190,
   194–195, 196, 197, 203,
   205–206, 208, 213, 214,
   216, 217, 219, 220,
   224–225, 238, 241,
   242, 261, 280, 281, 283,
   290, 295, 304, 305, 331,
   338, 356, 364
   Bagatelles for String
     Quartet Opus 9, 60–61,
     224
   Concerto for Nine
     Instruments, Opus 24,
     214, 224, 258

Five Movements for String
   Quartet Opus 5, 189
Five Pieces, 166
Four Songs, Opus 12, 60
Im Sommerwind, 58
   *Movements for String
     Quartet*, 124
Passacaglia, 291
Quartet, Opus 22, 111,
   204, 225
Second Cantata, 186
Six Pieces for Orchestra,
   Opus 6, 263
String Quartet, 58
Symphony, Opus 21,
   62, 159, 167, 183,
   187, 247
Variations for Piano,
   Opus 27, 63
Webern Society, 61
Weill, Kurt, 44
   Three Penny Opera, 44
Weill Hall, 362
Weiss, Adolphe, 42
Welles, Orson, 105
Wellesz, Egon, 31–32
Welty, Eudora, 200
Werfel, Franz, 105
Wessel, David, 356
West German Radio, 211, 253
White, Eric Walter, 67
Whitney, Mrs. Harry Payne,
   124
Whitney Museum, 203, 228
Widor, Charles-Marie, 120,
   121
Wiggen, Knut, 343
Wilhelm, Richard, 183
Wilhelm Hansen, 37
Williams, William Carlos, 347
Wolf, Hugo, 2
Wolff, Christian, 183, 214
   Four Pieces for Prepared
     Piano, 195, 211
Wolpe, Stefan, *143*, 258,
   364–365
Wood, Sir Henry, 25
Woodstock, 210–211
WPA, 50, 129, 200
Wuorinen, Charles, 276, 301,
   319, 329, 353, 363, 367,
   368
   The Politics of Harmony,
     301, 302, 303

Xenakis, Iannis, 350

Yale, 307, 311
Young, La Monte, 328
Yves Saint Laurent, 362

Zemlinsky, Alexander von, 11,
   12, 13, 15, 16, 19, 36,
   38, 44, 59
   Sarema, 11
Zillig, Winfried, 42
Zimmerman, Krystian, 357
Zmigrod, Joseph, 42